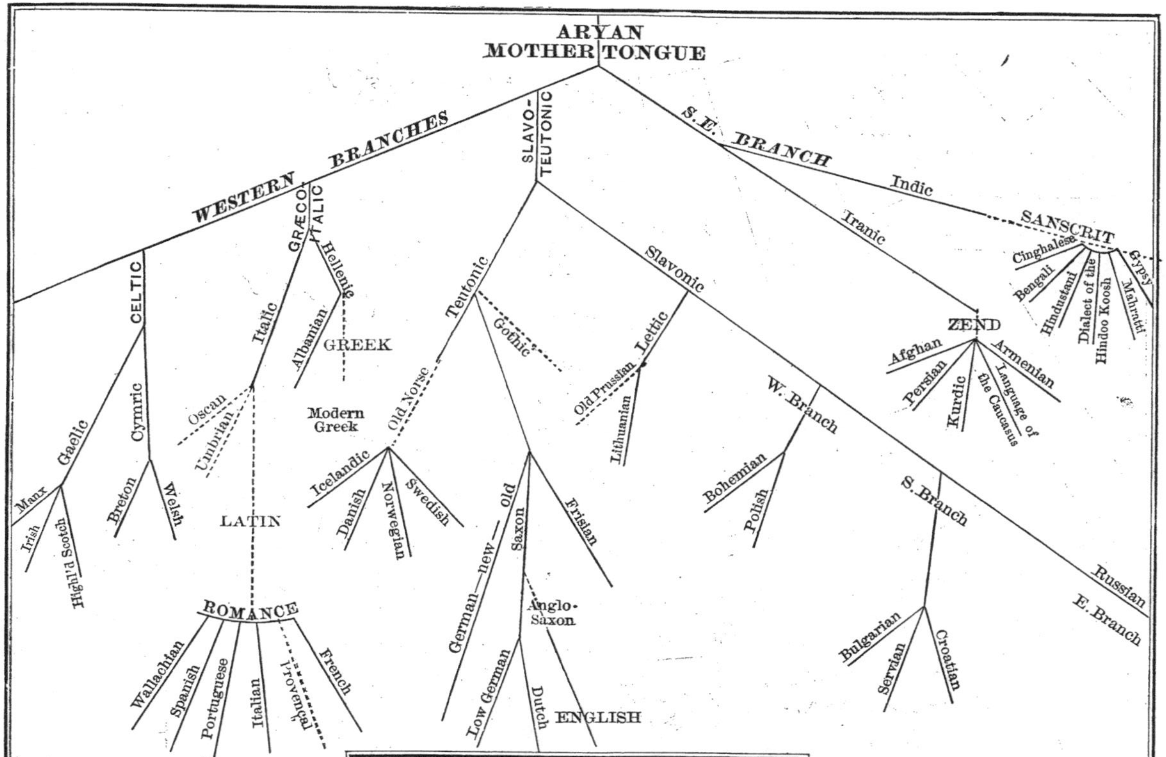

THE ARYAN FAMILY OF LANGUAGES

ARYAN MOTHER TONGUE

WESTERN BRANCHES

SLAVO-TEUTONIC

S.E. BRANCH

CELTIC

Gaelic

Manx

Irish

Highl'd Scotch

Cymric

Breton

Welsh

GRÆCO-ITALIC

Italic

Oscan

Umbrian

LATIN

ROMANCE

Wallachian

Spanish

Portuguese

Italian

Provençal

French

Hellenic

Albanian

GREEK

Modern Greek

Teutonic

Old Norse

Icelandic

Danish

Norwegian

Swedish

Gothic

German—new—old

Saxon

Low German

Dutch

Anglo-Saxon

ENGLISH

Frisian

Slavonic

Lettic

Old Prussian

Lithuanian

W. Branch

Bohemian

Polish

S. Branch

Bulgarian

Servian

Croatian

E. Branch

Russian

Indic

Iranic

ZEND

Afghan

Persian

Kurdic

Language of the Caucasus

Armenian

SANSCRIT

Cinghalese

Bengali

Hindustani

Dialect of the Hindoo Koosh

Mahratti

Gypsy

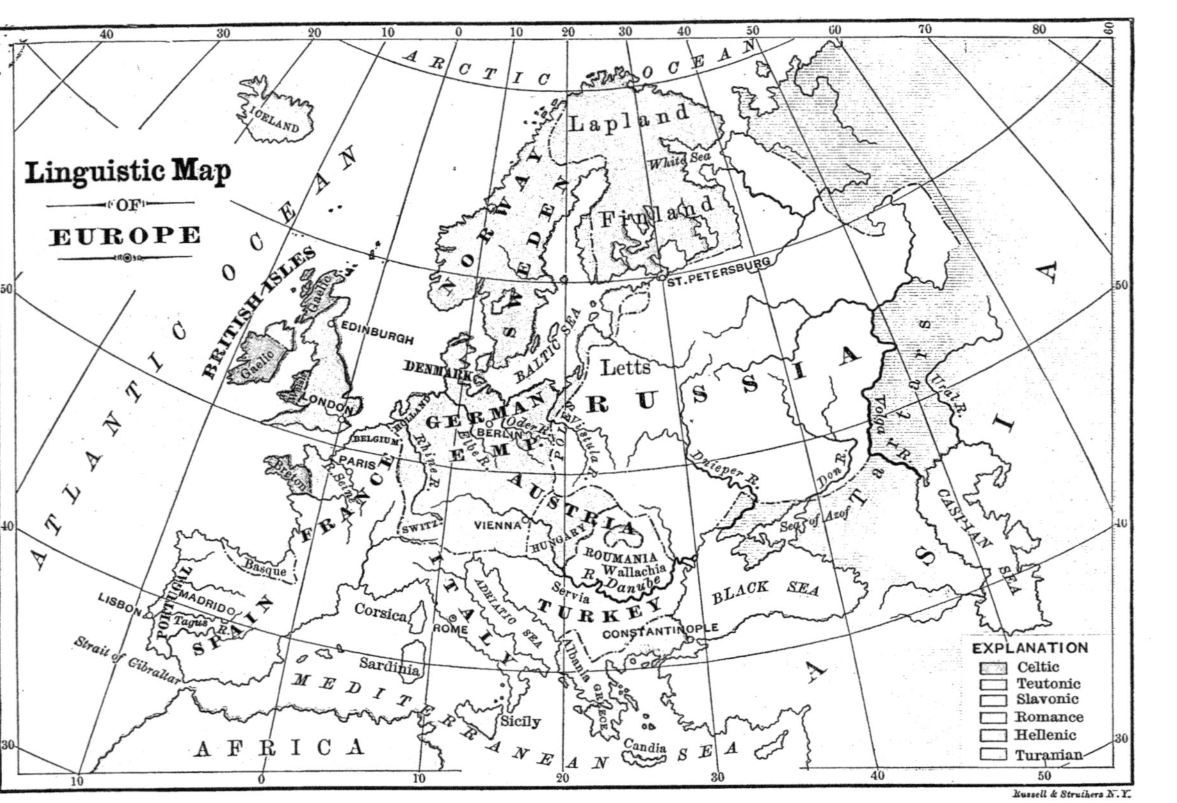
Linguistic Map
OF
EUROPE
ARCTIC OCEAN
ATLANTIC OCEAN
ICELAND
BRITISH ISLES
Gaelic
EDINBURGH
LONDON
NORWAY
SWEDEN
Lapland
White Sea
Finland
ST. PETERSBURG
BALTIC SEA
DENMARK
Letts
RUSSIA
HOLLAND
BELGIUM
GERMAN EMP.
BERLIN
Oder R.
Elbe R.
Rhine R.
Vistula R.
POLES
Dnieper R.
Don R.
Volga R.
Ural R.
Tatars
ASIA
CASPIAN SEA
Sea of Azof
PARIS
R. Seine
Breton
FRANCE
SWITZ.
VIENNA
AUSTRIA
HUNGARY
ROUMANIA
Wallachia
R. Danube
Servia
TURKEY
CONSTANTINOPLE
BLACK SEA
Basque
PORTUGAL
MADRID
LISBON
Tagus R.
SPAIN
Strait of Gibraltar
Corsica
ROME
ITALY
ADRIATIC SEA
Albania
GREECE
Sardinia
Sicily
Candia
MEDITERRANEAN SEA
AFRICA
EXPLANATION
Celtic
Teutonic
Slavonic
Romance
Hellenic
Turanian
Russell & Struthers N.Y.

ILLUSTRATED HISTORY

OF

ANCIENT LITERATURE,

ORIENTAL AND CLASSICAL.

BY

JOHN D. QUACKENBOS, A.M., M.D.,

AUTHOR OF "ILLUSTRATED SCHOOL HISTORY OF THE WORLD."

ACCOMPANIED WITH

ENGRAVINGS AND COLORED MAP.

NEW YORK:
HARPER & BROTHERS, PUBLISHERS,
FRANKLIN SQUARE.
1878.

PREFACE.

THE History of Literature, as a separate branch of the history of civilization, is of comparatively recent origin; the first work on the subject in any language dating no farther back than the sixteenth century of our era, and being little more than a crude catalogue of authors and their books. Yet who can deny the great importance of such history? When studied in connection with illustrative extracts from the masterpieces of which it treats, it furnishes a key to the intellectual development of our race, introduces us to the great minds that stand as beacon lights in successive ages, and with their wisdom widens the scope of knowledge, while it refines the taste and disciplines the judgment. Lord Bacon said but the truth, when he remarked that the history of the world without the history of letters would be as incomplete as a statue of Polyphemus deprived of his single eye.

Nor is this study without results of a direct practical bearing. Certainly all must appreciate the importance of understanding current allusions to the writers and literary works of other ages and countries, and must admit that some acquaintance at least with such writers and works is essential to a well-grounded knowledge of one's own language and a correct estimate of its literature. But when is such an acquaintance to be obtained, if not during a school or college course? The engrossing duties of after-life leave little time for the pursuit of liberal studies. And how is such an acquaintance to be obtained? All are not linguists, and the greater part must get it second-hand—must avail themselves of the labors of others who have delved in these unfamiliar fields. It may be stated as a broad fact that few will know anything of general literature who do not study its history systematically, as a part of the academic curriculum.

It is to facilitate and popularize this study by furnishing a complete and carefully condensed text-book on the subject, unencumbered by obscure names and wearisome details, that the volume now offered to the public has been prepared. It presents a full account of the literatures of ancient nations, and, treating of the origin and relationships of their respective languages, incidentally brings forward some of the most interesting facts of Comparative Philology. While the writings of Greece and Rome receive due attention, a new and, it is believed, peculiarly valuable feature of the book will be found in its treatment of ancient Oriental literature—particularly the Sanscrit and Persian. The labors of European scholars during the last quarter-century have thrown a chain of living interest around the subject, and awakened on this side of the Atlantic as well a thirst for further knowledge, which it is here attempted to satisfy. The principles of the Egyptian picture-writing (hieroglyphics) are also explained; and the vast literary treasures recently unearthed amid the ruins of the Nile Valley and elsewhere are described and illustrated.

In treating the subject, the author has aimed, while giving a clear outline of each literature as a whole, to make its great writers stand out in bold relief, and to associate them in the pupil's mind with the works that have made them immortal. With this view, brief biographies, not fragmentary or isolated, but grafted on the narrative where they naturally belong, are accompanied with short specimens, carefully selected to give the best idea of each author's style and genius. In the critical views as well as the historical facts presented, the latest authorities have been followed, and the aid of maps and illustrations has been freely resorted to for the better elucidation of points on which they could throw light.

The present volume has grown out of the author's experience in the lecture-room; and in the belief that it is of a scope and grade that will meet the popular want, he now offers it to high-schools, academies, and colleges. From such institutions he feels that no class should graduate in ignorance either of the Greek and Roman classics which have inspired the modern poet and philosopher, or of those precious remains of once great Oriental literatures that patient scholars of the nineteenth century have brought to light—that helped to shape the Greek mind itself in the morning of the world. He trusts that it may foster in the young admiration of the brilliant thoughts that sparkle in the pages of ancient lore, a love of literature, and a taste for philological investigations. If it be approved by the friends of education, he shall feel encouraged to continue his labors in this department by preparing a similar work on Modern Literature.

COLUMBIA COLLEGE, *June*, 1878.

CONTENTS.

INTRODUCTION.

(Pages 11-30.)

PART I.

ANCIENT ORIENTAL LITERATURES.

CHAPTER I.—HINDOO LITERATURE.

(Pages 31-60.)

CHAPTER II.—PERSIAN LITERATURE.

(Pages 60-67.)

Chapter III.—Chinese Literature.

Chapter IV.—Hebrew Literature.

Chapter V.—Chaldean, Assyrian, Arabic, and Phœnician Literatures.

Chapter VI.—Egyptian Literature.

PART II.

GRECIAN LITERATURE.

Chapter I.—Birth of Grecian Literature.

CHAPTER II.—AGE OF EPIC POETRY.

(Pages 139-156.)

CHAPTER III.—LYRIC POETRY.

(Pages 157-178.)

CHAPTER IV.—RISE OF GREEK PROSE.

(Pages 178-184.)

CHAPTER V.—GOLDEN AGE OF GRECIAN LITERATURE.

(Pages 184-262.)

CHAPTER VI.—THE ALEXANDRIAN PERIOD.

(Pages 262-280.)

CHAPTER VII.—LATER GREEK LITERATURE.

(Pages 280-302.)

PART III.

ROMAN LITERATURE.

HISTORY OF ANCIENT LITERATURE.

INTRODUCTION.

LITERATURE, in its broadest sense, comprises the written productions of all nations in all ages. It is the permanent expression of the intellectual power of man, and reflects the popular manners, the political condition, the moral and religious status. In its literary productions, a nation bequeaths to posterity an ever-speaking record of its inner life.

The history of literature traces the progress of the human mind from age to age, by landmarks erected by the mind itself. It represents the development of different phases of thought in written language, and shows their influence in moulding the public taste and morals. It investigates the connection between the literatures of different countries, considers the causes of their growth and their decay, and critically examines the works of individual authors.

Literature may be divided into two parts, Ancient and Modern. The former, to which this volume is devoted, includes the literatures of the ancient Oriental nations, the Greeks, and the Romans. To the second division belong the literatures of modern Europe, of the modern Oriental nations, and of America.

After considering the origin and relationship of languages,

we shall give a brief summary of the history of ancient literature as a whole, without national divisions; so that the reader, having previously followed the progress of letters from age to age and people to people, may be enabled to study more intelligently the separate literatures of the different countries.

ORIGIN AND RELATIONSHIP OF LANGUAGES.

The Dawn of History.—When the mist that envelops the early history of the world first rises, it discovers to our view, in parts of western Asia, communities more or less advanced in knowledge and the arts, gathered about certain centres of civilization; and others, of less culture, leading a wandering life, spent mostly, we may conjecture, in the chase, in predatory excursions, and the tending of herds. We find at this time a thrifty race, called Aryans, settled in the fair district between the Hindoo Koosh Mountains and the upper course of the Amoo River—the ancient Bactria (part of what is now Turkestan and Afghanistan; see Map, p. 15). The region watered by the rivers Euphrates and Tigris was occupied by the forefathers of the Chaldeans and Assyrians, the Jews and Arabians; while over the plains of Tartary, known as Turan, wandering tribes were spread—whence their name, Turanians, *swift horsemen.* Corresponding with these three divisions of the human race are three distinct families of languages, — the ARYAN or INDO-EUROPEAN, the SEMITIC, and the TURANIAN,—embracing more than one hundred and fifty tongues.

In Africa, also, civilization was a plant of early growth, Egypt ranking among the most ancient monarchies. Europe, however, in these primeval ages, was either a tenantless wilderness or the home of rude adventurers like the Lapps and Finns, of whom the Basques in the Pyrenees are perhaps the only remnants in the west.

THE ARYANS.

The Aryans have left no account of themselves sculptured on rocks or the walls of crumbling temples; but by careful study of the languages of Aryan origin we obtain, after the lapse of four thousand years, a glimpse of the social condition of those who spoke the mother-tongue among the mountains of Bactria. We infer that nouns similar in the various derived languages,—as father (*protector*), brother (*helper*), house, door, walls, boat, grain, etc.,—are the names of objects or notions familiar to the original family.* Thus utilizing language as a key to what would otherwise be locked up in the unknown past, we learn that the inhabitants of the fertile Bactrian valleys were devoted to agricultural pursuits. Tilling the ground was an honorable employment, the very name *Aryan* signifying *high-born, noble.* We have pictured to us law-abiding communities, grouped together in towns, ruled by chiefs and a king, recognizing family ties, entertaining exalted conceptions of woman, and a solemn regard for the marriage bond—the latter always a mark of high civilization.

Language also tells us that this interesting people preferred the arts of peace to war. With the dog for his companion, the shepherd folded his flocks of sheep; with the horse and ox for his servants, the landholder broke the soil with a plough of bronze. Pigs and fowls were raised; cattle formed the chief wealth; and the cows were milked by the *daughter* of the household—this name meaning *milk-maid.*

The Aryan drove from village to village in his wheeled car-

---

* A thousand words have thus been traced through the sister languages of Aryan birth—a number certainly adequate to the wants of primitive man, when we remember that of more than 100,000 words which constitute our present vocabulary but 3,000 are in common use. The Old Testament was translated with the help of only 5,642 English words. While Shakespeare's genius required 21,000 words for its expression, Milton's epic employs less than half that number.

riage, over well-constructed roads; worked the metals; plied the loom; moulded clay into pottery; and even navigated the neighboring waters in boats propelled by oars. He gave names to numbers as far as one hundred, was familiar with the principles of decimals, and took the moon for his guide in dividing the year into months.

A Supreme Being was worshipped in Bactria, the Great Unseen, the Creator and Governor of the world. In the reference to him of controversies that were difficult to settle, we trace the origin of the later trial by ordeal. Even some of our commonest stories are derived from fables current at least two thousand years B.C. in ancient Arya.

Aryan Migrations.—Few in number at first, the Aryans long lived peaceably together. But as the population grew denser, great bodies, either compelled to search for food in other lands or moved by a thirst for exploration, broke away at different periods from the cradle of their race, in quest of new abodes.

The first to leave were the Celts, who, passing between the Caspian Sea and the Black, made their way westward into Europe, and, conquering an indigenous population of supposed Turanian origin, possessed themselves of its fairest lands.* Following them, but by a route north of the Caspian, and ever pushing them toward the west, came the Slavonian and Teutonic tribes—the former, the ancestors of the Russians and Servians, Poles and Bohemians; the latter, of the Goths, Scandinavians, and German nations. Of the Aryans who thus migrated to the northwest, Max Müller says that they "have been the prominent actors in the great drama of history, and have carried to their fullest growth all the elements of active

* In common with the Celts, the North American Indians, Chinese, Egyptians, and other ancient nations, cherished a tradition that they had supplanted an original population—*the children of the soil*—of low intellectual powers, feeders on roots, hole-dwellers, serpent-eaters.

life with which our nature is endowed. They have perfected society and morals. They have become, after struggles with Semitic and Turanian races, the rulers of history; and it seems to be their mission to link all parts of the world together by the chains of civilization, commerce, and religion."

After the last emigration of Aryans to the west, the parent community extended its settlements southward into the Tableland of Iran (*e'rahn*) (modern Persia, Afghanistan, and Beloochistan; see Map), and finally, in consequence of a religious difference, separated into two great branches. One remained on the Iranian plateau, and was ultimately known in history as the Medes and Persians. The other made its way through the mountain-passes, crossed the upper Indus (at some uncertain date, between 2000 and 1400 B.C.), and in time effected the conquest of the rich peninsula of Hindostan. The invaders were the "fair-complexioned" Indo-Aryans, who spoke the polished Sanscrit, and among whom sprung up the institution of caste and many gross superstitions.

Aryan Languages.—Similarity in the words and grammatical structure of their languages proves that the Hindoos, the Persians, the Greeks and Romans, the Celtic races, the Slavonian and Teutonic nations,—all had a common origin; that the frozen Icelander and Indian fire-worshipper, the outcast Gypsy and the plaided Highlander, the English master and his Cooley servant, are brothers of the same stock. Their tongues have been derived from the same parent—a language full of poetic grandeur, older than Greek or Sanscrit, and containing the germs of both—a language which has perished.

Spoken as we have seen from India to the west of Europe, these tongues have been called INDO-EUROPEAN. They embrace the dialects of India and Persia; the Welsh, and the Celtic of Scotland and Ireland; the Latin and its derivatives, the Romance languages, viz., Italian, Spanish, Portuguese, French, Provençal, and Wallachian; Greek; Russian, Polish, and Bohemian; English, German, Dutch, Danish, and Swedish (see Linguistic Map of Europe and Chart, preceding the title-page). The relationship existing among these tongues of the Indo-European race—preëminently the race of progressive civilization—has been established by the study of their several grammars.

THE SEMITES.

The Semitic Languages, in like manner, may all be traced to a common source. To this group belong the Syriac, the Hebrew, the Arabic, the Ethiopic, the ancient Phœnician, and the Carthaginian; while the cuneiform inscriptions of Babylonia and Assyria are the written characters of a Semitic tongue common to those countries. (See Chart, p. 85.)

Philology has not followed the Semites to a home as limited as that of the Aryans; though tradition points to Armenia as their early domicile. It declares, however, the Semitic and the Aryan to be distinct families of speech, which, while both may be branches from a common parent stem, could not have been derived one from the other.

THE TURANIANS.

Turanian Dialects.—Here there is slighter evidence of relationship. The Turanian languages, though they seem to be members of the same original family, differ widely; for those who spoke them were nomads, wanderers over the globe, whose customs, laws, and dialects were modified with every change of habitation and condition. To this sporadic group belong the Mongolian tongues, the Turkish, Finnic, and Hungarian, together with certain Polynesian dialects; but the Chinese, Japanese, Australian, North American Indian, South African, and many others of the nine hundred languages spoken on the earth, bear hardly enough resemblance to these to be classed in the same family.

SYSTEMS OF WRITING.

Language is either spoken or written. Spoken language we find to have been used as a medium of communication between men in the earliest periods to which history carries us back. It is the expression of reason, and as such constitutes a line of demarcation between man and the lower animals. Without it, indeed, the brute can, to a certain extent, make known his emotions and desires. The house-dog, by the distinctive character of his bark, welcomes his master or threatens the intrusive stranger. The hen warns her chicks of danger by one set of signals, and calls them to feed by another.

The ant, discovering an inviting grain too heavy for itself alone, bears the intelligence to its fellows and promptly returns with aid. But such limited means of communication fall infinitely short of the perfect system which is exclusively man's birthright—which uses articulate sounds to represent ideas, and combines them so as to express every shade of thought.

Written Language.—Spoken Language lives only for the moment; words uttered to-day die and are forgotten to-morrow. To give permanency to his passing thoughts, when advancing civilization showed such permanency to be desirable, man devised Writing, the art of representing ideas by visible characters. Written Language is the vehicle of literature—the material in which the thinker embodies his conceptions for future generations, just as the sculptor gives permanent forms to his ideals in marble, or the painter on the glowing canvas.

Writing is either Ideographic or Phonetic. The Ideographic System represents material objects and abstract notions *directly*, by pictures or symbols. The Phonetic System uses certain characters to express the articulate sounds by which such objects or notions are denoted, and thus *indirectly*, through the two media of sounds and characters, indicates the objects or notions themselves.

IDEOGRAPHIC WRITING.—The earliest mode of conveying ideas of visible objects was by pictorial imitations. We have examples of it in the original hieroglyphics of Egypt and China, and the cuneiform letters borrowed from their Turanian inventors by the Assyrians and Persians. It was also practised by the Aztecs or ancient Mexicans, and the inhabitants of Central America. Thought-painting, as it may be called, has this advantage, that to a certain extent it is understood as well by the illiterate classes at home as by foreign nations speaking different tongues.

Hieroglyphics, at first purely *pictorial*, at length became *symbolic*, an action or idea being represented by the outline of some material object to which it was thought to bear analogy. A picture of two legs, for instance, stood for the act of walking; a battle was indicated by two men engaged in conflict; eternity, by a circle; brightness, by a combination of the sun and moon, thus ☉☽.

The hieroglyphic system was objectionable on account of the multitude of symbols required, as well as the impossibility of expressing grammatical relations. It therefore gradually went out of use, while its characters were borrowed to denote the sounds of spoken language. During the transition period, however, these characters in many cases retained also their original signification; as if we should denote by one and the same symbol (a picture of the animal) the dog, and the syllable *dog* in the word *dogmatical* —or by J (formed from the outline of a jay) both the idea *bird* and the sound of the letter *j*. This of course led to great confusion, and was long an insuperable obstacle to the interpretation of the cuneiform or *wedge-shaped* letters.

PHONETIC WRITING.—There are two systems of phonetic writing, the Syllabic and the Alphabetic. The characters of the former are used to represent *syllables*, or combinations of sounds (either words or parts of words) uttered by distinct impulses of the voice; those of the latter represent the elements of which these syllables are composed, or *letters*.

The characters by which the elementary sounds of any language are denoted, arranged in order, constitute its Alphabet. A perfect alphabet would be one in which every letter represented but one simple sound, and every simple sound was represented by but one letter—a perfection never yet attained.

It is to the Egyptians that the world is indebted for Alphabetic Writing. Their hieroglyphics, at first true pictures, then symbols corresponding to abstract ideas, finally became, as we have seen, the signs of articulate sounds. But in Egypt the phonetic system was imperfect, the same sound having several symbols, and the same symbol standing for many sounds. It was left for the Phœnicians to remedy these faults, and complete the work thus begun.

Brought into commercial relations with Egypt at an early date, this enterprising people at once saw the advantages of phonetic writing; and by rejecting the ideograms (pictures denoting material objects), but retaining and modifying the phonetic symbols used in that country, they perfected an alphabetic system. The Phœnician alphabet contained at first sixteen letters, to which six more were finally added.

Such is the most probable account of the origin of letters. Tradition variously ascribes their invention to Thoth an Egyptian, to Cadmus the Phœnician, to Odin the supreme deity of the Scandinavians, and to others. Of the varied exports of the Phœnicians, their alphabet was the most precious. Wherever their sails were spread, their letters were made known, and all nations sooner or later profited by this great Semitic invention. In the table on page 87 may be traced a decided resemblance between several of the Phœnician characters and the hieroglyphics in which they originated; also the successive changes by which they were modified in the earlier and later Greek and Latin letters—whence most of our English capitals.

Modes of Writing and Pointing.—As regards the direction in which their writing ran, ancient nations differed. In the Egyptian hieroglyphics there was no established order; but the figures of men and animals, facing the beginning of the lines, often gave a clue to the direction in which they were meant to be read. As a general rule, the Indo-Europeans wrote from left to right, the Semites from right to left. The Laws of Solon and other Greek writings of that period (about

600 B.C.) appeared in lines running alternately from right to left and from left to right, as an ox walks in ploughing; this "ox-turning system" (*boustrophedon*), however, was soon followed by our present method. The Chinese, Japanese, and Mongols, wrote in columns, which were read from the top of the page, and from right to left. In the ancient Mexican pictographs, similar columns were read from the bottom.

The ancients did not separate sentences, or their subdivisions, with points; but wrote their words together, leaving the meaning to be deciphered from the context. Rings, ovals, or squares, were sometimes drawn around proper names, and words were occasionally separated by some device—a diagonal bar or wedge \, as in ancient Persian inscriptions; or a letter placed on its side, as between the following words: CONJUGI⊢KARISSIMAE. In a Roman inscription found near Bath, England, a small *v* occurs after every word: JULIUSvVITALISvFABRI. A peculiar sign was used, in some cases, immediately before the name of a god or of a person.

In the third century B.C., a system of punctuation, devised by Aristophanes, a grammarian of Alexandria, became known to the Greeks. It employed a dot (.), which had the force of our period, colon, or comma, according as it was placed after the top, middle, or bottom of the final word. The better system of modern times was not invented till the sixteenth century.

ANCIENT WRITING MATERIALS.

Stylus and Tablets.—The first writing was done on rocks with sharp-pointed instruments of iron or bronze, to record great events. Next came tracings on bricks of soft clay, afterward hardened by baking; and then writing with a metal or ivory *stylus* on sheets of lead or layers of wax, from which erasures could be made, if needful, with the flattened end of the instrument.

Pliny speaks of leaden sheets, thus inscribed, rolled up in a cylindrical form when not in use. But under provocation the metallic stylus could be employed as a dagger; and when a Roman schoolmaster was killed by his pupils with their styles and heavy table-books, the dangerous instrument was banished, and superseded by a similar one of horn. The early shepherds, we are told, imitated this mode of writing, making thorns or awls do duty as styles, and scratching their songs on leather straps which they wound round their crooks.

Wooden tablets, glazed to receive coloring matter, were used by the Jews and early Egyptians, and the former wrote also with a diamond-tipped stylus on stone or metallic tables. The Greeks and Romans sometimes wired their tablets of citron-wood, beech, or fir, together at the back, so as to allow them to open like a modern book.

Calamus, or Reed.—A great advance was made when the stylus gave way to camel's-hair brushes or reeds (*calami*) sharpened and split like our pens, and the tablets were replaced with papyrus and parchment. The reeds in common use came from Egypt, but persons of fortune often wrote with a silver calamus. The ink employed was thicker and more lasting than ours; sometimes prepared from the black fluid of the cuttle-fish, but generally from lampblack and glue, or from soot, rosin, and pitch.—Chalk pencils were at one time manufactured by the Egyptians and Greeks.

With the reed and ink, bark came into use as a cheap writing material; hence the Latin word for bark, *liber*, meant also book. Leaves, too, were employed for this purpose, particularly those of the palm—whence, perhaps, the *leaf* of a book was so called. But for manuscripts designed for permanent preservation, papyrus had the decided preference.

Papyrus, or the *paper*-plant, the bulrush of Scripture, grew in the marshes and pools of Egypt. Its branchless stem rose from five to ten feet above the water, and was surmounted by a cluster of long, spike-shaped, drooping leaves. This plant was woven into sandals, mats, clothing, and even boats; was eaten, raw and boiled; was manufactured into furniture; and was burned for fuel and light; when prepared for writing purposes, it was invaluable. The part under the water was selected, the outer bark removed, and the delicate white layers found beneath were pressed together into sheets and dried. These were written on with red and black ink, and some of them were elaborately ornamented with many-colored figures.

EGYPTIAN PAPYRUS.

The finest papyrus was reserved for the priests, and never exported till they had used it. But the Romans, having invented a process for removing what was first written on it, imported it in large quantities; they also attempted its cultivation in the marshes of the Tiber, but without success. The Greeks did not use it extensively until the era of the Ptolemies.

Parchment was prepared from the skins of sheep and goats by polishing them with pumice-stone and then rubbing in fragrant oil. Its name, in Latin *pergamena,* would seem to indicate Pergamus in western Asia as the place of its origin; but centuries before that little kingdom became celebrated for its library of parchment volumes, this material, or something very like it, was known. Herodotus mentions its use in his time; and the Jews, as a pastoral people familiar with the art of dressing skins, wrote their first books on a kind of leather.

But if parchment was not invented at Pergamus, Eu'menes, king of that country, was certainly the first to make extensive use of it (175 B.C.). He had founded a splendid li-

Reading a Volumen, or Roll.

brary, which he determined should eclipse that of Alexandria. In the reign of Ptolemy Epiph'anes, king of Egypt, it was sought to prevent the transcription of books for the rival library by prohibiting the exportation of papyrus. This obliged Eumenes to resort to parchment as a substitute. From Pergamus it spread to Europe, finally superseding all other materials, and continuing in demand until the art of making paper cheaply from rags was invented in the fourteenth century.

Ancient manuscripts were put up in the form of rolls (*volu'mina* — whence *volumes*), made of sheets fastened together in a continuous strip, sometimes forty or fifty yards in length. This was wound round wooden cylinders, the ends of which were often set with jewels, or ornamented with knobs of ivory, silver, or gold. Titles were either suspended from these books like tags, or glued upon them as labels. An outside cover of parchment protected the scrolls, which, enclosed in cylindrical cases and placed horizontally on shelves ranged about a room, constituted an ancient library.

The Chinese, after writing for centuries, in common with their neighbors of India, on bark and dried palm-leaves, are believed to have discovered a process of preparing a pulp from cotton or bamboo, and to have manufactured it into paper as early as the commencement of our era. Perhaps, as observation of the silkworm spinning her cocoons led them to devise the art of weaving silk, they in like manner borrowed his cunning from the paper-making wasp, and thus early perfected an invention which has been of incalculable service to literature.

GENERAL VIEW OF THE HISTORY OF ANCIENT LITERATURE.

A comprehensive glance over the entire field whose treasures we are about to examine in detail, will enable us the better to appreciate and remember their relative age and value. Beginning, then, with the most distant periods, we find a literature developed in Mesopota'mia, Egypt, Iran, and China, as early as 2000 B.C. At that date, the valley of the Euphrates and Tigris was the seat of a civilized Turanian people, the inventors of the complex system of cuneiform writing, thought by some to be the oldest in the world. These Turanian Chaldees, mingled with a Semitic race, were then beginning to enjoy their golden age of letters; at the same time, the ancient Persians and Hindoos were composing hymns; the sages of China were busy on their sacred books; and Egypt had doubtless made considerable advance in both poetry and prose.

To trace the progress of literature in these remote times from century to century is impossible. Five hundred years, however, bring us to the Augustan era of romance and satire, epic and devotional poetry, in Egypt: they introduce us to Zoroas'ter, the founder or reformer of the ancient Persian religion, whose teachings are set forth in the Aves'ta; to the Ve'da, or Brahman Bible; to Moses and the Pentateuch; and to Phœnician theology, science, and poetry. Meanwhile Chaldean literature declines, and Assyrian letters come into view. During the next five centuries, poetry and science continue to flourish in Egypt, though not perhaps with their pristine vigor; Phœnicia maintains her literary reputation; the Veda grows; and Persian priests are occupied in enlarging and modifying their sacred texts.

1000 B.C. was the era of the great epics. The epic, or narrative poem, based on some important event (in Greek, ἔπος) or chain of events, though first appearing in Egypt—the mother-land of literature as well as science and art—was simultaneously brought to perfection, about this time, by the Greeks and Hindoos, Aryan nations holding no intercourse with each other and separated by at least three thousand miles. Homer's Iliad and Odyssey, the wonder of Hellas, were paralleled by two stupendous Indian poems, the Râmâyana (*rah-mah'-yă-nă*) and the Mahâbhârata (*mă-hah'bah'ră-tă*), the great masterpieces of Sanscrit poetry. To these, all dazzling with Oriental splendor, the epics of the Greek bard may yield in luxuriance of fancy and gorgeous imagery; but in power of description, sublimity of thought, and attractive simplicity of expression, Homer was without an equal.

While, then, the Semitic Hebrews and Phœnicians used prose as the vehicle of their earliest records of events, Greece and India, types of the Aryan stock, transmitted their legends to posterity in epic verse. Later times have not failed to perpetuate the taste, and measurably the ability; epic poetry has been cultivated by all the Indo-European nations, and to them it has been confined.—Contemporaneously with Homer, native poets were inditing ballads and pastorals in China, and the Hebrews enjoyed their golden age of secular and religious poetry; Egypt had entered on her literary, as well as her political, decline.

Henceforth our interest centres principally in Greece. Until 800 B.C., the poems of Homer and of Hesiod, his contemporary or immediate successor, constituted the bulk of Hellenic literature. Then began a transition to a poetry more natural—a poetry of the emotions—on themes that kindled love, anger, hatred, grief, hope; and for three centuries *lyrics* in different forms echoed throughout the land. Archil'ochus poured forth his caustic satires; Tyrtæus, his inspiriting war-songs; Sappho, her passionate strains; Anacreon, the joys of the wine-cup; Simon'ides breathed his touching laments; and Pindar stirred the soul with his grand odes, as with the sound of the trumpet. Prose also received attention, and Ionian authors took the initiative in systematic historical composition. Rude religious festivals suggested dramatic representations; and the pioneers in tragedy and comedy rode about the country, exhibiting their novel art on carts which carried the performers and their machinery.—Meanwhile in the East, Assyrian literature reached its highest development at Nineveh, to be buried beneath the ruins of that city, 625 B.C. Letters then revived at Babylon, and for nearly a century flourished there; Jewish poetry declined; and Confucius, the philosopher of transcendent wisdom, appeared in China.

Early in the 5th century, Greece plunged into a struggle for life or death with the Persian Empire—a struggle from which she emerged covered with glory, united and free. Her triumph is straightway sung in immortal verse, and historians arise to record her exploits. Athens, who faced the enemy at Marathon, Salamis, and Platæa, and drove him back crippled and disgraced to Asia, now becomes the leader of grateful Hellas, and the centre of literature and refinement. Blossom after blossom unfolds in her genial clime. She makes ample amends for her barrenness in the past by unprecedented fruitfulness, and gives to the nations a drama, lustrous with the names of Æschylus, Sophocles, Euripides (*es'ke-lus, sof'o-kleez, eu-rip'e-deez*)—the great tragic trio of antiquity. Comedy also, as represented by Aristophanes, is perfected in her theatre.

Then come the Peloponnesian War and the consequent humiliation of Athens; the overthrow of her democratic government, and the partial decline of literature, particularly poetry, with the fall of free institutions. Still, writers of genius are not wanting. The graphic pens of Thucydides and Xenophon lend additional graces to the history of Greece; Plato and Aristotle make her name immortal in philosophy; and the world's greatest orators electrify her assemblies with their eloquence. Demosthenes, prince of them all, stands forth as the champion of Grecian liberty, and thunders his Philippics at the wily Macedonian who would enthrall his country. But the star of Macedon was in the ascendant. Chærone'a decided the fate of Greece; and she who had withstood the legions of Xerxes, gave way before the invincible phalanx of Philip and Alexander.

A sad period of decadence followed. Alexandria, in Egypt, founded by the conqueror whose name it bore (332 B.C.), became the centre of learning as well as commerce; and Athens yielded to her fate, wasting her time in empty philosophical discussions and the pursuit of pleasure. Poetry languished, yet flashed out occasionally in epic or didactic form, bringing to mind the glories of the past. It is true that in the idyls of Theocritus (*little pictures of domestic life*) pastoral verse now bloomed for the first time on European soil, and with fine effect; but it was in far-off Syracuse, not in classic Greece. Here the deepening twilight was fatal to literary growth; and when Egypt fell beneath the power of Rome in the first century B.C., Greek letters sought a new asylum in the city of Romulus.

Turning to Rome, we find that she had long displayed an appreciation of Grecian genius as well as a striking talent for imitation. About the middle of the third century B.C., with little or no literature of her own, she gladly appropriated the foreign treasures held up before her admiring eyes by Liv′ius Androni′cus, a Tarentine Greek, whom the fortunes of war had made the slave of a Roman master. This most ancient of Latin poets put upon the stage versions of the Greek dramas, and with his translation of the Odyssey took his captors captive. Nævius and Ennius, following in the path thus opened, gave Italy its first epics; Ter′ence and Plautus made the people familiar with the humors of comedy; and Cato imparted dignity to Latin prose.

Oratory, for which the Romans had a natural aptitude, culminated in the speeches of Cicero, who ushered in the golden age. In his writings, as well as in the histories of Cæsar, Sallust, and Livy, prose now attracted with its finished periods. Nor was poetry less notably represented. Catullus, vehement and pathetic by turns, transplanted the ode and epigram to Italy; Lucre′tius threw into verse his ideal of philosophy; Tibullus excelled in simplicity and tenderness; while Virgil and Horace rivalled, as they doubtless imitated, the first poets of Greece.

Virgil's epic, the Æne'id, as remarkable for beauty as Homer's is for grandeur, secured to its author the first place among Latin poets; and next to him stands Horace, with his faultless mastery of metre and keen observation of men and manners. Their genius shed on the court of the first emperor, Augustus, a peculiar lustre, still recognized in our application of the epithet *Augustan* to the most brilliant period of a nation's literature.

It is not strange that under the tyranny of the Cæsars literary decay set in; yet Rome's silver age was kept bright by the labors of Persius and Juvenal, the unsparing satirists; Lucan, author of the epic Pharsalia; the grave and accurate historian Tacitus; the two Plinies; and Quintilian, the rhetorician. Taste, however, had sadly deteriorated; genius died with patriotism; and despots sought in vain to restore for their own corrupt purposes the ancient spirit which they had crushed out. At length the degenerate Latin writers laid aside their own manly tongue for Greek; and the list of the monuments of Roman genius was complete.

Such has been, in general, the course of every literature. We trace successively the birth of poetry; the gradual perfecting of prose; the ripening of simplicity into elegance; the perversion of elegance into affectation; the language and literature, losing the vigor of manhood, affected with the feebleness of age, and either succumbing at once to some great civil convulsion or perishing by a slow but no less certain living death. As with political, so with literary history:—

"This is the moral of all human tales;
'Tis but the same rehearsal of the past,—
First freedom, and then glory; when that fails,
Wealth, vice, corruption, barbarism at last;
And History, with all its volumes vast,
Hath but one page."

BYRON.

PART I.

ANCIENT ORIENTAL LITERATURES.

CHAPTER I.

HINDOO LITERATURE.

THE SANSCRIT LANGUAGE.

Characteristics.—Oldest of all the Indo-European tongues, and most closely resembling the common parent that is lost, is SANSCRIT—the language spoken by those fair-skinned Aryans who more than thirty centuries ago, swarming through the Hindoo Koosh passes, made the sunny plains of Hindostan their own (page 16). Sanscrit spread over most of the peninsula; and the meaning of the word, *perfected*, is significant of the flexibility, refinement, regularity, and philosophical system of grammar, by which the language was distinguished. In luxuriance of inflection it was unequalled. Its nouns were varied according to eight cases, and three numbers (singular, dual, and plural); and its verbs, which assumed causal, desiderative, and frequentative forms, were carried in conjugation through three voices, the active, middle, and passive. Its chief fault—a result of its very richness—lay in the frequent use of long compounds, particularly adjectives, presenting what seems to us a confused combination of ideas, sometimes ludicrously lengthened out; as in the expressions, "always-to-be-remembered-with-reverence patriot," "water-play-delighted-maiden-bathing-fragrant river-breezes" (that is, *river-breezes made fragrant by the bathing of maidens delighted with sporting in the water*).

Neither the parallelism of Hebrew poetry (page 89) nor the rhyme of modern times finds a place in Sanscrit verse; it is distinguished from prose, like Greek poetry, simply by a metrical arrangement of long and short syllables. The measured cadence gave great delight to the cultivated ear of the Hindoos. "There are two excellent things in the world," says one of their writers—"the friendship of the good, and the beauties of poetry."

Brahman Priest.

Sanscrit is now a dead language. About three hundred years before the Christian era, dialects derived from it took its place among the people, and it has since been kept alive only in the conversation and writings of the learned, as the sacred language of the Brahmans, or priestly caste.* Yet so extensive is its literature that it costs a Brahman half his life to master a portion of its sacred books alone.

Sanscrit Alphabet.—As to the origin of the Sanscrit alphabet, consisting of fifty letters, history is silent. It is believed that the entire early literature was preserved for centuries by

* The language of the Gypsies, descendants of those Hindoos who fled from the persecutions of Tamerlane, is a corrupted Sanscrit.

oral repetition. When their polished tongue was first expressed in written characters—derived directly or indirectly from the Phœnicians—so perfectly did these answer the purpose that the Hindoos styled their alphabet "the writing of the gods." The Sanscrit letters are still preserved in the written language of the pure Hindoos, but in that of the Mohammedan population have been replaced with the Arabic characters.

History of Sanscrit Researches.—Arabian translations of Sanscrit works were made as early as the reign of the Caliph Haroun'-al-Raschid, at Bagdad (800 A.D.), and appeared from time to time in the succeeding centuries. Europeans first knew of the existence of Sanscrit and its literature during the reign of Au'rungzebe (1658–1707), in whose time the French and English obtained a foothold in Hindostan. Before this, the Jesuit Nobili (*no'be-le*) had gone to India to study the sacred books with a view to the conversion of the Hindoos, and, having mastered them, boldly preached a new Veda; but he died on the scene of his labors, and Europe profited nothing by his researches. It was left for the Asiatic Society, organized at Calcutta in 1784 by Sir William Jones, to open the eyes of Europe to the importance and magnitude of Brahman literature, of which the translation of Sakoon'talâ (page 50) by this great orientalist gave a most favorable specimen.

Following in the footsteps of the English scholar just mentioned, the German critic Schlegel, in his "Language and Wisdom of the Indians" (1808) laid the permanent foundations of COMPARATIVE PHILOLOGY, a science of recent birth but one that has been of incalculable service to history, establishing the kinship of the Hindoos and Persians with the old Greeks and Romans, as well as the modern nations of the west, by striking resemblances in their respective tongues. Eminent scholars have since prosecuted the work with enthusiasm—especially Bopp, Humboldt, Pott, and Grimm among the Germans, the French savant Bournouf, Max Müller in England, and the American Whitney. Sanscrit is no longer a sealed volume. The leading European universities have their professors of that tongue, who lecture also on comparative grammar and the science of language.

SACRED LITERATURE OF THE HINDOOS.

The Veda.—The language of the ancient Indo-Aryans survives in the Ve′da, the oldest work of Indo-European literature, dating back to the prehistoric era of the Aryan race. The Veda, while rich in striking imagery, is marked by a beautiful simplicity of diction. In its language, we behold the most ancient form of our own tongue; in the hymns of its poets, those germs of Aryan intellectual development that no long time after bloomed in epic and idyl through the fertile valleys of India, bore immortal fruit on the soil of Greece and Rome, and have been brought to perfection in the grand productions of modern genius. The Veda is the first of thousands of Indian works; for Hindoo thought, undisturbed by Assyrian, Egyptian, or Macedonian conqueror, flowed on, ever creative, and still flows, an uninterrupted stream from the day of the Veda to the present.

The word *Veda* means *knowledge.* Though there is really but one—the Rig-Veda, or Veda of songs of praise—the name is applied also to three other collections of hymns. These are the Vedas of Chants, Sacrificial Rites, and Incantations; for the Hindoos were believers in the efficacy of sacrifices, some of which were prolonged for months and even years, as well as of talismans, charms, and incantations to ward off disease, bring riches, and inspire love. Each of the last-named Vedas is a medley of extracts from the Rig-Veda, transposed or combined into new hymns, with additions from outside sources.

To the metrical parts of the Vedas are attached the Brâhmanas, which abound in tedious descriptions of rites, and were written long after in prose to explain the hymns. There are also collections of rules for worship and sacrifice; and speculations on philosophy and religion, which display no little acuteness, for the Hindoo mind seems to have been prone to metaphysical investigation and ingenious in reasoning even to the verge of sophistry. Supplements to the Vedas contain abundant commentaries on their grammar and language, as well as astronomical facts — the latter mainly borrowed from other nations and not based on original researches or discoveries.

Finally, the Upave'das (*oo-pă-vā' dăz—appended*) treat of diseases and their cure, devotional music, the use of weapons, and the arts; while the Purânas (*poo-rah'năz*), of more recent birth, believed to have been revealed from heaven like the Vedas, present in verse the mythology of India and the history of its legendary age.

Religion of the Veda.—The Supreme Being first acknowledged by the Aryans was gradually lost sight of, and a worship of Nature arose. In the 1,028 hymns of the Rig-Veda, "thrice eleven" gods are invoked as intelligent beings, the principal of whom are Varuna (*vur'oo-nah*—god of waters), the sun, the moon, the day, fire, storms, the dawn, and the earth; and to "the three and thirty," offerings were made of butter, cakes, wine, and grain. They were immortal; clothed with power to answer prayer, and punish those who offended them. But as each great god is recognized as supreme in different hymns, it is with good reason thought that under various names, one great omnipotent Being is worshipped, called in the Veda "God above all gods," "that One alone who has upheld the spheres." "Wise poets," says the Rig-Veda, "make the Beautiful-winged, though he is one, manifold by words."*

* "He is the only master of the world; he fills heaven and earth. He gives life and strength: all the other gods seek for his blessing; death and immortality are but his shadow.

In the following hymn to Varuna is apparent the belief that evil-doing is hateful to the Almighty, that man is by nature prone to sin, and that God stands ready to exercise forgiveness.

HYMN TO VARUNA.

(We have given Max Müller's literal translation a dress of verse, the better to bring out the effect of the refrain.)

O Varuna, let me not yet enter the house of clay:
Mercy, Almighty one, thy mercy I pray!
If, like a cloud the sport of winds, I trembling go astray—
Mercy, Almighty one, thy mercy I pray!
Through want of strength, thou strong bright God, I've wandered from the way:
Mercy, Almighty one, thy mercy I pray!
Thirst comes upon the worshipper, though round the waters play:
Mercy, Almighty one, thy mercy I pray!
When we do wrong through thoughtlessness, thy hand of vengeance stay:
Transgressors of thy righteous law, thy mercy, God, we pray!

But of all the conceptions of the Vedic writers, that of the Dawn Goddess was the most poetical. Watching for the first flush in the eastern sky, her ancient worshippers, with their hands devoutly placed upon their foreheads, opened their hearts in strains of praise to the gloom-dispelling Dawn, the golden-hued Daughter of Heaven, leading on the sun with her modest smile, "like a radiant bride adorned by her mother for the bridegroom."

The sun is represented as a glorious prince, hastening after the Dawn-maiden and trying to discover her by a tiny slipper which she has dropped, and which is too small for another to wear; but the prince never overtakes the flying maid. This beautiful myth is the origin of the tale of Cinderella.

The mountains covered with frost, the ocean with its waves, the vast regions of heaven, proclaim his power.

By him the heaven and earth, space and the firmament, have been solidly founded: he spread abroad the light in the atmosphere.

Heaven and earth tremble for fear before him. He is God above all gods!"

RIG-VEDA.

The Veda contains no allusions to those corrupt practices which afterward became the distinguishing marks of Brahmanism. At this early period there was no belief in the transmigration of the souls of men into inferior animals; on the contrary, the Vedic Aryans looked for "excellent treasures in the sky." To caste, they were also strangers; idols were unknown; and suttee, the burning of the widow at her husband's funeral, was an unheard-of barbarity.

Social Life of the Vedic People.—The hymns of the Rig-Veda picture the manners and customs of an intellectual people, far advanced in the arts. Princely palaces are described, fortified cities, monarchs possessed of fabulous riches, ladies elegantly attired. There were poor as well as rich, workers in the various handicrafts; ship-building was practised, and naval expeditions were undertaken. Even at this remote day literary meetings were held.

Nor were the crimes and vices of later times unknown. Liars are denounced; thieves, robbers, and intoxicating drinks, are mentioned; while in one hymn, a gambler laments his ruin by "the tumbling dice," and warns others not to play, but rather to practise husbandry. Battles are sung, and waving banners, and chariots drawn by fleet horses.

The following extract from one of the secular hymns which are interspersed with those of a religious character, shows some knowledge of human nature:—

EVERY ONE TO HIS TASTE.

"Men's tastes and trades are multifarious,
And so their ends and aims are various.
The smith seeks something cracked to mend;
The doctor would have sick to tend.
The priest desires a devotee
From whom he may extract his fee.
Each craftsman makes and vends his ware,
And hopes the rich man's gold to share.
My sire's a doctor; I, a bard;
Corn grinds my mother, toiling hard.

All craving wealth, we each pursue,
By different means, the end in view,
Like people running after cows,
Which too far off have strayed to browse.
The draught-horse seeks an easy yoke,
The merry dearly like a joke,
Of lovers youthful belles are fond,
And thirsty frogs desire a pond."—MUIR.

LAW-BOOKS OF THE HINDOOS.

Code of Manu.—Of the many Indian treatises on the moral law still extant, the most ancient and important is the Institutes of Manu (*mun'oo*)—the time-hallowed monument of a period just subsequent to the Vedic age (variously placed at from 1280 to 880 B.C.). This code is written in verse, as were most Hindoo works, even scientific expositions. Four distinct castes are now recognized, ascending through the successive grades of laborers, farmers, warriors, and princes, to the highest, which consisted of the priests of Brahma, "the soul of the universe, whom eye, tongue, mind, cannot reach," from whose substance all men proceed and to whom all must return through various states of existence. The childlike religion of the Veda has disappeared.

The word *brahma* often occurs in the Vedas with the signification of worship, or hymn, the vehicle of worship. In the later Vedic poems it came to mean an object of worship, the universal but impersonal spiritual principle, all-pervading and self-existent. In Manu's Code, Brahma is endowed with personality, and a definite place is for the first time assigned him in the national religious system, as the creative spirit who made the universe before undiscerned discernible in the beginning. He, as the Creator, is united with the three-eyed thousand-named Siva (*se'vah*) the Destroyer, and Vishnu the Preserver, in the Hindoo triad. Vishnu was the first-begotten of Brahma, a benevolent being who, to overcome the malignant agents of evil, submitted to various incarnations or embodiments in human or animal form, known as *Av'atars*. Nine avatars, which the Hindoos believed to have taken place, were favorite themes of Sanscrit poetry; the tenth, still future, would result in the overthrow of the present state of things and the ushering in of a new and better era.

Moral Precepts. — The Institutes of Manu regulated the moral and social life of the people, prescribing certain rules for the government of society and the punishment of crimes. Purity of life was enjoined on all. One of the chief duties was to honor father and mother—the mother a thousand times the most—and the Brahman more than either. Widows are forbidden to remarry, and the duties of a wife are thus described :—

"The wife must always be in a cheerful temper, devoting herself to the good management of the household, taking great care of the furniture, and keeping down all expenses with a frugal hand. The husband to whom her father has given her, she must obsequiously honor while he lives and never neglect him when he dies. The husband gives bliss continually to his wife here below, and he will give her happiness in the next world. He must be constantly revered as a god by a virtuous wife, even if he does not observe approved usages, or is devoid of good qualities. A faithful wife, who wishes to attain heaven and dwell there with her husband, must never do anything unkind toward him, whether he be living or dead."

The following was the punishment for killing a cow, an animal treated with the honors due to a deity :—

"All day he must wait on a herd of cows, and stand quaffing the dust raised by their hoofs.

Free from passion, he must stand when they stand, follow when they move, lie down near them when they lie down.

By thus waiting on a herd for three months, he who has killed a cow atones for his guilt."

OTHER EXTRACTS FROM MANU.

"Greatness is not conferred by years nor by gray hairs, by wealth nor powerful kindred. Whoever has read the Veda, he always is great.

A Brahman beginning or ending a lecture on the Veda must always pronounce to himself the syllable OM*; for unless the syllable

* The mystical name formed of the three elements A U M, representing the three forms of the deity.

OM precede his learning will slip away from him, and unless it follow nothing will be long retained.

When one among all the organs sins, by that single failure all knowledge of God passes away; as the water flows through one hole in a leathern bottle.

The names of women should be agreeable, soft, clear, captivating the fancy, auspicious, ending in long vowels, resembling words of benediction."

EPIC POETRY.

Indian literature boasts of two grand epic poems—gems that would shine in the crown of a Homer or a Milton—the Râmâyana (*rah-mah'yă-nă*—Adventures of Râma) and the Mahâbhârata (*mă-hah'bah'ră-tă*—Great War of Bhârata), "the Iliad and Odyssey of Sanscrit poetry." The date of these epics is uncertain, though probably later than that of Manu's Code. Both contain ancient Vedic traditions, but mingled with these is much that is more recent. It is probable that the old songs and stories were current among the people ages before they were arrayed in their present dress by later poets, who gave them a different religious coloring to suit the Brahmanical doctrines. Their language is an improvement on that of the Veda in polish and softness; improvement would naturally result from oral repetition.

The Râmâyana, by the poet Vâlmiki (*vahl'me-ke*), relates the achievements of Râma (the name assumed by Vishnu in his seventh avatar, or incarnation), who descended to earth that he might destroy a demon-prince in Ceylon. Râma becomes the first-born of the monarch of Oude and heir-apparent to the throne, marries a lovely princess, Sîtâ (*se'tah*), whose hand others had vainly sought, and daily increases in popularity. But Râma's mother was not the only queen; a younger and more beautiful rival prevails on the old king to appoint her son his successor instead of Râma, and to banish the latter for fourteen years.

Loyal to his father, though he might have seized the crown by force, as his mother in her first disappointment bade him do, Râma set out for the wilderness, accompanied by his bride, who refused to remain behind in the luxurious capital. Soon after his father died of grief; whereupon the younger brother rejected the crown, and, seeking the exile in the jungle, saluted him as king. Râma, however, declined the honor, and, proceeding to fulfil his mission, slew the demon and conquered Ceylon. Then with his faithful wife he returned to Oude, to reign jointly with his brother and usher in a golden age.

The Râmâyana, in this fiction, is supposed to refer to the conquest of southern India and Ceylon by the Aryans. It so delighted the Hindoos that it was said, "He who sings and hears this epic continually has attained to the highest enjoyment, and will finally be equal to the gods."

FROM THE RÂMÂYANA.

Sîtâ, informed by her husband of his banishment, thus tenderly pleads to be the companion of his exile :—

"I will not be a charge to thee: the wood will give me roots,
The spring will yield me water, and the branch provide me fruits.
In hermit's humble mantle clad, and guarded by my lord,
I long to wander through the wood, the rivulet to ford,
To climb the rock, and gaze upon the lake that looks so cool;
And oh! the pleasant bathing in the clear and shaded pool,
With waters freshly running from the sweet perennial springs,
All lovely with the lotuses and wild swans' silver wings.
I would not live in heaven itself, and thou, my love, away;
A thousand years with thee, my love, would seem one blissful day.
Then take me with thee to the wood, nor leave me here alone:
I will not be a burthen sore to thee, mine own! mine own!"

But Râma seeks to dissuade her :—

"The forest life has fears and woes too many to be told:
Thirst, hunger, burning heat by day, by night the bitter cold.
Each moment on some deadly thing the heedless step may fall,
Where serpents with their venomed fangs and poisonous scorpions crawl;
There thro' the day the tiger roams, the panther and the boar,
And thro' the night the caverned hills echo the lion's roar;
There many a river deep and wide will bar thine onward way,

Where fearful crocodiles amid the foaming waters play.
The forest paths, my Sîtâ dear, are rough and hard to pass,
Tangled with knotted creeping plants, and thorns, and matted grass.
O'er many a league the wild woods stretch, and savage beasts abound;
No fruit or flower may there be seen, and water scarce is found;
No bed is there to rest the limbs, but stretched upon a heap
Of fallen leaves and gathered grass the homeless wretch must sleep.
No, such a life is not for thee; cast thou the thought away;
Here in the palace of the king in peace and safety stay.
Though far away from thee I go, and thou remainest here,
Still shalt thou live within the heart to which thou art so dear."

Yet Sîtâ still refuses to be parted from her husband, and with tearful eyes exclaims:—

"And death to me were sweeter far, with thine arms round me thrown,
Than life in thy father's palaces, in safety, but alone.
The wife's eternal duty is, as holy priests declare,
To follow where her husband goes, his weal and woe to share;
And for the true and loving wife remains the endless bliss
Of sharing all this life with him, and the life that follows this."

But, Râma being still inexorable, Sîtâ bursts forth in anger, upbraids him for his cruelty in deserting her, and finally, overcome by emotion, falls weeping at his feet. Then Râma raises her in his arms, and pours these soothing accents in her ear:—

"Oh! what is heaven without thee, love? With thee I'll live and die;
Never will Râma stoop to fear, though Brahma's self come nigh.
Obedience to my father's will now sends me to the wood;
For paramount of duties this is counted by the good.
Only to try thy mind, my love, thy prayer I first denied:
I never dreamed that aught could harm the lady by my side;
But yet I feared to suffer thee, so delicate and fair,
The troubles of a forest life and all its woes to share.
Now, as the glory of his life the saint can ne'er resign,
Thou too, devoted, brave, and true, shalt follow and be mine."

GRIFFITH.

As a favorable specimen of the florid description in which Hindoo imagination excels, we quote from the same epic,

THE DESCENT OF THE GANGES.

"From the high heaven burst Ganges forth, first on Siva's lofty crown;
Headlong then, and prone to earth, thundering rushed the cataract down.
Swarms of bright-hued fish came dashing; turtles, dolphins, in their mirth,
Fallen, or falling, glancing, flashing, to the many-gleaming earth;
And all the host of heaven came down, sprites and genii in amaze,
And each forsook his heavenly throne, upon that glorious scene to gaze.
On cars, like high-towered cities, seen, with elephants and coursers rode,
Or on soft-swinging palanquin lay wondering, each observant god.
As met in bright divan each god, and flashed their jewelled vestures' rays,
The coruscating ether glowed, as with a hundred suns ablaze.
And in ten thousand sparkles bright went flashing up the cloudy spray,
The snowy-flocking swans less white, within its glittering mists at play.
And headlong now poured down the flood, and now in silver circlets wound;
Then lake-like spread, all bright and broad, then gently, gently flowed around;
Then 'neath the caverned earth descending, then spouted up the boiling tide;
Then stream with stream, harmonious blending, swell bubbling up or smooth subside.
By that heaven-welling water's breast, the genii and the sages stood;
Its sanctifying dews they blest, and plunged within the lustral flood."—MILMAN.

The Mahâbhârata, one of the noblest creations of the Epic Muse, is a colossal poem by Vyâsa (*ve-ah'să*), containing more than 200,000 lines, and relating the history of a great struggle between two branches of an ancient royal family. Jealousy led to the separation of the rival parties, one of which, the Pândavas (*pahn'dă-văz*), cleared the jungle and founded the city of Delhi (*del'le*). But their enemies, the Kurus (*Koo'rooz*), resolving to dispossess them, challenged the Pândavas to a gambling match; the latter accepted, but were cheated out of all their possessions by the use of loaded dice, and driven into the wilderness. A savage war ensued, resulting in the triumph of the Pândavas, and their elevation over the neighboring rajahs.

The great Hindoo epics are both enlivened by charming episodes. The most beautiful of those interwoven in the Mahâbhârata are called "the Five Precious Gems." Of these, the magnificent philosophical poem entitled THE DIVINE SONG withdraws the reader for a while from the tumult of war, and introduces him to a profound theological dialogue between a disguised god and one of the principal combatants. It inculcates the existence of one Immutable, Eternal Being, and teems with grand thoughts not unlike those we should expect from a Christian teacher. The immortality of the soul is thus sublimely set forth by the deity, on the eve of a decisive battle, for the purpose of removing the scruples of the chief, while the latter humanely hesitates to precipitate the conflict in view of the slaughter that would ensue:—

"Ne'er was the time when I was not, nor thou, nor yonder kings of earth:
Hereafter, ne'er shall be the time, when one of us shall cease to be.
The soul, within its mortal frame, glides on thro' childhood, youth, and age;
Then in another form renewed, renews its stated course again.
All indestructible is He that spread the living universe;
And who is he that shall destroy the work of the Indestructible?
Corruptible these bodies are that wrap the everlasting soul—
The eternal, unimaginable soul. Whence on to battle, Bhârata!
For he that thinks to slay the soul, or he that thinks the soul is slain,
Are fondly both alike deceived: it is not slain—it slayeth not;
It is not born—it doth not die; past, present, future knows it not;
Ancient, eternal, and unchanged, it dies not with the dying frame.
Who knows it incorruptible, and everlasting, and unborn,
What heeds he whether he may slay, or fall himself in battle slain?
As their old garments men cast off, anon new raiment to assume,
So casts the soul its worn-out frame, and takes at once another form.
The weapon cannot pierce it through, nor wastes it the consuming fire;
The liquid waters melt it not, nor dries it up the parching wind;

Impenetrable and unburned; impermeable and undried;
Perpetual, ever-wandering, firm, indissoluble, permanent,
Invisible, unspeakable."—MILMAN.

But of all the episodes, that of Nala (*nul'ă*) and Damayanti is unsurpassed for pathos and tenderness of sentiment. King Nala, enamored of the "softly-smiling" Damayanti, "pearl among women," finds his love returned, and is accepted by her in preference to many other princes and even four of the gods. A jealous demon, however, possesses him, and causes him to lose at play everything except his bride, whom he cannot be prevailed upon to stake. Yet at last, in his madness, he deserts her in the forest, and Damayanti, after many strange adventures, reaches her father's court in safety. There she adopts the device of inviting suitors a second time to propose for her hand, in the hope of bringing her lost husband to her side if he should hear that there was danger of his losing her forever.

Nala, meanwhile, disguised as a charioteer, had entered the service of another king, who now sets forth to offer himself to the beauteous princess, driven by her husband. When they arrive Damayanti penetrates the disguise of the charioteer, and to prove the correctness of her suspicions, puts him to the severest test. She contrives to have his children brought before him. The father's heart is touched at once; he clasps them in his arms, and bursts into tears.

"Soon as he young Indrasena and her little brother saw,
Up he sprang, his arms wound round them, to his bosom folding both.
When he gazed upon the children, like the children of the gods,
All his heart o'erflowed with pity, and unwilling tears brake forth."

Not wishing, however, to reveal himself to a wife whom he thought false, he added by way of apology for his conduct,

"Oh! so like my own twin children was yon lovely infant pair,
Seeing them thus unexpected, have I broken out in tears."

Finally Nala makes himself known to Damayanti, and, convinced of her faithfulness, is reunited to her and regains his crown.

Such are the Indian epics and their episodes. They need but a skilful hand to file away their superfluities and reset their choicest gems together in fitting chaplets, that the names of their authors, Vâlmiki and Vyâsa, may be as familiar and as highly honored as those of Homer and Virgil.

LYRIC AND DIDACTIC POETRY.

Kâlidâsa.—In lyric poetry, embracing idyls and amatory pieces, Sanscrit is no less rich than in epic, whether quantity or quality be considered. Foremost in this department is Kâlidâsa (*kah'le-dah'să*), about whose life, and even his exact period, nothing is certainly known, but whose works have crowned him with immortality. He is the author of many charming verses; and his poem, "the Seasons," which draws fascinating pictures of the luxuriant landscapes of India, displaying on every page the poet's ardent love for the beauties of nature, has the honor of being the first book ever printed in Sanscrit.

AUTUMN.

FROM KÂLIDÂSA'S SEASONS.

"Welcome Autumn, lovely bride,
Full of beauty, full of pride!
Hear her anklets' silver ring:
'Tis the swans that round her sing.
Mark the glory of her face:
'Tis the lotus lends its grace.
See the garb around her thrown;
Look and wonder at her zone.
Robes of maize her limbs enfold,
Girt with rice like shining gold.
Streams are white with silver wings
Of the swans that autumn brings.
Lakes are sweet with opening flowers;
Gardens, gay with jasmine bowers;

While the woods, to charm the sight,
Show their bloom of purest white.
Vainly might the fairest try
With the charms around to vie.
How can India's graceful daughter
Match that swan upon the water?
Fair her arching brow above,
Swimming eyes that melt with love:
But that charming brow can never
Beat that ripple on the river;
And those eyes must still confess
Lilies' rarer loveliness.
Perfect are those rounded arms,
Aided by the bracelets' charms:
Fairer still those branches are,
And those creepers, better far,
Ring them round with many a fold,
Lovelier than gems and gold.
Now no more doth Indra's Bow
In the evening sunlight glow,
Nor his flag, the lightning's glare,
Flash across the murky air.
Beauty too has left the trees,
Which but now were wont to please:
Other darlings claim her care,
And she pours her blossoms there.

Now beneath the moonlight sweet,
Many troops of maidens meet.
Many a pleasant tale they tell
Of the youths that love them well;
Of the word, the flush, the glance,
The kiss, the sigh, the dalliance.

Not a youth can wander when
Jasmine blossoms scent the glen,
While the notes of many a bird
From the garden shades are heard,
But his melting soul must feel
Sweetest longing o'er it steal.
Not a maid can brush away
Morning dew-drops from the spray,
But she feels a sweet unrest
Wooingly disturb her breast.
As the breezes fresh and cool
From the lilies on the pool,
Sweet with all the fragrance there,
Play, like lovers, with her hair."

GRIFFITH.

Surpassing "the Seasons" in dignity and elegance, "the Cloud Messenger," by the same author, contains some fine flights of fancy. It tells how an inferior god, banished for twelve months to a sacred forest and thus separated from a wife whom he fondly loves, commits to a passing cloud a message for his goddess. He directs its imaginary journey through the sky, over forests and hills, to the city of the gods. There it will easily distinguish his wife, whom he paints to the cloud in glowing colors as the "first, best work of the Creator's hand," mourning over their separation.

"And sad and silent shalt thou find my wife,
Half of my soul and partner of my life;
Nipped by chill sorrow, as the flowers enfold
Their shrinking petals from the withering cold.
I view her now! Long weeping swells her eyes,
And those dear lips are dried by parching sighs.
Sad on her hand her pallid cheek declines,
And half unseen through veiling tresses shines;
As when a darkling night the moon enshrouds,
A few faint rays break straggling through the clouds."

He then intrusts the cloud with the tender words that he would breathe; bids it tell his beloved how he sees her in the rippling brooks, how

"O'er the rude stone her pictured beauties rise;"

and finally he charges his messenger to console her afflicted heart with assurances of his unabated love, and to hasten back with tidings that may relieve his soul of its anxiety. The cloud obeys; but meanwhile the supreme deity learns of the message, repents of his severity, restores the exile to his wife, and blesses the pair with ceaseless joy.

Kâlidâsa also wrote three epics of a romantic character, one of them on the adventures of Nala and his devoted Damayanti. Well does he merit the title conferred on him by his admiring countrymen,—"the Bridegroom of Poesy."

Jayadeva (*jī-ă-dā'vă*), a poet probably of more recent times, if not equal to Kâlidâsa, yet has given us in Gîtagovinda one of the most enchanting idyls ever written. In this Song of the Shepherd Govinda, the form assumed by the god Krishna, are set forth in voluptuous colors the adventures of the deity and nine shepherdesses, his beautiful attendants. The whole is supposed to be a mystical allegory.

The high estimation in which Jayadeva is held, may be inferred from the following eulogy by an Oriental critic: "Whatever is delightful in the modes of music, whatever is exquisite in the sweet art of love, whatever is graceful in the strains of poetry—all that let the happy and wise learn from the songs of Jayadeva."

Whittier has furnished us the following spirited version of a Hindoo lyric by a poet who flourished in the third century of our era, and who, if we may judge by his writings, had conceptions of God and duty not unworthy of a Christian bard.

GIVING AND TAKING.

"Who gives and hides the giving hand,
Nor counts on favor, fame, or praise,
Shall find his smallest gift outweighs
The burden of the sea and land.

Who gives to whom hath naught been given,
His gift in need, though small indeed,
As is the grass-blade's wind-blown seed,
Is large as earth, and rich as heaven.

Forget it not, O man, to whom
A gift shall fall while yet on earth;
Yea, even to thy sevenfold birth
Recall it in the lives to come.

Who dares to curse the hands that bless,
Shall know of sin the deadliest cost;
The patience of the heaven is lost
Beholding man's unthankfulness.

For he who breaks all laws may still
In Siva's mercy be forgiven;
But none can save, in earth or heaven,
The wretch who answers good with ill."

THE DRAMA.

The Sanscrit Shakespeare.—Not the least valuable of Sanscrit treasures is its dramatic poetry. Here, as in lyric verse, Kâlidâsa stands prëeminent, the Shakespeare of India. His title to this distinction rests mainly on his drama of Sakoon'-talâ, or the Lost Ring, which portrays the simple life and unsophisticated manners of his countrymen with all his characteristic tenderness of expression and rich imagination.

PLOT OF SAKOONTALÂ.—In early summer—the fitting season, sacred as it was to the god of love—the play of Sakoontalâ was wont to be acted in ancient India. The heroine, whose name the drama bears, was the daughter of a nymph, and dwelt at a hermitage in the jungle. Led to her retreat by chance in his pursuit of a deer, a neighboring rajah espies the "slender-waisted" forest maid, with two lovely companions, watering the shrubbery. Concealing himself among the trees, he plays eaves-dropper, and as he watches the trio he cannot restrain his admiration; "the woodland plants," he cries, "outshine the garden flowers." His heart is lost forthwith. Ordering his camp to be pitched near by, he wooes and finally weds Sakoontalâ, with the assurance that she shall "reign without a rival in his heart." Then leaving his bride a marriage-ring, engraved with his name, as a token of their union, the rajah goes back to his palace, promising that Sakoontalâ shall soon share his throne.

> "Repeat each day one letter of the name
> Engraven on this gem; ere thou hast reckoned
> The tale of syllables, my minister
> Shall come to lead thee to thy husband's palace."

Not long after his departure, a sage whose anger she has incurred pronounces a curse upon the pair,—"that he of whom she thought should think of her no more," should even forget her image, and that the spell should cease only at sight of the marriage-ring. This token of remembrance, however, was secured on her finger; and at length Sakoontalâ, re-assured by a favorable omen, leaves the sorrowing companions of her girlhood, and the venerable hermit, her reputed father, to seek her husband in his capital.

Arrived in safety, she gains access to the royal presence; but the king, laboring under the curse, fails to recognize her. Sakoontalâ is unveiled, and stands before him in all her beauty—a beauty that stirs him to exclaim:—

"What charms are here revealed before mine eyes!
Truly no blemish mars the symmetry
Of that fair form; yet can I ne'er believe
She is my wedded wife; and like a bee
That circles round the flower whose nectared cup
Teems with the dew of morning, I must pause
Ere eagerly I taste the proffered sweetness."

Then Sakoontalâ seeks her ring, but alas! it is not on her finger; she must have dropped it in the Ganges. In the midst of her confusion a nymph appears, and carries her off to a sacred retreat, where she gives birth to a son.

Meanwhile a fish is caught, in which is found the fatal ring, stamped with the rajah's name. It is restored to its owner, and at once the recollection of his long-forgotten Sakoontalâ flashes upon his mind. Overwhelmed with poignant regret for her loss, he abandons himself to melancholy for a time, calling on her beloved name, or trying to beguile his grief by tracing with his pencil her features now but too well remembered. At length ambition and piety unite to wake him from his lethargy. He embarks in a campaign against the giants, enemies of the gods; is victorious; and finds the consummation of happiness at last in a union with his long-lost wife, and with his son, whose name, Bhârata, becomes the most distinguished in the mythology of India.

English readers are enabled to enjoy the beauties of Sakoontalâ through the metrical version of Prof. Williams.

EXTRACTS FROM SAKOONTALÂ.

PARTING WORDS OF THE SAGE TO HIS ADOPTED DAUGHTER.

"This day my loved one leaves me, and my heart
Is heavy with its grief: the streams of sorrow,
Choked at the source, repress my faltering voice.
I have no words to speak; mine eyes are dimmed
By the dark shadows of the thoughts that rise
Within my soul. If such the force of grief
In an old hermit parted from his nursling,
What anguish must the stricken parent feel,
Bereft forever of an only daughter!

Weep not, my daughter, check the gathering tear
That lurks beneath thine eyelid, ere it flow
And weaken thy resolve; be firm and true—
True to thyself and me; the path of life
Will lead o'er hill and plain, o'er rough and smooth,
And all must feel the steepness of the way;
Tho' rugged be thy course, press boldly on.

Honor thy betters; ever be respectful
To those above thee. Should thy wedded lord
Treat thee with harshness, thou must never be
Harsh in return, but patient and submissive.
Be to thy menials courteous, and to all
Placed under thee considerate and kind:
Be never self-indulgent, but avoid
Excess in pleasure; and, when fortune smiles,
Be not puffed up. Thus to thy husband's house
Wilt thou a blessing prove, and not a curse.

How, O my child! shall my bereaved heart
Forget its bitterness, when, day by day,
Full in my sight shall grow the tender plants
Reared by thy care, or sprung from hallowed grain
Which thy loved hands have strewn around the door—
A frequent offering to our household gods."

THE KING AND SAKOONTALÂ'S PORTRAIT.

"My finger, burning with the glow of love,
Has left its impress on the painted tablet;
While here and there, alas! a scalding tear
Has fallen on the cheek and dimmed its brightness.

Go fetch the brush that I may finish it.
A sweet Sirisha blossom should be twined
Behind her ear, its perfumed crest depending
Toward her cheek; and resting on her bosom,
A lotus-fibre necklace, soft and bright
As an autumnal moonbeam, should be traced."

While gazing on the picture, the king in his infatuation mistakes for reality a bee which he has himself painted in the act of settling on the rosy lips of his love, and after attempting to drive it off is apprised of his error by an attendant, whom he thus addresses:—

"While all entranced I gazed upon her picture,
My loved one seemed to live before my eyes,
Till every fibre of my being thrilled
With rapturous emotion. Oh! 'twas cruel
To dissipate the day-dream, and transform
The blissful vision to a lifeless image.
Vain is the hope of meeting her in dreams,
For slumber, night by night, forsakes my couch.
And now that I would fain assuage my grief
By gazing on her portrait, here before me,
Tears of despairing love obscure my sight."

MONIER WILLIAMS.

Sakoontalâ may justly be called the pearl of Eastern dramatic poetry. It has been translated into every European tongue, and has elicited the admiration of all civilized nations. In the language of Goethe:—

"Would'st thou the young year's blossom and the fruits of its decline,
And all by which the soul is charmed, enraptured, feasted, fed—
Would'st thou the earth and heaven itself in one sole name combine?
I name thee, O Sakoontalâ! and all at once is said."

From the author of this drama we have two other pieces worthy of his fame, "the Hero and the Nymph" and a popular comedy. His era was the golden age of the Hindoo theatre.

Other noted plays, a few out of many, are "the Toy Cart," a domestic drama with a public underplot; "the Signet of the Minister," which had a political bearing; "the Stolen Marriage;" and an allegorical play, "the Moonrise of Science."

The Hindoo Drama, the invention of which was ascribed to an ancient sage inspired by Brahma himself, consisted at first of music, dancing, and pantomime. An outcome of the prevailing mythology, it was made a feature of the Indian festivals, and from very early rude beginnings of which we have no remains gradually progressed to the perfection with which Kâlidâsa invested it. Unfolding the inner life of the people and illustrating their peculiar institutions, it is at once interesting and valuable, original, and in its delineations of character strikingly true to nature. Love is its principal subject; and, what is markedly characteristic, its denouements are always happy. Tragedy is foreign to the Hindoo stage.

The Indian plays began and closed with a benediction or prayer; in many cases there was a preliminary account of the author, or a colloquy between the manager and one of the actors, leading the way to the play itself. The heroes were generally kings or deities. As foils to these, it was usual to introduce mountebanks or buffoons, and as such Brahmans were made to figure. The Hindoo dramatists did not hesitate to set forth their priests in a ridiculous light; a remarkable fact, when we remember that the drama in India was a semi-religious institution, and that the managers of companies were usually themselves Brahmans. The playwright who in Greece should have taken such liberties with his religious superiors would have run the risk of being driven from the stage, if indeed he were not more seriously handled by an indignant audience.

The consistency observed in managing the dialogue is noteworthy. The parts spoken by divinities and heroes, rulers and priests, are always in ancient Sanscrit; while the inferior personages and the female characters use the later and more familiar dialect. Want of acquaintance with the sacred language, which thus formed the staple of the classical plays, no doubt prevented the common people from fully understanding and enjoying dramatic representations; and hence the latter never attained that popularity which they had in other countries. They were the entertainment of the cultured class rather than the masses.

Another curious feature of the Hindoo drama was the absence of scenery, the plays being mostly represented in the open air, the courts of palaces, etc. The great advantage which the modern performer derives from fine scenic effects was entirely wanting. Changes of scene could be indicated only in the text, by minute descriptions of the new locality, thrown into the mouths of the speakers and left for the audience to fill out and remember. No shifting of scenes, for instance, as with us, would denote the entrance of one of the characters from out-doors into a drawing-room; but the personage entering, either in a soliloquy or in colloquy with some other, would immediately call attention to every little point — the threshold, the floor, the ceiling, the walls, the doors, the windows, the furniture—and the glowing fancy of his hearers would at once picture the scene as vividly as if it stood before them in reality.

The proprieties were strictly observed. To represent a death scene would have been intolerable; nor only so, but in the earlier and purer days no dramatist would introduce before his audience a scene of violence, eating, sleeping, or the performance of the marriage ceremony. Even kissing on the stage was repugnant to the Hindoo ideas of delicacy; so a charming love-scene in the Sakoontalâ breaks off just at the critical moment when the hero and heroine are about to interchange a token of affection.

As to the date of the dramas that have been mentioned,

they are supposed to have been written during the first ten centuries of the Christian Era; but here, as in the case of the epics and lyrics that preceded them, we are left to conjecture. Could we know more certainly what times they reflect, our pleasure in perusing them would be complete.

TALES AND FABLES.

India has long enjoyed the reputation, and not without reason, of having been the favorite home of fairy-tale and fable. From her storehouse of fictions, many waifs have crept into the literatures of both Europe and Asia, and striking the popular taste have attained wide currency. Tongues have changed, dynasties have fallen; but these stories by unknown hands still live in the nursery, influencing the pliant minds of the children of to-day as they have done those of the last twenty centuries.

The Sanscrit has two great collections of fables, — the Pânkatantra, *Five Stories* (more properly *Five Sections*); and the Hitopadêsa, *Friendly Advice*, a compilation from the former by the sage Pilpay (*pil'pi*). The latter, translated into many languages, has almost rivalled in circulation the Bible itself. In the following fable from "the Friendly Advice" will be seen the germ of La Fontaine's charming imitation, "the Milkmaid and the Pitcher of Milk;" both point the same moral as our own cautionary proverb, "Don't count your chickens before they are hatched."

THE STUPID BRAHMAN.

"In the town of Devikotta there lived a Brahman of the name of Devasarman. At the feast of the great equinox he received a plateful of rice. He took it, went into a potter's shop, which was full of crockery, and, overcome by the heat, he lay down in a corner and began to doze. In order to protect his plate of rice, he kept a stick in his hand; and he began to think: 'Now if I sell this plate of rice, I shall receive ten cowries. I shall then, on the spot, buy pots and plates, and after having increased my capital again and again I shall buy and sell betel nuts and dresses till I grow enormously rich. Then I shall marry four wives, and the youngest and prettiest of the four I shall make a great pet of. Then the other wives will be so angry and begin to quarrel. But I shall be in a great rage, and take a stick, and give them a good flogging.'

While he said this, suiting the action to the thought, he laid about him with his stick; the plate of rice was smashed to pieces, and many of the pots in the shop were broken. The potter, hearing the noise, ran in; and when he saw his pots broken, gave the Brahman a good scolding and drove him out of the shop.

Therefore I say, 'He who rejoices over plans for the future will come to grief, like the Brahman who broke the pots.'"—MAX MÜLLER.

Of the numerous collections of tales and romances, the best known is "the Ocean of the Rivers of Narratives," the original of that more familiar compilation, the Arabian Nights.

HISTORY, GRAMMAR, ETC.

Sanscrit is also worthily represented in other departments of literature; on the fine arts we have nothing worthy of notice, but science has not been neglected, while historical, grammatical, and philosophical works, complete the category of its productions. Its chronicles, however, obscured as they are by myths without number, are comparatively valueless; but one deserves the name of history, the Chronicle of Cashmere, or the Stream of the Kings, extending from the fabulous ages to the reign of Akbar, who reduced that province in the 16th century.

But in grammar we must certainly award to Sanscrit the very first place. Commentaries on the constructions of the Veda, dating from 750 B.C., embody the earliest attempts at grammatical and critical investigation with which we are acquainted; and in the digest of Pânini (*pah'ne-ne*) (500 B.C.) we have the first systematic grammar that the world ever produced—a book remarkable for its completeness, declared by Max Müller to be "the perfection of an empirical analysis of language, unsurpassed—nay, even unapproached, by anything in the grammatical literature of other nations."

In connection with the literature of India, we may also mention inscriptions on monuments, in temples and grottoes, and on plates of marble and copper. These are worthy of study mainly in view of the historical information they may afford.

BUDDHIST LITERATURE.

About 500 B.C., a new and purer religion was preached in India by a monk of royal birth, afterward called Buddha (*the Enlightened*). It met with a hearty reception from the people, for it taught men to live in charity with their neighbors, to reverence their parents, to practise truth and morality; above all, it overthrew the institution of caste, and abolished the foolish system of Brahman sacrifices. The riches and fleeting pleasures of this world, Buddha proclaimed unworthy of pursuit, representing life itself as a burden, and promising his followers a paradise of eternal rest* beyond the grave. No wonder that thousands declared in favor of the new faith, which during a struggle of many cen-

A Buddhist Priest.

* *Nirvâna*—according to some an everlasting slumber of thought, or total annihilation. The literal meaning of the word is *blowing out*, as of a light.

turies disputed with Brahmanism for the supremacy of India. Pushing out to the northeast, it made its way into Thibet, China, and Japan; and at the present day has more followers than any other religious system, their number being estimated at 300,000,000.

The sacred books of the Buddhists are called the Tripitaka (*three baskets*); one is metaphysical, another disciplinary, and the third contains the discourses of Buddha. They are written in a dialect of Sanscrit, and are made up of nearly 600,000 stanzas, containing five times as much matter as our Bible.

EXTRACTS FROM THE BUDDHIST SCRIPTURES.

"The succoring of mother and father, the cherishing of child and wife, and the following of a lawful calling,—this is the greatest blessing.

The giving of alms, the abstaining from sins, the eschewing of intoxicating drink, diligence in good deeds, reverence and humility, contentment and gratitude,—this is the greatest blessing.

He who lives for pleasure only, his senses uncontrolled, idle and weak, the tempter will certainly overcome him as the wind throws down a weak tree.

Like a beautiful flower, full of color but without scent, are the fine but fruitless words of him who does not act accordingly.

As the bee collects nectar, and departs without injuring the flower, or its color and scent, so let the sage dwell on earth.

Let no man think lightly of evil, saying in his heart, 'It will not come near unto me.' Even by the falling of water-drops a water-pot is filled; the fool becomes full of evil, even if he gathers it little by little.

Let us live happily then, though we call nothing our own; not hating those who hate us, free from greed among the greedy. We shall then be like the bright gods, feeding on happiness."

NOTES ON HINDOO LITERATURE, ETC.

The literature of India incalculably vast, and its individual works voluminous. The Mahâbhârata six times as long as the Iliad, Odyssey, and Æneid united; the Râmâyana half this size. The eighteen Purânas contain 1,600,000 lines. The library of one of the kings said to have numbered so many books that a hundred Brahmans were employed in taking care of it, and a thousand dromedaries were required to convey it from place to place; twenty years were consumed in condensing its contents, by the royal command, into an encyclopædia of 12,000 volumes. Sir William Jones computed that the longest life would not suffice for the perusal of all the Sanscrit writings.—First century B.C. believed to have been an Augustan age of Indian literature.

Writing apparently unknown to the ancient Hindoos before the time of Pâni-ni. No mention anywhere made, in the early works, of writing materials, pen or brush, paper, bark, or skin. The Vedic hymns sung or repeated probably for a thousand years before they were committed to writing. The use of the alphabet long regarded as impious. First letters appear in Buddhist inscriptions of the 3d century B.C. Later Indian manuscripts, beautifully inscribed on palm leaves. The letters of the Sanscrit alphabet thought to be the oldest forms of our Arabic figures, which came originally from India, as did also our decimal system.

Chess one of the earliest inventions of the Hindoos—called chess (*king*) from the principal piece. The Brahman inventor, so the story goes, asked of the reigning emperor as his reward, a single grain of wheat for the first square of the chess-board, two for the second, four for the third, and so on to the sixty-fourth; apparently a modest price, but one that it would have taken yearc to pay with the wheat crop of the whole world. Elephants, horses, foot-soldiers, and chariots, the original chess-men. From India, the game found its way into China, Japan, and Persia, and finally into Europe.—Throwing dice, also, a favorite pastime; the "Game of Four Crowns," with playing-cards, early known to the Hindoos.

Square copper money coined in the 3d century B.C., and stamped with inscriptions in a Sanscrit dialect.

CHAPTER II.

PERSIAN LITERATURE.

Zend.—Sprung from the same ancient Aryan tongue as the Sanscrit of India, and distinguished by the same richness of inflection, is Zend (*living*), the earliest language of Persia, still preserved to us in the Persian Scriptures known as the Avesta. The Veda and the Avesta have been described as "two rivers flowing from one fountain-head;" and beyond a doubt the Vedic Aryans and the Zend-speaking Persians were originally one community, conversing in a common tongue.

The Avesta was first made known to Europeans by a French

orientalist, Anquetil Duperron (*ongk-teel' deu-pa-rong'*), who went to India for the express purpose of discovering the sacred books of the Parsees. With great difficulty he at length possessed himself of the much-desired Zend manuscripts, and in 1771, after long and patient effort, he gave his countrymen the first translation of the Avesta into a European tongue. The language has since been carefully studied, but cannot be said even yet to have been mastered. Time wrought many changes in it; the Persian of Xerxes' reign differed much more from the Zend of antiquity than our present language does from the English of Chaucer. Further modifications and the introduction of Arabic elements have made modern Persian still more unlike the ancient vernacular.

The sacred writings of Persia just referred to are among the oldest and most important in the whole range of Indo-European literature. They contain the doctrines of Zoroaster (*golden splendor*), the Bactrian sage who reformed the religious system of his country.

Zoroaster is believed to have flourished about 1500 B.C. Nothing is known of his life or history. Yet, through more than thirty centuries his influence has been felt; and to-day, though they have dwindled to perhaps 150,000 souls, his followers constitute a thrifty and intelligent population in India and Persia. These Parsees, or Fire-worshippers (called by the Mohammedans *Guebres*, or infidels), still burn the eternal fire, kindled as they believe from heaven, not for idolatrous worship, but as an emblem of Ormazd, the Almighty source of light. They are descendants of those Zoroastrians whom Darius and Xerxes, having stretched their empire to the deserts of India, launched against Europe in the mightiest armies ever raised by man, threatening to plant their purer faith amid the ruined shrines of Greece.

At a later date, when the Caliph Omar converted Persia to Mohammedanism with the sword (641 A.D.), their forefathers clung to the ancient faith, and found an asylum across the Indus or in the deserts of their native land.

The Avesta (*sacred text*) contains the only existing monuments of a once extensive literature. It is divided into distinct parts, made up of separate pieces and fragments, which, repeated orally from generation to generation, were probably collected and reduced to writing in their present form ten centuries after the period of Zoroaster (500 B.C.). The compositions in question are chiefly professed revelations and instructions to mankind, confessions, prayers to the Supreme Being and various inferior deities, and metrical hymns (*Gâthâs*), simple and some of them so grand as to be deemed the productions of Zoroaster himself.

Zoroaster is represented in the Avesta as conversing with Ormazd, who, in answer to the inquiries of the sage, reveals his will, and prescribes the moral and ceremonial law. Thus, in the following passage, Zoroaster questions Ormazd :—

"O Ormazd, most holy spirit, creator of existent worlds, truth-loving! What, O Ormazd, was the Word which existed before the heaven, before the water, before the cow, before the tree, before the fire, before the truthful man, before the spirits and animals, before all the existent universe?"

Then Ormazd replies: "I will tell thee, most holy Zoroaster, what was the whole of the Creative Word. It existed before the heaven, before the water, before the cow, before the tree, before the fire, before the truthful man, before the spirits and animals, before all the existent universe. Such is the whole of the Creative Word, which, even when unpronounced and unrecited, outweighs a thousand breathed prayers, which are not pronounced, nor recited, nor sung. And he who in this world, O most holy Zoroaster, remembers the whole of the Creative Word, or utters it, or sings it, I will lead his soul thrice across the bridge of the better world, to the better existence, to the better truth, to the better days. I pronounced this Speech which contains the Word and its working to accomplish the creation of this heaven, before the creation of the earth, of the tree, of the four-footed cow, before the birth of the truthful man."

"He is a holy man," says Ormazd elsewhere, "who constructs upon the earth a habitation in which he maintains fire, cattle, his wife, his children, and flocks and herds. He who makes the earth produce grain, who cultivates the fruits of the fields, he maintains purity; he promotes the law of Ormazd as much as if he offered a hundred sacrifices."

Avestan Philosophy.—The Avesta seems to recognize one eternal Supreme Being, infinite and omnipotent. This was Ormazd (*Spiritual Wise One*), whom Zoroaster invokes as the source of light and purity, "true, lucid, shining," all-perfect, all-powerful, all-beautiful, all-wise." Opposed to Ormazd was a principle of darkness and evil, called Ah'riman (*Sinful-minded*). The theory of evolution finds no support in the Avesta, which contains an account of the creation of the universe strikingly like that of Moses. Traditions of the fall of man through the falsehood of Ahriman, and of a universal deluge, are also handed down.

Zoroaster's mission was to exhort men to follow the right and forsake the wrong. "Choose one of these two spirits, the Good or the Base," he said; "you cannot serve both." Again:—

"Of these two spirits, the evil one chose the worst deeds; the Kind Spirit, he whose garment is the immovable sky, chose what is right; as they also do who faithfully please Ormazd by good works.

Hear with your ears what is best, perceive with your mind what is pure, so that every man may choose for himself his tenets before the great doom.

Let our mind, then, O bliss-conferring Truth! be there where wisdom abides. Let us be of those who further the well-being of mankind.

Then indeed will be the fall of pernicious Falsehood; but in the beautiful abode of the Good Spirit will be gathered forever those who dwell in good report.

O men! if you cling to these commandments which the Wise One has given, which are a torment to the wicked and a blessing to the righteous, then through them will you have the victory."

Like Buddha, the Persian reformer raised his voice against the priesthood, and the corruptions which had crept into the national religion. Devil-worship, which had come into vogue as a means of averting the evil supposed to be wrought by wicked spirits, he specially denounced, recognizing in sin the cause of all human sorrow, and urging men to wage uncompromising warfare with the powers of darkness, relying for aid on the Good Spirit. "Give offering and praise," says the Avesta, "to that Lord who made men greater than all earthly beings, and through the gift of speech created them to rule the creatures, *as warriors against the evil spirits.*" Fire was invoked as the symbol of Divinity, and the sun as "the eye of Ormazd;" but idolatry Zoroaster and his disciples abhorred.

Ormazd was the rewarder of the good, the punisher of the bad. Those who obeyed him, and were "pure in thoughts, pure in words, pure in actions," were admitted at death into *Paradise*, "the House of the Angels' Hymns," where all was brightness: the wicked were consigned to a region of everlasting darkness and woe, "the House of Destruction." Of all the religions of human origin, Zoroaster's, though not free from superstition and cumbrous rites, approaches nearest to the truth. It was gladly accepted by the people, and did much to elevate them and improve their condition. We have thrown into verse the following

HYMN TO ORMAZD.

Praise to Ormazd, great Creator,
He it was the cattle made;
Lord of purity and goodness,
Trees and water, sun and shade.
Unto him belongs the kingdom,
Unto him the might belongs;
Unto him, as first of beings,
Light-creator, float our songs.

Him we praise, Ahurian Mazda,
With our life and bodies praise;
Purer than the purest, fairest,
Bright through never-ending days.
What is good and what is brilliant,
That we reverence in thee—
Thy good spirit, thy good kingdom,
Wisdom, law, and equity.

Persian Inscriptions.—In a flower-clad plain of southwestern Persia, shut in from the outer world by lofty hills, and now dotted with pleasant villages, once stood the great palace of Persep'olis, the wonder of the world for its magnificence—which Alexander, in a fit of drunken fury, reduced to a heap of ruins with his wanton torch (331 B.C.). Yet, though silent and deserted, "the piles of fallen Persepolis" speak to us, not only with their strange sculptures, but also through the inscriptions carved upon them in cuneiform letters, originally adorned with gold.

MOUNTAIN RECORD OF DARIUS.

Not far from these ruins is the famous rock of Behistun, 1,700 feet high, and inscribed with the same arrow-headed, wedge-shaped characters. Some of these, protected from the weather by a varnish of flint, have been wonderfully preserved to the present time.

This mountain-record was set up by Darius I. (516–515 B.C.), who, in the shadow of the palace-walls of Persepolis, was wont to sit upon a throne of gold, canopied by a vine of the same precious metal bearing clusters of priceless gems. It is his triumphal tablet, graven with figures of himself and several conquered princes. It records his victories, asserts his hereditary right to the throne, and enumerates the provinces of his vast empire, in nearly a thousand lines of cuneiform characters—in three different languages, the Persian, Scythian, and Babylonian—that it might be understood by all his subjects.

Here the Persian monarch announces his dignity, while he attributes the glory of it all to the God Supreme :—

> "I am Darius, the Great King, the King of Kings, the King of Persia, the King of the dependent provinces, the son of Hystaspes.
>
> By the grace of Ormazd I am King. Ormazd has granted me my empire. The countries which have fallen into my hands, by the grace of Ormazd I have become king of them.
>
> Within these countries, whoever was good, him have I cherished and protected; whoever was evil, him have I utterly destroyed. By the grace of Ormazd, these countries have obeyed my laws. By the grace of Ormazd, I hold this empire."

Other inscriptions were cut by order of Xerxes, whose royal name and title they formally declare; but there are none of any later date.

Cuneiform letters were also employed by other nations, as will be hereafter seen (page 105). The Persian writing is the least complicated, and is in the Zend language, but Zend in a later stage of development than the primitive tongue of the Avesta.

NOTES ON PERSIAN LITERATURE, ETC.

Ancient Persian records made on leather; parchment the favorite writing material, the high price of papyrus preventing its adoption. Bricks seldom used for inscriptions. A running hand, different from the cuneiform, probably in use among the people for ordinary purposes, as every educated person could undoubtedly write: no trace of this left.

The kings of Persia founders of a library consisting of historical records, state archives, and royal ordinances. "The house of the rolls" at Babylon is mentioned in the book of Ezra as being searched, during the reign of Darius, for a certain volume supposed to contain a decree of Cyrus, providing for the rebuilding of the Temple at Jerusalem.

The old priestly order of Media a..d Persia, known as Ma'gi; devoted to scientific studies, in which they attained such eminence that they were believed to possess supernatural powers—whence our word *magic*. The "wise men" of the New Testament by some supposed to be Persian Magi.

The Zoroastrian religion, which was on the wane, restored and maintained in the third century after Christ by the Sassan'idæ, who measured swords successfully with the Roman emperors, and extended the power of Persia. The coins of this dynasty stamped on one side with five altars, which seem to have been carried before the kings in processions as emblematical of their faith.

Most of the ancient Persian literature lost during the struggle with Alexander the Great, and subsequent wars and convulsions.

CHAPTER III.

CHINESE LITERATURE.

Chinese Language.—From the Persian Gâthâs and Vedic hymns, let us now turn to the prose writings of the Chinese philosophers, plain, grave, and moral in their tone. The language in which their tenets have been preserved differs materially from the musical Sanscrit and its sister Zend.

Modern Chinese, which has changed but little from the ancient tongue and is the least developed of all existing languages, is monosyllabic; i. e. each syllable conveys a complete idea, all its words are expressed by single separate sounds. Of these elements, or *roots*, it contains 450; changes of emphasis and intonation, accompanied with corresponding changes in meaning, increase this number to 1,263.

Chinese may be called a language without grammar, as it

dispenses with inflection and conjugation, and leaves the relations of words and their functions as different parts of speech to be determined by the arrangement. Thus *sin* means *honor*, *honorable*, *honorably*, or *to be honorable*, according to its position in the sentence. Plurality and gender are generally indicated by adding roots with a modifying signification. Son in Chinese is *man-child;* daughter, *woman-child;* a mare is called a *mother-horse;* people is the word *surnames* with *a hundred* prefixed. This grouping together of roots is carried to great lengths. Writing materials is expressed by two words denoting *four precious objects* (paper, brush, ink, and palette); a trader is *a buying-selling-man;* a knife is a *sword's-son;* while difference of opinion is expressed by four words meaning *I east, thou west.*

Characters used in Writing.—The written characters of the Chinese were originally outline pictures of visible objects; specimens are presented below. A crescent (1) stood for the moon; three peaks (2), for a mountain; (3) is a tortoise, (4) a fish, (5) a field. Pictographs were frequently combined to represent a single idea. The notion of song, for instance, was conveyed by a mouth and a bird (6); that of tears, by the symbols for eye and water; beauty and goodness, by the representation of a virgin and an infant.

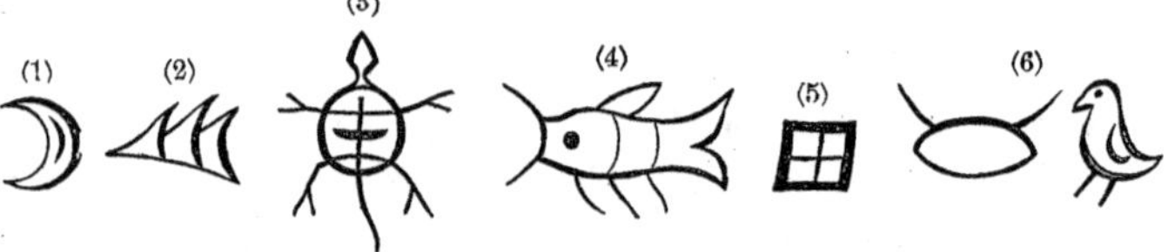

A phonetic symbol is often joined with a pure hieroglyphic in one and the same character; as in the case of the sign for a rapid stream, which is composed of the ideogram for water and a symbol denoting the sound of a torrent. And quite necessary is the ideographic element: the one sound *tschoo*, for example, means ape, whirlpool, island, silk, deep, a wine, a kind of plant, to enclose, to help, to quarrel, to walk, to answer. It would be next to impossible to interpret the written symbol correctly, were not a separate ideogram adopted for each idea. This necessary device, however, involved the wholesale multiplication of characters. Over 40,000 are contained in the fullest dictionaries; but three-fourths of this number are almost wholly unknown, and only about 5,000 are in common use.

It is interesting to notice how, in the course of ages, the old hieroglyphics have been transformed into the present characters. The symbol representing the verb to listen, two folding-doors and an ear between them is now written 聞. Two shells exactly alike originally stood for two friends; this symbol has been changed to 朋. A mountain is now 山; a field 田. The most complicated modern character is made by fifty-two strokes of the pen.

Antiquity of Chinese Literature.—China prides herself on her antiquity, and her literature carries us back to the remotest past. From those early days to the present the chain is almost unbroken, notwithstanding the irreparable loss sustained when the ruthless Ching Wang destroyed the great bulk of Chinese literature (220–205 B.C.). This emperor is noted for his erection of the Great Wall, and notorious for his contempt of learning. Thinking to reconcile the masses to his despotism by keeping them in ignorance, and to deceive posterity with the belief that he had founded the empire, he ordered all books, except those on husbandry, divination, and medicine, to be burned. Any person found with a book in his possession was condemned to labor four years on the Great

Wall, and several hundred scholars who resisted the royal decree were buried alive.

The dynasty of "the book-burner," however, was not long after overthrown; and among the succeeding princes was found a "restorer of literature," who collected and preserved for future generations the writings which, concealed by the people in the walls of their houses or buried beneath the beds of streams, had escaped destruction. To his praiseworthy efforts we are indebted for all that remains of the ancient literature,—the Sacred Books of China, edited by Confu'cius her admirable philosopher, as well as for the works of Confucius himself and his disciples.

Confucius, to whom we are thus introduced, the *reverend master*, the beloved teacher of his countrymen, stands out in bold relief as the most distinguished personage in Chinese history. His birth, which took place 551 B.C., was mysteriously predicted, as legend tells us, on a precious stone found in his father's garden: "A child is about to be born, pure as the crystal wave; he shall be a king, but without territorial dominion." Wonderfully has this prophecy been fulfilled; the child, as we shall see, became a king whose subjects were numbered by hundreds of millions.

Born in an evil age, when corruption had undermined the government, and misrule and violence were everywhere rife, Confucius early dedicated himself to the cause of social and political reform. At twenty-two he entered upon his work as a teacher, thoroughly fitted for the high vocation, for he had been so eager after knowledge as to feel no toil in its pursuit, and sometimes even to forget his food. His merits were recognized; and when at last he was raised to the position of prime-minister, he labored in season and out of season for the welfare of his people—and with the best results. But then, as now, princes were ungrateful, and the neglect of his sovereign led to his resignation. Henceforth the mission of Confucius, no less useful if humbler than before, was simply to disseminate his precepts, wandering from state to state among the fifteen millions who constituted the population of what was then China. Occupied thus and with the study of the Sacred Books, he finally found rest in his native state, and there passed his declining years in the midst of loving disciples, "unconscious," as he tells us, "that he had reached old age." He died at seventy-three, lamenting that, despite his prolonged efforts, so little had been accomplished toward elevating the moral standard of the nation.

Yet after his death, his influence was destined far to exceed his most sanguine longings; it has been greater than that of any other human teacher. No other has ever spoken to so many millions, or received such honors from posterity. For more than twenty centuries, his precepts have been taught in the schools of China (and each little village has its common school); at stated times, every scholar, on entering in the morning, still bows in adoration before a tablet sacred to Confucius. The learned can repeat page after page from his classical books; and scores of his maxims are familiar to the masses, who have positively no other moral law to guide them. His tomb, approached by an avenue of cypresses through a gate of exquisite workmanship, is inscribed with the words, "The most sagely ancient Teacher; the all-accomplished, all-informed King." About the spot are imperial tablets "with glowing tributes to the one man whom China delights to honor;" and in the city near by live 50,000 of his descendants, constituting a distinct class —the head of the family holding large

CONFUCIAN PRIEST.

estates as "Duke by imperial appointment and hereditary right, continuator of the sage." There is a temple of Confucius in every city, and Confucian priests superintend various ceremonies for both mandarins and common people.

Tenets of Confucius.—Confucius claimed no divine inspiration; he founded no new religion. To him the Almighty was "the Unknown God," and there was no Paul to declare him to the philosopher. He avoided referring to a personal Supreme Being, and thought that the study of themselves should suffice for men. As to death and a future state, he was equally reticent. "While you do not know life," he said to an inquiring disciple, "what can you know about death?" With polygamy, then an institution of his country, he found no fault; and for women as such he appears to have had no kindly word, or very elevated regard.

The aim of Confucius was to inculcate certain lofty principles of conduct, to govern men in their relations to each other and to the ruling powers. Respect for learning, filial piety,* and veneration for the men and institutions of ancient days, were corner-stones of his system, and are still deeply impressed on the Chinese mind. His golden rule "What you do not like when done to yourself, do not to others"—expressed in written language by a single ideogram—was the *one word* he specially commended as embodying the sum and substance of duty.

* We find one phase of this in the worship of ancestral tablets. These are of wood, a foot high, and bear the name of the departed ancestor, the hour of his birth, and that of his decease. They are worshipped twice a month with tapers and burning incense. Death is believed to liberate three spirits from the tenement of clay; while one of these occupies the grave, and another seeks the invisible world, the third is supposed to take up its habitation in the tablet erected by filial reverence. The accompanying engraving shows one of these ancestral tablets with its inscription in Chinese.

The practical workings of this rule, as enforced by the authority of the great master, were recently exemplified in the case of an American traveller. As he and his companion were passing through a Chinese town, their strange faces and unusual costumes attracted a crowd, and hooting seemed likely to be followed by serious violence. With admirable presence of mind, one of the strangers faced the throng, and amid a shower of mud and stones exclaimed: "Is this the way, O people! that you obey the precepts of your philosophers, to treat strangers within your walls tenderly? Have you forgotten the saying of your great master Confucius,—"That which I wish another not to do to me, I must not do to him?" The effect was electric. In a moment every hand was lowered, and the recent assailants sought as best they could to make amends for their rudeness.

The Chinese Classics comprise the Sacred Books already alluded to, viz., the Five King; also the Four Shoo, or Books of the Philosophers (Confucius and the writers of his school). *King* is the equivalent of our word *text*, and the Five Sacred Texts are the YIH King, Book of Changes; the SHOO King, Book of History; the SHE King, Book of Poetry; the LE KE King, Book of Rites; and the Spring and Autumn, an historical record of events in the native state of Confucius, from 721 to 480 B.C. It was written by that philosopher himself, who so entitled it because "its commendations were life-giving like spring, and its censures life-withering like autumn." The first four King, which rank with the most ancient creations of the human mind, were compiled and published by Confucius; the Book of Rites, originally drawn up by the ruler of Chow in the twelfth century B.C., received additions from subsequent writers.

Little is known of the true nature of the mysterious Book of Changes; it apparently relates to divination. The Shoo King gives us the history of China from the earliest periods to about 720 B.C., and contains, besides, discourses on music, astronomy, and the principles of government. Part of it was dictated from memory by a blind man after the destruction of the original tablets.

In the She King, we have a collection of 305 odes and hymns. Many of them, more than three thousand years old, were written while the Chinese Empire was as yet a mere bundle of feudal states; here, as in all other lands, the first grand thoughts of the people were cast in the mould of poetry. The odes are in rhyme, and mirror the every-day life and simple manners of antiquity—often in a highly metaphorical style, but with a dignity and attractiveness which the later poetry fails to exhibit. They paint pleasing pictures of rural quiet, contain delicate touches of nature, and in some few cases display a high appreciation of woman's worth; on the whole, however, the status assigned to the gentler sex is low. Extracts from the Book of Poetry follow.

FESTAL ODE.

(Celebrating a feast given by an ancient king.)

"See how the rushes spring
Thickly along the way!
Ye browsing herds, no foot
Upon those rushes lay!
Grown to their height ere long,
They soft and rich shall shine;
Close as the rushes grow,
Should brethren all combine.
Let all at feast appear,
None absent, none thought mean.
Mats for the young be spread!
On stools let elders lean!

Lo! double mats are spread,
And stools are featly set.
Servants in waiting stand;
See! host and guests are met.
He pledges them; they him;
He drinks, again they fill.

Sauces and pickles come,
  Roast meat, and broiled; and still
Palates and tripe are brought.
  Then lutes and drums appear,
Singers fine concord make—
  The joyous feasters hear.

The feasting o'er, from bow,
  Lacquered and strong and bright,
Four well-poised shafts each sends,
  That in the target light.
The guests are ranged as they
  The mark have nearest hit.
They shoot again; the shafts
  Are fairly lodged in it.
Their bearing then is judged;
  Each takes his final place,
As mild propriety
  Has round him thrown its grace.

The long-descended king
  Presides and ends the feast.
With spirits sweet and strong
  From vase he cheers each guest.
And for the old he prays,
  While all with rapture glow,
That they the wrinkled back
  And whitening hair may show;
Striving with mutual help
  In virtue's onward ways,
That brightest happiness
  May crown their latest days."

LEGGE.

PASTORAL ODE.

(An industrious wife wakens her husband at early dawn.)

"'Get up, husband, here's the day!'
'Not yet, wife, the dawn's still gray.'
'Get up, sir, and on the right,
See the morning-star shines bright.
Shake off slumber, and prepare
Ducks and geese to shoot and snare.

All your darts and line may kill,
I will dress for you with skill.

Thus a blithesome hour we'll pass,
  Brightened by a cheerful glass;
While your lute its aid imparts,
  To gratify and soothe our hearts.'"

LEGGE.

ODE TO A BRIDE.

"Gay child of Spring, the garden's Queen,
  Yon peach-tree charms the roving sight;
Its fragrant leaves, how richly green!
  Its blossoms, how divinely bright!

So softly smiles the blooming bride,
  By love and conscious virtue led,
O'er her new mansion to preside,
  And placid joys around her spread."

SIR WILLIAM JONES.

The Book of Rites prescribes rules of conduct for all occasions, from the most important down to a mere interchange of greetings. With Chinamen ceremonial is everything, and the influence which this book has exerted on manners and society for three thousand years cannot be estimated. It is still the standard of etiquette, a governing board at Pekin being charged with the duty of enforcing its rigid observance.

Spring and Autumn, professedly written in the interests of morality and good order, to inspire wicked officials and undutiful sons with wholesome terror, disappoints us in the reading. It is made up of short, unconnected sentences, stating isolated facts (some of them quite insignificant) in the baldest manner, without any attempt at rhetorical excellence or any expression of condemnation or praise. Whether a temple is struck by lightning, or a father is murdered by his son, or locusts appear, or some glorious exploit is performed, or the ruler goes on a journey, or the sun is eclipsed—it is just stated in so many words—nothing more. The historical style of Confucius is certainly not striking, and we fail to see why the guilty should have "quaked with fear" when his annals appeared.

The Four Shoo are constituted as follows: 1. The Confucian Analects (literary fragments). 2. The Great Learning. 3. The Doctrine of the Mean (as opposed to extremes—the Moderate). 4. The works of Mencius, or the philosopher Meng, a disciple of Confucius, and second only to his master among the sages of China.

The Analects consist of the sayings of Confucius, as they occur in conversations with his followers. Sententious, simple, and sometimes signally beautiful, they contain the very marrow of wisdom based upon observation and experience. They shine among the laconics of the world. A few specimens are subjoined.

EXTRACTS FROM THE ANALECTS.

"The Master said: 'In the Book of Poetry are three hundred pieces, but the design of all may be embraced in one sentence—Have no depraved thoughts.'

There are cases in which the blade springs, but the plant does not go on to flower. There are cases where it flowers, but no fruit is subsequently produced.

Learning without thought is labor lost; thought without learning is perilous.

Worship as if the Deity were present.

Good government obtains when those who are near are made happy, and those who are far off are attracted.

Three friendships are advantageous,—friendship with the upright, friendship with the sincere, and friendship with the man of observation. Three are injurious,—friendship with the man of specious airs, friendship with the insinuatingly soft, and friendship with the glib-tongued.

To see what is right and not to do it, is want of courage.

The cautious seldom err.

If I am building a mountain, and stop before the last basketful of earth is placed on the summit, I have failed of my work. But if I have placed but one basketful on the plain and go on, I am really building a mountain.

Shall I teach you what knowledge is? When you know a thing, to hold that you know it; and when you do not know a thing, to confess your ignorance—is knowledge.

Extravagance leads to insubordination, and parsimony to meanness. It is better to be mean than insubordinate.

Learn the past, and you will know the future.

A poor man who flatters not and a rich man who is not proud, are passable characters; but they are not equal to the poor who are yet cheerful, and the rich who yet love the rules of propriety.

When you transgress, fear not to return.

Were I to say that the departed were possessed of consciousness, pious sons might dissipate their fortunes in festivals of the dead; and were I to deny their consciousness, heartless sons might leave their fathers unburied.

With coarse rice to eat, water to drink, and my bended arm for a pillow—I have still happiness even with these; but riches and honors acquired by unrighteousness are to me as a floating cloud.

What the superior man seeks is in himself; what the small man seeks is in others."

The Great Learning, based on the teachings of Confucius, and ascribed to one or more of his followers, evinces political sagacity in its suggestions for the perfecting of government, insisting that the welfare of the people should be the single aim, and scouting the idea of any divine right in kings to rule except in accordance with the principles of justice and virtue.

EXTRACTS FROM THE GREAT LEARNING.

"The ancients who wished to establish illustrious virtue throughout the empire, first ordered well their own states. Wishing to order well their states, they first regulated their families. Wishing to regulate their families, they first cultivated their persons. Wishing to cultivate their persons, they first rectified their hearts.

From the loving example of one family, a whole state becomes loving; and from its courtesies, the whole state becomes courteous: while from the ambition and perverseness of one man, the whole state may be led to rebellious disorder: such is the nature of influence. This verifies the saying: 'Affairs may be ruined by a single sentence; a kingdom may be settled by its one man.'

It is not possible for one to teach others, while he cannot teach his own family. There is filial piety, there is fraternal submission, there is kindness. Therefore the ruler, without going beyond his family, completes the lessons for the state.

Never has there been a case of the sovereign loving benevolence, and the people not loving righteousness. Never has there been a case where the people loved righteousness, and the affairs of the sovereign have not been carried to completion.

What a man dislikes in his superiors, let him not display in the treatment of his inferiors; what he dislikes in inferiors, let him not display in the service of his superiors. What he hates in those who are before him, let him not therewith precede those who are behind him. What he is unwilling to receive on the right, let him not bestow on the left. This is what is called 'The principle with which, as with a measuring-square, to regulate one's conduct.'"

The Doctrine of the Mean was written by the grandson of Confucius, who in his boyhood listened to the wise instructions of the sage, and professed himself ready to carry "the bundle of firewood his grandsire had gathered and prepared," thus leading Confucius to exclaim with delight: "My undertakings will not come to naught; they will be carried on, and flourish." The philosophy of this work is obscure; for while it presents examples of filial piety, and draws an ideal of the perfect man, "possessed of all sagely qualities," who alone is able to "accord with the course of the Mean," its language with reference to that Mean is decidedly mystical. Thus:—

"While there are no stirrings of pleasure, anger, sorrow, or joy, the mind may be said to be in a state of EQUILIBRIUM. When those feelings have been stirred and act in their due degree, there ensues what may be called the state of HARMONY. This equilibrium is the great root from which grow all the human actings in the world, and this harmony is the universal path which they all should pursue.

Let the states of equilibrium and harmony exist in perfection, and a happy order will prevail throughout heaven and earth, and all things will flourish.

The Master said:—'Perfect is the virtue which is according to the Mean. Rare have they long been among the people, who could practise it! I know how it is that the path of the Mean is not walked in: the knowing go beyond it, and the stupid do not come up to it.'"

Mencius, author of the fourth Shoo, lived in a degenerate age, but without fear or favor threw himself into the arena to wrestle with wickedness. In the society around him he found many fitting marks for his shafts of humor and satire. Purification of heart was his remedy for evil; the sinlessness of childhood, his standard of moral purity. "The great man," said Mencius, "is he who does not lose his child's heart."

Virtue and benevolence are insisted on in the voluminous works of this philosopher—the Plato of Chinese literature as Confucius was its Socrates*—a benevolence that should not only provide for the physical wants of the people, but also secure their education and moral advancement. We glean the following pointed sentences from the

SAYINGS OF MENCIUS.

"I like life and I also like righteousness. If I cannot keep the two together, I will let life go and choose righteousness.

When one by force subdues men, they do not submit to him in heart, but because their strength is not adequate to resist. When one subdues men by virtue, in their heart's core they are pleased, and sincerely submit, as was the case with the seventy disciples in their submission to Confucius.

The noblest thing in the world is the people. To them the spirits of the earth and the fruits of the earth are inferior. The prince is least important of all.

Benevolence brings glory, its opposite brings disgrace.

That whereby man differs from the animals is small. Superior men preserve it, while the mass of men cast it away.

There is a way to get the kingdom; get the people, and the kingdom is got. There is a way to get the people; get their hearts, and the people are got. The people turn to a benevolent rule as water flows downward.

Mencius said: 'The richest fruit of benevolence is the service of one's parents; of righteousness, the service of one's elder brother; of wisdom, the knowing those two things and not departing from them.'"

Spirit of the Chinese Classics. — One prevailing spirit breathes through the nine classical books of the Chinese —a spirit of conservatism. Confucius nowhere encourages men to take independent flights into the realms of original thought. He ignores the future, and exalts the past. His motto was not *Go up higher*, but *Walk in the trodden paths.*

---

* The two Chinese philosophers remind us of the two Greeks, not only by the moral tone of their teachings, but by their relative positions as master and follower. Nor were their respective eras widely apart; compare their dates—

The master, Confucius, 551–478 B.C. The master, Socrates, 470–399 B.C.

The disciple, Mencius, 370–288 B.C. The pupil, Plato, 429–348 B.C.

WORSHIPPING THE ANCESTRAL TABLET (p. 72).

He sought to reclaim from sin and folly, but only by winning to the purer practices of that venerable antiquity which he so blindly admired. Beyond the old landmarks, he cared not even to point the way.

It is hardly strange that under such leadership the nation became wedded to formalism, wrapped itself in a complacent aversion to novelty or progress, eschewed dealings with the outer world, and in a word came to an intellectual standstill for four and twenty centuries.

Other Works.—There are numerous commentaries on the old classics, some themselves quite ancient; but they are mere reproductions or servile imitations of the original texts.

Different, however, are the works of Lao-Tse, who was contemporary with Confucius, and whose writings are so mystical that the matter-of-fact Confucius declared himself unable to comprehend them. He made something which he calls Tao the mainspring of the universe, the source and ultimate destination of all things. Many of his followers, to whom he recommended self-denial and retirement, became recluses; their philosophy was perpetuated, and Taoism is still professed to some extent in China.

Having little imagination for works of fiction and no genius for the higher departments of poetry, the ancient Chinese produced nothing of special note—nothing, at least, that has come down to us—except what has been mentioned. We have indeed numerous chronicles of the various dynasties, industriously and no doubt accurately compiled; but they lack the graces of style, and possess little interest for the general European reader. The Bamboo Annals, found in a royal tomb 284 A.D., is the oldest of these chronicles that have thus far come to light.

We are also told that before the Christian Era numerous treatises were written on philosophy, mathematics, medicine, military affairs, husbandry, law, and geography; but many of these perished in the convulsions which afterward shook the empire.

With the languages of Siam, Burmah, and Thibet—all monosyllabic like the Chinese — are also connected literatures of considerable antiquity. In both Burmah and Siam the drama, often licentious, has always been popular, its exhibitions being sometimes prolonged for days. Burmah has records that purport to carry back its history almost to the Christian Era. The best writings of the Siamese are imitations of Hindoo fictions, while the literature of Thibet is largely made up of commentaries on the Tripitaka.

NOTES ON CHINESE LITERATURE, ETC.

Bamboo tablets and the stylus, the ancient writing implements; these in the reign of Ching Wang, the book-burner, superseded by the brush, and paper made of closely woven silk. Silk paper, found too expensive, replaced in turn by paper made of the inner bark of trees, old rags, and worn-out fishing-nets. Books multiply in consequence. At the Christian Era, the imperial library contained 11,332 sections filled with books on all subjects, but no great productions of genius. The old classics still in the front rank.

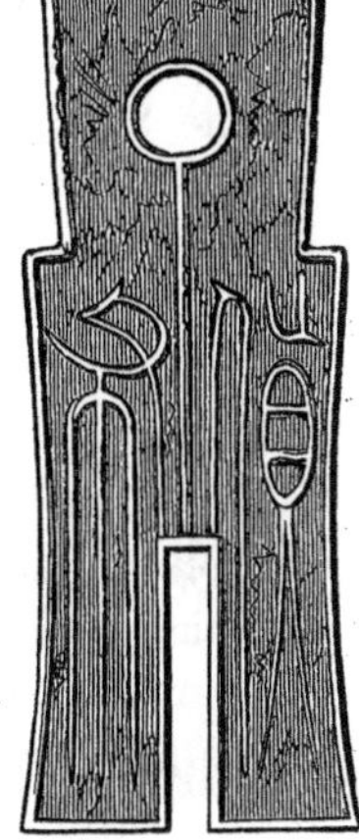

Specimen Cash.

Printing practised in China 600 A.D., nearly 900 years before its invention in Europe. Movable types invented by a blacksmith between 1000 and 1100 A.D. The types, made of clay hardened in the fire, reduced to an exact level by a smooth board, and then cemented to an iron plate with a mixture of resin and wax. The production of books thus greatly facilitated. Chinese books at the present day not printed from movable types, but from wooden blocks of the size of the page, on which the characters are cut in relief.

Bronze pieces called *cash,* worth one-tenth of a cent, coined as early as the 12th century B.C.; strung on cords through holes with which they are pierced; in later times worn as amulets.

The golden age of China's later ancient literature, the period of the Tang dynasty (620–907 A.D.), when the imperial armies penetrated to Samarcand and Bokhara in Turkestan. Le Taipih, the Chinese Anacreon, the greatest poet of this period; but even he seldom rises above mediocrity.

CHAPTER IV.

HEBREW LITERATURE.

The Semitic Languages, enumerated on page 16, have certain peculiarities in common :—

They are triliteral, i. e. three consonants enter into the composition of every root.

Consonants only are represented by letters; vowels, indicated by points, play a subordinate part. The latter vary according to the relation to be expressed; while the consonant root, which conveys the leading idea, remains unchanged. Thus, in Arabic, the notion of bloodshed is expressed by the triple root *q t l: quatl* is murder; *quitl*, enemy; *uqtul* means to kill; *quatala*, he kills. The picturesque compounds, so convenient in the Indo-European languages, are here wanting.

The Semitic verb is deficient in mood-forms, and has in general only two tenses, which represent action completed and action continuing. Case, as a rule, is left undistinguished; and grammar, on the whole, is crude and imperfect. Brevity is gained, but at the expense of precision.

Distribution of the Semitic Tongues.—The terms Arama'ic, Hebra'ic, and Ar'abic, designate the three great divisions of the Semitic family of languages; and it may here be noticed that these are much more alike than the Aryan tongues.

Aramaic (from the Hebrew Arâm—*highlands*) was spoken in northern Syria, Mesopotamia, and Babylonia. A dialect of it, the Jews gradually adopted after their return from captivity at Babylon (536 B.C.), retaining the Hebrew as their sacred language, but speaking and writing in Aramaic somewhat modified by Greek. Aramaic, therefore, was the tongue in which our Lord and his disciples conversed.

The Hebraic was spread over Palestine, and included the ancient Phœnician and Carthaginian, with the dialects of the Ammonites, Moabites, and Philis'tines. Samaritan was a mixture of this with the Aramaic spoken by those foreign settlers introduced into the land of Israel by the Assyrians, to replace the Ten Tribes whom they had transplanted beyond the Euphrates.

The softer Arabic, musical by reason of its preponderance of vowel sounds, was carried from Arabia into Africa, where it was long the language of the cultivated Ethiopians, and where it still survives in its derivative, the Abyssinian.

The Ancient Hebrew shares the imperfections of the Semitic

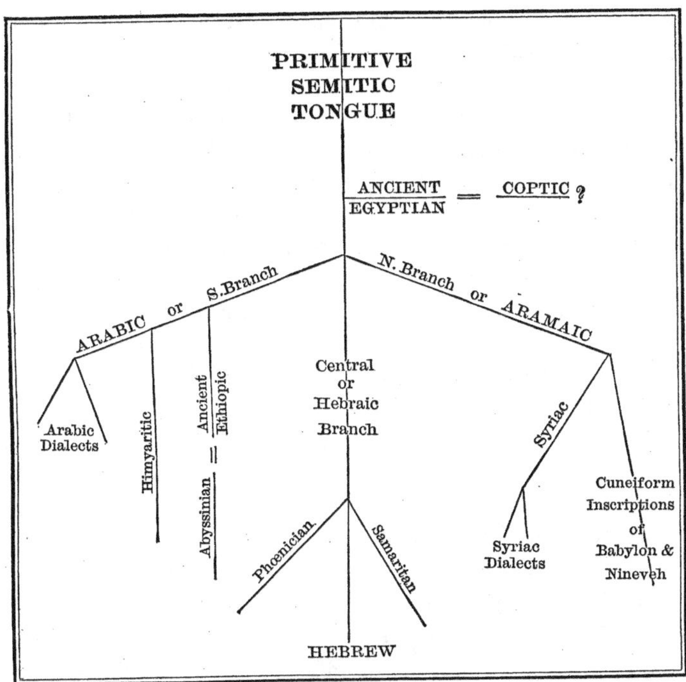

THE SEMITIC FAMILY OF LANGUAGES.

group to which it belongs. It is one of the oldest members of this family, and was long thought to have been the original language of the human race. Its name is derived by some from Heber, ancestor of Abraham and consequently of the people who spoke the classical tongue of the Old Testament; while by many it is believed to mean *belonging to the other side*, that is, of the Jordan—an epithet applicable to the Chosen People as coming from beyond that river to dispossess the Canaanitish tribes.

In the days of the patriarch Abraham, whose father dwelt in "Ur of the Chaldees" (see Map, p. 105) about 2000 B.C., the Semitic dialects differed slightly, if at all; for Abraham, crossing the Euphrates into Canaan, had no difficulty in making himself understood, and afterward, when Jacob went back to Mesopotamia, he conversed readily with the people.

The meagre vocabulary and other defects of the Hebrew are counterbalanced by its euphony, simplicity, and power of poetical expression. Conciseness is its crowning merit. A single sonorous word often conveys an idea that would require a clause of four or five words in English. The whole range of literature in other fields affords no such examples of majestic thought, grand imagery, and impetuous, heart-warming outpourings of soul, as the poetry of that sublime Hebrew tongue which was developed by a simple race of shepherds beneath the mild skies of western Asia.

The Hebrew Alphabet.—The Hebrews early profited by the invention of their Phœnician kinsmen, borrowing from them an alphabet which, as may be seen on the opposite page, they changed little from the original. After the Captivity (588–536 B.C.), the more elegant *square* characters of the Babylonians took the place of the ancient letters; the latter, however, for reasons political as well as religious, were reproduced on the shekels coined during the period of Jewish independence under the Maccabees (168–37 B.C.), by which time the written language was universally expressed in Aramaic characters.

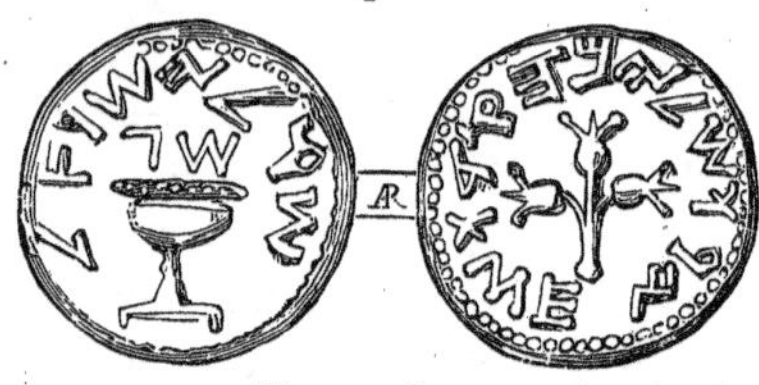

Hebrew Shekel.

The oldest Hebrew alphabet (see Table) contained no more than ten or twelve letters; the number was afterward increased to twenty-two—consonants all. These were qualified by vowel sounds, denoted by *vowel-points* (·- ·.̣ .·. T) placed over or under the consonants to which they belonged. Capitals there were none.—While some have held that the names

ANCIENT ALPHABETS.

Hebrew Names of Letters.	Meaning in English.	English Equivalent.	Conjectural Hieroglyphic Original.	Ancient Phœnician.	Old Hebrew.	Square Hebrew.	Old and Later Greek.		Old and Later Latin.	
Aleph	Ox	A				א		Α		A
Beth	House	B				ב		Β		B
Gimel	Camel	G				ג		Γ		C
Daleth	Door	D				ד		Δ		D
He	Window	H, E				ה		Ε		E
Vau	Hook	V				ו				F
Zayin	Weapon	Z				ז		Ζ		Z
Cheth	Fence	Ch				ח		Η		H
Teth	Snake	Th				ט		Θ		
Yod	Hand	Y, I, J				י		Ι		I
Kaph	Bent Hand	C, Ch				כ ך		Κ		K
Lamed	Ox-goad	L				ל		Λ		L
Mem	Water	M				מ ם		Μ		M
Nun	Fish	N				נ ן		Ν		N
Samech	Prop	S				ס		Ξ		
Ayin	Eye	O				ע		Ο		O
Pe	Mouth	P, Ph				פ ף		Π		P
Tsadhe	Hook	Ts				צ ץ				
Koph	Back of Head	K, Q				ק				Q
Resh	Head	R				ר		Ρ		R
Shin	Tooth	Sh				ש		Σ		S
Tau	Sign (Cross)	T, Th				ת		Τ		T

of the letters were given them arbitrarily, merely to facilitate the memorizing of the alphabet, others believe that a connection existed between their names and their forms: that, for example, A, called *Aleph* (ox), was originally a rough picture of an ox's head; that B was the representation of a house or tent, such being the meaning of its name *Beth*, etc.

Spirit of Hebrew Poetry.—The most ancient Semitic poetry is found in the pure musical Hebrew of the oldest books of the Bible. Nearly one half of the Old Testament was in verse, mainly lyrical, ranging from the simplest song or dirge to the sublimest strains of prophecy; yet didactic poetry has also a place, for in it were embodied the proverbs of Israel's wise men.

Other literatures boast of their epics and dramas; but the Hebrew, without either, has exerted a far more exalted influence on the human mind than any other. In vain do we search the Veda and the Avesta for conceptions as grand as those in the Scriptures. God is apprehended in all his majesty by the Hebrew bards, and speaks through them to nations that are yet to be. The Bible poets wrote not merely for the purpose of pleasing; as teachers and prophets, they had a divine mission and a loftier aim. The graces of rhetoric were employed to present their impressive subjects in the strongest and clearest light. Frequent metaphors embellished their style, and striking personifications endowed it with life and energy. Imagery drawn from the picturesque scenes about them,—the hills, the streams, the plains of Palestine,—or from their every-day employments as tillers and herdsmen, they used without stint; while *parallelism*, whether it consisted in the repetition of the same sentiment or in a contrasting of opposite ideas, was a peculiar beauty of their poetry.

Their language significant and striking, their thoughts lofty and solemn, their tone severely moral, their themes of the deepest interest to man, what wonder that the Hebrew poets tower above the sublimest writers of other times and countries? "Whatever in our literature," says Taylor, "possesses most of simple majesty and force, whatever is most fully fraught with feeling, whatever draws away the soul from its cleaving to the dust and lifts the thoughts toward a brighter sphere—all such elements we owe directly or indirectly to the Hebrew Scriptures, especially to those parts that are in spirit and form poetic."

Parallelism has been mentioned as a distinctive feature of Hebrew poetry. This is defined by Bishop Lowth as "a certain equality, resemblance, or relationship between the members of a period, so that things shall answer to things and words to words, as if fitted to each other by a kind of rule or measure."

Parallelism may be either cumulative, antithetical, or constructive. In the first, a proposition, after having been once stated, is repeated in equivalent words of similar construction, as in Isaiah, lv., 6, 7:—

"Seek ye the Lord, while he may be found;
Call ye upon him, while he is near.

Let the wicked forsake his way,
And the unrighteous man his thoughts:

And let him return unto the Lord, and he will have mercy upon him;
And to our God, for he will abundantly pardon."

Antithetical parallelism is similar, except that the two periods correspond with each other by an opposition of sentiments and terms; as in Proverbs, xxvii., 6:—

"Faithful are the wounds of a friend;
But deceitful are the kisses of an enemy."

In the third kind of parallelism, there is neither correspondence nor opposition in the sentiment, but simply a similarity of construction in the two periods, as in Psalm xix., 8, 9:—

"The statutes of the Lord are right, rejoicing the heart;
The commandment of the Lord is pure, enlightening the eyes.

The fear of the Lord is clean, enduring forever;
The judgments of the Lord are true and righteous altogether."

DAWN OF HEBREW LITERATURE.

There is good reason for believing that the ancient Hebrews had an extensive literature; but out of their "multitude of books," all that have descended to us are those of the Old Testament. Their secular poetical and prose works are wholly lost.

The Books of Moses.—The earliest Hebrew writer of whom we have positive knowledge was Moses, author of the greater part of the Pentateuch* (*five volumes*—the first five books of the Bible), or, as it was called by the Jews, the Book of the Law.

The first book of the Pentateuch, Genesis (*the generation*), tells us all that we know of the Creation, the Deluge, the Confusion of languages, the Dispersion, and the lives of the patriarchs, whose history it sketches till the death of Joseph in Egypt, keeping everywhere prominent the relation of Jehovah to the chosen race.

Exodus (*the going out*) continues the story of the Hebrews from the death of Joseph, relates their oppression under the Pharaoh Ram'eses the Great, their miraculous escape from the land of bondage in the reign of his successor, and the promulgation of the commandments on Mount Sinai. It is in this book that we catch our first glimpse of Hebrew poetry in

* Some hold that the Pentateuch was compiled by Moses from extant writings of an earlier period; others believe it to have been reduced to its present form at a much later date; while many theologians ascribe it all to Moses, except the part that relates to his death and a few interpolated sentences. Its authenticity as part of God's Word has been disputed from time to time, and particularly in these later days; but neither Jews nor Christians doubt its inspiration, though they admit that in parts its meaning may have been misconceived. We have here to do with it, as with other parts of the Bible, simply as a *literary* work.

the Song of Moses and his sister Miriam—a magnificent triumphal ode, the most ancient in any language. The rescued host pour forth in unison their joy and gratitude ; while in response the exulting prophetess, timbrel in hand, leads the women of Israel, on the shore of that sea which had engulfed their enemies, to celebrate their deliverance with sacred dance and rapturous verse. (See Exodus, chapter xv.)

Leviticus (the book *pertaining to the Levites*) consists of regulations relative to worship and sacrifice, together with historical items touching the consecration of Aaron, his first offering, and the destruction of two of his sons for their impiety. Here is developed the theocratic system that lay at the base of Hebrew society.

Numbers takes its name from the *numbering* of the Israelites in the wilderness of Sinai ; it gives an account of this census, and continues their history during thirty-seven years of subsequent wandering, up to their arrival on the borders of the Promised Land. In this book there are several brief specimens of poetry, commemorative of victory, of the digging of a well in the wilderness, etc.

In Deuteronomy (*the second law*) the law is repeated and explained by Moses in three fervid discourses, just before the entrance of the Hebrews into Canaan. The Pentateuch closes with a simple but inexpressibly grand outburst of the Hebrew legislator in song (chapter xxxii.), the blessings he pronounces upon the twelve tribes, and an account of his death.

Of the facts presented in these first five books of the Old Testament, some are confirmed by hieroglyphic inscriptions and the traditions of different nations ; but of the greater part we should have had no knowledge without the inspired narrative. Aside, therefore, from its religious bearing, the Pentateuch is invaluable as an historical record of primeval ages ; while its clear, concise, dignified style, rich with noble thoughts expressed in the venerable manner of antiquity, is worthy of its sublime subjects.

The Historical Books.—The Pentateuch is followed by the historical books of Scripture, which, though extending into the silver age, will for convenience' sake be here considered together. With the Pentateuch they form a complete summary of national history, in which are interwoven religious matters that explain and illustrate it. We may glance briefly at their authorship and contents.

The Book of Joshua, supposed to have been written by Joshua himself or soon after his death, covers a period of twenty-five years (about 1425 B.C.); it relates to the conquest of Canaan and the partition of that promised land among the twelve tribes, closing with the farewell exhortation and death of the great leader. Judges, ascribed to the Prophet Samuel, continues the history of the nation to about 1100 B.C.; it tells how the Jews, as a punishment for their apostasy, were at different times reduced to servitude by their heathen enemies, and on their repentance delivered by heroes who became their Judges. Ruth, regarded by the ancient Jews as belonging to the Book of Judges, is of unknown date and authorship, though attributed by some to Samuel. It is an exquisite idyl of domestic life, designed to show the origin of King David.

The Books of Samuel, the first portion of which Samuel probably composed himself, give an account of the magistracy of that prophet and the reigns of Saul and David. The Books of the Kings dwell upon the glorious reign of Solomon, and then take us through the divided lines of Israel and Judah, till both were finally overthrown and carried into captivity; Jewish tradition points to Jeremiah as the author of these books. Ezra seems to have written most of the Chronicles, which is supplementary to the Kings; he was also the author of the book that bears his name. This and Nehemiah describe the return of the Jews from their captivity in Babylon, and the restoration of the temple-worship at Jerusalem. The Book of Esther, possibly from the pen of Mordecai, one of the personages of the story, is devoted to a touching episode of the reign of Ahasuerus, king of Persia, supposed to be identical with Xerxes, the son of Darius Hystaspis.

The Book of Job is worthy of special mention, as the most artistic specimen of Hebrew genius. Whether this unique poem was the work of Job himself in his later days, or of some other whose name is lost, its author was evidently proficient in all the scientific knowledge of his time. The hero, a native of northern Arabia, whose name has become a synonym for patient suffering, is reduced to the very depths by family bereavements, bodily anguish, and the well-meant reproaches of his friends; yet his faith in God is unshaken, and in the end that faith is amply vindicated and rewarded.

Bold imagery, vividness of description, life-like delineations of lofty passion as well as the gentler emotions, combined with master-touches of dramatic art, stamp this poem as the greatest in Oriental literature. Its passages relating to the war-horse, behemoth, and leviathan (chapters xxxix., xl., xli.), are cited by writers on the sublime as among the grandest illustrations of their subject; and its descriptions of the Deity, as manifested in his works, exhibit the noblest conceptions of the Infinite that man's finite intellect is capable of forming.

GOLDEN AGE OF HEBREW POETRY.

The Psalms.—The flourishing period of DAVID (1085–1015 B.C.) ushers in the Augustan age of Hebrew poetry. The Lyric was then carried to perfection by the poet-king himself and his contemporaries in their Psalms,—"those delicate, fragrant, and lovely flowers," as Luther calls them, "springing up out of all manner of beautiful joyous thoughts toward God and his goodness." The strains of "Israel's sweet psalmist," who began as a shepherd-lad to cultivate the arts of music and poetry, breathe a spirit of plaintive tenderness that distinguishes them from the statelier productions of other contributors to Hebrew psalmody.

A utopian theory of the great Plato, but one that he declared could be carried out only by "a god or some divine one," was the training of the Grecian youth in odes like the Psalms: and this—the religious instruction of the people—was the very object of the Hebrew lyrics. The plan of the Greek philosopher had been put in practice centuries before his day in Palestine, and on a far grander scale than ever he imagined. In the royal city of Jerusalem, four thousand musicians appointed by David chanted hymns of triumph and praise, to the accompaniment of harp and flute; while in the gorgeous temple of David's son, the sublime worship of Jehovah challenges description.

For three thousand years, these Hebrew anthems, unapproached by the religious songs of any other age or people, have been the glory of the Jewish and the Christian Church, eloquently testifying that "there has been one people among the nations—one among the millions of the worshippers of stocks—taught of God."

Most of the Psalms date from David's time; but one (Psalm xc.) carries us as far back as Moses, and others were as late as the Captivity; they thus cover a period of nearly ten centuries. They were probably arranged as we now have them in the fifth century B.C.

Elegiac Poetry.—King David was also a writer of elegy, that kind of song in which the Hebrew poets and prophets poured out their grief in the unaffected language of nature. Some of his Psalms are beautiful specimens of this species of poetry, especially Psalm xlii., "As the hart panteth after the water-brooks," composed during his exile among the mountains of Lebanon. Another exquisite and pathetic elegy of this poet, rendered below in English verse by Lowth, is the

LAMENTATION FOR SAUL AND JONATHAN.

"Thy glory, Israel, droops its languid head,
  On Gilboa's heights thy rising beauty dies;
In sordid piles there sleep the illustrious dead,
  The mighty victor fall'n and vanquished lies.

Yet dumb be Grief; hushed be her clam'rous voice!
  Tell not in Gath the tidings of our shame!
Lest proud Philistia in our woes rejoice,
  And rude barbarians blast fair Israel's fame.

The sword of Saul ne'er spent its force in air;
  The shaft of Jonathan brought low the brave;
In life united equal fates they share,
  In death united share one common grave.

Daughters of Judah! mourn the fatal day,
  In sable grief attend your monarch's urn;
To solemn notes attune the pensive lay,
  And weep those joys that never shall return.

With various wealth he made your tents o'erflow,
  In princely pride your charms profusely dressed;
Bade the rich robe with ardent purple glow,
  And sparkling gems adorn the tissued vest.

On Gilboa's heights the mighty vanquished lies,
  The son of Saul, the generous and the just;
Let streaming sorrow ever fill these eyes,
  Let sacred tears bedew a brother's dust.

Thy firm regard revered thy David's name,
  And kindest thoughts in kindest acts expressed;
Not brighter glows the pure and generous flame
  That lives within the tender virgin's breast.

But vain the tear and vain the bursting sigh,
  Though Sion's echoes with our grief resound;
The mighty victors fall'n and vanquished lie,
  And war's refulgent weapons strew the ground."

Didactic Poetry.—In the golden age, didactic poetry also reached the acme of perfection. The Proverbs that then flowed from the inspired pen of SOLOMON, prince of didactic writers as his father was of lyric poets, are too well known, with all their richness of practical wisdom, to require more than a passing mention. Expressed concisely in energetic words, according to the different forms of parallelism, these moral precepts are indeed "like apples of gold in baskets of silver."

Of the same general scope as the Proverbs, and by the same author, is Ecclesiastes, or the Preacher. In this book is shown the vanity of earthly pleasures; and the whole duty of man is summed up in the sentence, "Fear God and keep his commandments." The Book of Ecclesiastes has been attributed to Solomon's latter days; the Proverbs, to his prime; while that sweet pastoral, the Song of Songs—singularly beautiful, whether taken literally as an exponent of happy wedded love, or allegorically as delineating the mutual attachment of God and his people—was the joyous outburst of his youth. Solomon was also the author of a thousand canticles and various works on miscellaneous subjects; books of making which, he tells us, there was no end.

Prophetic Poetry of the Golden Age.—The writings of the earlier prophets, florid with high-wrought imagery, revived for a time the waning glories of the golden age. Foremost of this class in eloquence of diction, sublimity of thought, and versatility of genius, stands ISAIAH. Majesty united with elaborate finish; a harmony that delights the soul; a variety that imparts freshness without detracting from dignity; simplicity and unvarying purity of language,—conspire to make the lyric verse of "the Evangelical Prophet" the most appropriate embodiment of the awful messages of God to the Jews, the promise of a Messiah and universal peace.

After a career of nearly seventy years, Isaiah sealed his great work with his blood in the reign of the idolatrous Manasseh (698–643 B.C.). His mind has been pronounced "one of the most sublime and variously gifted instruments which the Spirit of God has ever employed to pour forth its Voice upon the world."

Even the minor prophets, if we except Jonah the oldest, exhibit in their compositions unwonted grandeur and elegance: Hosea, with his sententious style; Amos, "the herdman and gatherer of sycamore fruit;" Joel and Micah; Habakkuk, whose fervent prayer to the Almighty is graced with the loftiest embellishments, and Nahum, perhaps the boldest and most ardent of all.

And so the Golden Age of Hebrew Literature ends. We know only its sacred poetry, and much indeed of this has disappeared.* The harvest and vintage songs which wakened the echoes amid the vales of Palestine, the pastorals that accompanied the shepherd's pipe on the hill-sides of Ephraim, all are lost forever; "the voice of mirth and the voice of gladness, the voice of the bridegroom and the bride," were forgotten in the streets of Jerusalem, when the land was desolate under the Babylonian and "the daughters of music were brought low."

SILVER AGE.

The Prophets.—The names of three great prophets—Jeremiah, Ezekiel, and Daniel—illuminate the first page in the history of the decline of Hebrew literature. But in their writings, and notably so in those of the later minor prophets, poetry was evidently on the wane. They lived in a degenerate day. About half of the prophecy of Jeremiah, denouncing the judgment of Heaven on the disobedient people, is poetry; he lacks the pomp and majesty of Isaiah, but excels in stirring the gentler emotions.

His Lamentations are beautiful elegies on the fall of his country and the desecration of the temple; every letter seems "written with a tear and every word the sound of a broken

* For example, the Book of Jasher, which appears to have been a collection of songs in praise of the just and upright—the subject of endless discussions.

heart." The verses of the several chapters in the original begin with consecutive letters of the alphabet, that they may be the more easily memorized, for it was intended that the sins and sufferings of the Jewish nation should never be forgotten. Can anything be more touching than the personification of Jerusalem, sitting as a solitary widow on the ground and mourning for her children?

"Is this nothing to all you who pass along the way? behold and see
If there be any sorrow like unto my sorrow, which is inflicted on me;
Which Jehovah inflicted on me in the day of the violence of his wrath.
For these things I weep, my eyes stream with water,
Because the comforter is far away that should tranquillize my soul.
My children are desolate, because the enemy was strong."

Ezekiel and Daniel were carried captives to Babylon, where they made known their prophetic visions. The former wrote partly in poetry, characterized by a rough vehemence peculiar to himself. The Book of Daniel, in which history is combined with prophecy, is in prose, and a portion of it in the Chaldee language.

Another writer of distinguished merit, belonging to this age, was the scribe and priest Ezra (already mentioned), who was

THE TOMB OF EZRA.

permitted to return from Babylon to Jerusalem with a company of his people, 458 B.C. He settled the canon of Scripture, restoring and editing the whole of the Old Testament.

The Apocrypha (*secret writings*) consist chiefly of the stories of To'bit and Judith, the first and second books of Esdras and of the Maccabees, Ba'ruch, the Wisdom of Solomon, and Ecclesiasticus or the Wisdom of the Son of Sirach. Composed during the three centuries immediately preceding the Christian Era, they bear internal evidence, in their lack of the ancient poetical power, of belonging to an age of literary decline. They were mostly included in the canon of Scripture by the Council of Trent in 1545, but are rejected by Protestants as uninspired.

Ecclesiasticus, best of the Apocryphal books, is full of moral, political, and religious precepts, its object being to teach true wisdom and its style resembling the didactic poetry of Solomon. The following fine passage, versified by Lowth, personifies

WISDOM.

"Wisdom shall raise her loud exulting voice,
And midst her people glory and rejoice;
Oft the Almighty's awful presence near,
Her dulcet sounds angelic choirs shall hear.

Me before time itself He gave to-day,
Nor shall my spirit faint or feel decay;
I bowed before Him in His hallowed shrine,
And Sion's pride and Sion's strength was mine.
Did I not tall as those fair cedars grow,
Which grace our Lebanon's exalted brow?
Did I not lofty as the cypress rise,
Which seems from Hermon's heights to meet the skies?
Fresh as Engaddi's palm that scents the air,
Like rose of Jericho, so sweet, so fair;
Green as the verdant olive of the groves,
Straight as the plane-tree which the streamlet loves,
Richer than vineyards rise my sacred bowers,
Sweeter than roses bloom my vernal flowers;
Fair love is mine, and hope, and gentle fear;
Me science hallows, as a parent dear.

Come, who aspire beneath my shade to live;
Come, all my fragrance, all my fruits receive!
Sweeter than honey are the strains I sing,
Sweeter than honey-comb the dower I bring;
Me, taste who will, shall feel increased desire,
Who drinks shall still my flowing cups require;
He whose firm heart my precepts still obeys,
With safety walks through life's perplexing maze;
Who cautious follows where my footsteps lead,
No cares shall feel, no mighty terrors dread.

Small was my stream when first I rolled along,
In clear meanders Eden's vales among;
With fresh'ning draughts each tender plant I fed,
And bade each flow'ret raise its blushing head;
But soon my torrent o'er its margin rose,
Where late a brook, behold an ocean flows!
For Wisdom's blessings shall o'er earth extend,
Blessings that know no bound, that know no end."

The Talmud.—Our treatise would be incomplete without some notice of the mysterious book whose name heads this paragraph,—the Talmud. Comparatively unknown except in name for centuries, it was repeatedly suppressed in the Dark Ages by popes, kings, and emperors, as likely to be dangerous to Christianity.

Talmud means *learning*. It is essentially a digest of law, civil and criminal, and a collection of traditions orally preserved. It consists of two parts, viz., the Mishna, or earlier text; and the Gemara (*ghe-mah'ră*), a commentary on the Mishna. The age that gave birth to the Talmud was the period after the Captivity, when a passionate love for their sacred and national writings animated the Jews restored to their country and its institutions. Hundreds of learned men, all great in their day, who treasured in their memories the traditions of a thousand years, contributed to its pages.

The Talmud was a cyclopædia treating of every subject, even down to gardening and the manual arts; it depicts incidentally the social life of the people, not of the Jews alone, but of other nations also. It is enlivened by parables, jests, and fairy-tales, ethical sayings, and proverbs; the style is now poetical, anon sublime; and there may be gathered amid its wilderness of themes "some of the richest and most precious fruits of human thought and fancy."

After two unsuccessful attempts, the Talmud was finally systemized in a code by the Saint Jehuda (about 200 A.D.). A remarkable correspondence exists between it and the Gospel writings, explained by the fact that both reflect in a measure the same times.

EXTRACTS FROM THE TALMUD.

"Turn the Bible and turn it again, for everything is in it.

Bless God for the evil as well as the good. When you hear of a death, say 'Blessed is the righteous Judge.'

Even when the gates of heaven are shut to prayer, they are open to tears.

When the righteous die, it is the earth that loses. The lost jewel will always be a jewel, but the possessor who has lost it—well may he weep.

Life is a passing shadow, says the Scripture. Is it the shadow of a tower, of a tree? A shadow that prevails for a while? No, it is the shadow of a bird in his flight; away flies the bird, and there is neither bird nor shadow.

Teach thy tongue to say, 'I do not know.'

If a word spoken in its time is worth one piece of money, silence in its time is worth two.

The ass complains of the cold even in July.

Four shall not enter Paradise: the scoffer, the liar, the hypocrite, and the slanderer. To slander is to murder.

The camel wanted to have horns, and they took away his ears.

Thy friend has a friend, and thy friend's friend has a friend: be discreet.

The soldiers fight, and the kings are heroes.

Love your wife like yourself, honor her more than yourself. Whoso lives unmarried, lives without joy, without comfort, without blessing. He who forsakes the love of his youth, God's altar weeps for him. It is woman alone through whom God's blessings are vouchsafed to a house. She teaches the children, speeds the husband to the place of worship, welcomes him when he returns, keeps the house godly and pure, and God's blessings rest upon all these things. He who marries for money, his children shall be a curse to him.

Men should be careful lest they cause women to weep, for God counts their tears.

The world is saved by the breath of school-children.

When the thief has no opportunity of stealing, he considers himself an honest man. The thief invokes God while he breaks into the house.

Get your living by skinning carcasses in the street, if you cannot otherwise; and do not say, 'I am a great man, this work would not befit my dignity.' Not the place honors the man, but the man the place.

Youth is a garland of roses; age is a crown of thorns.

The day is short and the work is great. It is not incumbent upon thee to complete the work: but thou must not therefore cease from it. If thou hast worked much, great shall be thy reward; for the Master who employed thee is faithful in his payment. But know that the true reward is not of this world."—DEUTSCH.

RETURNING THE JEWELS.

"Rabbi Meir, the great teacher, was sitting on the Sabbath-day and instructing the people in the Synagogue. In the meantime, his two sons died; they were both fine of growth and enlightened in the law. His wife carried them into the attic, laid them on the bed, and spread a white cloth over their dead bodies.

In the evening, Rabbi Meir came home. 'Where are my sons,' inquired he, 'that I may give them my blessing?'—'They went to the Synagogue,' was the reply.—'I looked round,' returned he, 'and did not perceive them.'

She reached him a cup; he praised the Lord at the close of the Sabbath, drank, and asked again, 'Where are my sons, that they also may drink of the wine of blessing?'—'They cannot be far off,' said she, and set before him something to eat. When he had given thanks after the repast, she said: 'Rabbi, grant me a request.'—'Speak, my love!' answered he.

'A few days ago, a person gave me some jewels to take care of, and now he asks for them again; shall I give them back to him?'—'This my wife should not need to ask,' said Rabbi Meir. 'Wouldst thou hesitate to return every one his own?'—'Oh! no,' replied she, 'but I would not return them without thy knowledge.'

Soon after she led him to the attic, approached, and took the cloth off the dead bodies. 'Oh! my sons!' exclaimed the father sorrowfully, 'My sons!' She turned away and wept.

At length she took his hand, and said: 'Rabbi, hast thou not taught me that we must not refuse to return that which hath been intrusted to our care? Behold, the Lord gave and the Lord hath taken away; praised be the name of the Lord.'

'The name of the Lord be praised!' rejoined Rabbi Meir. 'It is well said: He who hath a virtuous wife hath a greater treasure than costly pearls. She openeth her mouth with wisdom, and on her tongue is the law of kindness.'"

THE PAINTED FLOWERS.

"The power of Solomon had spread his wisdom to the remotest parts of the known world. Queen Sheba, attracted by the splendor of his reputation, visited this poetical king at his own court. There, one day, to exercise the sagacity of the monarch, Sheba presented herself at the foot of the throne: in each hand she held a wreath; the one was composed of natural, and the other of artificial flowers. Art, in constructing the mimetic wreath, had exquisitely emulated the lively hues of nature; so that, at the distance it was held by the queen for the inspection of the king, it was deemed impossible for him to decide, as her question required, which wreath was the production of nature, and which the work of art.

The sagacious Solomon seemed perplexed; yet to be vanquished, though in a trifle, by a trifling woman, irritated his pride. The son of David, he who had written treatises on the vegetable productions 'from the cedar to the hyssop,' to acknowledge himself outwitted by a woman, with shreds of paper and glazed paintings! The honor of the monarch's reputation for divine sagacity seemed diminished, and the whole Jewish court looked solemn and melancholy.

At length an expedient presented itself to the king; and one, it must be confessed, worthy of the naturalist. Observing a cluster of bees hovering about a window, he commanded that it should be opened. It was opened; the bees rushed into the court, and alighted immediately on one of the wreaths, while not a single one fixed on the other. The baffled Sheba had one more reason to be astonished at the wisdom of Solomon."—D'ISRAELI.

NOTES ON WRITING, EDUCATION, ETC., AMONG THE HEBREWS.

The art of writing practised by the Hebrews at a very remote period. In primitive times, records of important events cut in stone; the letters sometimes filled with plaster or melted lead. Engraving also practised with the stylus on rough tablets of boxwood, earthenware, or bone. Leather early employed; the Law written on skins (of "clean animals or birds") in golden characters. The skins rolled round one or two wooden cylinders, the scroll then tied with a thread and sealed. Parchment written on with reed pens, which, together with a knife for sharpening them and an ink of lamp-black dissolved in gall-juice, were carried in an inkhorn suspended from the girdle. Letter-writing in vogue from the time of David.

Many ancient Jewish cities far advanced in art and literature. Reading and writing from the first not confined to the learned, for the people were required to write precepts of the Law upon their door-posts, and on crossing the Jordan were commanded to place certain inscriptions on great stones very plainly, that they might be read by all. *Scribes* in readiness to serve those who could not write. Schools established in different localities in the prophetical age, in which "the sons of the prophets" lived a kind of monastic life, studying their laws and institutions along with poetry and music.

After the Captivity, education recognized as all-important, and at length made compulsory. The Jews in consequence soon noted for learning and scholarship. $2,500,000 paid by Ptolemy Philadelphus (260 B.C.) to seventy Jewish doctors for translating the Old Testament into Greek, at Alexandria; hence the *Septuagint*, as it is called, or version of the *Seventy*. By 80 B.C., Palestine filled with flourishing schools. *Jerusalem was destroyed because the instruction of the young was neglected—Revere a teacher even more than your father—A scholar is greater than a prophet*—common sayings among the Jews. Colleges maintained where lectures were delivered, and the Socratic method of debate was pursued. Every student trained to some trade, the ripest scholars working with their own hands as tent-makers, weavers, carpenters, bakers, cooks, etc. A large library at Jerusalem composed of volumes in history, royal letters, and various works of the prophets. The most learned of the later Platonists the Jew Phi'lo (20 B.C.–50 A.D.), who tried to reconcile the Platonic philosophy with the teachings of the Hebrew Scriptures.

Riddles, enigmas, and play upon words, the chief sources of amusement among the Hebrews. Dice mentioned in the Talmud. Public games unknown. Fishing with nets and hooks, favorite sports. Dancing practised as a religious rite; the stage on which it was performed in the temples styled the *choir:* each Psalm perhaps accompanied by a suitable dance.

CHAPTER V.

CHALDEAN, ASSYRIAN, ARABIC, AND PHŒNICIAN LITERATURES.

Cuneiform Letters.—North of the Persian Gulf, and drained by the rivers Euphrates and Tigris, lay Chalde'a, or Babylonia, the "Land of Shi'nar" (*country of the two rivers*). Here arose the earliest cities, amid a population principally Turanian and Semitic, with a limited intermixture of the Aryan element. A Semitic dialect prevailed among the people at large; but the Turanian Chaldees, to whom Babylonia was indebted for its aboriginal civilization, through the centuries of their ascendency, political and intellectual, not only kept alive their native tongue in conversation with each other, but inscribing it on imperishable monuments caused it to endure through all time.

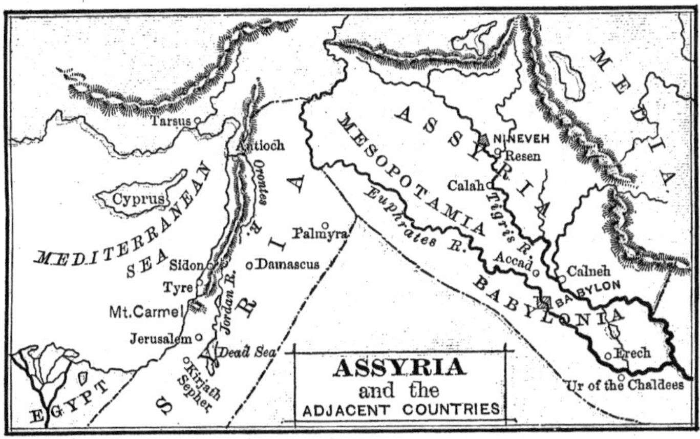

To these Turanians, the honor of having invented cuneiform letters must be conceded; an honor, indeed, when we remember that theirs was possibly the most ancient device for embodying human thought. The characters, variously called wedge-formed, arrow-headed, nail-shaped, and swallow-tailed, they appear to have brought with them into the Euphrates valley from the more northerly country which they previously occupied; and their Semitic co-residents in Babylonia were not slow in adopting the ingenious system which they had elaborated.

The cuneiform letters, like the hieroglyphics, were at first rude representations of objects, but in most cases the resemblance to the original was soon lost in the attempt to simplify. In some few instances, however, it may be readily detected;

as in 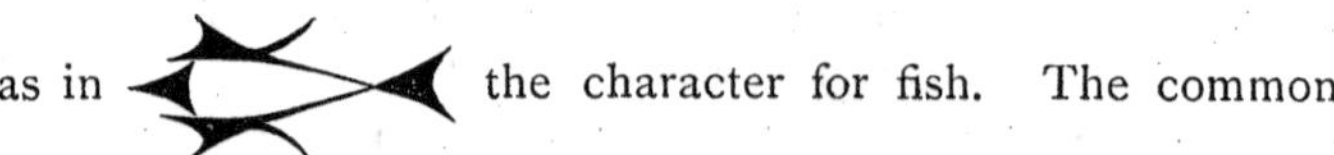 the character for fish. The common signs eventually acquired phonetic values, the whole number of characters employed amounting to about four hundred.

When by the victory of Alexander at Arbe'la (331 B.C.) the great Persian Empire fell, cuneiform writing ceased to be practised, and cuneiform literature was buried in the mounds of Assyria and Babylonia for two thousand years. During the present century, it has been disinterred by inquisitive scholars, whose labors have resulted in the restoration of a forgotten history, through the wonderful literature of a people long known only in name.

ASSYRIO-BABYLONIAN LITERATURE.

Writing Materials.—The cuneiform letters heretofore spoken of as in use among the Persians at a later date (p. 66) were doubtless originally intended to be cut on rocks with chisels, and hence were angular instead of round. But the ancient Babylonians preferred bricks and tablets of clay, on which, when moist and soft, they traced their legends, annals, and scientific items, with an ivory or bronze stylus, hardening the surface thus inscribed by baking. The tablets, from one inch in length upward, are pillow-shaped and covered with characters so minute as to be almost illegible without a glass. After baking, to insure their preservation, they were usually coated with thin clay, and on this the inscription below was duplicated.

The Assyrians used similar tablets, and besides carved their records exquisitely on the stone panels of their palaces, and on human-headed bulls of colossal size. The tablets above described, together with terra-cotta cylinders, formed the books of this inventive nation, who also engraved with wonderful delicacy glass, metals, the amethyst, jasper, and onyx.

ASSYRIAN TABLET.

Stone slabs were generally reserved for royal inscriptions; the literary classes of Assyria preferred the cheaper clay, on which they could write more rapidly and quite as legibly with their triangular instruments. Something like paper or parchment seems to have been used to a very limited extent; but if so, it has entirely disappeared. It is also thought that the Chaldeans may have practised a simple method of printing, as wedge-like types of stone have been found among the ruins of their cities.

Golden Age of Babylonian Literature (2000–1550 B.C.).—Very little of the Assyrio-Babylonian literature has as yet been recovered. A mine of literary wealth in the valley of the Euphrates still awaits the persevering student, for before 2000 B.C. important works were written in Chaldea. In the twentieth century, a golden age dawned on this ancient land; its great cities became centres of literary refinement, as well as of commerce and art, and a lofty poetical style characterized the writings of the time. Standard texts on religion, science, and remote history were then and shortly thereafter produced, the copying of which appears to have satisfied the ambition of subsequent generations.

The oldest known specimen of Chaldean writing is a set of bricks, discovered near the site of E′rech (see Map, p. 105). They are thought to have been made about 2008 B.C. As these bricks illustrate the most ancient cuneiform character, two of them are here presented, accompanied with a translation.

CHALDEAN BRICKS.

"Beltis, his lady, has caused Urukh, the pious chief and king of Ur, king of the land of Accad, to build a temple to her."

FROM A TABLET OF BABYLONIAN LAWS.

"A certain man's brother-in-law hired workmen, and on his foundation built an enclosure. From the house the judge expelled him.

His father and his mother a man shall not deny.

A decision. A son says to his mother: 'Thou art not my mother.' His hair is cut off; in the city they exclude him from earth and water, and in the house imprison him.

A decision. A mother says to her son: 'Thou art not my son.' They imprison her.

A decision. A woman says to her husband: 'Thou art not my husband.' Into the river they throw her.

A decision. A husband says to his wife: 'Thou art not my wife.' Half a ma'neh (thirty ounces) of silver he weighs out in payment.

A decision. A master kills his slaves, cuts them to pieces, injures their offspring, drives them from the land. His hand every day a half measure of corn measures out."

Babylonian literature was rich in the departments of law, mathematics, astrology, grammar, and history. Nor was fiction wanting; fables, in which the lower animals carried on spirited dialogues, were favorites with the people. At a very early date, the inscribed tablets and cylinders were collected, and the chief cities were made the seats of libraries.

From a volume of Chaldean hymns, somewhat similar to the Rig-Veda, are taken the following verses to the Babylonian Venus :—

PRAYER OF THE HEART TO ISTAR.

"Light of heaven, who like the fire dawnest on the world, art thou!
Goddess in the earth, who dawnest like the earth, art thou!
To the house of men in thy descending thou goest: prosperity approaches thee.
Day is thy servant, heaven thy canopy.
Princess of the four cities, head of the sea, heaven is thy canopy.
Exalted of the Sun-god, heaven is thy canopy!
For my father the Moon-god, revolver of the seasons, sanctuaries I build, a temple I build.
For my brother the Sun-god, revolver of the seasons, sanctuaries I build, a temple I build.
In the beginning the goddess spoke thus to men:
The Lady of Heaven, the divinity of the zenith, am I!
The Lady of Heaven, the divinity of the dawn, am I!
The Queen of Heaven, the opener of the locks of the high heaven, my begetter.
O Istar! Lady of Heaven! may thy heart rest.
O Lady, Queen of Heaven! may thy liver be magnified.
O Lady, Queen of the land of the four rivers of Erech! may thy heart rest.
O Lady, Queen of Babylon! may thy liver be magnified!
O Lady, Queen of the Temple of the Resting-place of the World! may thy heart rest."—A. H. SAYCE.

The Babylonians believed in omens. They gathered auguries from dreams, inspection of the hand, the time of birth, and various phenomena, establishing a national system of divination not without its amusing features. For instance, we have the following

OMENS CONNECTED WITH DOGS.

"If a blue dog enters into a palace, that palace is burned.

If a yellow dog enters into the palace, exit from that palace will be baleful.

If a spotted dog enters into the palace, that palace its peace to the enemy gives.

If a dog to the palace goes and on a bed lies down, that palace none with his hand takes.

If a dog to the palace goes and on the royal parasol lies down, that palace its peace to the enemy gives.

If a white dog into a temple enters, the foundation of that temple is not stable.

If a yellow dog into a temple enters, that temple sees plenty.
If a spotted dog into a temple enters, that temple do its gods love."

Many charms and exorcisms appear in the ancient language of Babylonia, disease being attributed to possession by evil spirits. Specimens follow.

BABYLONIAN EXORCISMS.

"Wasting, want of health, the evil spirit of the ulcer, spreading quinsy of the throat, the violent and noxious ulcer. Spirit of Heaven! remember; Spirit of Earth! remember.

Sickness of the stomach, sickness of the heart, palpitation of the heart, sickness of the head, noxious colic, the agitation of terror, lingering sickness, nightmare. Spirit of Heaven! remember; Spirit of Earth! remember.

Poisonous spittle of the mouth which is noxious to the voice, phlegm which is destructive, tubercles of the lungs. Spirit of Heaven! remember; Spirit of Earth! remember."

Chambers of Records at Nineveh.—The Semites who, as the sacred historian informs us, left the land of Shinar to found Nineveh and the neighboring cities, carried with them the civilization and literary culture of the Chaldeans. The earliest permanent seat of letters was Ca'lah (see Map, p. 105), where, during the reign of Shalmane'ser II. (858–823 B.C.) many clay tablets borrowed from the Babylonians were copied by Assyrian scribes. This same king erected at Calah an obelisk of black marble, containing a narrative of his wars illustrated by reliefs—one of the few Assyrian monuments of its kind commemorative of national triumphs.

The library thus begun at Calah was enlarged under succeeding kings. Removed at length to Nineveh, it there attained vast proportions through the efforts of that munificent patron of literature, Sardanapa'lus II., Assyria's greatest monarch (667–647 B.C.). The number of engraved tablets reached ten thousand.

Here were grammars* and lexicons, law-books and scien-

* The grammatical literature of the Assyrians is equalled only by that of the Hindoos and the Greeks.

tific treatises, histories, astronomical and arithmetical works, songs, prayers, hymns sometimes approaching the Hebrew sacred lyrics in sublimity, books of charms and omens, natural histories, botanies, and geographies — a complete encyclopædia of ancient literature. The books of this curious collection were carefully arranged according to their subjects, numbered, catalogued, and placed in charge of librarians. They were public property, intended for the instruction of the people.

BLACK OBELISK OF SHALMANESER.

Such was the library of Sardanapalus — principally copied from Babylonian texts; such, it was buried beneath the ruins of the palace when "the gates of the rivers were opened and Nineveh became a desolation;" such, it lay amid the débris for centuries, "while the cormorant and the bittern lodged in the upper lintels."

But the mounds that so long covered the site of Nineveh have recently surrendered their treasures. Clouds that environed the history of the past have been dissipated; ancient nations, for ages wrapped in obscurity, we no longer "see through a glass, darkly;" and the narrative of the inspired writers of the Bible has been in many places confirmed by the inscriptions disentombed in the East. Among the most interesting fragments found scattered through the ruined "Chambers of Records" of the Assyrian palace, are the tablets relating to the Creation, the Fall of Man, and the Deluge, copied from Babylonian records hundreds of years older than the Pentateuch.

FROM THE CHALDEAN ACCOUNT OF THE DELUGE.

(Compiled originally about 2000 B.C.)

"The flood reached to heaven: the bright earth to a waste was turned. It destroyed all life from the face of the earth, the strong deluge over the people. Brother saw not brother, they did not know the people. In heaven, the gods feared the tempest and sought refuge; they ascended to the heaven of the King of angels and spirits.

Six days and nights passed; the wind, deluge, and storm, overwhelmed. On the seventh day, in its course, was calmed the storm; and all the deluge, which had destroyed like an earthquake, quieted. The sea he caused to dry, and the wind and deluge ended.

I perceived the sea making a tossing; and the whole of mankind turned to corruption; like reeds the corpses floated. I opened the window, and the light broke over my face; it passed. I sat down and wept; over my face flowed my tears. I perceived the shore at the boundary of the sea. To the country of Nizir went the ship. The mountain of Nizir stopped the ship; and to pass over, it was not able. The first day, and the second day, the mountain of Nizir the same. The third day, and the fourth day, the mountain of Nizir the same. The fifth and sixth, the mountain of Nizir the same. On the seventh day, in the course of it, I sent forth a dove, and it left. The dove went and turned, and a resting-place it did not find, and it returned.

I sent forth a swallow, and it left. The swallow went and turned, and a resting-place it did not find, and it returned.

I sent forth a raven, and it left. The raven went, and the decrease of the water it saw, and it did eat, it swam, and wandered away, and did not return.

I sent the animals forth to the four winds. I poured out a libation. I built an altar on the peak of the mountain."—GEORGE SMITH.

SPECIMENS OF ASSYRIAN SACRED POETRY.

A PRAYER FOR THE KING.

"Length of days,
Long, lasting years,
A strong sword,
A long life,
Extended years of glory,
Preëminence among kings,

Grant ye to the King my Lord,
Who has given such gifts
To his gods.

The bounds vast and wide of his empire,
And of his rule,
May he enlarge and may he complete,
Holding over all kings supremacy,
And royalty, and empire.
May he attain to gray hairs and old age.

And after the life of these days,
In the feasts of the Silver Mountain, the heavenly courts,
The abode of blessedness:
And in the Light
Of the Happy Fields,
May he dwell a life
Eternal, holy,
In the presence of the gods
Who inhabit Assyria."—H. F. TALBOT.

Here is undoubtedly expressed a belief in the soul's immortality, which also appears in the following prayer for the spirit of a dying man:—

"Like a bird may it fly to a lofty place!
To the holy hands of its god may it ascend!"

A PENITENTIAL PSALM.

"O my Lord! my sins are many, my trespasses are great; and the wrath of the gods has plagued me with disease, and with sickness and sorrow.

I fainted: but no one stretched forth his hand!
I groaned: but no one drew nigh!
I cried aloud: but no one heard!
O Lord! do not abandon thy servant!
In the waters of the great storm, seize his hand!
The sins which he has committed, turn thou to righteousness."—H. F. TALBOT.

Like their Babylonian kinsmen, the Assyrians put faith in charms, incantations, and exorcisms, using sometimes magic ties or knots. The following is a prescription for giving consolation in the hour of death:—

"Take a woman's linen kerchief; bind it round the right hand, loose it from the left hand. Knot it with seven knots; do so twice. Sprinkle it with bright wine. Bind it round the head of the sick man. Bind it round his hands and feet, like manacles and fetters. Sit down on his bed. Sprinkle holy water over him. He shall hear the voice of Hea, Davkina* shall protect him, and the Eldest Son of Heaven shall find him a happy habitation."

TRANSLATION OF A LETTER.

(Written in Assyria more than 2,500 years ago, by an officer named Bel-basa, to Sennacherib.)

To the King my Lord,

From thy servant Bel-basa:

May there be peace to the King my Lord; may the gods Nebo and Merodach greatly bless the Lord my King.

Concerning the palace of the queen which is in the city of Kalzi, which the King has appointed us; the house is decaying, the house is opening its foundation, its bricks are bulging. When will the King, our Lord, command the master of works? An order let him make, that he may come and the foundation that he may strengthen.

ARABIC LITERATURE.

Himyaritic Inscriptions.—The high-spirited war-loving tribes that roved over the tablelands of Arabia, as well as the more refined inhabitants of her ports on the Red Sea, doubtless cultivated letters. We may suppose the former to have given their florid fancies vent in pastorals, rude songs for the desert bivouac, or triumphal odes. More finished species of poetry would have been congenial to the courtly residents of the cities, whose knowledge of the world was extended by trading expeditions to India, and along the African coast as far as the Mozambique Channel.

Yet of this probable literature we possess little that is older than the era of Mohammed (600 A.D.), at which time the Arabians awoke to a new life, for centuries leading the van of the nations in the march of literature and science. But the little that we have is not without interest.

---

* God and goddess of the sea and of the lower regions.

At least eighteen hundred years before the Christian Era, descendants of Joktan, called Sabæans and afterward Himyarites, established themselves in southwestern Arabia; but not until about 800 B.C. do they appear to have gained permanent dominion over the neighboring tribes. Inscriptions in their language, the Himyaritic, a Semitic tongue closely related to the Arabic, if not sufficiently like it to be called by the same name, have been found in the lower part of the Arabian peninsula on walls, tombs, dikes, and bronze tablets.

These are the oldest known Arabic writings, and are believed by scholars to represent the golden age of the Himyarite monarchy (100 B.C.–500 A.D.). Gems have also been discovered, inscribed with these same characters.

PHŒNICIAN LITERATURE.

Its Lost Treasures.—In the most ancient records, the narrow strip of coast between the Lib'anus Mountains and the Mediterranean was recognized as an important centre of civilization. Its cities were seats of art and commerce; Africa, Sicily, and Spain, were dotted with its colonies and trading-stations; the sails of its merchantmen sparkled on every sea; its language was known throughout the ancient world.

It cannot be that a nation so advanced in knowledge was without a literature; and if works on their philosophy and religion, on history, geography, navigation, and agriculture, didactic poems and love-songs, constitute a literature, vast indeed was that of the Phœnicians. No department of science or belles-lettres appears to have been overlooked by their authors.

The famous "Book City," Kir'jath-Se'pher, which, during the conquest of Canaan, was taken by Othniel the future Judge, is thought to have been a Phœnician town. Its name implies that it was a repository of books, probably public records and works on law—perhaps an Athens to the nations of

Canaan, whither their youth flocked to consult its libraries and receive instruction at its academies. Its valuable collection of manuscripts was doubtless committed to the flames by the Hebrew conqueror.

In like manner, the whole constellation of Phœnician hymns, and lyrics, and prose pieces, has become extinct, except a lonely star left here and there in the works of foreign authors; or a faint light glimmering on some coin or tablet, gem or tombstone.

The only important Phœnician writer known to us is Sanchoni'athon. Fragments of his History, written perhaps in the fourteenth century B.C., have survived through a Greek translation. In accounting for the origin of the universe, Sanchoniathon taught the theory of evolution, that "from certain animals not having sensation, intelligent animals were produced."

Phœnician Carthage also developed an extensive literature. The records of the city were kept by native historians; and we know that Ma'go's great work on agriculture, in twenty-eight parts, was highly appreciated at Rome, and there rendered into Latin. When the city of Hannibal fell before her more powerful rival, her vast library was scattered among the African allies of the Romans, and lost to history.

An interesting relic of Carthaginian literature is the Circumnavigation of Hanno, the history of a voyage undertaken in the sixth century B.C. to the coasts of Libya—the oldest history of a voyage existing. This work of Hanno, which used to hang in a temple at Carthage, describes a savage people called *Gorillas*, whose bodies were covered with hair and who defended themselves with stones. The narrator says: "Three women were taken, but they attacked their conductors with their teeth and hands, and could not be prevailed on to accompany us. Having killed them, we flayed them, and brought their skins with us to Carthage."

NOTES ON ASSYRIO-BABYLONIAN LITERATURE.

Oldest Chaldean book, a work on astrology written before 2000 B.C. The golden age, 2000–1850 B.C.; oral traditions collected and committed to writing; tile-libraries in all the principal Chaldean cities. Decline begins 1550 B.C. The term *Chaldean* long synonymous with *man of learning.*

Rise of Assyrian literature, 1500 B.C.; confined to archives and records for a number of centuries. Renaissance under Sardanapalus I. and his son Shalmane'-ser II. (885–823 B.C.). Enlargement of the national library in the reign of Tig'-lath-Pile'ser II. (745–727 B.C.) and of Sargon (722–705 B.C.), followed by a revival of the study of ancient literature. Copies made of the masterpieces of antiquity. Reign of Sardanapalus II. (667–647 B.C.), the golden age of Assyrian letters. Fall of Nineveh, 625 B.C.

Babylon succeeds as the seat of power and the centre of literature in western Asia; attains the height of its glory under Nebuchadnezzar (604–561 B.C.). Great revival of ancient learning: "the Lady of Kingdoms" soon boasts of a library emulating in extent and variety that of her former rival Nineveh. Little of this later Babylonian literature recovered: its restoration left for future laborers in the field of philology.

During these centuries, a wild poetry probably flourished on the highland wastes of Arabia, and Phœnician cities attained literary greatness.—Coins made of British tin, the money of Phœnician commerce.

CHAPTER VI.

EGYPTIAN LITERATURE.

The Egyptian Language.—There yet remains one field of Oriental literature for us to visit, and it is specially interesting on account of the valuable treasures it long concealed. These have recently been brought to light in the writings of that people who settled the fertile valley of the Nile in prehistoric times, and adorned the land of Egypt with pyramids and obelisks inscribed with their mysterious characters.

Some have found in the ancient Egyptian a resemblance to the Indo-European tongues, and argue that it was an offshoot from an original parent-stock in which Semitic and Aryan were blended before they separated into distinct languages. Between the Egyptian and the Semitic tongues, however, there is a much more striking likeness and a more probable relationship.

EGYPTIAN WRITING.

Hieroglyphics.—There is little doubt that the Egyptians practised writing in the days of Me'nes, founder of their monarchy, more than forty centuries ago. The earliest characters were colored pictures, called hieroglyphics (*sacred carvings*) by the Greeks, who erroneously believed them to have been used by the priestly caste alone. Just as we have adapted our letters to a running hand, so the hieroglyphic was soon abridged into the *hieratic* character, suitable for rapid writing. This in turn, in the seventh century B.C., gave place to the still simpler *demotic*, or popular hand, the letters of which, mainly phonetic, bore no likeness to the original pictures.

As stated on page 19, the hieroglyphic characters were partly pictorial and partly symbolical. Thus, the figure of a man with upraised hands symbolized praise; a reed with an ink-pot, writing; an enraged monkey, anger. Day was denoted by a drawing of the sun; bravery, by the head of a lion; adoration, by a box with burning incense; cunning, by a jackal. A frog suggested the notion of large numbers; while a tadpole implied a million.

This picture-writing, not in itself complete, was supplemented to a certain extent with a phonetic system. An object for which there was no appropriate symbol was represented by the sign of any other object that had the same name when spoken; as if we should denote the mint where money is coined by a painting of the plant so called,—or pike, both the weapon and the fish, by a picture of either. Serious confusion resulted from this practice; till at last it fortunately occurred to some thinker to substitute for the numberless symbols and pictures in use signs corresponding to the few simple sounds employed in spoken language. These, often repeated in different combinations, would answer every requirement.

Still the system was far from perfect, for, as a rule, the vowel sounds were not represented; only by the context, for instance, could it be told whether *s t r* was meant for *star*, *store*, *stair*, or *straw*. Another difficulty lay in the fact that the same consonant was represented by different signs—pictures of objects whose names commenced with the letter in question. In writing London, the Egyptians might represent *L* by the figure of a *l*amb, a *l*eaf, or a *l*ion. From this group of characters, it would be necessary to select the one most appropriate; the lion would be taken for the *l* in *London*, the leaf for the *l* in *lotus*, the lamb for the *l* in *lady*.

To add to the confusion, the old ideographic characters were all the time measurably used along with the phonetic signs. It is not to be wondered at that the Egyptians themselves were puzzled to read their own complicated writing, and introduced *determinatives* as guides to the reader. For example, the drawing of an open mouth was attached to a character to indicate that its phonetic value must be taken; the representation of a surveying-instrument distinguished the names of Egyptian towns; that of a mountain, a thing unknown in the Nile valley, marked foreign localities.

The Rosetta Stone.—The finding of the Rosetta Stone in 1799 paved the way for the brilliant discoveries of the French savant Champollion (*sham-pol'le-on*), before whose time the vast literature of Egypt had been locked up from the world. A French officer, while erecting works at Rosetta in the delta of the Nile during Napoleon's Egyptian campaign, unearthed a piece of black basalt, which contained, in equivalent inscriptions in hieroglyphics and Greek letters, a decree conferring divine honors on Ptolemy V., a monarch of the second century B.C. The meaning of the Greek text being known,

THE ROSETTA STONE.

the hieroglyphics through it were translated ; patient study determined the signification of the separate characters, and a key was thus obtained to other Egyptian inscriptions. The famous Rosetta Stone, resting on a block of red porphyry, now ornaments the Egyptian gallery of the British Museum.

Champollion thus succeeded in solving a problem that had baffled alike Greeks, Romans, and all subsequent nations.* It has been truly said that he opened the door to "a library of stones and papyri in myriads of volumes," in which every

* It is but just to say that Gustav Seyffarth, the eminent German archæologist, still living (in New York, 1878), as long ago as 1826 published a system of interpretation differing from Champollion's, which he claims that the later Egyptologists have virtually adopted.

branch of literature is represented. The crumbling walls scattered throughout "the Monumental Land" now utter intelligible words; the very implements and toys have their stories to tell; and many a tomb has yielded up its brittle treasure of papyrus, its eulogy or legend, its history or hymn.

Monuments and Papyri.—The ancient Egyptians exceeded all other nations in their fondness for writing. The chisel was kept busy in graving monuments of granite. The reed or goose-quill, with ink-pot and palette, was in constant requisition, committing their records to rolls of papyrus sometimes a hundred feet long; and not unfrequently the processions of men, birds, insects, and reptiles, in profile, were illuminated with high colors and gold wrought in artistic vignettes.

Golden Age of Egyptian Literature.—If we look for a progressive development of Egyptian literature, we shall be disappointed. A wonderful sameness pervades every period, with the exception of that which has been called the Ramessid, from one of the greatest Pharaohs, Ram'eses II., at whose court Moses was brought up "in all the wisdom of the Egyptians" (15th century B.C.). Great national triumphs helped to make the reign of this Rameses, the Sesostris of the Greeks, a golden age of art and literature. His court at hundred-gated Thebes was adorned by men of genius, among them the poet and romance-writer Enna, with his simple and majestic style. At their head was the Master of the Rolls, Kagabu the Elegant, who kept the great library founded at the capital by his royal master, and inscribed "Dispensary of the Soul."

LITERARY REMAINS.

Religious Works.—The ancient Egyptians are spoken of by Herodotus as "surpassing all others in the reverence they paid the gods." Their social life, institutions, and government, all bore a religious impress; and even art seems to have been cultivated mainly to glorify the deities or invest the monarchs with divine honors. The bulk of Egyptian literature, therefore, is of a religious character.

Thanks to the custom of enclosing with the embalmed body in the mummy-case papyrus texts from the Book of the Dead or Funeral Ritual, this old Bible of the Egyptians, the greatest of all their theological works, has been preserved to us. The copying of this sacred book, and illuminating it according to the rank or fortune of the dead man, afforded profitable employment to a multitude of priests.

The Book of the Dead contains 166 chapters. It is introduced by a sublime dialogue between Osi'ris, god of the lower world, and the disembodied soul, at the moment of death. The funeral ceremonies are then prescribed; after which come the pilgrimage of the soul through the land of the dead—its battles with serpents and monsters, and the charms by which they may be vanquished—its various transformations—the terrible trial in the judgment-hall of Osiris, where the heart of the deceased is weighed in the balance—and the final admission of its owner, if not found wanting, to everlasting bliss. Thus it will be seen that the immortality of the soul was a cardinal article of Egyptian belief.

EXTRACT FROM THE BOOK OF THE DEAD.

THE SOUL'S DECLARATION OF INNOCENCE IN THE JUDGMENT-HALL.

"O ye Lords of Truth! I have brought you truth. I have not privily done evil against mankind. I have not afflicted the miserable. I have not told falsehoods. I have had no acquaintance with sin. I have not made the laboring man do more than his daily task. I have not been idle. I have not been intoxicated. I have not been immoral. I have not calumniated a slave to his master. I have not caused hunger. I have not made to weep. I have not murdered. I have not defrauded.

I have not eaten the sacred bread in the temples. I have not cheated in the weight of the balance. I have not withheld milk from the mouths of sucklings. I have not slandered any one. I have not netted sacred birds. I have not caught the fish which typify them. I have not stopped running water. I have not robbed the gods of their offered haunches. I have not stopped a god from his manifestation. I have made to the gods the offerings that were their due. I have given food to the hungry, drink to the thirsty, and clothes to the naked. I am pure! I am pure!"—BIRCH AND PLEYTE.

Human nature, in its faults and vices, as portrayed in the above passage, seems to have been much the same 3,500 years ago as at the present day; the high-toned moral principles here implied are certainly worthy of all admiration.

This Book of the Dead is almost the sole survivor of many sacred works on science, religion, music, and law, called Hermetic Books, from Hermes Trismegistus (*thrice greatest*), their reputed author and the traditional founder of all Egyptian institutions. The Book of the Breaths of Life, which treats of the resurrection and the subsequent existence of the soul, is another curious work. Copies of it were buried with the mummies of certain priests and priestesses.

FROM THE BOOK OF THE BREATHS OF LIFE.

"Hail to thee, ——— (*name of the deceased*)!
Thine individuality is permanent.
Thy body is durable.
Thy mummy doth germinate.
Thou art not repulsed from heaven, neither from earth.
Thou dost breathe for ever and ever.
Thy flesh is on thy bones,
Like unto thy form on earth.
Thou dost drink, thou eatest with thy mouth.
Thou receivest bread with the souls of the gods.
Thy soul doth breathe for ever and ever.

O ye gods that dwell in the Lower Heaven,
Hearken unto the voice of ———!
He is near unto you.
There is no fault in him. He liveth in the truth.
Let him enter then into the Lower Heaven!
He hath received the Book of the Breaths of Life,
That he may breathe with his soul,
And that he may make any transformation at will;
That his soul may go wherever it desireth,
Living on the earth for ever and ever."—DE HORRACK.

Hymns.—Grand hymns to the Egyptian deities have also been recovered, displaying a purer faith than that with which this ancient people has been generally credited. The various gods addressed seem to have been regarded as only different manifestations of one uncreated Supreme Being.

HYMN OF THE RAMESSID AGE.

"Glory to thee who hast begotten all that exists!
Who hast made man;
Who hast made the gods, and all the beasts of the field;
Who makest man to live;
Who hast no being second to thee.
Lord of generation! thou hast given the breath of life,
Thou makest the world to move in its seasons,
And orderest the course of the Nile, whose ways are secret.
He is the light of the world.
He shooteth in the green herb,
And maketh the corn, the grass, and the trees of the field.
He giveth to sons the dignity of their fathers."—CHABAS.

The genius of the early Egyptian lyric poets may be estimated from the following verses discovered on a monumental tablet among the ruins of Thebes. They are represented as addressed by Amen (*ah'men*), the supreme god of that city, to Thothmes III., under whom (1600 B.C.) Egypt rose to the zenith of her military greatness, and according to a popular saying of the day "placed her frontier where it pleased herself." The hymn is peculiarly beautiful in the original, by reason of the harmonious cadence of its periods, and that parallelism or "balance of clauses and ideas" which is largely characteristic of Oriental poetry, and which the Egyptians are thought to have invented.

HYMN TO THOTHMES III.

"I am come—to thee have I given to strike down Syrian princes;
Under thy feet they lie throughout the breadth of their country.
Like to the Lord of Light, I made them see thy glory,
Blinding their eyes with light, the earthly image of Amen.

I am come—to thee have I given to strike down Asian people;
Captive now thou hast led the proud Assyrian chieftains;
Decked in royal robes, I made them see thy glory;
All in glittering arms and fighting high in thy war-car.

I am come—to thee have I given to strike down western nations;
Cyprus both and the Ases have heard thy name with terror.
Like a strong-horned bull, I made them see thy glory,
Strong with piercing horns, so that none can stand before him.

I am come—to thee have I given to strike down Libyan archers;
All the isles of the Greeks submit to the force of thy spirit.
Like a lion in prey, I made them see thy glory,
Couched by the corpse he has made down in the rocky valley.

I am come—to thee have I given to strike down the ends of the ocean;
In the grasp of thy hand is the circling zone of waters;
Like the soaring eagle, I made them see thy glory,
Whose far-seeing eye there is none can hope to escape from."

Secular Poetry was at the same time cultivated in ancient Egypt; the people delighted in odes and ballads. The accompanying harvest-song, presented in the original hieroglyphics with their equivalents in English words, was found on an ancient tomb:—

HARVEST SONG.

Thresh for yourselves,
Thresh for yourselves,
Thresh for yourselves, O oxen!
Thresh for yourselves,
Thresh for yourselves,
Measures of grain for yourselves,
Measures of grain for your masters.

The Egyptian Iliad.—There are also extant five copies of an epic poem by Pentaour, a writer of the golden age, one on papyrus, the others in hieroglyphics on temple-walls. This Iliad of Egypt, the only representative of its class in all the literature that has been recovered, celebrates the prowess of Rameses the Great in a war with the Hittites. The grand central scene, vividly portrayed by the hand of a master-artist, discloses the king, forsaken by his cowardly troops in the heat of battle, calling on the god Amen for aid, and with his assistance discomfiting single-handed the hostile multitude. Then he bursts forth into a eulogy of his own bravery, loading the fugitives with reproaches, and contrasting their cowardice with the fiery spirit of his trusty horses that had borne him safely through the battle.

From this relic of the age of taste and literary culture in ancient Egypt, the following extract is taken. Rameses, surrounded by the chariots of the Hittites, thus calls upon his god:—

"Who art thou, then, my father Amen; art thou a father that forgetteth his son? Have I done aught without thee? Did I not march at thy word? Have I not offered thee myriads of sacrifices? Have I not filled thy house with prisoners, and built thee a temple to last for millions of years? I have offered thee all the world. I set up the obelisks of Elephantine;* by me were the eternal stones set up. Assuredly wretched is the lot of him that resists thy counsel; blessed is he that knoweth thee, for thy deeds are the fruit of a heart full of love.

Behold! I am in the midst of a host of strangers, and no man is with me. All my men of war have forsaken me, and when I called them there was none to listen to my voice. But I prefer Amen to a million of soldiers, to ten thousand horsemen, to myriads of assembled brothers and sons. The designs of man are nothing: Amen overrules them."

Moral Treatises.—Piety, charity, and filial obedience, were esteemed as leading virtues in Egypt, and were inculcated in moral treatises, letters, and dialogues. Before 2000 B.C., the

* One now stands in the *Place de la Concorde*, Paris.

great sage, Prince Ptah-hotep prepared a handbook on practical morality, full of wise maxims, prescribing rules of conduct for the young, and recommending the practice of obedience, honesty, and benevolence, though in a style unconnected and weakened by repetitions.

Ptah-hotep's curious treatise, which recalls the Proverbs of Solomon, is preserved in the famous Prisse papyrus,* by some considered the oldest book in the world.

ANCIENT EGYPTIAN PROVERBS.

"That man is happy who lives on his own labor.

If thou become great after being small, and gain fortune by toil, and art therefore placed at the head of thy city, be not proud of thy riches, which are thine by the gift of God. Thy neighbor is not inferior to thee; be to him as a companion.

Slay not, lest thou be thyself in peril of being slain.

Love thy wife, and cherish her as long as thou livest; be no tyrant; flattery acts upon her better than rudeness, and will make her contented and diligent.

Curse not thy master before God.

Gossip is abominable.

If a beggar is made rich, the magistrates will praise him.

If thou art wise, bring up thy son to fear God.

Redeem not thy life with that of thy neighbor.

Fairer is obedience than all things, when it is rendered freely. Very fair is it when a son receives the word of his father; therefore shall his life be long in the land. His fame shall be known to all men.

Walk not with a fool."

Scientific Literature.—We have every reason to believe that the Egyptians attained a high degree of scientific knowledge, even at a period far beyond the reach of our investigations. Undoubtedly many books were written on science, to study which the deepest thinkers among the Greeks regarded a journey into Egypt as well worth their while. With the exception, however, of a papyrus on geometry, dating about 1100 B.C., and some medical treatises, nothing has come to light.

* M. Prisse first published this papyrus in France; hence its name.

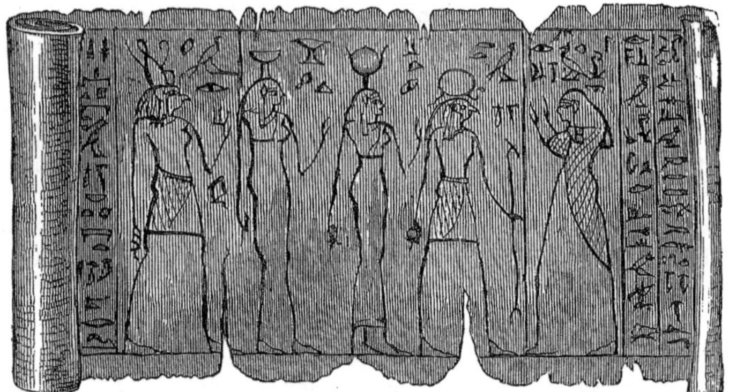

PAPYRUS, FROM THE COLLECTION OF THE NEW YORK HISTORICAL SOCIETY.

Judging from the medical writings that have been found, it would seem that the Egyptian physicians had a superficial acquaintance with the principles of physiology, and administered various ointments, draughts, the milk of animals, honey, vinegar, and herbs. They were adepts in surgery, and practised specialties; mummies have been found with gold fillings in their teeth, and bandaged as skilfully as by an expert of to-day. Such was the reputation of Egyptian practitioners that they were sent for from distant countries.

In later times, medical science was tinctured with magic. Superstitious rites accompanied the administering of medicines; charms and love-philters came into vogue; bits of papyri containing magical formulæ were worn as amulets; and the sensible remedies of early times were crowded aside by foolish prescriptions for acquiring happiness, making friends, obtaining dreams, etc.

AMULET.

Fiction and Satire.—Works of the imagination would not seem to be in harmony with the grave Egyptian character,—nor would satires and caricatures; yet all three find a place in this comprehensive literature. Even kings did not escape the pen and brush of the satirist. The tale and romance, generally the vehicle for some religious doctrine, constituted a favorite branch of literature in the Ramessid age.

The poet Enna has left us a novel, written more than 3,000 years ago for the amusement of the crown-prince, who afterward perished with his host in the Red Sea. It is entitled "the Tale of the Two Brothers," and is perhaps "the oldest fairy story in the world." It sets forth the rustic life of two devoted brothers; the false accusation of one by the wife of the other; the flight of the accused, after a warning given him by his faithful cattle; his pursuit by the elder brother, who is resolved to avenge the alleged outrage; the interference, in behalf of the innocent, of a god who creates between pursuer and pursued a stream full of crocodiles; and many strange adventures on the part of the fugitive, followed by the reunion of the brothers, the elevation of the younger to the throne of Egypt, and of the elder to the proud position of hereditary prince.

Other works of fiction are "the Romance of Setna," showing the danger of appropriating sacred books; "the Tale of the Doomed Prince" (who, it was decreed by the Fates when they came to greet him at his birth, was to die by a serpent, a crocodile, or a dog); and "the Tale of the Garden of Flowers," illustrative of Egyptian social life.

In the department of letter-writing, Egyptian literature was especially rich. There were also legal documents, histories, biographical sketches, and travels. Nor must fables be forgotten, in which the animals are represented as conversing, as in the following:—

THE LION AND THE MOUSE.

MOUSE.—"O Pharaoh! if you eat me, you will not be satisfied, your hunger will remain. Give me life as I gave it to you in the day of your straits, in your evil day.

Remember the hunters; one had a net to catch you, and the other a rope. There was also a pit dug before the lion, he fell in and was a prisoner in the pit; he was pledged by his feet. Then came the little mouse opposite him, and released him. Now therefore reward me: I am the little mouse."

Such is the literature which the sands of Egypt have yielded to modern research—a literature which, itself of greater antiquity, furnished models even to the nations that we call ancient. While these later nations, judging from the remains that have thus far come to our knowledge, certainly improved on their masters in artistic finish and grandeur of conception, it must be remembered that we have not yet fully sounded the depths of Egyptian literature. We know not what masterpieces may still lie hid beneath the sand, or bear the mummy company in some undiscovered tomb. We are, indeed, justified in expecting greater works from the land that was the fount of Greek inspiration; the dayspring of knowledge to the Chosen People, in whose mysterious hieroglyphics perhaps Moses wrote the Pentateuch; whose religion bears in many points a strange analogy to ours; whose lasting structures are emblematic of the soul's immortality; and whose lotus-blossoms, reopening every morning, symbolize the resurrection from the night of death.

NOTES ON EGYPTIAN EDUCATION, ETC.

Egyptian education in the hands of priests, who gave instruction in the schools of Thebes and Memphis to members of their own and the warrior caste. Religion, belles-lettres, science, and music, the branches taught; particular attention bestowed upon mathematical studies. The rudiments of education imparted to children by their parents or in common schools, and supplemented with a severe course of physical training. Reading and writing great accomplishments among the lower classes, who were generally unlearned. In the earliest periods, education recognized as the great agent of civilization; the proudest offices within reach of the scholar. No mention made of the education of women, but girls were doubtless fitted by some system of mental training for the public positions they were afterward allowed to fill.

Manual labor despised by the aristocratic orders, who looked with contempt even upon painting and sculpture. Dancing, gymnastic exercises, games (one like our chequers), fishing in preserves, spearing the hippopotamus from canoes, and hunting wild fowl in the marshes, favorite pastimes. Ladies present at the sports. A keen eye for humor manifested in the fondness of the Egyptians for caricature, from which even their representations of funeral ceremonies were not exempt.

Gold rings and engraved gems used as currency. Precious stones carved with the sacred beetle of Egypt, the media of exchange throughout the Mediterranean countries.

SYNCHRONISTIC TABLE OF ORIENTAL LITERATURE.

	India.	Persia.	The Hebrews.	Assyria and Babylonia.	Egypt.	China.
B.C. 2000	Earliest Vedic Hymns written.	Earliest metrical songs.	**Abraham.**	Birth of Chaldean Literature. Cuneiform Writing. Golden Age.	Ptah-hotep's Moral Treatise. Hermetic Books. Papyri and Inscriptions.	The
	Vedic	Gâthâs.	**Job.**	Rise of Assyrian		Five
1500	Age.	**Zoroaster.**		Literature.		
			Moses and the Pentateuch.		Ramessid Era.	"King."
		A succession of Persian priests	Early Lyrics and Secular	Archives and Records.	Epic Poetry, Fiction, Satire, Hymns.	
1200	Code of **Manu.**	enlarging and modifying the	Poetry.			Odes
		Sacred	Golden Age. Psalms of		Scientific Works on various subjects.	and Pastoral
1000	Epics.	Literature.	**David.** **Solomon's** Proverbs.			Poetry.
	Hymns. Lyrics.			Renaissance.		
			Prophetic Poetry.	Golden Age of Assyrian Literature.	Demotic Writing introduced.	
500	**Pânini.** Grammar.	Compilation of the Avesta.	**Ezra.**			**Confucius.**

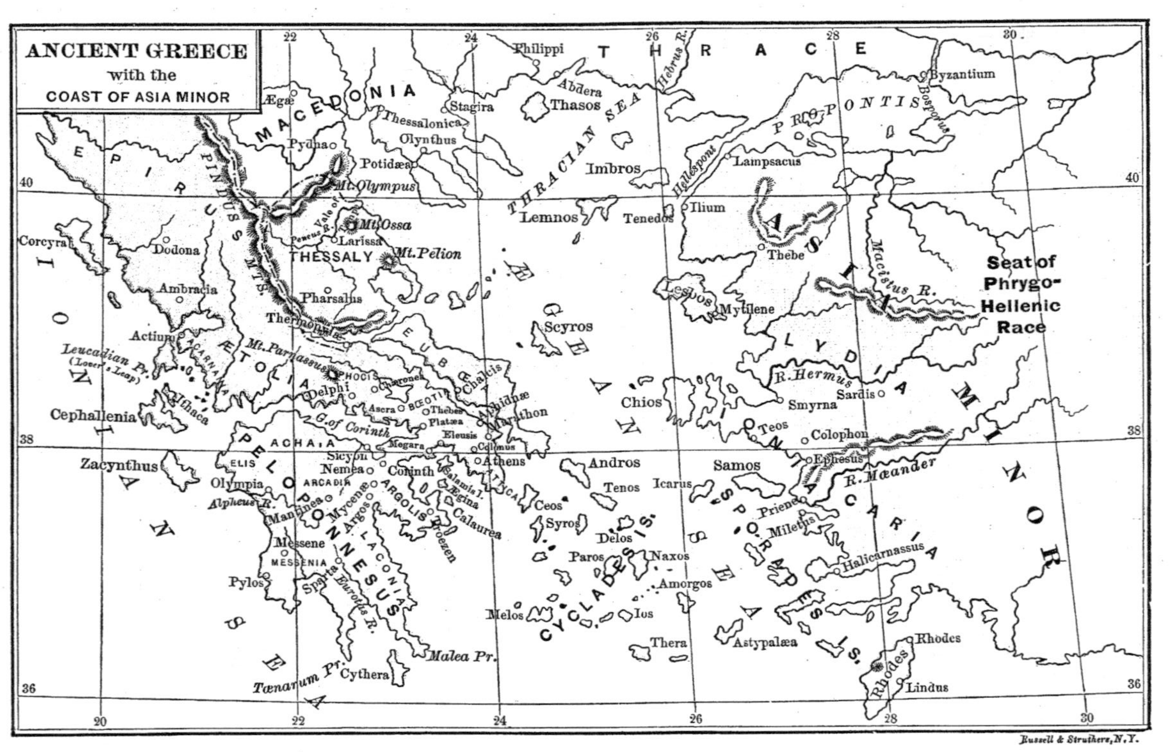

ANCIENT GREECE
with the
COAST OF ASIA MINOR
THRACE
MACEDONIA
EPIRUS
THESSALY
PINDUS MTS.
ÆTOLIA
ACARNANIA
PHOCIS
BŒOTIA
ATTICA
ACHAIA
ELIS
ARCADIA
ARGOLIS
MESSENIA
LACONIA
PELOPONNESUS
ASIA MINOR
LYDIA
CARIA
IONIA
PROPONTIS
THRACIAN SEA
ÆGEAN SEA
IONIAN SEA
CYCLADES IS.
SPORADES IS.
Seat of
Phrygo-
Hellenic
Race
Byzantium
Bosporus
Hellespont
Hebrus R.
Philippi
Abdera
Thasos
Stagira
Thessalonica
Olynthus
Potidæa
Pydna
Ægæ
Mt. Olympus
Vale of
Peneus R.
Mt. Ossa
Mt. Pelion
Larissa
Pharsalus
Thermopylæ
Mt. Parnassus
Delphi
Dodona
Ambracia
Actium
Corcyra
Leucadian Pr.
(Lover's Leap)
Cephallenia
Ithaca
Zacynthus
Olympia
Alpheus R.
Pylos
Messene
Mantinea
Sparta
Eurotas R.
Tænarum Pr.
Cythera
Malea Pr.
Mycenæ
Argos
Trœzen
Calauria
Ægina
Salamis I.
Athens
Colonus
Eleusis
Marathon
Platæa
Thebes
Ascra
Chæronea
Megara
Corinth
Sicyon
Nemea
G. of Corinth
Eubœa
Chalcis
Aulis
Scyros
Lemnos
Imbros
Tenedos
Ilium
Lampsacus
Thebe
Lesbos
Mytilene
Macistus R.
Sardis
Smyrna
R. Hermus
Teos
Colophon
Ephesus
R. Mæander
Priene
Miletus
Halicarnassus
Chios
Samos
Icarus
Andros
Tenos
Delos
Naxos
Paros
Syros
Ceos
Melos
Ios
Amorgos
Thera
Astypalæa
Rhodes
Lindus
Russell & Struthers, N.Y.

PART II.

GRECIAN LITERATURE.

CHAPTER I.

BIRTH OF GRECIAN LITERATURE.

Early Settlement of Greece.—While Chaldea and Assyria were rising to greatness, while Phœnicia was winning for herself maritime supremacy, and wonders in art and science were spreading the renown of Egypt throughout the earth, a simple agricultural people was quietly moving westward toward Greece and Italy. In very early times, Aryan tribes known as *Pelasgic* quitted their habitations in southwestern Bactria (Map, p. 15), and made their way through Persia and Mesopotamia into Asia Minor. Here, on rich table-lands irrigated by the head-waters of streams flowing into the Black Sea and the Mediterranean, among the gold-bearing mountains and vine-grown valleys of Phrygia (see Map), they cultivated their grain, pastured their sheep, made permanent settlements, and rapidly grew into a great nation. These Pelasgic tribes were the ancestors of the Greeks and Romans.

The same general causes that led to emigration from the mother-country crowded toward the coast communities of this Phrygian people, and ultimately obliged them to seek new homes in the west. Perhaps, paddling from island to island in rude galleys, some crossed the Æge′an; perhaps, passing the Hellespont, some picked their way through Thrace and Macedonia, entered the defiles of the northern mountains, and spread over Greece; while others, more adventurous, pushed their course still farther, and peopled the Italian peninsula.

The Pelasgic tribes were probably the first occupants of Greece and Italy. Earlier emigrants from Asia appear to have found all they desired in the accessible districts of central Europe, and not to have climbed the steep ranges that hemmed in those regions on the south. The Greeks themselves claimed with pride to have sprung from the earth; and a golden grasshopper, worn in the hair as an ornament by the Athenians, pointed to this belief in their *autochthony.*

The Hellenes.—Fresh bodies of Pelasgians continued to arrive from Asia Minor, until all Greece was populated with a thrifty race of husbandmen and shepherds. Upon this primitive Pelasgian stock was afterward engrafted a branch called Hellenic, identical with it in origin, but forced to a higher state of development in the garden of Asiatic culture, and ready to burst into blossom on the soil of Greece. The new-comers were the Helle'nes, a people of greater vigor, physical and intellectual. Mingling with their Pelasgian kinsmen in the Grecian peninsula, they formed a new nation, endowed with fresh life; and the Pelasgic dialect, modified and energized by their more cultivated tongue, was converted into GREEK.

The Greeks had a popular proverb, *do nothing too much,* which they applied in writing as in acting. Pruning away too great exuberance and repressing the Oriental tendency to exaggerate, they reduced everything to the standard of a rigid but elegant correctness. More artistic than the Hindoos, less luxuriant in imagination but with a chaster and severer taste, they established a literature richly furnished in every department, whose influence can be traced in the works of genius that stand out in every age and country. As Professor Jebb says, "the thoughts of the great Greek thinkers have been bearing fruit in the world ever since they were first uttered."

Thus in Greece, Aryan energy, freed from the trammels of Oriental despotism, seems first to have found its true development. The facilities which this country enjoyed for intercourse with Egypt and Phœnicia, enabled it to draw from the learning of one, to copy the enterprise and adopt the inventions of the other. This accounts for its having been the seat of the earliest European civilization.

At a later period, we find the Hellenes separated into three great families—the Æolians, occupying generally the north of Greece; the Ionians, distributed over the central portions; and the Dorians, settled in the south (the Peloponnesus, *island of Pelops*). Connected with these three divisions were as many dialects—Æolic, Ionic, and Doric Greek—of which, Ionic was the softest and most polished. This Ionic, refined and perfected, became what is known as Attic Greek; it was the language of Athens in the golden age of her art and poetry, and for centuries was understood by the educated classes throughout a great part of the civilized world.

These Hellenic dialects were also spoken on the islands of the Ægean and the coast of Asia Minor; for the tide of emigration set back again toward the Asiatic shores, and Æolians, Ionians, and Dorians, returned in great colonies to the neighborhood of their early home.

Ancient Greek is the most musical language of the Indo-European group. Sanscrit indeed excels it in regularity, but offends the ear with its sameness, the constant recurrence of *a* sounds wearying the European reader. No such monotonous repetition mars the harmony of Greek, which, on the other hand, presents a pleasing variety in its vowel sounds, its numerous diphthongs, and consonant combinations. Nor is this variety to be wondered at, for tribes differing in their habits and intellectual traits, mingling on the shores of the Ægean, contributed different elements to the common language. Above all, the Greeks were gifted with a delicate ear, which led them, in the oral transmission of their earliest poetry, to soften all harshness in their tongue and make it melody itself.

In common with Sanscrit, Greek was well adapted to the formation of compound words by the combining of primitives; but this facility for combination was turned to account only so far as was consistent with clearness and taste; the unwieldy polysyllabic compounds of Sanscrit were wanting. The Greek rivals its Indian sister in luxuriance of inflection also, having five cases, three numbers, and three voices for the verb. Accents were used in later days to denote the peculiar key or tone of voice; for the Greeks appreciated the subtle difference between *tone* (accent) and *quantity* in pronunciation, a distinction unrecognized in modern languages.

Greek is universally admired for its dignity, versatility, and precision; its blending of strength and elegance, unity and variety. It is suited to all departments of composition; to the effective expression of the various emotions; to stately prose or simple verse. Its perfection at so early a period, particularly in view of the social condition of the people who spoke it, is a phenomenon which we vainly seek to explain.

The Greek Alphabet.—The Phœnician letters were adopted by the Greeks, legend ascribing their introduction to Cadmus, the storied founder of Thebes (1500 B.C.). Some changes were made in these; new characters were added by the Ionians; and about 400 B.C. the resulting alphabet, consisting of twenty-four letters, was officially adopted at Athens. The resemblance between the Greek and the Phœnician alphabet is obvious; see Table, p. 87.

That there was Pelasgian picture-writing in Greece before the Phœnician alphabet reached that country, is by no means improbable.

The Beginnings of Greek Poetry are found in the sacred ode, the metrical response of the oracle, the festal song, and the ballad immortalizing the deeds of heroes during the mythical ages. The art of poetry was coeval with the first settlement of the peninsula; but its higher development followed the transfusion of Hellenic genius into the older Pelasgian race.

The earliest forms of poetry were hymns to the deities. The religion of the Greeks was a worship of Nature. Imagination peopled every nook of their picturesque land with supernatural beings; and each was propitiated with song, from the wood-nymph supposed to reside in the spreading oak to the sun-god Apollo, who, with the Nine Muses, the goddesses of poetry, abode on snow-crowned Parnassus.

To Mother Earth (Deme'ter) were poured forth strains of glowing gratitude for her bounty; the Mother of the Gods (Cyb'ele) was worshipped with wilder verse, accompanied with the sound of cymbals and riotous dances; the god of wine (Diony'sus or Bacchus) was hymned with lively lays in praise of revelry; and so the burden of sacred song varied with the character of the divinity. When spring clothed the earth with beauty, the hymns were joyous; in autumn they breathed a spirit of sadness, and at the grape-harvest was sung a plaintive ditty, the Li'nus, as a coranach for the death of Nature. The perishing of vegetation before the blighting breath of approaching winter was symbolized by the fate of the beauteous youth Linus torn and devoured by furious dogs. Of similar allegorical significance were many of the hymns.

The delights and sorrows of domestic life also found utterance in verse; when the bride was escorted to her new home the nuptial song was sung, and for the dead the funeral dirge was chanted. At first this was no doubt done with solemn pomp, as a religious ceremony; but the tendency in Greece was to popularize song, and both dirge and bridal hymn in time lost their mere ritual complexion, and became changed in the mouths of the people into free outpourings of emotion.

The bard now aimed at entertaining his listeners; he filled an important place at banquets and festivals, where, in short poems, he chanted to the accompaniment of flute or lyre the adventures of heroes, or so transformed old traditions that he was looked upon as their maker (*poie'tes, poet*). All Greece honored him, regardless of his nationality. Whether Æolian, Dorian, or Ionian, he contributed equally to Hellenic fame, and was entitled to the sympathy and support of all Hellenes. Indeed, he was invested with a sacred character, for he was regarded as divinely inspired.

Thus was laid the foundation of Greek letters. From such rude beginnings, the Greek imagination, by strides unparalleled in history, mounted to the grandest heights ever attained in poetry. Moreover, to original Greek genius we owe the different varieties of literary composition,—epic, lyric, and dramatic poetry, history, criticism, and oratory. Without the Grecian models, nowhere has marked superiority been attained; the originals themselves have never been surpassed.

Tradition has given us the names of many poets belonging to the fabulous age; but their dates are unknown, their very existence may be questioned.

LEGENDARY POETS OF GREECE.

ORPHEUS, the Thracian minstrel, inventor of religious poetry.

THAM'YRIS, deprived of his sight and poetical talent for challenging the Muses to a trial of skill on the lyre.

EUMOLPUS, a Thracian priest; reputed founder of the Eleusinian Mysteries.

O'LEN, earliest prophet of Apollo.

CHRYSOTH'EMIS, the Cretan.

MUSÆUS (*inspired by the Muses*), a son or disciple of Orpheus.

AMPHI'ON, taught of the god Mercury; raised stones into the walls of Thebes by the strains of his lyre.

PHILAMMON, son of Apollo, and inventor of choral music.

PAMPHOS, author of the first Linus.

OLYMPUS, introducer of the flute.

PHEMON'OE, first priestess at the Delphic shrine, inventor of hexameters.

CHAPTER II.

AGE OF EPIC POETRY.

HOMER AND HIS WORKS.

Homer.—The oldest literary productions of Greece extant are the poems of Homer, the most ancient monuments of Aryan poetry west of the Persian Gulf. About 1000 B.C., among the legion of ballad-writers, the reciters of battle-songs, myths, and traditions (known as Rhapsodists—*ode-stitchers*), there arose an Ionian poet who soon towered head and shoulders above them all—a giant among the giants of literature—HOMER, of unique genius and world-wide fame.

As to Homer's life, we must ever remain in the dark. For the honor of giving him birth, seven cities of antiquity disputed,* Smyrna seeming to have the best claim. If we may believe tradition, he gave early evidence of his divine powers. Chance took him on a sea-voyage, during which he visited many countries, among them Ithaca, the home of Ulysses, one of his heroes. On the island of Chi'os, his favorite resort, he is thought to have written his epics the Il'iad and Od'yssey, the first in early manhood, the second in old age.

Legend relates that Homer, twice warned by an oracle to *beware of the young men's riddle*, went ashore one day on I'os, an island of the Cyc'lades, and there, noticing some boys who had been fishing, asked them, "What luck?" "What we caught we left, what we could not catch we carried with us,"

---

* "Septem urbes certant de stirpe insignis Homeri,—
Smyrna, Rhodos, Colophon, Salamis, Chios, Argos, Athenæ."

For all places mentioned in the history of Grecian literature, see Map, p. 132.

was the reply. Unable to guess the riddle, the old poet died of vexation. According to another account, disease carried him off. He was buried on the sea-shore at Ios, where in after years this epitaph marked his tomb:—

"Here Homer the Divine, in earthy bed,
Poet of heroes, rests his sacred head."

Homer's Style.—Homer's Iliad was the first Greek poem in which were combined ingenuity of plot, unity of subject, and a faithful delineation of character throughout. He deals with heroes, but they are men of like passions with ourselves. The Odyssey, if less sublime, in its pathos and fine touches of nature shows the same rich gifts of genius as the older poem of loftier flight. Both works are written in hexameter verse, the true metre of the ancient epic.

The distinguishing features of Homer's style are clearness, a vigor which makes us feel we are in the presence of a master, and a childlike simplicity that well accords with his sublime themes. His fidelity to nature is matched only by Shakespeare's; and imagery, profuse as it is rich, lifelike, and appropriate, lights up every page. Simile is Homer's own figure; and transporting pictures flash ever and anon across the scene, called up by his magic wand. For example:—

"As when, high-fed with grain, a stall-bound steed
Snaps his strong cord, and flies, from bondage freed,
Strikes with resounding hoof the earth, and flies
Where the wide champaign spread before him lies,
Seeks the remembered haunts, on fire to lave
His glowing limbs, and dash amid the wave,
High rears his crest, and tossing with disdain
Wide o'er his shoulders spreads his stream of mane,
And fierce in beauty, graceful in his speed,
Snuffs his known fellows in the distant mead:
Thus Hector—"

"As a young olive, in some sylvan scene,
Crowned by fresh fountains with eternal green,
Lifts its gay head in snowy flowerets fair,
And plays and dances to the gentle air;

When lo! by blasts uprooted, whirled around,
Low lies the plant, extended on the ground:
Thus in his beauty young Euphorbus lay."

Homer astonishes us with his universal knowledge. He names every part of a vessel technically with all the accuracy of a veteran seaman; he is as conversant with the details of a sacrifice as the officiating priest; he describes a conflict between two warriors with the precision of a master of fence; he sketches the forms and usages of palaces as if born and bred in kings' courts, and is equally familiar with the manners of the meanest hind. Everywhere he is at home.

Other poets* may be stars in the firmament, but Homer, as Longi′nus says, is the sun in the zenith. His poetry is all nature, life, action, fire. It breathes an atmosphere of pure morality, and furnishes ideal characters long held up as models to the Grecian youth, who learned his verses by heart and in some cases could even repeat his entire poems. Human genius has left on earth at intervals of centuries a few imperishable monuments; none nobler among these than the marvellous Greek epics.

Plan of the Iliad.—The Iliad, a poem of twenty-four books, is a tale of the siege of Troy (Il′ium), a city on the coast of Asia Minor (probable date of the siege, 1194–1184 B.C.). The cause of the war was the perfidious conduct of Paris, son of Priam, the Trojan monarch. Hospitably entertained at the court of Menela′us, king of Sparta, he eloped with Helen, the wife of his host, the most beautiful of women, and carried her off to Asia with the treasures of her husband. To avenge this outrage, Menelaus, supported by Nestor the sage of Py′los, called upon the Greek princes, collected an armament of a thousand ships, the command of which was conferred upon

* In this category we do not mean to include our own Shakespeare; Homer's pedestal is no loftier than his.

his brother Agamemnon, and set sail for Troy. A war of ten years followed, which ended in the capture of the city by stratagem, the slaughter of Priam and his family, and the enslavement of many of the Trojans.

The special subject of the Iliad is the wrath of the Thessalian Achilles (*a-kil'leez*), the leading warrior of the Grecian host, and the time of the action is near the close of the war. Agamemnon, compelled to restore to her father, a priest of Apollo, the captive maid Chryse'is who had fallen to his share, seizes upon Brise'is, a virgin allotted to Achilles. A quarrel results, and Achilles withdraws from the camp.

Emboldened by his absence, the Trojans redouble their efforts. Misfortunes to the Greek cause follow; and though many heroes second only to Achilles—the stalwart Ajax, the cunning Ulysses, king of Ithaca, Menelaus, and Diomede—exert themselves to turn the tide of battle, the Greek host is made keenly to feel the loss of its puissant champion. Jupiter, king of heaven, sides with the Trojans; and Hector "of the dancing helm-crest" drives the besiegers to their ships.

At length Achilles, still unwilling to join in the fray himself, allows Patro'clus, his bosom-friend, to lead his Myrmidons to the rescue. Arrayed in the armor of the Thessalian chief, Patroclus puts to flight the deceived Trojans; but, pursuing them too far, receives a death-wound from the hand of Hector. The news of his friend's fall fills Achilles with thirst for revenge. A reconciliation is effected with Agamemnon; Achilles returns to the field; the enemy are thrown into confusion; and Hector, pierced by his spear, is dragged in triumph at Achilles' chariot-wheels. The wrath of the Greek hero is finally appeased by the sacrifice of twelve Trojan captives at the funeral of Patroclus.

To redeem the body of his son, old Priam, alone and unarmed, enters the Grecian camp, is well received by Achilles, who melts into pity at the sight of the grief-stricken suppliant, accomplishes his purpose, and returns to Troy with Hector's corpse. This meeting between Achilles and Priam is counted among the finest scenes.—The Iliad closes with the obsequies of Hector.

Achilles, the central figure of the poem, over whose grave Alexander wept jealous tears, was the impersonation of youthful beauty and physical prowess. Brave, generous, passionate, devoted in his friendship but awful in his implacable anger, in him we are brought face to face with the ideal of Greek chivalry. Hector, the magnanimous Trojan hero, was the type of moral courage and domestic virtue. He appears as the affectionate husband, the loving father, kind even to fallen Helen. Homer has painted with exquisite touch a parting scene between Hector and his consort Androm'ache, possessed of every wifely virtue. This passage, herewith presented, is pronounced the most beautiful in the Iliad.

PARTING OF HECTOR AND ANDROMACHE.

"Hector left in haste
The mansion, and retraced his way between
The rows of stately dwellings, traversing
The mighty city. When at length he reached
The Scæan gates, that issue on the field,
His spouse, the nobly dowered Andromache,
Came forth to meet him—daughter of the prince
Eëtion, who, among the woody slopes
Of Placos, in the Hypoplacian town
Of Thebè,* ruled Cilicia and her sons,
And gave his child to Hector great in arms.
She came attended by a maid, who bore
A tender child—a babe too young to speak—
Upon her bosom; Hector's only son,
Beautiful as a star, whom Hector called
Scamandrius, but all else Astyanax,—
The city's lord,—since Hector stood the sole
Defence of Troy. The father on his child
Looked with a silent smile. Andromache

* A city southeast of Troy, situated at the base of Mount Pla'cos, and hence called Hypoplacian (*under Placos*).

Pressed to his side meanwhile, and all in tears
Clung to his hand, and, thus beginning, said:—

'Too brave! thy valor yet will cause thy death.
Thou hast no pity on thy tender child,
Nor me, unhappy one, who soon must be
Thy widow. All the Greeks will rush on thee
To take thy life. A happier lot were mine,
If I must lose thee, to go down to earth,
For I shall have no hope when thou art gone,—
Nothing but sorrow. Father have I none,
And no dear mother. Great Achilles slew
My father, when he sacked the populous town
Of the Cilicians,—Thebè with high gates.
'Twas there he smote Eëtion, yet forbore
To make his arms a spoil; he dared not that,
But burned the dead with his bright armor on,
And raised a mound above him. Mountain nymphs,
Daughters of ægis-bearing* Jupiter,
Came to the spot and planted it with elms.
Seven brothers had I in my father's house,
And all went down to Hades in one day;
Achilles the swift-footed slew them all
Among their slow-paced bullocks and white sheep.
My mother, princess on the woody slopes
Of Placos, with his spoils he bore away,
And only for large ransom gave her back.
But her Diana, archer-queen, struck down
Within her father's palace. Hector, thou
Art father and dear mother now to me,
And brother and my youthful spouse besides.
In pity keep within the fortress here,
Nor make thy child an orphan nor thy wife
A widow.'

Then answered Hector, great in war: 'All this
I bear in mind, dear wife; but I should stand
Ashamed before the men and long-robed dames
Of Troy, were I to keep aloof and shun
The conflict, coward-like. Not thus my heart
Prompts me, for greatly have I learned to dare
And strike among the foremost sons of Troy,
Upholding my great father's fame and mine;
Yet well in my undoubting mind I know

---

* The ægis was Jupiter's shield, which inspired fear, and caused darkness, clouds, and storms.

The day shall come in which our sacred Troy,
And Priam, and the people over whom
Spear-bearing Priam rules, shall perish all.
But not the sorrows of the Trojan race,
Nor those of Hecuba* herself, nor those
Of royal Priam, nor the woes that wait
My brothers many and brave,—who all at last,
Slain by the pitiless foe, shall lie in dust,—
Grieve me so much as thine, when some mailed Greek
Shall lead thee weeping hence, and take from thee
Thy day of freedom. Thou in Argos then
Shalt, at another's bidding, ply the loom,
And from the fountain of Messeis draw
Water, or from the Hypereian spring,
Constrained, unwilling try thy cruel lot.
And then shall some one say who sees thee weep,
"This was the wife of Hector, most renowned
Of the horse-taming Trojans, when they fought
Around their city." So shall some one say,
And thou shalt grieve the more, lamenting him
Who haply might have kept afar the day
Of thy captivity. Oh! let the earth
Be heaped above my head in death, before
I hear thy cries as thou art borne away!'

So speaking, mighty Hector stretched his arms
To take the boy; the boy shrank crying back
To his fair nurse's bosom, scared to see
His father helmeted in glittering brass,
And eying with affright the horse-hair plume
That grimly nodded from the lofty crest.
At this both parents in their fondness laughed;
And hastily the mighty Hector took
The helmet from his brow, and laid it down
Gleaming upon the ground; and, having kissed
His darling son and tossed him up in play,
Prayed thus to Jove, and all the gods of heaven :—
'O Jupiter and all ye deities,
Vouchsafe that this my son may yet become
Among the Trojans eminent like me,
And nobly rule in Ilium. May they say,
"This man is greater than his father was!"
When they behold him from the battle-field
Bring back the bloody spoil of the slain foe,—
That so his mother may be glad at heart.'

---

* His mother, Priam's wife, king of Troy.

So speaking, to the arms of his dear spouse
He gave the boy; she on her fragrant breast
Received him, weeping as she smiled. The chief
Beheld, and, moved with tender pity, smoothed
Her forehead gently with his hand and said:—
'Sorrow not thus, beloved one, for me.
No living man can send me to the shades
Before my time; no man of woman born,
Coward or brave, can shun his destiny.
But go thou home, and tend thy labors there,—
The web, the distaff,—and command thy maids
To speed the work. The cares of war pertain
To all men born in Troy, and most to me.'

Thus speaking, mighty Hector took again
His helmet, shadowed with the horse-hair plume,
While homeward his beloved consort went,
Oft looking back and shedding many tears.
Soon was she in the spacious palace-halls
Of the man-queller Hector. There she found
A troop of maidens,—with them all she shared
Her grief; and all in his own house bewailed
The living Hector whom they thought no more
To see returning from the battle-field,
Safe from the rage and weapons of the Greeks."

BRYANT.

The ancients implicitly believed the story of the Iliad, but modern scepticism has doubted its truth and questioned the authenticity of the poem itself. The German critic Wolf and others have even gone so far as to deny that any such person as Homer ever existed, contending that the name means simply a *fitter together* or *compiler*, and that the great epic is a mosaic of romantic legends by different rhapsodists, for years kept from perishing merely by oral repetition.

Such, however, is the continuity of the narrative, the identity of style, the consistency in carrying out the several characters, that this theory, ingeniously as it has been urged, lacks credibility. We see no reason to doubt that, despite a few minor discrepancies, one great intellect gave birth in the main to both these epics; that whatever foundations for them may have been laid in previous ballads, the glorious superstructures were reared by one master-builder. It is easier to believe that there was one transcendent genius, than that there were half a dozen of uniform poetic power, competent to have had a hand in works so glorious—works displaying perfect unity of design, and taste so faultless that from them, as standards, have been deduced the very principles of criticism and laws of epic poetry.

Besides the internal evidence of its authenticity, the historical facts woven into the Iliad have just received unexpected confirmation in the discoveries of Dr. Schliemann, a German explorer who claims to have unearthed the Ilium of Homer, and to have found among its ruins gold and amber ornaments once worn by King Priam.

Plan of the Odyssey.—In the Odyssey, divided like the Iliad into twenty-four books, Homer has immortalized the story of the return-voyage of Ulysses (*Odysseus* in Greek) from Troy to Ithaca. After a series of remarkable adventures and hair-breadth escapes, the hero is cast on the lovely island of the sea-nymph Calypso, who, becoming enamored of him, detains him for seven years. During this time, a number of insolent suitors force themselves upon Ulysses' faithful wife Penelope, take up their residence at her court, and there lead a riotous life, hoping that the queen will bestow her hand on one of them and thus make him lord of Ithaca. They even plan the murder of her son Telem'achus.

Admonished by Jupiter, Calypso reluctantly allows Ulysses to depart, and he finally reaches Ithaca in safety. Disguised as a beggar, he enters his palace after an absence of twenty years, to endure the insults of the suitors, but to concert with his son for their overthrow.

On the following day, a great festival is held, and Penelope agrees to give her hand to him who shall send an arrow from Ulysses' bow through a row of twelve rings. The suitors try in turn without success; but the beggar, obtaining possession of the bow, draws the shaft to its head and accomplishes the feat. Then turning on the trembling suitors, he showers his arrows among them, and none escape. The true-hearted Penelope is restored to him whom she had wept as lost, and husband and wife sit down together to talk over the sorrows of the past.

"She told him of the scorn and wrong
 She long had suffered in her house,
From the detested suitor throng,
 Each wooing her to be his spouse;
How, for their feasts, her sheep and kine
Were slaughtered, while they quaffed her wine
 In plentiful carouse.

And he, the noble wanderer, spoke
 Of many a deed of peril sore,
Of men who fell beneath his stroke,
 Of all the sorrowing tasks he bore.
She listened with delighted ear;
Sleep never came her eyelids near,
 Till all the tale was o'er."

Ulysses next discovers himself to his father; and they two, with their friends, succeed in putting down the adherents of the suitors and restoring peace to the kingdom.

Among the most beautiful passages of the Odyssey is that in which the poet introduces us to the happy household of Alcinoüs, king of an island on which Ulysses was thrown. Charming is the simple sketch he gives of the unaffected princess of this isle, just before her marriage, driving her maidens to the river in her father's chariot, to wash the robes of state, lunch, and disport upon the bank while the clothes are drying. The royal mother superintends the weaving, the royal daughter the washing. We quote Homer's description of the

PALACE AND GARDEN OF ALCINOÜS.

"Ulysses, then, toward the palace moved
Of King Alcinoüs, but immersed in thought
Stood first and paused, ere with his foot he pressed

The brazen threshold; for a light he saw,
As of the sun or moon, illuming clear
The palace of Phæacia's mighty king.
  Walls plated bright with brass on either side
Stretched from the portal to the interior house,
With azure cornice crowned; the doors were gold,
Which shut the palace fast; silver the posts
Reared on a brazen threshold, and above,
The lintels, silver architraved with gold.
Mastiffs, in gold and silver, lined the approach
On either side, by art celestial framed
Of Vulcan, guardians of Alcinoüs' gate
Forever, unobnoxious to decay.
Sheer from the threshold to the inner house
Fixed thrones the walls, through all their length, adorned,
With mantles overspread of subtlest warp
Transparent, work of many a female hand.
On these the princes of Phæacia sat,
Holding perpetual feasts, while golden youths
On all the sumptuous altars stood, their hands
With burning torches charged, which, night by night,
Shed radiance over all the festive throng.
  Full fifty female menials served the king
In household offices; the rapid mills
These turning, pulverize the mellowed grain;
Those, seated orderly, the purple fleece
Wind off, or ply the loom, restless as leaves
Of lofty poplars fluttering in the breeze;
Bright as with oil the new-wrought texture shone.

  Without the court, and to the gates adjoined,
A spacious garden lay, fenced all around
Secure, four acres measuring complete.
There grew luxuriant many a lofty tree,
Pomegranate, pear, the apple blushing bright,
The honeyed fig, and unctuous olive smooth.
Those fruits nor winter's cold nor summer's heat
Fear ever, fail not, wither not, but hang
Perennial, whose unceasing zephyr breathes
Gently on all, enlarging these, and those
Maturing genial; in an endless course
Pears after pears to full dimensions swell,
Figs follow figs, grapes clustering grow again
Where clusters grew, and (every apple stripped)
The boughs soon tempt the gatherer as before.
  There too, well-rooted, and of fruit profuse,
His vineyard grows; part, wide-extended, basks
In the sun's beams; the arid level glows;

In part they gather, and in part they tread
The wine-press, while, before the eye, the grapes
Here put their blossom forth, there gather fast
Their blackness. On the garden's verge extreme
Flowers of all hues smile all the year, arranged
With neatest art judicious, and amid
The lovely scene two fountains welling forth,
One visits, into every part diffused,
The garden ground, the other soft beneath
The threshold steals into the palace court,
Whence every citizen his vase supplies.
Such were the ample blessings on the house
Of King Alcinoüs by the gods bestowed."—COWPER.

Minor Poems of Homer.—The Iliad and the Odyssey are the only authentic productions of Homer. To their author, however, have been attributed about thirty hymns and several minor poems, which have little claim to so distinguished an origin. Of these, "the Margites," a satire on a blockhead who knew much "but everything knew ill," was probably the work of some clever Athenian in an age when epic poetry was a thing of the past; the poem is no longer extant.

"The Battle of the Frogs and Mice," a mock heroic of comparatively modern birth, is still preserved and appreciated. It is a witty burlesque on the Iliad (perhaps the earliest burlesque extant), written in a bold and flowing style. The plot is brief. A mouse, Crumb-snatcher, son of the Mice-king, flying from an enemy, reaches a pool over which a courteous frog, Puff-cheek, undertakes to carry him. But during the passage a water-snake appears; the frightened frog dives to escape his foe, and thoughtlessly leaves his newly-made friend to drown. The mice gather to avenge the loss of their prince; a great battle ensues, and but for the interference of Jupiter the frogs would have been annihilated.

The so-called HOMERIC HYMNS, which the ancients believed to be the work of Homer, if somewhat inferior in age to the Iliad and Odyssey, are undoubtedly older than the pieces named above. Those addressed to Apollo, Mercury, Venus, and Ceres, the finest in the collection, are regular poems of some length; the others are simple eulogies or brief preludes to longer pieces. The Hymn to Venus has a tenderness and warmth not unworthy of Homer. The one in honor of Ceres relates the abduction of her daughter Pros'erpine by Pluto, king of the lower world, the mother's search for the stolen maiden, her anger on discovering the ravisher, and the final arrangement that the goddess shall enjoy the society of her daughter during two-thirds of the year. As a favorable specimen of its style, we cite the lines that follow:—

THE ABDUCTION OF PROSERPINE.

"In Nysia's vale, with nymphs a lovely train,
Sprung from the hoary father of the main,
Fair Proserpine consumed the fleeting hours
In pleasing sports, and plucked the gaudy flowers.
Around them wide the flamy crocus glows,
Through leaves of verdure blooms the opening rose;
The hyacinth declines his fragrant head,
And purple violets deck th' enamelled mead.
The fair Narcissus far above the rest,
By magic formed, in beauty rose confessed.
So Jove, t' ensnare the virgin's thoughtless mind,
And please the ruler of the shades, designed.
He caused it from the opening earth to rise,
Sweet to the scent, alluring to the eyes.
Never did mortal or celestial power
Behold such vivid tints adorn a flower.
From the deep root a hundred branches sprung,
And to the winds ambrosial odors flung;
Which, lightly wafted on the wings of air,
The gladdened earth and heaven's wide circuit share.
The joy-dispensing fragrance spreads around,
And ocean's briny swell with smiles is crowned.

Pleased at the sight, nor deeming danger nigh,
The fair beheld it with desiring eye:
Her eager hand she stretched to seize the flower,
(Beauteous illusion of the ethereal power!)
When, dreadful to behold, the rocking ground
Disparted—widely yawned a gulf profound!
Forth rushing from the black abyss, arose
The gloomy monarch of the realm of woes,

Pluto, from Saturn sprung. The trembling maid
He seized, and to his golden car conveyed.
Borne by immortal steeds the chariot flies:
And thus she pours her supplicating cries:—
'Assist, protect me, thou who reign'st above,
Supreme and best of gods, paternal Jove!'
But ah! in vain the hapless virgin rears
Her wild complaint: nor god nor mortal hears!
Not to the white-armed nymphs with beauty crowned,
Her loved companions, reached the mournful sound."

HOLE.

There are also various fragments styled Homeric, supposed to have been dropped from the poet's genuine or spurious works. Among these is the beautiful couplet quoted by Plato:—

"Asked and unasked, thy blessings give, O Lord!
The evil, though we ask it, from us ward."

Cyclic Poets.—After the death of Homer, a host of imitators sprung up in Greece and Asia Minor. Rhapsodists by profession, as they wandered among the Grecian cities reciting the Homeric poems, their attention was naturally directed to epic composition, and they sought to supply in verse like Homer's what the Iliad and Odyssey had left untold. Confining themselves to the Cycle (*circle*) of the Trojan War, they were called *Cyc'lic* poets.

One bard sung of the preparations made by the Grecian chiefs and the events of the war prior to Achilles' withdrawal; two others took up the narrative where the Iliad left it, and described the sack of Troy; a fourth celebrated the return voyages of the Greek heroes; a fifth supplemented the Odyssey with the later history of Ulysses. Fragments only of these Cyclic epics survive.

HESIOD AND HIS WORKS.

Hesiod.—Homer was an Ionian of Asia Minor. Shortly after his time, or, as some think, contemporaneously with him, a new school of epic poetry appeared in the mother-country.

Its founder was Hesiod, who, like Homer, wrote in the Ionic dialect.

Hesiod was born at Ascra in Bœotia, and brought up in the midst of rural life at the base of Mount Helicon. Here first he held free converse with the Muses. On his father's death, he was defrauded of his portion of the estate by his younger brother Perses, who bribed the judges charged with making the division. Hesiod felt the wrong keenly, yet seems to have regarded his unnatural brother with fraternal interest; for one object of his poem entitled "Works and Days," was to reclaim Perses from dissolute improvidence and incite him to a life of industry.

The first portion of this work is devoted to moral lessons; some in a proverbial form, and others illustrated by narratives and fables. The latter part contains practical directions for the husbandman, and also treats of the art of navigation, important to the Bœotian farmer because much of his produce was shipped to other countries. The whole abounds in excellent precepts for every-day life, and forms the earliest specimen of didactic poetry among the Greeks. For ages its lines were committed to memory and recited as part of the course of ethics in their schools.

FROM HESIOD'S WORKS AND DAYS.

RIGHT AND WRONG.

"Wrong, if he yield to its abhorred control,
Shall pierce like iron to the poor man's soul:
Wrong weighs the rich man's conscience to the dust,
When his foot stumbles on the way unjust.
Far different is the path, a path of light,
That guides the feet to equitable right:
The end of righteousness, enduring long,
Exceeds the short prosperity of wrong.
The fool by suffering his experience buys;
The penalty of folly makes him wise.
But they who never from the right have strayed,
Who as the citizen the stranger aid,

They and their cities flourish: genial Peace
Dwells in their borders; and their youth increase:
Nor Jove, whose radiant eyes behold afar,
Hangs forth in heaven the signs of grievous war.
Nor scathe nor famine on the righteous prey;
Feasts, strewn by earth, employ their easy day:
Rich are their mountain oaks; the topmost trees
With clustering acorns full, the trunks with hiving bees.
Still flourish they, nor tempt with ships the main;
The fruits of earth are poured from every plain.
But o'er the wicked race, to whom belong
The thought of evil, and the deed of wrong,
Saturnian Jove, of wide beholding eyes,
Bids the dark signs of retribution rise.
The god sends down his angry plagues from high,
Famine and pestilence: in heaps they die.
Again, in vengeance of his wrath he falls
On their great hosts, and breaks their tottering walls;
Arrests their navies on the ocean's plain,
And whelms their strength with mountains of the main."

ELTON.

SOME OF HESIOD'S PROVERBS.

"Than wife that's good man finds no greater gain,
But feast-frequenting mates are simply bane.

Invisible, the gods are ever nigh.
Senseless is he who dares with power contend.

Know then this awful truth: it is not given
To elude the wisdom of omniscient Heaven.

Toil, and the slothful man shall envy thee.
The more children, the more cares.
Sometimes a day is a step-mother, sometimes a mother.

Whoever forgeth for another ill,
With it himself is overtaken still.

The procrastinator has ever to contend with loss.
The idler never shall his garners fill.
The lips of moderate speech with grace are hung.

When on your home falls unforeseen distress,
Half-clothed come neighbors; kinsmen stay to dress.

Justice is a virgin pure.
The road to vice is broad and easy; that of virtue, difficult, long, and steep.

Fools! not to know how better for the soul,
An honest half than an ill-gotten whole.

Oh! gorged with gold, ye kingly judges hear!
Make straight your paths; your crooked judgments fear.

How richer he who dines on herbs with health
Of heart, than knaves with all their wines and wealth.

He who nor knows himself, nor will take rule
From those who do, is either knave or fool."

Next in importance to the "Works and Days" is "the Theogony," devoted to the genealogy and history of the Grecian gods, thirty thousand in number. Whatever interest this poem may have possessed for the believer in the Greek mythology, to the reader of the present day it is for the most part tedious, though relieved by occasional grand descriptions of battles between the celestial personages. "The Shield of Hercules" also bears the name of Hesiod; and of works ascribed to him, but not now extant, there are about a dozen.

Hesiod mentions a poetical contest between himself and another, which took place at the funeral of Amphid'amas, king of Eubœa, and in which he obtained a tripod as a prize. Tradition mentions Homer as his competitor on that occasion, and even gives the inscription placed on the tripod by the victor:—

"This Hesiod vows to th' Heliconian Nine,
In Chalcis won, from Homer the divine."

But this part of the story rests on insufficient evidence.

Hesiod is said to have been slain, during a visit to the Locrian town of Œnoë, by two brothers, in revenge for an insult offered to their sister by Hesiod's companion, which caused her to destroy herself. The poet's body, thrown into the sea, was brought to shore by his dog, or as some say by dolphins. Thereupon the indignant people put the murderers to death and razed their dwellings to the ground—an incident which shows the sacredness attached to the vocation of the bard in those early times.

Though Hesiod ranks far below Homer, and indeed is often commonplace, yet at times his style exhibits enthusiasm and even rises to sublimity. We must respect him for the pure morality of his teachings.

POETS OF THE EPIC CYCLE.

ARCTI'NUS OF MILE'TUS.
His poem of 9,100 verses had Memnon, an Ethiopian chief, for its hero. It treated of the part taken in the Trojan War by the Amazons, who arrived after Hector's funeral; the death of their queen, Penthesile'a, at the hand of Achilles; the fall of Achilles himself; and the sack of Troy.

LES'CHES OF MYTILE'NE.
Author of the *Little Iliad*, a supplement to the greater work of that name; it took up the narrative where Homer leaves off, and carried it to the fall of Troy.

STASI'NUS OF CYPRUS.
Wrote the *Cypria*, in eleven books, narrating the events that preceded the Trojan War, and the incidents of the first nine years of the siege.

A'GIAS THE TRŒZENIAN.
His epic in five books, called *Nostoi* (the Returns), was descriptive of the home-voyages of the Greek heroes.

EU'GAMON OF CYRE'NE.
The *Telegonia*, a continuation of the Odyssey to the death of Ulysses, who falls by the hand of Teleg'onus, his son by Cir'ce.

NOTES ON GREEK WRITING, ETC.

The language of epic poetry perhaps once the common tongue of the people, and merely elaborated by the bards. The art of writing, old in Greece; while there is no positive evidence of its being known before 800 B.C., the historian Herodotus (450 B.C.) speaks as if it had been familiar to his countrymen for hundreds of years. Homer's epics, though by some thought to have been handed down by oral repetition, probably written on metallic or wooden tablets by their author. Hesiod's works originally committed to leaden tables and deposited in the temple of the Bœotian Muses.

Greek papyrus-factories on the Nile, 650 B.C. Writing first extensively used by priests and bards, particularly at the temple of Delphi.

CHAPTER III.

LYRIC POETRY.

Rise of Lyric Poetry.—For more than two hundred years after Homer and Hesiod, no one worthy of the name of poet appeared in Greece. Greek genius seemed to have exhausted itself. A few feeble imitators of the great master, and epic poetry was no more. The spirit of the Iliad and the Odyssey died with the monarchies whose chieftains they immortalized. When popular governments arose, the bard no longer celebrated the gods and demigods of the past, or traced the genealogies of kings, but sung the glories of his country, or poured forth without restraint the emotions of his soul. Thus lyric poetry was the child of liberty.

Varieties.—At the beginning of the seventh century B.C., there was a new birth of poesy; Grecian song burst forth once more, from hearts throbbing with enthusiasm at the triumph of free institutions. Solemn dirges and stately hymns chanted by olive-crowned youth bearing offerings to the gods, were no longer paramount; ballads full of human feeling, lyrics appealing directly to the people—to the patriot, the artisan, the shepherd, the lover, the pleasure-seeker—struck chords that vibrated in many hearts. Feasts afforded frequent occasions for outbursts of national feeling, it being the custom of the guests to pass a branch of myrtle from hand to hand, each as he received it repeating an appropriate verse.

A favorite banquet-song of the fifth century B.C. was the following eulogy of Harmo'dius and Aristogi'ton, the Athenian heroes who slew the tyrant Hipparchus :—

"In a wreath of myrtle I'll wear my glaive,
Like Harmodius and Aristogi'ton brave,
Who striking the tyrant down,
Made Athens a freeman's town.
Harmodius, our darling, thou art not dead!
Thou liv'st in the isles of the blest, 'tis said,
With Achilles first in speed,
And Tydi'des Diomede.

In a wreath of myrtle I'll wear my glaive,
Like Harmodius and Aristogiton brave,
When the twain on Athena's day
Did the tyrant Hipparchus slay.
For aye shall your fame in the land be told,
Harmodius and Aristogiton bold,
Who, striking the tyrant down,
Made Athens a freeman's town."

PROF. CONINGTON.

The flower-songs of the Greeks were especially beautiful; children enjoyed their nursery rhymes; while in the Lay of the Swallow, the penniless bard, chanting at the gate, sought an avenue to the charity of his rich neighbor.

FROM THE LAY OF THE SWALLOW.

"The swallow is here, the swallow is here,
She comes to proclaim the reviving year;
With her jet-black hood, and her milk-white breast,
She is come, she is come, at our behest,
The harbinger of the beautiful spring,
To claim your generous offering.
Let your bountiful door its wealth outpour,
What is little to you is to us great store;
A bunch of dry figs, and a savory cruse
Of pottage the swallow will not refuse;
With a basket of cheese and a barley cake,
And a cup of red wine our thirst to slake."—MURE.

The creations of the lyric muse are graceful, touching, and true to nature. We regret not to exchange the sublime heights of epic poetry for an humbler field in which we may commune with the joys and sorrows, the hopes and fears, of humanity. Here, as Tegner says, Greek poetry arises "slender, smooth, erect like the palm-tree with its rich yet symmetrical crown; and a nightingale sits among the leaves and sings."

THE ELEGY.

The Ionians, first to free themselves from kingly rule, gave to the Hellenic world the earliest forms of lyric poetry,—the elegiac couplet and the lighter iambic verse appropriate to satire. These twin-born metres, of Ionian parentage, grew up side by side in Greece. In the elegiac couplet, a dactylic line of five feet or their equivalent followed the sonorous hexameter,* constituting a livelier measure than the old heroic verse, which consisted of hexameters alone.

The Greek elegy was not necessarily plaintive; on the contrary, it did good service in rousing to action in time of war, and gave fitting expression to the spirit of the banquet-hall.

Callinus.—The inventor of this metre was Calli'nus of Eph'esus, in Ionia, who flourished between 730 and 678 B.C. He attempted by it to excite his countrymen against a horde of barbarian invaders; but the people were too much enervated by intercourse with the effeminate nations of Asia to respond to his thrilling strains.

The following is a fragment of Callinus, perhaps the oldest war-elegy in existence:—

"How long will ye slumber? When will ye take heart,
And fear the reproach of your neighbors at hand?
Fy! comrades, to think ye have peace for your part,
Whilst the sword and the arrow are wasting our land!
Shame! grasp the shield close! cover well the bold breast!
Aloft raise the spear as ye march on the foe!
With no thought of retreat, with no terror confessed,
Hurl your last dart in dying, or strike your last blow!

---

* The following lines, with their long and short syllables distinguished and arranged as in the dactylic hexameter and pentameter, will give an idea of the cadence of the elegiac couplet:—

"Gīve mĕ sŏme | mōre," săys thĕ | mīsĕrlȳ | mān, thoŭgh ăs | rīch ăs ă | Crœ̄sŭs;
Nēvĕr ĕ|noūgh ĭn hĭs | stōre, || īf hĕ căn | gēt ăny̆ | mōre.

Oh! 'tis noble and glorious to fight for our all—
For our country, our children, the wife of our love!
Death comes not the sooner! no soldier shall fall
Ere his thread is spun out by the sisters above.
Once to die is man's doom; rush, rush to the fight!
He cannot escape, though his blood were Jove's own;
For a while let him cheat the shrill arrow by flight:
Fate will catch him at last in his chamber alone.
Unlamented he dies—unregretted? not so,
When, the tower of his country, in death falls the brave;
Thrice hallowed his name amongst all, high or low,
As with blessings alive, so with tears in the grave."

H. N. COLERIDGE.

Tyrtæus.—Another proficient in this variety of elegy was Tyrtæus, supposed to have been born in the Attic town of Aphidnæ. He led the Spartans in the Second Messenian War (685 - 668 B.C.), they having, by the direction of an oracle, sent to Athens for a general, to secure the success which had before been denied them. The story is that the jealous Athenians despatched to their neighbors a deformed schoolmaster, the cripple Tyrtæus, in the belief that his services would be of little value; but they mistook. The greatest military genius could not have accomplished more; for Tyrtæus, by his wise counsels and inspiriting war-songs, made his soldiers invincible. Messenia fell, and her citizens became slaves to the Spartans. Nor, afterward, was the poetry of Tyrtæus less efficacious in quelling civil dissensions and establishing domestic peace. In every respect, "the Muse of Sparta," as he was called, proved to be to his adopted country the blessing promised by the oracle.

Tyrtæus is said to have invented the trumpet, and introduced it as a companion to the flute, then the chief instrument in use. Some have interpreted the lameness of the bard as signifying his limping measure, the second line of the elegiac couplet being, as we have seen, a foot shorter than the first.

Of the many productions of Tyrtæus, consisting of marching-songs, as well as warlike and political elegies, only a few fragments survive. His poems, characterized by terseness and impassioned power, were long popular among the Spartans, who, on a campaign, were wont to recite them after each evening meal to kindle afresh their martial fire.

BATTLE-HYMN OF TYRTÆUS.

"Our country's voice invites the brave
The glorious toils of war to try;
Cursed be the coward, or the slave,
Who shuns the fight, who fears to die.

Obedient to the high command,
Full fraught with patriotic fire,
Descends a small but trusty band,
And scarce restrains the impatient ire.

Behold! the hostile crowds advance;
Unyielding, we their might oppose;
With helm to helm, and lance to lance,
In awful pomp we meet our foes.

Unawed by fear, untaught to yield,
We boldly tread the ensanguined plain;
And scorn to quit the martial field,
Though drenched in blood, though heaped with slain.

For, though stern Death assail the brave,
His virtues endless life shall claim;
His fame shall mock the invidious grave,
To times unborn a sacred name."—LOWTH.

THE SATIRE.

Archilochus of Pa'ros (728–660 B.C.) was the first great satirist, the inventor of that rapid, loosely-constructed iambic measure so admirably adapted to his withering lampoons. The son of a slave-woman, Archil'ochus was treated with indignity in his native island; so bidding adieu to "the figs and fishy life" of Paros in early youth, he sailed with a colony to Tha'sos in the northern Ægean. His new home, however, disappointed his expectations; its gold-mines yielded not the fortune he had dreamed of, and he denounced it as "the sink of all Hellenic ills." The colonists becoming engaged in war with a neighboring people, a pitched battle proved too severe an ordeal for the poet's courage, and dropping his shield he fled.

Perhaps it was for this cowardly action, perhaps on account of his empty purse, that when he returned to Paros, one of its fair daughters, who had been his boyhood's love, refused him her hand. Her father, also, denied his suit; whereupon the furious poet poured forth in stinging verses such a torrent of violent invective upon the girl and her whole family, that she, her father, and her sisters, are said to have taken refuge from his scurrilous attacks in suicide.

The public odium thus excited drove Archilochus from Paros. But the brand of cowardice was upon him. The Spartans, whose mothers, pointing to the battle-field, were wont to say "Return with your shields or upon them," disdained the man who could write,

"That shield some Saian decks, which, 'gainst my grain,
I left—fair, flawless shield—beside the wood.
Well, let it go! I and my purse remain:
To-morrow's bull-skin may be just as good."

Insult met him at every step, till a poetical victory at the Olympic Games restored him to popular favor. He went back to Paros, an old man, to redeem his reputation as a soldier by dying in battle with the Naxians. Then all Greece awoke to the greatness of his genius; and the prediction of an oracle before his birth, that he would be "immortal among men in the glory of his song," was fulfilled.

Fertility of invention, and an intimate acquaintance with human nature, were conspicuous in the poetry of Archilochus. Elegies and love-songs flowed from his pen, and his philosophical poetry gained for him from Plato the epithet of "Wisest;" but it was in satire that classical writers conceded to him the highest rank. Archilochus likens himself to a hedgehog bristling with quills, whose "one great resource is worth all the devices of more powerful animals." From his birthplace, ill-natured satire has been called *Parian verse.*

So little remains of the writings of this author that we can hardly decide whether his countrymen judged aright in reckoning him second only to Homer. The two represented distinct departments of poetry; each in his own, it was claimed, fell little short of perfection. Where Homer praised, Archilochus reviled. Their birthdays were celebrated in one grand festival, and a single double-faced statue perpetuated the memory of the Epic Poet and the Parian Satirist.

ARCHILOCHUS TO HIS SOUL.

"My soul, my soul, by cares past all relief
Distracted sore, bear up! with manly breast
And dauntless mien, each fresh assault of grief
Encountering. By hostile weapons pressed,
Stand firm. Let no unlooked-for triumph move
To empty exultation, no defeat
Cast down. But still let moderation prove
Of life's uncertain cup the bitter and the sweet."

MURE.

Greek satire had other representatives, whose names will be found at the end of this chapter; but their genius was of a lower grade.

ÆOLIC AND DORIC SCHOOLS.

Lyric poetry was the peculiar province of the Æolian and Dorian Greeks, who carried it to perfection. The Æolic writers were replete with intense passion, and employed lively metres of simple structure. The Dorian lyric, intended to be sung by choruses or to choral dances on great occasions, funerals, marriages, or public festivals, was a much more majestic, but at the same time a more intricate and artificial composition. The most distinguished composers of the Æolic School were Alcæus and Sappho; of the Doric, Simonides and Pindar.

Alcæus flourished in the latter part of the seventh century B.C. He was a noble of Lesbos, and lived in the stirring times when the constitutional and the aristocratic party contended for the sovereignty. In this struggle Alcæus appears as the deadly foe of democratic rule; when his friend Pittacus was clothed with supreme authority by the people, Alcæus directed against him the keenest shafts of his satire. Pittacus defeated him in an attempt to overthrow the government, but generously spared his life, saying, "Forgiveness is better than revenge." Of the poet's subsequent career we are ignorant.

The ancients were loud in their praises of Alcæus. His poems were polished, full of vehemence and passion, sublime in their denunciations of tyranny and encomiums of freedom. Love and wine were two of his favorite topics; yet even his jovial pieces were pervaded by a loftiness of sentiment foreign to mere sensual songs. Among his most beautiful compositions were the odes to Sappho, whose love he once sought, but whose genius soared to greater heights than his. We take from Alcæus

THE CONSTITUTION OF A STATE.

"What constitutes a state?
Not high-raised battlement or labored mound,
Thick wall or moated gate;
Not cities fair, with spires and turrets crowned:
No:—Men, high-minded men,
With powers as far above dull brutes endued,
In forest, brake, or den,
As beasts excel cold rocks and brambles rude—
Men who their duties know,
Know too their rights, and knowing, dare maintain;
Prevent the long-aimed blow,
And crush the tyrant, while they rend the chain."

SIR WILLIAM JONES.

The Lesbian Poetesses.—Lesbos was the centre of lyric song. To its shores, the waves of ocean are fabled to have borne the lyre of Orpheus, which the people hung in Apollo's temple: thus traditionally distinguished by fate, it became renowned as the home of Grecian poetesses.

The Lesbian women were not confined to domestic duties, but were allowed to take part in public affairs. They founded societies for the cultivation of their literary tastes, and before all Greece vindicated the genius of their sex. And Lesbos was the very clime for poetry to ripen in. The love of the beautiful was fed on every side. The island was a paradise of groves and rivulets, of blossoms and perfumes. Among its olive-clad hills, at its fountains set in violets and fringed with fern, under its stately pines, and in its temples shining with ivory and gold, its poetesses received their inspiration.

Sappho.—Greatest of these, and queen of her sex in intellectual endowments, was Sappho, "the Lesbian Nightingale," "spotless, sweetly-smiling, violet-wreathed," as Alcæus fondly described her, whom all Greece knew as *The Poetess.*

In her history it is difficult to separate the true from the fabulous. Born at Mytile'ne, the capital of the island, in the latter part of the seventh century B.C., she was deprived of a mother's care at the age of six. In early womanhood, a new calamity befell her in the loss of her husband, and thenceforth she devoted her genius to letters, making the elevation of her countrywomen the great object of her life. Her reputation soon spread throughout Greece. Mytilene became the seat of a brilliant sisterhood eager in the study of the polished arts; sparkling conversation enlivened its meetings; music and poetry were the branches its members specially cultivated; love was the common subject of their verse; their lives were above reproach. In the centre of this constellation of gifted women blazed Sappho, "Star of Lesbian Song." Greece, captivated by her sweet numbers, accorded her a place by Homer's side—then raised her to the level of its goddesses as "the Tenth Muse."

Ancient story made Sappho the victim of disappointed love.

Overcome with passion for Pha'on, a beautiful Mytilenean youth notorious for his heart-breaking propensities, and finding Phaon indifferent to her advances, she is said to have thrown herself from the Leuca'dian promontory * and drowned her passion in the Ionian Sea. There is, however, no evidence

THE LOVER'S LEAP.

* The Leucadian promontory projects from the southern shore of the island of Leucadia, off the coast of Acarnania (see Map, p. 132). On the bluff stood a temple of Apollo, to whom, in very ancient times, human sacrifices were yearly offered, a victim being hurled from the rock into the sea below. The priests some-

to support the story; on the contrary, the poetess seems to have been implicated with Alcæus in a conspiracy against Pittacus, who then ruled in Lesbos, and to have been banished in consequence. She is thought to have found an asylum in Sicily.

SAPPHO'S STYLE.—Simplicity, tenderness, concentrated passion, and brilliancy of description, are characteristic of Sappho's verse. Her poetry is the very language of harmony; no more musical measures than hers were known to the Greeks. Her favorite stanza, an invention of her own, consisted of four lines with a cadence like the following:—

Tenderest mistress | of the heart's emotion,
Over whom love sweeps | as the mighty ocean,
Unto thee pour we | all our soul's devotion,
Glorious Sappho!

In depicting love, Sappho is unmatched. Her utterances, indeed, were so intense as to be misconstrued by the sensual Greeks of a later day, and give rise to reports injurious to her good name; or possibly she may have been confounded with another Sappho, of a different character; but we have no doubt that her life was as pure as her poetry is charming. Her imagery, when imagery she used, Sappho gathered from the

---

times took the place of these unfortunates, but on such occasions carefully avoided danger by fastening to their persons flocks of live birds, the flapping of whose pinions during the descent broke their fall. This rite was gradually modified; and at one time we find the leap from the cliff used as an ordeal to test the guilt of suspected persons.

In Sappho's day it was customary for those suffering the pangs of unrequited affection to take the Lover's Leap from the precipice, after secretly uttering their vows in the sanctuary of the god. Some, intent on suicide, were dashed to pieces on the rocks below or perished in the waves; others took the precaution to buoy themselves up with feathers or bladders, trusting to a plunge in the cold sea or the bruises they might receive, to cure their passion. Queen Artemisia, of Halicarnassus, lost her life in taking the Lover's Leap, after putting out the eyes of the youth who would not return her attachment; and one case is recorded in which a man four times resorted to this perilous remedy.—The modern Greek sailor still calls the promontory "the Lady's Cape."

bright-tinted flowers, the starry skies, and fragrant zephyrs of Lesbos, where, as she sung,

> "Through orchard plots, with fragrance crowned,
> The clear cold fountain murmuring flows;
> And forest leaves, with rustling sound,
> Invite to soft repose."

Judging from her fragments, we must admit that in her peculiar department Sappho stands without a peer. Indeed, her own graceful lines may well be applied to herself:—

> "The stars that round the beauteous moon
> Attendant wait, cast into shade
> Their ineffectual lustres, soon
> As she, in full-orbed majesty arrayed,
> Her silver radiance showers
> Upon this world of ours,"—

for the lesser lights of lyric poesy pale in the lustre of her genius.

Addison, in his Spectator, makes the following remarks on Sappho, which are fully justified by the praises of ancient critics:—"Among the mutilated poets of antiquity, there are none whose fragments are so beautiful as those of Sappho. One may see, by what is left, that she followed nature in all her thoughts, without descending to those little points, conceits, and turns of wit, with which many of our modern lyrics are so miserably infected. Her soul seems to have been made up of love and poetry. She felt the passion in all its warmth and described it in all its symptoms. I do not know, by the character that is given of her works, whether it is not for the benefit of mankind that they are lost. They were filled with such bewitching tenderness and rapture, that it might have been dangerous to have given them a reading."

It is told that a physician, by studying the symptoms of love as described by Sappho, detected in the mysterious sickness of the young Anti′ochus, son of the king of Syria, a hidden passion for his step-mother. The treatment was in accordance with the diagnosis, the disease disappearing when the anxious father relinquished to the youth the beautiful object of his affections.

Sappho's description of the raptures of love, commended by all critics from Longinus down, is certainly a nonpareil. It has been thus translated by Ambrose Philips, a friend of Addison's :—

A LOVE SONG.

"Blest as th' immortal gods is he,
The youth who fondly sits by thee,
And hears, and sees thee all the while
Softly speak and sweetly smile.

'Twas this deprived my soul of rest,
And raised such tumults in my breast;
For while I gazed in transport tost,
My breath was gone, my voice was lost.

My bosom glowed: the subtle flame
Ran quick through all my vital frame;
O'er my dim eyes a darkness hung;
My ears with hollow murmurs rung.

In dewy damps my limbs were chill'd;
My blood with gentle horrors thrill'd;
My feeble pulse forgot to play;
I fainted, sunk, and died away."

The grave Solon paid our authoress a delicate compliment. Having heard his nephew recite one of her poems, he is said to have exclaimed that he would not willingly die till he had learned it by heart.

The works of Sappho, comprised in nine books, embraced love-lays, elegies, bridal songs sometimes extended into miniature dramas, and amorous hymns to Venus and Cupid. The remnants are principally erotic pieces. We present below the Hymn to Venus, preserved entire, in which the writer delicately makes the goddess her confidante, and modestly discloses the secret of her misplaced affections.

HYMN TO VENUS.

"O Venus, beauty of the skies,
To whom a thousand temples rise,
Gayly false in gentle smiles,
Full of love-perplexing wiles;
O goddess! from my heart remove
The wasting cares and pains of love.

If ever thou hast kindly heard
A song in soft distress preferred,
Propitious to my tuneful vow,
O gentle goddess! hear me now.
Descend, thou bright immortal guest,
In all thy radiant charms confessed.

Thou once didst leave almighty Jove,
And all the golden roofs above:
The car thy wanton sparrows drew,
Hovering in air they lightly flew;
As to my bower they winged their way,
I saw their quivering pinions play.

The birds dismissed (while you remain),
Bore back their empty car again.
Then you, with looks divinely mild,
In every heavenly feature smiled,
And asked what new complaints I made,
And why I called you to my aid:

What frenzy in my bosom raged,
And by what cure to be assuaged:
What gentle youth I would allure;
Whom in my artful toils secure:
Who does thy tender heart subdue,
Tell me, my Sappho, tell me, who?

Though now he shuns thy longing arms,
He soon shall court thy slighted charms;
Though now thy offerings he despise,
He soon to thee shall sacrifice;
Though now he freeze, he soon shall burn,
And be thy victim in his turn.

Celestial visitant, once more
Thy needful presence I implore!

In pity come and ease my grief,
Bring my distempered soul relief;
Favor thy suppliant's hidden fires,
And give me all my heart desires."
AMBROSE PHILIPS.

THE ROSE.

"Did Jove a queen of flowers decree,
The rose the queen of flowers should be;
Of flowers the eye; of plants the gem;
The meadow's blush; earth's diadem;
Glory of colors on the gaze
Lightening in its beauty's blaze.
It breathes of Love; it blooms the guest
Of Venus' ever-fragrant breast.
In gaudy pomp its petals spread;
Light foliage trembles round its head;
With vermeil blossoms fresh and fair
It laughs to the voluptuous air."—ELTON.

Sappho's Pupils.—Doubtless many went forth from Sappho's school to reflect, in their own accomplishments, the brilliancy of their mistress. History has preserved the names of two of her pupils—Damoph'yla of Asia Minor, noted for a Hymn to Diana; and ERINNA, a Rhodian maid who shone among the brightest lights of Sappho's circle, and, if we may believe the story, died of a broken heart when compelled by her parents to exchange the delights of literature for the drudgery of the spinning-wheel. This cruel treatment Erinna made the subject of an affecting lament, "the Spindle," a poem of three hundred hexameters, on which her reputation rests. Her death at the age of nineteen cheated the world of a writer who promised to rival Homer himself.

"The Spindle" is lost; but the following epigram on a virgin of Lesbos, who died on the day appointed for her marriage, speaks for Erinna:—

"The virgin Myrtis' sepulchre am I;
Creep softly to the pillar'd mount of woe;
And whisper to the grave, in earth below,
'Grave! thou art envious in thy cruelty!'

To thee, now gazing here, her barbarous fate
These bride's adornments tell; that, with the fire
Of Hymen's torch, which led her to the gate,
Her husband burned the maid upon her pyre:
Yes, Hymen! thou didst change the marriage-song
To the shrill wailing of the mourners' throng."

A pointed epitaph in the Greek Anthology shows the estimation in which the poetess was held by her countrymen:—

"These are Erinna's songs: how sweet, though slight!
For she was but a girl of nineteen years;
Yet stronger far than what most men can write:
Had death delayed, whose fame had equalled hers?"

Anacreon.—In the sixth century, Te'os, a seaport of Ionia, gave birth to the society poet, Anacreon; who, though an Ionian, wrote rather in the style of the Æolian lyrics. His verses, however, while soft and graceful, were marked by levity, and lacked the dignity and depth of the Æolic school. "The Muse, good humor, love, and wine," Anacreon tells us, were his themes; accordingly his songs, brimming with sensuality, grew in popular estimation as Greece degenerated in public morality.

When his native city fell a prey to Cyrus the Persian, Anacreon with the other inhabitants set sail for Thrace (540 B.C.). From Thrace, while yet in his youth, he withdrew to the island of Sa'mos whose tyrant, Polyc'rates, was a munificent patron of literature and art. Amid the gayety of the Samian court, the witty and pleasure-loving poet found a congenial home, Polycrates making him an intimate companion and confiding to him important state secrets. But the ruler of Samos was treacherously put to death by a Persian satrap; about which time, Anacreon was invited to Athens by the tyrant Hipparchus, who sent his royal trireme to bring his poet-laureate across the Ægean.

At Athens, Anacreon for a time gave free rein to his passions, joining a set of boon companions who basked in the sunshine of royal favor. His voluptuous career was cut short by the assassination of Hipparchus, and he returned to Teos (repeopled during his absence), to be choked by a grape-seed at the advanced age of eighty-five—or, if we are to take the story figuratively, to fall a victim to his irrepressible love of the bottle.

A statue of a drunken old man on the Athenian acropolis kept alive in the minds of the people as well the graceful odes of Anacreon as his prevailing weakness. His friend Simonides wrote an epitaph to his memory, in which we catch a glimpse of the exciting whirl of pleasures that made up his existence:—

"Bland mother of the grape! all-gladdening vine!
Teeming inebriate joy! whose tendrils bloom
Crisp-woven in winding trail, now green entwine
This pillar's top, this mount, Anacreon's tomb.
As lover of the feast, the untempered bowl,
While the full draught was reeling in his soul,
He smote upon the harp, whose melodies
Were tuned to girlish loves, till midnight fled;
Now, fallen to earth, embower him as he lies,
Thy purpling clusters blushing o'er his head:
Still be fresh dew upon the branches hung,
Like that which breathed from his enchanting tongue."

The name of Anacreon is attached to about sixty odes, but they are all probably from five hundred to a thousand years later than he. Yet, if they are not by his hand, they breathe his spirit. As a sample of these Anacreontics, we give a paraphrase of

CUPID AND THE BEE.

Young Cupid once a rose caressed,
And sportively its leaflets pressed.
The witching thing, so fair to view
One could not but believe it true,
Warmed, on its bosom false, a bee,
Which stung the boy-god in his glee.
Sobbing, he raised his pinions bright,
And flew unto the isle of light,

Where, in her beauty, myrtle-crowned,
The Paphian goddess sat enthroned.
Her Cupid sought, and to her breast
His wounded finger, weeping, pressed.
"O mother! kiss me," was his cry—
"O mother! save me, or I die;
A winged little snake or bee
With cruel sting has wounded me!"

The blooming goddess in her arms
Folded and kissed his budding charms;
To her soft bosom pressed her pride,
And then with truthful words replied:
"If thus a little insect thing
Can pain thee with its tiny sting,
How languish, think you, those who smart
Beneath my Cupid's cruel dart?
How fatal must that poison prove
That rankles on the shafts of Love!"

Simonides (556–467 B.C.), who brought into high repute the Doric or Choral School while he also composed in the Ionic dialect, was born in Ceos, an island of the Cyclades. He was one of a brilliant coterie of poets attracted to Athens by the munificence of Hipparchus; and after the assassination of the latter he withdrew to Thessaly, to find rich and powerful patrons there on whom to lavish his eulogies; for Simonides was the first poet that set a price upon his talents and turned his panegyrics into gold. He who, when small pay was offered, disdained to celebrate a mule victorious in the race on the plea that it was an ass's daughter, when the price was raised found in the "child of thunder-footed steeds" no unfit subject for his facile Muse.

In connection with this rather unpoetical eye to business, we are told that once Simonides, having extolled in verse one of his Thessalian patrons, was refused more than half the promised price and referred for the balance to the gods Castor and Pollux, whose praises filled most of the poem. The Thessalian noble was still laughing at his ruse for evading payment, when Simonides was summoned from the room to speak with two strangers. Hastening out, he found that they had vanished; but no sooner had he withdrawn from the apartment than the roof fell and killed all whom he had left there. Thus the twin deities discharged their indebtedness to the poet.

The evening of his days Simonides passed in Syracuse, the ornament of Hi'ero's court, the recipient of royal favors during his life, and at his death of the highest funeral honors. It was here that the poet, who was somewhat of a philosopher, confessed his inability to answer the question of the Syracusan monarch, "What is God?"

Simonides was remarkably successful in adapting the elegy to funeral songs and epitaphs, and thus embalming Grecian heroism for the contemplation of future ages. He lived in the time of the Persian War, and commemorated its worthies. The tomb of the three hundred who fell at Thermopylæ for the liberties of Greece bore this grand inscription from his pen: "Go, stranger, and tell the Lacedæmonians that we lie here in obedience to their laws." In his workshop the epigram was wrought to perfection. "The Simonidean tears" seemed to well up from the very depths of the heart. Among all the epigrammatists known to literature, none have excelled him whom Plato styled "the divine Simonides;" who was "the voice of Hellas—the genius of Fame, sculpturing with a pen of adamant, in letters of indelible gold, the achievements to which the whole world owes its civilization." Fifty-six times, the last time at the age of eighty, he bore away from all competitors the prize of poetry.

Besides dirges and epigrams, hymns, prayers, pæans, and processional odes, flowed from the prolific pen of Simonides. Long a chorus-teacher in the land of his birth, he was peculiarly fitted for the composition of solemn choral poetry. "The Lament of Danaë," his finest surviving work, is a noble specimen of the Greek lyric. It describes the Argive princess set adrift with her child in an ark upon the stormy billows by her inhuman parent. Tenderly she folds the sleeping boy in her arms, and prays Father Zeus that like him the sea may sleep.

DANAË'S LAMENT.

"Closed in the fine-wrought chest,
She felt the rising wind the waters move.
Then, by new fear possessed,
With action wild
And cheeks bedewed, she stretched her arms of love
Toward Perseus: 'O my child,
What sorrow wrings my breast!
While thou art sunk so deep
In infancy's calm sleep;
Launched in this joyless ark,
Bronze-fastened, glimmering-dark,
Yet, pillowed on thy tangled hair,
Thou slumberest, nor dost care
For billows past thee bounding
Nor breezes shrilly sounding.
Laid in thy mantle red, sweet face, how fair!
Ah! but if Fear
Had aught of fear for thee,
Thou even to me
Wouldst turn thy tender ear.
But now I bid thee rest, my babe; sleep still!
Rest, O thou sea! Rest, rest, unbounded ill!
Zeus, Father, some relief, some change from thee!
Am I too bold? For *his* sake, pardon me!'"

EPITAPH ON THE NIECE OF HIPPARCHUS.

"Archedicè, the daughter of King Hippias,
Who in his time
Of all the potentates of Greece was prime,
This dust doth hide;
Daughter, wife, sister, mother, unto kings she was,
Yet free from pride."—HOBBES.

Pindar, the friend and pupil of Simonides, the greatest master of the Doric School, adorned the golden age of Grecian literature, and will there be considered as the representative of lyric poetry.

MINOR ELEGIAC AND IAMBIC POETS.

MIMNERMUS of Colophon (634–590 B.C.), the first to adapt the elegiac couplet to plaintive and erotic themes: he bewails the enslavement of his degenerate country by Lydia. Old age the terror of the poet; life without "the gold-haired goddess" of love not worth living; a characteristic saying of his, "When the flower of youth is past, it is best to die at once; may death strike me at my sixtieth year."

SOLON, the Athenian lawgiver (638–559 B.C.), the first *gnomic* poet: embodied his moral maxims (*gnomes*) in elegiac verse: also a master of the martial elegy, as his famous "Salaminian Ode" shows. Plato declared that if Solon had devoted his genius to the Muses, Homer might not have stood alone in his glory.

THEOGNIS (583–495 B.C.), a noble of Meg'ara, who opposed the democratic faction, and was in consequence expelled from the state and deprived of his hereditary lands by the Commons. He sang his songs in elegiac verse. Distinguished also as a gnomic poet. The following thoughts are culled from among his sayings:—"Wealth is almighty."—"Easy among men is the practice of wickedness, but hard the method of goodness."—"No one descends to Hades with his riches, nor can he by paying ransom escape death."—"Prefer to live piously on small means to being rich on what is gotten unjustly."

PHOCYL'IDES of Miletus (550–490 B.C.), an Ionian gnomic poet whose didactic couplets, generally marked by sound sense, sometimes breathing a worldly spirit, began with the introductory phrase, "And this too is Phocylides'." The following are maxims of his:—"First get your living, and then think of getting virtue."—"A small city set upon a rock and well-governed is better than all foolish Nineveh."

XENOPH'ANES of Colophon (about 540 B.C.), founder of the Eleatic sect of philosophers: also an elegiac poet: condemns the effeminacy of his countrymen, and derides a prevailing preference for physical over intellectual culture.

THE SATIRISTS.

SIMONIDES THE ELDER, of Amorgus (660 B.C.), "the Iambographer:" style flowing and polished: masterpiece, a satire on women—"Even though they seem to be good, when one has got one she becomes a plague."

HIP'PONAX of Ephesus (540 B.C.), the father of parody, and inventor of the choliambic measure, or limping iambic, in which the last foot was a spondee. He attacked the luxury and vice of his day, sparing neither friend nor relative; it is told that by his crushing satire a sculptor who had caricatured his ugly person was driven to suicide. It was Hipponax who said: "Woman gives two days of happiness to man, the day of her bridal and the day of her funeral." The stranger who passed his tomb was warned:

"Wake not the sleeping wasp, for though he's dead,
Still straight and sure his crooked lines are sped."

MINOR POETS OF THE CHORAL SCHOOL.

ALCMAN (671–631 B.C.), Sparta's jovial lyric poet, an emancipated Lydian slave.

STESICH'ORUS of Sicily (632–560 B.C.), inventor of the choric system; named from his occupation *Stesi-chorus*, leader of the chorus. His greatness foreshadowed by a nightingale that alighted on his infant lips and burst into song: hymns, fables, pastorals: the earliest Greek novelist; his love tales and romances narrated in verse.

TERPANDER the Lesbian (about 650 B.C.), the founder of Greek musical science, and inventor of the heptachord, or seven-stringed lyre.

IB'YCUS, of Rhegium in southern Italy (540 B.C.), lived in Samos as the friend of Polycrates. His odes principally erotic: from the warmth of his passion, Ibycus was styled "the love-maddened."

BACCHYL'IDES (470 B.C.), the nephew of Simonides of Ceos: hymns, epigrams, etc., in Doric: style highly polished: a specimen epigram is,

"The touchstone tries the purity of gold,
And by all-conquering truth man's worth and wit are told."

TIMOC'REON OF RHODES (471 B.C.), lyric poet and satirist.

CHAPTER IV.

RISE OF GREEK PROSE.

Earliest Prose Writings.—For several centuries, the literature of Greece was confined to poetry. In Hellas, as elsewhere, verse for a time at first so charmingly and completely filled the popular ear that there was no desire, no room, for prose. But, as new necessities arose, poetry could not suffice for Greece; not with epic and lyric voice alone were her men of genius to gain a hearing from the world. National achievements must be recorded; the people must be appealed to in the agora; the curtain of metaphysics must be raised; and so History, Oratory, and Philosophy appeared upon the stage. To these practical new-comers, the plain garb of prose was found more appropriate than the broidery of verse.

Moreover, the introduction of facilities for writing favored the development of prose literature; for, unlike poetry, it needed a written form to give it permanence. When the art of writing became familiar, and men with its help could rapidly inscribe their thoughts for others still more rapidly to read, prose, as a distinct branch of composition, was born; and its birth marked an era in the intellectual growth of the Greeks.

Ever since the introduction of letters, prose had doubtless been used more or less in despatches, records, laws, and official documents. Pherecy'des of Sy'ros and Cadmus of Miletus (about 550 B.C.) were the first to secure its recognition as a department of polite literature, the one embodying in it his philosophical doctrines, the other the fabulous history of his native land—with homely strength, if not with artistic finish.

Era of the Sages.—In the period during which prose gained its first foothold flourished the Seven Sages of Greece (665–540 B.C.). Revolutions were then the order of the day, the people were beginning actively to assert their rights, and political questions of vital interest absorbed the attention of thinkers. The flights of fancy became fewer, as these grave problems presented themselves. Philosophers strove to solve them at home; patriots went abroad to study foreign institutions; and all awoke to the discovery that "knowledge is power."

The Seven Sages were gnomic poets, as well as philosophers and statesmen. Their moral and political maxims they usually threw into verse; but those inscribed on plates of metal and deposited in the temple of Apollo at Delphi, were in prose. In their proverbs, whether prose or poetry, we discern the dawn of moral philosophy.

SOLON.—The greatest of the Seven Sages were Solon and Thales. Solon of Athens was born about 638 B.C. After extensive travels and studies, he drew up for the Athenians (594 B.C.) the famous code called by his name, which reformed many abuses and secured to the people a liberal government. His laws were written in prose on the polished faces of triangular wooden prisms. These were set in frames, and turned on pivots by persons who wished to consult them. The state copy was carved on four-sided blocks of brass, and kept in the Acropolis.

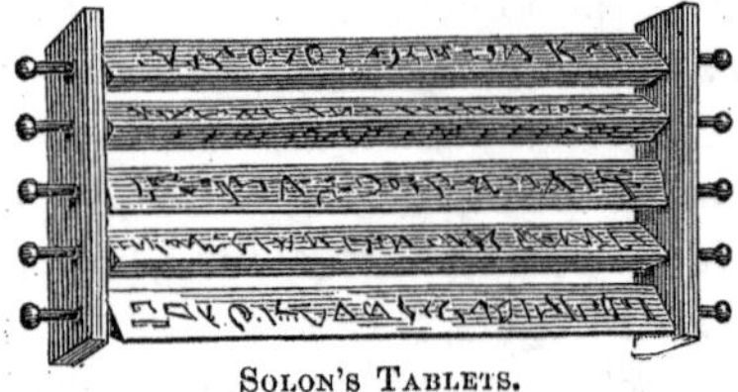

SOLON'S TABLETS.

After Solon's code was adopted, that it might be the better enforced, its author is said to have absented himself from Athens for ten years, visiting among other courts that of Crœsus, King of Lydia. To this visit, Crœsus owed his life; for afterward, when chained to the stake by Cyrus the Persian, the truth of one of Solon's remarks,—that no man can be accounted happy while he still lives,—flashed upon his mind, and he thrice called upon the name of the Athenian sage. Cyrus demanded an explanation of his words, and, struck with the truth of Solon's saying, revoked the order of execution and made Crœsus his friend.

THALES, of Miletus in Ionia (640–550 B.C.), was the founder of Greek philosophy. Water, according to his theory, was the source of all things; without this element, he truly said, his own body would fall into dust. This doctrine he is supposed to have derived from the Egyptians, who worshipped the Nile as a god, being dependent on its annual inundations for their crops.

In mathematical science and astronomy, Thales was an adept. His knowledge of the latter enabled him to predict a solar eclipse, which took place 610 B.C., and to divide the year into three hundred and sixty-five days. If he was an author, not a line of what he wrote has survived.

Fable. — An outgrowth of these practical times was the

Fable, or Allegory, in which the lower animals were introduced as speakers, with the object of satirizing the follies of mankind, or of conveying some useful moral more pointedly than by means of dry argument.

Destitute of the outward form of poetry, while in a measure retaining its imagery, fable may be regarded as a stepping-stone from the early lyrics to the stately prose of a later period. It at once became popular, as did also a kindred class of humorous tales, the characters of which were inanimate objects endowed with the power of speech. An earthen pot, for example, is represented as clamoring loudly against the woman who broke it; and she, as bidding it "cease its plaints and show its wisdom by buying a copper ring to bind itself together."

ÆSOP.—The great fabulist of Greece, and indeed of all time, was Æsop. Born a Phrygian slave about 620 B.C., he passed from one master to another till at last his wit gained him freedom. Thus left to choose his own course, he became a student in foreign lands. Athens was his home for a number of years; and there, in his well-known fable of "the Frogs asking Jupiter for a King," he read a lesson both to Pisistratus the Tyrant and to the people who imagined themselves oppressed under his government.

By special invitation, Æsop spent some time at the court of Crœsus. Here he made the acquaintance of Solon, who had incurred that monarch's displeasure by speaking lightly of his vaunted wealth; and he is said to have admonished the Athenian sage that a wise man should resolve either not to converse with kings at all, or to converse with them agreeably."—"Nay," replied Solon, "he should either not converse with them at all, or converse with them usefully."

Crœsus commissioned Æsop to go to Delphi for the purpose of sacrificing to Apollo and distributing a sum of money among the citizens. But Æsop quarrelled with the Delphians, and taking it upon himself to withhold from them the Lydian gold, was seized by the enraged people and hurled from a precipice. Legend says that the murderers brought upon themselves the vengeance of heaven in the form of mysterious plagues.

While these particulars of Æsop's life rest on rather dubious authority, it is certain that as a fable-writer he was deservedly appreciated in ancient Greece. At Athens, Æsop's Fables became indispensable to a polite education. Their author does not appear to have committed them to writing; they passed from mouth to mouth for generations, undergoing more or less change. Hence we have left only the substance of those pointed stories over which the Athenians went into transports, and which Socrates amused himself by turning into verse during his imprisonment. The young folks of every age, with whom Æsop has always been a favorite, would applaud the Athenians for placing the statue of the world's great fabulist before those of their Seven Sages.

When the people of Samos were on the point of executing a public officer who had robbed the treasury, they were induced to spare the offender by Æsop's spicy fable of

THE FOX AND THE HEDGEHOG.

A Fox, while crossing a river, was driven by the stream into a narrow gorge, and lay there for a long time unable to get out, covered with myriads of horse-flies that had fastened upon him. A Hedgehog, who was wandering in that direction, saw him, and taking compassion on him, asked if he should drive away the flies that were so tormenting him. But the Fox begged him to do nothing of the sort.

"Why not?" asked the Hedgehog.

"Because," replied the Fox, "these flies that are upon me now are already full, and draw but little blood; but should you remove them, a swarm of fresh and hungry ones will come, who will not leave a drop of blood in my body."—JAMES.

Progress of Greek Prose.—An impetus was given to the development of Greek prose by the praiseworthy efforts of

Pisistratus (537–527 B.C.), who gathered the first library in Greece, collected and edited the poems of Homer, and imitated his kinsman Solon in laboring to elevate the literary taste of the people. During his administration and that of his sons Hippias and Hipparchus, also patrons of letters, prose literature took deep root throughout the Ionian colonies, where history and philosophy had many representatives.

The style of these early writers was for the most part fragmentary, dry, and inelegant. It soon improved, however, grew into favor, and in the hands of the profound thinkers, fluent historians, and persuasive orators of Greece, was wrought into models which are still the admiration of the world.

EARLY PROSE WRITERS.

PHILOSOPHERS.

ANAXIMANDER (born 610 B.C.), first map-drawer, and introducer of the sundial. He represented the earth as cylindrical, and as the centre about which the stars and planets revolved; its inhabitants as the result of fermentation caused by the action of the sun's rays on its marshes. His "Treatise on Nature" (547 B.C.), the first work on biology and the earliest philosophical essay written in Greek.

ANAXIM'ENES (born 556 B.C.) made the earth a leaf-shaped mass floating in the air; the sun and moon flat circular bodies; *air* the elementary principle from which all things were made and to which they returned: the soul, air.

HERACLI'TUS of Ephesus (505 B.C.) rejected the nature-worship of his countrymen, and believed in an all-wise, omnipresent Power. He is recorded to have wept continually over the sins of men; hence called the weeping philosopher. *Fire* the first principle. "No man," said he in allusion to the never-ceasing changes in the world, "can wade twice in the same stream."

HISTORIANS.

CADMUS of Miletus (540 B.C.): "Primeval History of Miletus and Ionia."

ACUSILA'US the Argive (525 B.C.): "Genealogies," a prose translation of Hesiod's "Theogony," altered in parts to suit the theories of the author.

HECATÆUS the Milesian (520 – 479 B.C.), "the far-travelled man:" "Genealogies," a history of the mythical heroes of Greece; and a "Description of the Earth," containing a summary of his own travels and explorations.

CHARON of Lampsacus (500–450 B.C.), the first historian to record authentic events: "History of the Persian War," "Annals of Lampsacus," "Chronicles of the Spartan Kings."

HELLANI'CUS of Mўtilene, a noted compiler.

XANTHUS the Lydian: "The Lydiaca," a history of Lydia in four volumes.

SEVEN SAGES AND THEIR MOTTOES.

SOLON of Athens: "Know thyself."

CHI'LO of Sparta: "Consider the end."

THALES of Miletus: "Who hateth suretyship is sure."

BIAS of Priene: "Most men are bad."

CLEOBU'LUS of Lindus: "Avoid extremes."

PIT'TACUS of Mytilene: "Seize time by the forelock."

PERIANDER of Corinth: "Nothing is impossible to industry."

CHAPTER V.

GOLDEN AGE OF GRECIAN LITERATURE.

(480–330 B.C.)

The Attic Period.—In their wars with the Persians (492–479 B.C.), the Hellenic people fully demonstrated their military superiority, vindicating their manhood on the fields of Marathon and Platæa, and in the sea-fight with Xerxes at Salamis. Under the stimulus of these national triumphs, conducing to national unity, as well as of the free institutions now generally established, the Greek mind was awakened to renewed action; literature made unprecedented growth, and in the fifth century B.C. matured its choicest products.

Athens, the laurel-crowned saviour of Greece, hitherto but an indifferent contributor to art and poetry, now became the centre of letters, aspiring through her statesman Pericles (469–429 B.C.) to both literary and political supremacy. Her Attic dialect, nervous but not rough, harmonious without a too effeminate softness—the perfection of the Greek language—materially helped to make her the "mother of eloquence," the home of poets and philosophers, the school of the nations; while Pericles extended her imperial dominion over many cities and islands, and filled her coffers with their tribute. Her sculptor Phidias devoted his genius to the erection and decoration of public edifices; his grand creations in marble adorned her fanes; and the Parthenon, whose classic beauty has passed into a proverb, owed to him its graceful embellishments as well as its renowned statue of Minerva. Another colossal image of the goddess surmounted the Athenian Acropolis, which was crowned with noble temples; and votaries of the sister art added to the attractions of the city with their brush and colors.

It was at this noonday of Attic glory that Grecian literature reached its meridian. Then lyric verse climbed to heights before unattained; and dramatic poetry, tragic and comic, held its listeners spell-bound. History found distinguished representatives in Herodotus the Ionian, and later in Thucydides and Xenophon, the Athenians. Philosophy, in no other age or clime, has had worthier teachers than Socrates, Plato, and Aristotle; while the art of persuasion seemed to be impersonated in Pericles, Isoc'rates, Æschines (*es'ke-neez*), Demosthenes—all true sons of Attica.

LYRIC POETRY.

Pindar.—Lyric poetry culminated in the sublime odes of Pindar, who ushered in the golden age. Pindar was born of noble parents about 520 B.C., near Thebes, a city of Bœotia. The celestials are fabled to have danced at his birth, and the dropping of honey on his infant lips by a swarm of bees was interpreted as an omen of a brilliant literary career.

An early display of poetical talent led his father to yield to the boy's desire and send him to Athens for instruction; thence he returned to Thebes, to study under the direction of the Bœotian poetesses, Myrtis and Corinna, who gave the finishing touches to his education. At the age of twenty, he composed an ode which established his reputation throughout Greece, and brought him into great request with princes and heroes who craved immortality for victories at the national games. Corinna was the rival of his youth; though she reproached Myrtis for entering the lists against Pindar, she was herself tempted to contend with her former pupil, and five times bore away from him the fillet of victory.

Pindar made choral poetry his profession, and was handsomely paid out of the treasuries of the Greek princes and free cities for laudatory odes written to their order. But he never descended to flattery or falsehood; on the contrary, he leavened his panegyrics with salutary advice, and fearlessly denounced pride, cupidity, and tyranny, even in monarchs. To the king of Cyrene, for example, whose tyranny afterward cost him his throne, he said: "It is easy for a fool to shake the stability of a city, but it is hard to place it again on its foundations."

Pindar's home was at Thebes, near Dirce's fountain;* but he travelled much in Greece. For a time he was the honored guest of the Athenians; and no wonder, for when his native city sided with Persia in the deadly struggle with that empire, the poet condemned so pusillanimous a course and upheld Athens in her resistance, styling her "the Pillar of Greece." It is told that he received from the Athenians a gift of 10,000 drachmas ($1,800), and that when the Thebans mulcted him for the bold expression of his views, the former generously paid the fine. At Delphi, which Pindar often visited, the people contributed their finest fruits for his entertainment by

* From which he has been called "the Dircean Swan."

order of the priestess; and an iron chair was set apart for his use in the temple, where he was wont to sit and sing the praises of Apollo, god of poetry. He lived four years with Hiero, and doubtless sojourned with others of his patrons. But Pindar was no boon companion of kings like Simonides, and while he accepted their costly presents he never forfeited the respect of his countrymen.

Pindar died at the age of eighty, in the theatre, it is related, amid the acclamations of the audience. He had been taking part as usual, and overcome with weariness, rested his head on the knees of a favorite pupil, and fell into a slumber from which his friends vainly strove to wake him. A tradition, more in accordance with the Greek love of the marvellous, informs us that a few days before he died Proserpine (goddess of the lower world) appeared to him, and having reproached him for slighting her in his odes, announced that he should soon compose a song in her honor within the confines of her own kingdom. Shortly after, Pindar's death occurred; and on the following day, Thebes resounded with a hymn to Proserpine sung by an old woman, who declared the poet's ghost had dictated it to her in a dream.

Statues were erected to Pindar at Athens and in the hippodrome of Thebes; a hundred years after, when Alexander the Great destroyed the latter city in consequence of its rebellion, he bade his soldiers spare the house hallowed by having once been the residence of the Theban bard. Statues and dwelling have since passed away, and the only surviving monument of Pindar is that reared by himself in the deathless odes he has left us.

THE PINDARIC ODE.—Pindar's fertile pen enriched every department of lyric poetry; but all his compositions are lost except a few fragments of pæans and dirges, with forty-five Triumphal Odes (which we have entire) written to commemorate victories at the Great Games of Greece.

These games were celebrated at Olympia, Delphi, Neme'a, and on the Corinthian Isthmus: they consisted of athletic sports, races, literary and musical contests. All Greece was represented at them. Peasant and prince, trader and priest, poet and historian, painter and sculptor, hurried to the exciting scene as contestants or spectators; and the simple crown of olive or laurel, pine or parsley, that was placed on the conqueror's brow, was valued beyond price. All that was needed to complete the triumph was an ode in its honor from the Great Lyrist. This, when obtained, was sung at an honorary banquet or solemn procession, amid great rejoicings; and was annually rehearsed in the victor's native town to the accompaniment of soul-stirring music—for his family, town, and state, participated in the victor's glory.

PINDAR'S STYLE is original, chaste, full of splendor and majestic energy. The Theban eagle, as he has often been called, soaring to the sun, seems to disdain the commonplace in his solitary flight. His style, however, is not faultless. The over-boldness of his metaphors confuses; his massing of magnificent images and high-sounding epithets wearies; his Doric condensation obscures his meaning; his metre is too complicated for the uneducated ear, and his transitions are so abrupt that the reader has difficulty in finding the connection. His subjects were hard to treat; but Pindar found material and lent variety to his odes by skilfully interweaving legendary lore, history, and fragments of mythology. This was by Corinna's advice; but her young pupil carried it to such excess in his first attempt that his fair teacher warned him, "One should sow with the hand, not with the whole sack."

Pindar's tone is everywhere moral. He merits indeed the title of "Sacerdotal Poet;" for he upheld the religion of Greece in its purity, rejecting all sensual notions of "the blessed ones," and asserting his faith in their holiness and justice. He taught the immortality of the soul; "things of a day" are men, but after death there is in store "a gladsome life." His belief in an existence beyond the grave is indicated in the following lines from one of his dirges. And here be it observed that no translation can do justice to Pindar; the Doric diamonds cease to flash when removed from their Doric setting.

"Shines for them the sun's warm glow,
When 'tis darkness here below;
And the ground before their towers,
Meadow-land with purple flowers,
Teems with incense-bearing treen,
Teems with fruit of golden sheen.
Some in steed and wrestling feat,
Some in dice take pleasure sweet,
Some in harping: at their side
Blooms the spring in all her pride.
Fragrance all about is blown
O'er that country of desire,
Ever as rich gifts are thrown
Freely on the far-seen fire,
Blazing from the altar-stone.
But the souls of the profane
Far from heaven removed below,
Flit on earth in murderous pain,
'Neath the unyielding yoke of woe;
While pious spirits tenanting the sky
Chant praises to the mighty one on high."

CONINGTON.

The more characteristic extract given below consists of portions of the Seventh Olympic Ode, in which the poet sings the praises of Diag'oras of Rhodes for having gained a victory with the cestus (made of leather thongs and worn round the hands in boxing). This ode was so much admired by the Rhodians that they wrote it in golden letters on the wall of Minerva's temple at Lindus. It relates the birth of their patron goddess and the story of their own origin, closing with an invocation to Jupiter, who was worshipped on Ataby'ris, a mountain of the island. Here stood a temple, dedicated to him, containing the fabulous brazen bulls that bellowed when any calamity threatened.

ODE TO DIAGORAS.

"As when a sire the golden bowl,
All foaming with the dew of wine,
Takes with a liberal hand and soul,
Chief gem where all his treasures shine—
Then tends the beverage (hallowed first
By prayers to all the powers above)
To slake the youthful bridegroom's thirst,
In honor of connubial love;
The social pledge he bears on high,
And, homeward as his course he bends,
Blesses the fond connubial tie,
Admired by all his circling friends;

E'en thus I bring the nectared strain,
The Muses' gift, to those who gain
The Pythian and Olympic crown;
Thrice blest, to whom 'tis given to share
The arduous fruit of mental care,
Cheered by the voice of high renown!
Full many a victor in the fray
My life-inspiring strains survey—
Which bid the sweet-toned lyre its music raise,
And wake the sounding flutes through all their notes of praise.

And now, Diagoras, to thee
They breathe united melody.
When Rhodes, the warlike isle, is sung,
Apollo's bride from Venus sprung;
He too, the hero brave and bold,
With hardy frame of giant mould,
Who, by Alphe'us' sacred tide,
And where Castalia's waters glide,
First in the cestus' manly fray,
Bore the triumphant prize away.
Let Damage'tus next, his sire,
To justice dear, the strain inspire.
Fixed on that isle which three fair cities grace,
Where Embolus protects wide Asia's coast,
They dwell united with the Argive host.

In that blest isle secure at last,
'Twas thine, Tlepolemus, to meet
For each afflictive trial past
A recompense and respite sweet.

Chief of Tirynthian hosts, to thee,
As to a present deity,
The fumes of slaughtered sheep arise
In all the pomp of sacrifice:
Awarded by thy just decree,
The victor gains his verdant prize—
That crown whose double honors glow,
Diagoras, around thy brow;
On which four times the Isthmian pine,
And twice the Nemean olive shine:
While Athens on her rocky throne
Made her illustrious wreath his own.

Trophies of many a well-fought field
He won in glory's sacred cause,
The Theban tripod, brazen shield
At Argos, and Arcadia's vase.
Her palms Bœotia's genuine contests yield;
Six times Ægina's prize he gained,
As oft Pellene's robe obtained,
And graved in characters of fame,
Thy column, Megara, records his name.

Great sire of all, immortal Jove!
On Atabyris' mount enshrined,
Oh! still may thy propitious mind
The encomiastic hymn approve,
Which celebrates in lawful strain
The victor on Olympia's plain,
Whose valorous arm the cestus knows to wield.

Protected by thy constant care,
In citizens' and strangers' eyes
Still more exalted shall he rise
Whose virtuous deeds thy favor share:
Since he, to violence and fraud unknown,
Treads the straight paths of equity alone;
His fathers' counsels mindful to pursue,
And keep their bright example still in view.
Then let not inactivity disgrace
The well-earned fame of thine illustrious race,
Who sprang from great Calli′anax, and crown
The Erat′idæ with splendor all their own.
With joy and festal hymns the streets resound—
But soon, as shifts the ever-varying gale,
The storms of adverse fortune may assail—
Then, Rhodians, be your mirth with sober temperance crowned."—WHEELWRIGHT.

Antimachus.—An elegiac poet of the golden age was Antim'achus of Col'ophon, whose "Ly'de," an elegy on his lost love, enjoyed considerable celebrity. When, however, Antimachus undertook to read his long "Theba'is" to an audience, their patience became exhausted and one after another departed, until finally he had but a single listener left,—the young Plato.

DRAMATIC POETRY.

Rise of the Attic Drama.—The Greek drama, like the Hindoo, had a religious origin. In the festivals of Bacchus, the wine-god, which consisted of licentious dances and songs round his altar by persons disguised in goat-skins as fauns and satyrs (beings half-man and half-goat), we must look for its earliest phase. From the dress of those who composed the chorus, or because a goat was sacrificed, or a goat-skin of wine awarded to the poet who wrote the best ode for the occasion, such ode was called a *tragedy* (*goat-song*); and the name was afterward extended to the entire department of dramatic poetry to which these rude hymns gave rise.

Comedy, on the contrary, was elaborated from the *village-songs* rife during the gala-days of the vintage, when companies of noisy revellers,* their cheeks stained with wine-lees, went about from town to town, plunging into all kinds of excesses, and garnishing their songs with jokes at the expense of the spectators.

The Father of Greek tragedy was THESPIS, the Athenian, who refined the coarse Bacchanalian orgies, and introduced a single actor (generally sustaining the part himself), to alternate with the chorus or enter into a dialogue with its leaders (536 B.C.). Between the hymns, the poet, having smeared his face with paint, would mount a table and recite with copious

---

* Some derive our word *comedy* from *kōmos*, the Greek term for a band of revellers.

gestures some mythological legend, perhaps relating to Bacchus.

With a trained chorus, Thespis strolled about Greece, stopping at the towns to give his exhibitions on the wagon which carried his machinery and skin-clad troupe. Dancing was a prominent feature of his entertainments. His pupil Phryn′icus improved the performance by exchanging myths for real events and introducing female characters; but the recitations were still disconnected and the plays lacked method; albeit Phrynicus was fined by the Athenians for moving their feelings too deeply by one of his pieces.

Birth of Tragedy.—Out of these rude materials, Æschylus, who was born about ten years after the first Thespian exhibition, constructed genuine tragedy. He added a second actor and remodelled the chorus, making it secondary to the dialogue, and instituting a connection between its songs and the events represented on the stage. Appropriate theatrical costumes, stationary scenery, painted masks, and thick-soled buskins to increase the height of the performers, complete the list of his innovations. Thus the goat-song of early days developed into the true drama (*action*), the crowning effort of Greek genius. Athens had the honor of creating and perfecting it; while in other departments of verse she fell behind her neighbors, in dramatic poetry she eclipsed them all.

The love of the theatre grew into a passion at Athens. When the first rude structure of boards gave way under the weight of the audience, her citizens erected a permanent edifice of semicircular form, whose seats, rising in tiers, were hewn in the rocky side of the Acropolis. This new theatre accommodated thirty thousand persons, who sat under the shadow of Athens' patron-goddess, and with reverent gaze watched actors and chorus go through their parts round the altar of Bacchus.

The performances took place by day, and in the open air,

the theatre not being roofed. They began immediately after the morning meal, and on great occasions seats were secured and occupied during the preceding night. It was the custom of those who desired a comfortable sitting to bring their own cushions. Tickets of admission at first cost one drachma (18 cents); but Pericles reduced the price to six cents, and thus placed dramatic entertainments within the reach of the poorest citizens. The audience sometimes remained in the theatre twelve hours, gossiping during the intervals, and refreshing themselves with cake, wine, and sweetmeats.—In ancient Greece, the actor's profession was lucrative and highly honorable; dramatic authors not unfrequently performed parts in their own plays.

Under the favoring skies of Athens the drama advanced to perfection with marvellous rapidity. In the hands of Æschylus it was all grandeur; Sophocles invested it with beauty, and Euripides with pathos. These three tragic poets, almost contemporaries, were the brightest ornaments of the Attic capital, where there were many bright. Their triumphs cover a period of seventy-eight years (484–406 B.C.), including the proud age of Pericles, but extending beyond it till the Peloponnesian War had deprived Athens of her supremacy. Simultaneously with Sophocles and Euripides flourished Aristophanes, under whom comedy reached its climax.

It has been computed that during the golden age 250 dramatic poets flourished, who produced more than 3,400 plays. Out of this vast number, only 44 have survived to our time.

Æschylus (525–456 B.C.).—Eleusis, a hamlet of Attica, was the birthplace of Æschylus. It is related that in his youth he was charged with watching grapes, and overcome by slumber, saw Bacchus in his dreams, who bade him devote himself to tragedy. The boy forgot not the injunction; he applied himself diligently to study, and in his twenty-fifth year contended, though unsuccessfully, for the chaplet of ivy.

Ten years afterward, he acquitted himself so bravely in the battle of Marathon as to receive a special prize, and have his deeds immortalized in a painting which was hung in the theatre at Athens. He also won distinction at Salamis and Platæa; and the name of one of his brothers was long remembered in connection with the sinking of the Persian admiral's galley. During the flourishing period of Athenian history that followed, the literary reputation of Æschylus became as great as his military renown. He was the hero of thirteen poetical victories.

In 468 B.C. Æschylus left Athens for the court of Hiero, the Syracusan prince, round which so many great men clustered. According to some, the unjust award of the tragic prize to Sophocles, for political reasons, was the cause of his going. The more probable account is that his exile followed a public accusation of impiety, for disclosing certain religious mysteries in one of his plays. The popular excitement ran high; the poet was attacked with stones, when his brother happily averted the fury of the mob by uncovering before them the stump of his own arm, which had been mutilated at Salamis in defence of his country.

Hiero received our author hospitably; and the poet made return by writing for him a drama called "the Women of Etna." Æschylus may have visited Athens after this; but if so, he returned to Sicily to die, in the sixty-ninth year of his age. While he sat in a field near Gela absorbed in thought, so the fable goes, an eagle, hovering over the spot with a tortoise in its talons, let the tortoise fall on his bald crown, which it mistook for a shining cobble-stone, for the purpose of breaking the shell. The bird's aim was true; and the blow fractured the poet's skull. Thus, in fulfilment of an oracular prediction, Æschylus received his death-stroke from heaven.

In sublimity and power of dealing with the terrible, Æschylus is unequalled. Even the resources of the versatile Greek tongue were hardly adequate to the expression of his conceptions. He found congenial subjects only among the gods and demigods of mythology or the tragical events of the heroic period. His genius enabled him to give life and shape to the vast and the supernatural, as few others have done—and most effectively, though his plot is always simple.

Sir Walter Scott thus speaks of Æschylus in his Essay on the Drama:—"At his summons, the mysterious and tremendous volume of destiny, in which are inscribed the dooms of gods and men, seemed to display its leaves of iron before the appalled spectators; the more than mortal voices of deities, Titans, and departed heroes, were heard in awful conference; Olympus bowed, and its divinities descended; earth yawned, and gave up the pale spectres of the dead; and the yet more undefined and grisly forms of those infernal deities who struck horror into the gods themselves. All this could only be dared and done by a poet of the highest order."

But seven of the seventy-five tragedies of Æschylus are extant. Of these, "Prometheus Chained" is considered the greatest, and from it we have selected our extracts. The opening scene is laid on the grim ocean's shore near frowning Caucasus, to which, in obedience to Jove's command, the giant Prometheus is to be chained. For thirty thousand years a vulture is to tear his vitals, constantly growing out afresh, as a punishment for his having given fire to mortals, and taught them useful arts in opposition to the will of heaven. Strength and Force, grandly personified, drag the victim to the place of torture; and Vulcan, the god of fire, rivets his fetters to the rock. The chorus is composed of sea-nymphs, who come to offer their sympathy to the sufferer and advise him to submit; but Prometheus, who is the embodiment of stern independence, fortitude, and decision, endures unyieldingly to the last. Even amid "the thunder's deepening roar, blazing wreaths of lightning, and eddying sands whirled on high," while the earth rocks to its centre, and "boisterous billows rise, confounding sea and sky," he hurls a proud defiance at his oppressors.

SCENE FROM PROMETHEUS CHAINED.

STROPHE.

"Thy dire disasters, unexampled wrongs,
I weep, Prometheus.
From its soft founts distilled, the flowing tear
My cheek bedashes.
'Tis hard, most hard! By self-made laws Jove rules,
And 'gainst the host of primal gods he points
The lordly spear.

ANTISTROPHE.

With echoing groans the ambient waste bewails
Thy fate, Prometheus;
The neighboring tribes of holy Asia weep
For thee, Prometheus.
For thee and thine! names mighty and revered
Of yore, now shamed, dishonored, and cast down,
And chained with thee.

STROPHE.

And Colchis, with her belted daughters, weeps
For thee, Prometheus;
And Scythian tribes, on earth's remotest verge,
Where lone Mæotis* spreads her wintry waters,
Do weep for thee.

ANTISTROPHE.

The flower of Araby's wandering warriors weep
For thee, Prometheus;
And they who high their airy holds have perched
On Caucasus' ridge, with pointed lances bristling,
Do weep for thee.

---

* The Sea of Azof.

EPODE.

One only vexed like thee, and even as thou
In adamant bound,
A Titan, and a god scorned by the gods,
Atlas I knew.
He on his shoulders the surpassing weight
Of the celestial pole stoutly upbore,
And groaned beneath.
Roars billowy Ocean, and the Deep sucks back
Its waters when he sobs; from earth's dark caves
Deep hell resounds;
The fountains of the holy-streaming rivers
Do moan with him.

PROMETHEUS.—Deem me not self-willed nor with pride
high-strung,
That I am dumb; my heart is gnawed to see
Myself thus mocked and jeered. These gods, to whom
Owe they their green advancement but to me?
But this ye know; and, not to teach the taught,
I'll speak of it no more. Of human kind,
My great offence in aiding them, in teaching
The babe to speak, and rousing torpid mind
To take the grasp of itself—of this I'll talk;
Meaning to mortal men no blame, but only
The true recital of mine own deserts.
For, soothly, having eyes to see they saw not,
And hearing heard not; but, like dreamy phantoms,
A random life they led from year to year,
All blindly floundering on. No craft they knew
With woven brick or jointed beam to pile
The sunward porch; but in the dark earth burrowed
And housed, like tiny ants in sunless caves.
No signs they knew to mark the wintry year:
The flower-strewn Spring, and the fruit-laden Summer,
Uncalendared, unregistered, returned—
Till I the difficult art of the stars revealed,
Their risings and their settings. Numbers, too,
I taught them (a most choice device), and how
By marshalled signs to fix their shifting thoughts,
That Memory, mother of Muses, might achieve
Her wondrous works. I first slaved to the yoke
Both ox and ass. I, the rein-loving steeds
(Of wealth's gay-flaunting pomp the chiefest pride)
Joined to the car; and bade them ease the toils
Of laboring men vicarious. I the first
Upon the lint-winged car of mariner

Was launched, sea-wandering. Such wise arts I found,
To soothe the ills of man's ephemeral life;
But for myself, plunged in this depth of woe,
No prop I find.

CHORUS.—Sad chance! Thy wit hath slipt
From its firm footing then when needed most,
Like some unlearned leech who many healed,
But being sick himself, from all his store,
Cannot cull out one medicinal drug.

PROMETHEUS.—Hear me yet further; and in hearing marvel,
What arts and curious shifts my wit devised.
Chiefest of all, the cure of dire disease
Men owe to me. Nor healing food, nor drink,
Nor unguent knew they, but did slowly wither
And waste away for lack of pharmacy,
Till taught by me to mix the soothing drug
And check corruption's march. I fixed the art
Of divination with its various phase
Of dim revealings, making dreams speak truth,
Stray voices, and encounters by the way
Significant; the flight of taloned birds
On right and left I marked—these fraught with ban,
With blissful augury those. I first did wrap
In the smooth fat the thighs; first burnt the loins,
And from the flickering flame taught men to spell
No easy lore, and cleared the fire-faced signs*
Obscure before. Yet more: I probed the earth,
To yield its hidden wealth to help man's weakness—
Iron, copper, silver, gold. None but a fool,
A prating fool, will stint me of this praise.
And thus, with one short word to sum the tale,
Prometheus taught all arts to mortal men."

JOHN STUART BLACKIE.

Prometheus may be regarded as typifying the spirit of progress, bound by the shackles of inevitable destiny, chafing under its enslavement, but enduring contumely and suffering rather than yield to tyranny. The weird wail of Io on leaving Prometheus, wrung from her by the persecution of Juno, is thus rendered by Mrs. Browning, with all the wildness and fire of the original:—

* The sacrificial flame, from which omens were taken.

"Io.—Eleleu! Eleleu!
How the spasm and the pain,
And the fire on the brain,
Strike me burning through!
How the sting of the curse, all aflame as it flew,
Pricks me onward again!
How my heart, in its terror, is spurning my breast!
And my eyes, like the wheels of a chariot, roll round;
I am whirled from my course, to the east and the west,
In the whirlwind of frenzy all madly inwound—
And my mouth is unbridled for anguish and hate,
And my words beat in vain, in wild storms of unrest,
On the sea of desolate fate."

EXTANT PLAYS OF ÆSCHYLUS.

PROMETHEUS CHAINED.

SEVEN AGAINST THEBES. Founded on the siege of Thebes by seven Argive chiefs, who espouse the cause of Polyni'ces against his brother Ete'ocles, the latter having seized the crown contrary to agreement. A great favorite, and the poet's special pride.

THE PERSIANS. Subject, the overthrow of Xerxes: thought to be the oldest Greek drama extant.

THE SUPPLIANTS. Danaus and his fifty daughters solicit of the king of Argos protection from their enemies. The weakest of the seven.

AGAMEMNON. The murder of Agamemnon, on his return from Troy, by his wife Clytemnestra and her paramour Ægisthus, is the material part of the plot.

CHOËPHORÆ (libation-bearers). Based on the avenging of the crime by Orestes, Agamemnon's son, who slays his mother and her guilty partner.

THE FURIES. Here we have the pursuit of the parricide by the Furies.—Clytemnestra, the Lady Macbeth of the Greek stage; her deep-laid plan, her cunning welcome of her husband, the fatal strokes dealt by her own hand, her fiendish glorying in the deed of blood,—touched with masterly skill.

The three tragedies last named constitute what is called a *trilogy*, or group of three dramas founded upon one story. "Prometheus Chained" was one of a trilogy, of which the other two members are lost.

Sophocles (495–405 B.C.), the rival of Æschylus, was born at Colo'nus, an Attic borough a short mile from the capital. He was fortunate in having a father able to give him a liberal education, and entered the service of the Muses at an early age. His skill in music and the exercises of the gymnasium won him many a garland; and when hardly sixteen, unrobed and crowned, he led the choir of boys with his ivory lyre in the chant of triumph which the Athenians poured forth round the trophy raised at Salamis.

Sophocles made his début as a tragic writer in that successful contest with Æschylus which, some think, cost Athens her grand old dramatist. Fame spread the news, and Greece looked to Sophocles as the coming man. A succession of plays extended his popularity. He added nineteen prizes to the one wrested from Æschylus in 468 B.C. In the year 440 he completed the drama of "Antig'one," the oldest of his seven surviving tragedies, which secured for him an important official position. The "Antigone" ushered in the most active portion of its author's literary life, during which eighty-one of his pieces were written. Although history throws little light on this period of his career, we know that, unlike his great contemporaries, he never left his native city to enjoy the munificence of foreign patrons. The Greek theatre was indebted to him for a third actor, improvements in scenery, and a further modification of the chorus, which no longer took an active part in the play.

In his eightieth year, Sophocles was charged with imbecility by an ungrateful son, who regarded with jealous eyes his partiality for a favorite grandchild, and hoped in this way to obtain control of his property. The defence of the alleged dotard was to read before his judges a choral song from a play which he had just finished—"Œdipus at Colonus" (p. 206). The vindication was complete; the judges at once rendered a decision in the old poet's favor, and in a burst of enthusiasm bore him home in triumph. He died at the age of ninety. Some tell us that while he was repeating the pathetic plaints of his "Antigone," his breath suddenly ceased; others, that after gaining a tragic victory, he died of excessive joy as the crown was placed on his brow. He left the Athenians 113 dramas.

STYLE OF SOPHOCLES.—As Æschylus is the impersonation of grandeur, so is Sophocles of beauty and harmony. He descends from the sublime heights Æschylus loved to tread, and, appealing to our sympathy with humanity, finds his way into the secret chambers of the heart. His language is pure; his style, elegant, dignified, vivacious—faultless; in allusion to his sweet diction, he was called by the ancients *the Bee of Attica.* The type of manly beauty and intellectual power, æsthetic culture and lofty morality, it seems as if Sophocles had been "specially created to represent Greek art in its most refined and exquisitely balanced perfection."

THE MASTERPIECE OF SOPHOCLES is "King Œdipus." Laïus, a Theban monarch, told by an oracle (such was the legend) that his children would be the cause of his death, had his infant son Œdipus exposed on Mount Cithæron, hoping thus to escape his destiny. But the boy was discovered by some herdsmen and carried to Corinth, where he grew to man's estate as the adopted son and heir of the king.

Warned at the Delphic shrine to beware of his native land lest he should imbrue his hands in his father's blood, and believing Corinth to be his birthplace, he withdrew to Thebes; but on the way he met Laïus, and, not knowing who he was, killed him in a quarrel. Arrived at Thebes, he won the hand of the widow Jocasta, his own mother, who bore him four children. All went well for a time. At length, however, an epidemic broke out; and the oracle assigned as its cause the presence of the late king's murderer. Œdipus strained every nerve to discover the offender, and at last, to his horror, fastened the crime, and the more terrible guilt of parricide, upon himself. Unhappy Jocasta hanged herself in the palace, and Œdipus in his frenzy beat out his eyes with her gold-embossed buckles.

The play opens at Thebes, during the plague. Œdipus, in conversation with a priest and Creon, Jocasta's brother, is informed of Apollo's will,—that, to avert the evil, the land must be purified by the punishment of the assassin. After the catastrophe above related, blinded Œdipus bemoans his lot in heart-rending utterances, but finally accepts his fate with resignation. We give the

CLOSING SCENE OF KING ŒDIPUS.

[*Enter Creon.*]

"CREON.—I have not come, O Œdipus, to scorn,
Nor to reproach thee for thy former crimes;
But ye, if ye have lost your sense of shame
For mortal men, yet reverence the light
Of him, our King, the Sun-god, source of life,
Nor sight so foul expose unveiled to view,
Which neither earth, nor shower from heaven, nor light,
Can see and welcome. But with utmost speed
Convey him in; for nearest kin alone
Can meetly see and hear their kindred's ills.
ŒDIPUS.—Oh! by the gods! since thou, beyond my hopes,
Dost come all noble unto me all base,
In one thing hearken. For thy good I ask.
CREON.—And what request seek'st thou so wistfully?
ŒDIPUS.—Cast me with all thy speed from out this land,
Where never more a man may look on me!
CREON.—Be sure I would have done so, but I wished
To learn what now the God will bid us do.
ŒDIPUS.—The oracle was surely clear enough
That I, the parricide, the pest, should die.
CREON.—So ran the words. But in our present need
'Tis better to learn surely what to do.
ŒDIPUS.—And will ye ask for one so vile as I?
CREON.—Yea, now thou too would'st trust the voice of God.
ŒDIPUS.—And this I charge thee, yea, and supplicate:
For her within, provide what tomb thou wilt,
For for thine own most meetly thou wilt care.
But never let this city of my fathers
Be sentenced to receive me as its guest;
But suffer me on yon lone hills to dwell,
Where stands Cithæron, chosen as my tomb
While still I lived, by mother and by sire,
That I may die by those who sought to kill.
And for my boys, O Creon, lay no charge
Of them upon me. They are grown, nor need,
Where'er they be, feel lack of means to live.
But for my two poor girls, all desolate,

To whom their table never brought a meal
Without my presence, but whate'er I touched
They still partook of with me—these I care for.
Yea, let me touch them with my hands, and weep
To them my sorrows. Grant it, O my prince!
O born of noble nature!
Could I but touch them with my hands, I feel
Still I should have them mine, as when I saw.

[*Enter Antigone and Ismene.*]

What say I? What is this?
Do I not hear, ye gods! their dear, loved tones,
Broken with sobs, and Creon, pitying me,
Hath sent the dearest of my children to me?
Is it not so?

CREON.—It is so. I am he who gives thee this,
Knowing the joy thou hadst in them of old.

ŒDIPUS.—Good luck have thou! And may the Powers on high
Guard thy path better than they guarded mine!
Where are ye, O my children? Come, oh! come
To these your brother's hands, which but now tore
Your father's eyes, that once were bright to see,
Who, O my children, blind and knowing naught,
Became your father—how, I may not tell.
I weep for you, though sight is mine no more,
Picturing in mind the sad and dreary life
Which waits you in the world in years to come;
For to what friendly gatherings will ye go,
Or festive joys, from whence, for stately show,
Once yours, ye shall not home return in tears?
Who is there, O my children, rash enough
To make his own the shame that then will fall
On those who bore me, and on you as well?
What evil fails us here? Such shame as this
Will men lay on you, and who then will dare
To make you his in marriage? None, not one,
My children! but ye needs must waste away,
Unwedded, childless. Thou, Menœceus' son,
Since thou alone art left a father to them,
Suffer them not to wander husbandless,
Nor let thy kindred beg their daily bread;
But look on them with pity, seeing them
At their age, but for thee, deprived of all.
O noble soul, I pray thee, touch my hand
In token of consent. And ye, my girls,
Had ye the minds to hearken, I would fain
Give ye much counsel. As it is, pray for me

To live where'er is meet; and for yourselves
A brighter life than his ye call your sire.
CREON.—Enough of tears and words. Go thou within.
ŒDIPUS.—I needs must yield, however hard it be.
CREON.—In their right season, all things prosper best.
ŒDIPUS.—Know'st thou my wish?
CREON.— Speak, and I then shall hear.
ŒDIPUS.—That thou should'st send me far away from home?
CREON.—Thou askest what the gods alone can give.
ŒDIPUS.—And yet I go most hated of the gods.
CREON.—And therefore it may chance thou gain'st thy wish.
ŒDIPUS.—And dost thou promise, then, to grant it me?
CREON.—I am not wont to utter idle words.
ŒDIPUS.—Lead me then hence.
CREON.— Go thou, but leave the girls.
ŒDIPUS.—Ah! take them not from me.
CREON.— Thou must not think
To have thy way in all things all thy life.
Thou hadst it once, yet went it ill with thee.

CHORUS.—Ye men of Thebes, behold this Œdipus,
Who knew the famous riddle* and was noblest,
Who envied no one's fortune and success:
And lo! in what a sea of direst woe
He now is plunged. From hence the lesson draw,
To reckon no man happy till ye see
The closing day; until he pass the bourn
Which severs life from death, unscathed by woe."—PLUMPTRE.

Œdipus ended his days in exile at Colonus, where he was received by Theseus, the hero of Attica, and attended to the last by his faithful daughter Antigone. His death is the subject of the play "Œdipus at Colonus," written at the close of the poet's life and reflecting the gentleness and serenity of his last days. It contains one of the gems of Sophocles—that chorus which has immortalized the lovely scenery about Colonus—which the old poet recited before the Athenian judges to prove his sanity. Bulwer furnishes us a spirited version of this famous passage:—The chorus informs the outcast Œdipus that he has come to Colonus,

---

* The riddle proposed by the Sphinx: "What animal is that which goes on four feet in the morning, two at noon, and three at evening?" The answer of Œdipus was, *Man.*

"Where ever and aye, through the greenest vale,
Gush the wailing notes of the nightingale,
From her home where the dark-hued ivy weaves
With the grove of the god a night of leaves;
And the vines blossom out from the lonely glade,
And the suns of the summer are dim in the shade,
And the storms of the winter have never a breeze,
That can shiver a leaf from the charmèd trees;
For there, oh! ever there
With that fair mountain throng,
Who his sweet nurses were,
Wild Bacchus holds his court, the conscious woods among!
Daintily, ever there,
Crown of the mighty goddesses of old,
Clustering Narcissus with his glorious hues
Springs from his bath of heaven's delicious dews,
And the gay crocus sheds his rays of gold.
And wandering there forever
The fountains are at play,
And Cephissus feeds his river
From their sweet urns, day by day;
The river knows no dearth;
Adown the vale the lapsing waters glide,
And the pure rain of that pellucid tide
Calls the rife beauty from the heart of earth;
While by the banks the Muses' choral train
Are duly heard—and there Love checks her golden rein."

EXTANT PLAYS OF SOPHOCLES.

King Œdipus: this and the next two tragedies form a trilogy.

Œdipus at Colonus: well adapted to flatter the local pride of the Athenians.

Antigone: based on the story of "the Seven against Thebes." Antigone was the daughter of Œdipus. Her uncle, King Creon, forbids the burial of her brother Polyni'ces, the instigator of the war and one of its victims. Sisterly affection proves stronger than fear of the royal decree; Antigone performs the last sad offices for her brother, and is entombed alive for her disobedience.

The Trachinian Women: subject, the poisoning of Hercules by his wife Deïanira.

Electra: called from the heroine, Electra, daughter of Agamemnon, who is overpowered by hatred for her unnatural mother and Ægisthus. The plot culminates with the slaughter of the guilty pair by Orestes the avenger. Finest passage, the meeting between Orestes and his sister.

Ajax: founded upon the madness of Ajax in consequence of the bestowal of Achilles' arms on Ulysses in preference to himself; his suicide and funeral.

PHILOCTE'TES: the hero was a Thessalian prince, whom the Greeks treacherously abandoned on the island of Lemnos. Afterward, when informed by the oracle that Troy would not fall until the arrows of Hercules, which Philoctetes had, were brought to bear on its defenders, they induced him to take part in the war.

Euripides.—In 480 B.C., on the island of Salamis, while the battle that was to decide the future of Greece raged in the neighboring waters, Euripides first saw the light. Æschylus, in his prime, was at the time bravely fighting on an Athenian galley; while Sophocles, but fifteen years of age, stood ready, should the gods grant his countrymen success, to celebrate the victory with the arts in which he excelled.

The third of the illustrious tragic trio was carefully trained; painting, rhetoric, and philosophy, besides the customary gymnastic exercises, engaged his attention; and he had not attained his eighteenth year when he finished his first drama. Not, however, until 441 B.C. did he, by winning the tragic prize, verify a prediction made before his birth that he would be crowned with sacred chaplets.

His reputation was now secure; and though he was exposed to bitter partisan attacks, his plays became widely popular. The philosopher Socrates always went to see them performed, and is even suspected of having had a hand in their composition. So great was the estimation in which they were held at Syracuse, that, after the surrender of the Athenian armies which had attempted the reduction of that city (413 B.C.), such of the soldiers as could teach their captors verses of Euripides were exempted from the cruelties inflicted on their fellows, and sent home to thank the author for their liberty. Athens itself is said to have been saved nine years later, when the Spartan general Lysander was minded to lay it in ashes, by the singing of a chorus of Euripides at the triumphal banquet; who could raise his hand against the city of one that had discoursed poetry so sweet?

Like his brother tragedians, Euripides drew his subjects from the mythical history of his country. His plays numbered seventy-five, some say ninety-two; and the best of them rank with the best pieces on the roll of dramatic literature. He composed slowly and with care. On one occasion, it is related, when he had completed only four verses in three days, Euripides was told by a poetaster that in the same time *he* had produced a hundred. "And yours," replied the great man, "will live for three days; mine, forever."

Euripides spent the last two years of his life at the Macedonian court, then the abode of many illustrious men. He went there in search of rest, but found that he had only exchanged persecution at home for jealousy abroad. The honors heaped upon him by the Macedonian prince, together with his own superior genius, raised him up enemies. In the king's savage hounds, if we may credit the legend, they saw the means of removing an obnoxious rival; and while Euripides was walking in his patron's garden, he was attacked and fatally mangled by the fierce brutes (406 B.C.).

Athens felt the loss, and went into mourning at news of his death; vainly she supplicated the Macedonian king for his ashes. They were magnificently interred at Pella; while his country was forced to remain content with a statue, and a cenotaph on which was inscribed, "All Greece is the monument of Euripides." His verses, as he predicted, were immortal; admiration of them led an epigrammatist to write:

> "If it be true that in the grave the dead
> Have sense and knowledge, as some men have said,
> I'd hang myself to see Euripides."

With Euripides, the glory of the Athenian stage descended

into the tomb; and Tragedy found no one worthy to fill his place till Shakespeare's day.

Style of Euripides.—Sophocles once remarked that he represented men as they ought to be, Euripides as they are. This holding of the mirror up to nature was what Athenian taste began to demand; Euripides had the tact to see what was wanted, and the genius to make the innovation successfully. His heroes and heroines talked and acted like men and women of the day; hence he has been accused of degrading his art by introducing the commonplace into his dramas, of lowering Greek tragedy to the level of every-day life.

A more serious charge also was laid at his door—that of impiety. Euripides rejected the faith of his fathers; we need not, therefore, look in his plays for the religious fervor of Æschylus, or even for the high moral tone of Sophocles. In one of his lines the doctrine of mental reservation appears,

"My tongue took an oath, but my mind is unsworn"—

a sentiment which led to his prosecution for justifying perjury.

While Euripides was inferior to Æschylus in majesty, to Sophocles in symmetry and finish, he surpassed both in delineating character, and particularly in representing the human passions. He was the most pathetic of the three, and in the portraiture of woman stands second to no poet, ancient or modern. His heroines are his master-figures. Traces of art are sometimes apparent in his writings, and occasionally he verges on the sensational.

The Mede'a is the *chef d'œuvre* of this author. Its plot is derived from the story of Medea, a Colchian princess proficient in sorcery. She won the love of the Greek prince Jason, who came to Colchis in the ship Argo to obtain possession of the Golden Fleece, helped him to secure the object of his search, and eloped with him to Greece. But when Jason beheld the fair Glaucè, daughter of the King of Corinth, he resolved to thrust aside Medea in favor of his new love, forgetful of the dark power of the enchantress.

The opening scene is laid at Corinth, after the nuptials of Jason and Glaucè. The infidelity of her husband has transformed Medea into a tigress, whose conflicting passions the poet touches with consummate skill—the anger of the dishonored wife, the love of the tender mother, the steeling of the woman's heart against its deep affection, the all-absorbing thirst for vengeance.

The play ends with Medea's terrible revenge. Banished by the king from Corinth, she begs for one day of preparation, in which she sends to the bride a costly robe and golden wreath poisoned by her fell arts. The unsuspecting Glaucè smilingly arrays herself in these presents; but her smiles give place to shrieks of agony as the enchanted garments burn into her flesh and the chaplet blazes in her hair. Her father tries to save her, and perishes in her flaming embrace. Medea completes her work by the murder of her two children—Jason's sons—and after jeering at her husband's grief disappears with the corpses in a chariot whirled through the air by dragons.

One of the most affecting passages in Euripides is found in

MEDEA'S LAST WORDS TO HER SONS.

"O children, children! you have still a city,
A home, where, lost to me and all my woe,
You will live out your lives without a mother!
But I—lo! I am for another land,
Leaving the joy of you: to see you happy,
To deck your marriage-bed, to greet your bride,
To light your wedding-torch, shall not be mine!
O me! thrice wretched in my own self-will!
In vain then, dear my children! did I rear you;
In vain I travailed, and with wearing sorrow

Bore bitter anguish in the hour of childbirth!
Yea, of a sooth, I had great hope of you,
That you should cherish my old age, and deck
My corpse with loving hands, and make me blessed
'Mid women in my death. But now, ah me!
Hath perished that sweet dream. For long without you
I shall drag out a dreary doleful age,
And you shall never see your mother more
With your dear eyes: for all your life is changed.
Woe! woe!
Why gaze you at me with your eyes, my children?
Why smile your last sweet smile? Ah me! ah me!
What shall I do? My heart dissolves within me,
Friends, when I see the glad eyes of my sons!
I cannot. No: my will that was so steady,
Farewell to it. They too shall go with me:
Why should I wound their sire with what wounds them,
Heaping tenfold his woes on my own head?
No, no, I shall not. Perish my proud will.

Yet whence this weakness? Do I wish to reap
The scorn that springs from enemies unpunished?
Dare it I must. What craven fool am I,
To let soft thoughts flow trickling from my soul!
Go, boys, into the house: and he who may not
Be present at my solemn sacrifice—
Let him see to it. My hand shall not falter.
Ah! ah!
Nay, do not, O my heart! do not this thing!
Suffer them, O poor fool; yea, spare thy children!
There in thy exile they will gladden thee.
Not so: by all the plagues of nethermost hell
It shall not be that I, that I should suffer
My foes to triumph and insult my sons!
Die must they: this must be, and since it must,
I, I myself will slay them, I who bore them.
So is it fixed, and there is no escape.
Even as I speak, the crown is on her head,
The bride is dying in her robes, I know it.
But since this path most piteous I tread,
Sending them forth on paths more piteous far,
I will embrace my children. O my sons!
Give, give your mother your dear hands to kiss.
O dearest hands, and mouths most dear to me,
And forms and noble faces of my sons!
Be happy even there: what here was yours,
Your father robs you of. O delicate scent!
O tender touch and sweet breath of my boys!

Go, go, go—leave me! Lo, I cannot bear
To look on you: my woes have overwhelmed me."
SYMONDS.

EXTANT PLAYS OF EURIPIDES.

ALCESTIS, first represented 438 B.C.
MEDEA, " 431 "
HIPPOL'YTUS, " 428 "
HECUBA, " 423 "
HERACLI'DÆ, " 421 "
THE SUPPLIANTS.
ION.
THE RAGING HERCULES.
ANDROMACHE.
THE TROJAN WOMEN, 415 B.C.: pathetic by reason of the plaints of the captive women.
ELECTRA, first represented 413 B.C.
HELEN, " 412 "
IPHIGENI'A AT TAURIS.
ORESTES, 408 B.C.: demoralizing in its portraiture of crime.
THE PHŒNICIAN WOMEN.
THE FEMALE BACCHANALIANS: produced at the Macedonian court.
IPHIGENIA AT AULIS: not acted till after the author's death.
CYCLOPS: a satyric drama (chorus of satyrs).

Lost Tragedies.—Dramatic literature has sustained an irreparable loss, not only in the missing plays of the three great masters, but also in those numberless works of their contemporaries and occasionally successful competitors now buried in oblivion. From the allusions of two or three Greek authors, a few meagre particulars may be gleaned, now of one, now of another—but they only serve to make us more painfully conscious of our loss.

Greek Comedy.—Comedy was older than tragedy in Greece. Thirty years before the time of Thespis, Susa'rion of Meg'ara, in his burlesque exhibitions, improved somewhat on the extempore jests and village-songs of the Bacchic revellers, and hence has been called the inventor of comedy. Susarion was no great lover of the fair sex, if we may judge by an ungallant sentiment of his which has been preserved: "Woman is a curse, but we cannot conduct our household affairs without this curse; therefore to marry is an evil, and not to marry is an evil." Perhaps he had taken to wife a Xantippe.

The poet Epicharmus, also of Megara, but the Sicilian city of that name, first committed his effusions to writing; he was the author of thirty-five comedies, some of them on subjects not mythological.

The development of comedy, however, was interrupted. The Tragic Muse enforced her claims at the expense of her elder sister, and the latter was for a season neglected. But the flourishing era of republican Athens, when the poet was free to lash whom he chose, saw comedy restored to the favor of the satire-loving people. It may be said to have been perfected by Aristophanes. He not only ridiculed the follies and vices of the day, laid bare family secrets on the stage, and edified his audiences by caricaturing the rich and great with masks and costumes which reproduced their peculiarities, but fearlessly assailed the government. When all others shrunk from playing so dangerous a rôle, he himself performed the part of the insolent demagogue Cleon (originally a leather-dresser), whom he mercilessly "cut into sandal-strips" in his "Knights."

Even the gods were not slighted by the comic poets. The gourmand Hercules devours as fast as the cook can prepare victuals; Prometheus is protected from the elements by an umbrella; Bacchus swaggers as a fop and coward. Comedy in the hands of Aristophanes and his contemporaries was to the Athenians what our press is to us, but went still further. Always personal and sometimes scurrilous in its attacks, too often coarse and licentious in its tone, it yet doubtless accomplished much good in restraining political ambition, checking public corruption, and modifying the prevailing faults of society.

Aristophanes.—The oldest comedies extant are those of Aristophanes, a citizen of Athens by birth or adoption, born about the middle of the fifth century B.C. If he was an adopted son, Athens had good reason to be proud of her protégé. His society was sought by the learned and great. He became the idol of the people, who fined such as brought libel-suits against him, and voted him an olive crown for exposing the misconduct of their rulers.

Nor was his fame confined to Athens. All Greece, and Sicily too, laughed at his humorous sallies. The Persian king enjoyed his pungent satires, and regarded him as such a power in Greece that when Spartan ambassadors sought an alliance with Persia against their Athenian rivals, the king asked on which side the comic poet was arrayed; for, said he, "the party whose cause Aristophanes espouses will certainly win."

Aristophanes was loyal to the true interests of his country, and declined the flattering invitations of Dionysius to dwell in ease at Syracuse with the luminaries of his age. He longed for the glorious Athens of the past, and attacked whatever conflicted with his conservative ideas. None escaped his well-aimed shafts. He was specially severe on the Sophists, a new class of teachers at Athens, whose forte lay in chopping logic and splitting hairs, and who taught the tricks of rhetoric rather than practical morality. In his "Clouds" he derides their sharp practices and unsound system of education, striking them over the head of Socrates, the exponent of true philosophy, whose life was devoted to combating the false teachings of these very pretenders.

That Socrates was merely the scape-goat is plain, for he and Aristophanes were intimate friends. When the play was first exhibited, the philosopher, who was in the audience, took it all in good part, and even rose that the people might compare him with the caricature presented, which exaggerated his eccentricities of dress and figure—his pug-nose, thick lips, shabby garments, and absent-minded stare. The chorus of changing clouds symbolized the meretricious charms of sophistry.

"THE CLOUDS" opens in the sleeping-apartment of Strepsi'ades, an Athenian citizen, his son Pheidippides occupying a pallet near him. The slaves of the household are abed in an adjoining room. Strepsiades, oppressed by debt incurred through the extravagance of his "precious son," a fast young man addicted to fast horses, is disturbed by the recollection of numerous outstanding bills and notes about to mature. He wakes before daylight and calls a slave :—

"Boy! light a lamp;
Bring me my pocket-book, that I may see
How my accounts stand, and just cast them up. [*Slave obeys.*]
Let's see now. First, here's Prasias, fifty pounds.
Now, what's that for? When did I borrow that?
Ah! when I bought that gray. O dear! O dear!
I shall grow gray enough, if this goes on.
PHEIDIPPIDES [*talking in his sleep*].—That's not fair,
Philo! Keep your own side of the course!
STREPSIADES.—Ay, there he goes! that's what is ruining me;
He's always racing, even in his dreams.
PHEIDIPPIDES [*awaking*].—Good heavens! my dear father,
What makes you groan and toss so all night long?
STREPSIADES.—There's a sheriff's officer at me—in the bedclothes.
PHEIDIPPIDES.—Lie quiet, sir, do pray, and let me sleep.
STREPSIADES.—Sleep, if you like; but these debts, I can tell you,
Will fall on your own head some day, young man.
Heugh! may those match-makers come to an evil end
Who drew me into marrying your good mother!
There I was, living a quiet life in the country,—
Shaved once a week, maybe, wore my old clothes—
Full of my sheep, and goats, and bees, and vineyards,
And I must marry the fine niece of Megacles.
Marry a fine town-belle, all airs and graces!
A pretty pair we were to come together—
I smelling of the vineyard and sheep-shearing,
She with her scents, and essences, and cosmetics,
And all the deviltries of modern fashion.
Not a bad housekeeper though, I will say that—
SLAVE [*examining the lamp, which is going out*].—This lamp has got no oil in it.
STREPSIADES.— Deuce take you,
Why did you light that thirsty beast of a lamp?
Come here, and you shall catch it.
SLAVE.— Catch it—why?
STREPSIADES [*boxes his ears*].—For putting such a thick wick in, to be sure.
Well, in due time, this boy of ours was born
To me and my grand lady. First of all,
We got to loggerheads about his name;
She would have something that had got a *horse* in it--

Xanthippus—or Charippus—or Philippides;
I was for his grandfather's name—Pheidonides.*
Well, for some time we squabbled; then at last
We came to a compromise upon Pheid-ippides.
This boy—she'd take him in her lap and fondle him,
And say, 'Ah! when it grows up to be a man,
It shall drive horses, like its uncle Megacles,
And wear a red cloak, it shall.' Then I would say,
'He shall wear a good sheep-skin coat, like his own father,
And drive his goats to market from the farm.'"

Strepsiades finally bethinks him of a plan for paying his debts. He will have his son trained by the Sophists; and when the creditors bring the case into court, Pheidippides shall plead his cause, and defeat them with fallacious arguments even in the face of a thousand witnesses. Father and son at once arise, dress, and walk out in the direction of the Sophists' school. Arrived in front of it, Strepsiades remarks:—

"That's the great Thinking-school of our new philosophers;
There live the men who teach that heaven around us
Is a vast oven, and we the charcoal in it.
And they teach too—for a consideration, mind—
To plead a cause and win it, right or wrong.
PHEIDIPPIDES [*carelessly*].—Who are these fellows?
STREPSIADES.— I don't quite remember
The name they call themselves, it's such a long one;
Very hard thinkers—but they're first-rate men.
PHEIDIPPIDES.—Faugh! vulgar fellows—I know 'em.
Dirty vagabonds,
Like Socrates there and Chærephon; a low set.
STREPSIADES.—Pray hold your tongue—don't show your ignorance,
But, if you care at all for your old father,
Be one of them; now do, and cut the turf.
PHEIDIPPIDES.—Not I, by Bacchus! not if you would give me
That team of Arabs which Leogoras drives.
STREPSIADES.—Do, my dear boy, I beg you—go and be taught.
PHEIDIPPIDES.—What shall I learn there?
STREPSIADES.—Learn? Why, they do say
That these men have the secret of both Arguments,
The honest Argument (if there be such a thing) and the other;

* *Hippos* means a *horse* in Greek; *pheidon, economical.*

Now this last—this false Argument, you understand—
Will make the veriest rascal win his cause.
So if you'll go and learn for us this glorious art,
The debts I owe for you will all be cleared;
For I shan't pay a single man a farthing.
  PHEIDIPPIDES.—No—I can't do it. Studying hard, you see,
Spoils the complexion. How could I show my face
Among the knights, looking a beast, like those fellows?
  STREPSIADES.—Then, sir, henceforth I swear, so help me Ceres,
I won't maintain you—you, nor your bays, nor your chestnuts.
Go to the dogs—or anywhere—out of my house!"

Failing to induce his son to enter the Thinking-school, Strepsiades resolves himself to master the fashionable Argument that "pays no bills;" he has an interview with Socrates, and is introduced to the Clouds, the new goddesses of this misty philosophy.

One of the most beautiful passages of the play—having the ring of the true metal—is the chorus of Clouds responding to the call of Socrates—first, behind the scenes, in the distance; then nearer; then rising from the lips of twenty-four gauze-clad nymphs, who descend upon the stage as personifications of the ethereal deities.

CHORUS OF CLOUDS (*in the distance*).

"Eternal clouds!
Rise we to mortal view,
Embodied in bright shapes of dewy sheen,
Leaving the depths serene
Where our loud-sounding Father Ocean dwells,
For the wood-crownèd summits of the hills:
Thence shall our glance command
The beetling crags which sentinel the land,
The teeming earth,
The crops we bring to birth;
Thence shall we hear
The music of the ever-flowing streams,
The low deep thunders of the booming sea.
Lo, the bright Eye of Day unwearied beams!
Shedding our veil of storms
From our immortal forms,
We scan with keen-eyed gaze this nether sphere."

CHORUS OF CLOUDS (*nearer*).

"Sisters who bring the showers,
Let us arise and greet
This glorious land, for Pallas' dwelling meet,
Rich in brave men, beloved of Cecrops old;
Where Faith and Reverence reign,
Where comes no foot profane,
When for the mystic rites the Holy Doors unfold.
There gifts are duly paid
To the great gods, and pious prayers are said;
Tall temples rise, and statues heavenly fair.
There at each holy tide,
With coronals and song,
The glad processions to the altars throng;
There in the jocund spring,
Great Bacchus, festive king,
With dance and tuneful flute his Chorus leads along."

W. L. COLLINS.

But though the Clouds assist Socrates in teaching Strepsiades, the pupil proves an utter dunce. Finally, in a moment of impatience, Socrates kicks him out of the school.

At last Pheidippides is prevailed upon to study with the Sophists. He proves an apt scholar, rapidly developing into an unprincipled scamp. When his education as a sharper is completed, he brings to bear his specious arguments against the creditors, and cheats them out of their dues. So far, so good; but his notions of filial duty have also been greatly modified by the instructions of Socrates. A quarrel arising in the family, he hesitates not to fall upon his father with a cudgel, and threatens to do the same by his mother if she provokes him.

With a curse upon Socrates, the outraged old gentleman calls his slaves, hurries to the Thinking-school, and sets fire to the building. Thus the play ends.

Beneath the pleasantry of Aristophanes is a substratum of solid sense; as is apparent in "the Birds," an ingenious play in which the woodland songsters take characters. It was produced at a time when the Athenians, puffed up with vanity, confidently looked for the reduction of Sicily and the dominion of Greece. Aristophanes alone, at this critical period, ventured to raise the note of warning, and satirize their foolish ambition. The choruses in this drama ring with the sweet music of the wild woods; they were rendered by twenty-four performers plumed so as to represent as many different kinds of birds. The Hoopoe thus calls his fellows to a mass-meeting:—

"Hoop! hoop!
Come in a troop,
Come at a call
One and all,
Birds of a feather,
All together.
Birds of an humble gentle bill
Smooth and shrill,
Dieted on seeds and grain,
Rioting on the furrowed plain,
Pecking, hopping,
Picking, popping,
Among the barley newly sown.
Birds of bolder, louder tone,
Lodging in the shrubs and bushes,
Mavises and Thrushes.
On the summer berries browsing,
On the garden fruits carousing,
All the grubs and vermin smouzing.

You that in an humbler station,
With an active occupation,
Haunt the lowly watery mead,
Warring against the native breed,
The gnats and flies, your enemies;
In the level marshy plain
Of Marathon pursued and slain.

You that in a squadron driving
From the seas are seen arriving,
With the Cormorants and Mews,
Haste to land and hear the news!
All the feathered airy nation,
Birds of every size and station,
Are convened in convocation.

For an envoy, queer and shrewd,
Means to address the multitude,
And submit to their decision
A surprising proposition,
For the welfare of the state.
Come in a flurry,
With a hurry, scurry,
Hurry to the meeting and attend to the debate."

FRERE.

STYLE OF ARISTOPHANES.—In weighing the merits of Aristophanes, it must be remembered that many of his peculiar beauties cannot be translated, and that we lose his local hits from our inability to see things from an Athenian standpoint. He is often indelicate in his allusions; he is as ready with town slang and the cant of the shop as with the most elegant phrase. But Attic salt seasons the whole, and none ever handled the versatile Greek tongue more deftly. In his command of language, he is equalled only by Plato, who felt the comic poet's power when he said that in the soul of Aristophanes the Graces sought an imperishable shrine. Amid all his humor and buffoonery sparkles genius of the highest order. His aim seems to have been to elevate his art. Some of the improvements he claimed to have introduced, are thus set forth in an address which he puts into the mouth of the leader of the chorus in his "Peace:"—

"It was he that indignantly swept from the stage the paltry ignoble device
Of a Hercules needy and seedy and greedy, a vagabond sturdy and stout,
Now baking his bread, now swindling instead, now beaten and battered about.
And freedom he gave to the lacrimose slave who was wont with a howl to rush in,
And all for the sake of a joke which they make on the wounds which disfigure his skin.
Such vulgar contemptible lumber at once he bade from the drama depart,
And then, like an edifice stately and grand, he raised and ennobled the art."

THOROLD ROGERS.

Aristophanes outlived the license of the old comedy, which died with liberty. When in 404 B.C. the popular government was overthrown, and Thirty Tyrants, supported by Sparta, lorded it over Athens, a statute was passed making personal attacks on the stage capital offences; an actor who defied the law was actually starved to death. Thenceforth the comic poet dared not individualize the object of his satire; he tilted against vice and folly in general, or thrust at his intended victims indirectly under assumed names.

Aristophanes died about 380 B.C. No other comic poet could vie with him during his lifetime; none worthy to be his successor arose after his death, for "Nature broke the mould in which he was cast." Of fifty-four comedies from his pen, eleven remain entire.

The Acharnians.......... 425 B.C.
The Knights.............. 424 "
The Clouds............... 423 "
The Wasps................ 422 "
The persons constituting the chorus were girt in tightly about the waist, to make them as wasp-like as possible in appearance; skewers did service as stings.
Peace..................... 421 "
The Birds................. 414 "
Lysistrata................ 411 "
The Women celebrating the Feast of Ceres.. 411 "
Ridicule of Euripides is the staple of this play.
The Frogs................. 405 B.C.
Here again Euripides is the butt. The chorus was made up to represent frogs, whose croakings were imitated.
The Women met in Assembly.................... 392 "
Certain strong-minded female communists, advocates of women's rights, seize on the government and undertake the reformation of public abuses. This play contains the longest word known, made up of 77 syllables and 169 letters.
Plutus.................... 388 "

HISTORY.

During this halcyon age of Greek poetry, prose also was cultivated, and in the century following the Persian Wars it was brought to maturity. After the victories that secured her freedom, Greece felt the need of a national historian to record the story of her struggles and triumphs. The earliest narrators, as has been shown, confined themselves to mythology and tradition: the times now demanded an artist who could paint with faithful pencil on living canvas those scenes that were the glory of Hellas—and in Herodotus of Halicarnassus that artist appeared.

Herodotus (born 484 B.C.).—Halicarnassus was the capital of a Dorian confederacy of states in southern Asia Minor. Its queen Artemisia supported Xerxes in his quarrel with Greece; and although the Athenians, provoked that a woman should take the field against them, offered an immense reward for her capture, she escaped the perils of war, and carried her kingdom safely through the political troubles of the time.

The parents of Herodotus were persons of rank and property. His writings prove him to have been well read in the literature of his country. Though not an Ionian born, he adopted the Ionic dialect—the dress in which Greek prose first appeared.

Herodotus spent the best twenty years of his life in travelling over the greater part of the known world, studying the history, geography, and customs of the countries he visited. Thebes and Memphis, Tyre and Jerusalem, Babylon and Ecbat'ana—with all he made personal acquaintance, extending his tour as far west as the Greek settlements in Italy, and as far south as the first cataract of the Nile.

The marvellousness of the stories he collected brought down upon Herodotus the ridicule of his fellow-citizens; so quitting Halicarnassus when about thirty-seven years of age, he settled at Athens. Here, it is related, he read his history, still in the rough, to the admiring people, who voted him a handsome reward. Here also he seems to have become intimate with Sophocles and his great contemporaries; and here, perhaps, his ambition was kindled to add another star to the galaxy that made Athens the glory of the world.

Not long, however, did Herodotus remain at the capital. As one of a band of colonists sent out by Pericles in 443 B.C., he crossed to Italy, and aided in founding the town of Thurii, near the ruins of Syb'aris (see Map, p. 304). At Thurii he spent his last years in revising, enlarging, and polishing his history; yet we are not to believe that he ceased to indulge his passion for travelling when Sicily and southern Italy lay so invitingly before him. He died at the age of sixty, leaving the great work of his life unfinished.

The main subject of our author's work is the Græco-Persian War and the triumph of his country. His narrative is from time to time relieved by delightful episodes. Indeed, we owe to him not a few of those romantic tales that invest ancient history with its peculiar charm; while modern research has verified many of the wonder-stories that provoked the derision of his countrymen. Nor do his digressions mar the unity of his history, which is planned and developed as skilfully as a drama of Sophocles.

The style of Herodotus is poetical, clear, familiar, fascinating, and marked by a pleasing variety. "His animation," says Macaulay, "his simple-hearted tenderness, his wonderful talent for description and dialogue, and the pure sweet flow of his language, place him at the head of narrators." His history is the first work of its kind that has descended to us entire. It is divided into nine books, said to have been read by the author at the Olympic Games, and there to have received the names of the Nine Muses, which they still bear.* Certainly no names could have been more appropriately connected with a work that has entitled its author to be called through all time "the Father of History."—Extracts follow:—

---

* An epigram of later date thus accounted for their names:—

"The Muses to Herodotus one day came, nine of them, and dined;
And in return, their host to pay, left each a book behind."

XERXES AND THE PILOT.

"It is said that Xerxes, leaving Athens, came to a city called Eïon, on the banks of the Stry'mon. Hence he proceeded no farther by land, but, intrusting the conduct of his forces to Hydarnes, with orders to march them to the Hellespont, he went on board a Phœnician vessel to cross over into Asia. After he had embarked, a heavy and tempestuous wind set in from the lake; which, on account of the great number of Persians on board, attendant upon Xerxes, made the situation of the vessel extremely dangerous. The king, in a transport of terror, inquired aloud of the pilot if he thought they were safe.

'By no means,' was the answer, 'unless we could be rid of some of this multitude.'

Upon this Xerxes exclaimed, 'Persians, let me now see which of you loves his prince; my safety, it seems, depends on you.'

As soon as he had spoken, they first bowed themselves before him, and then leaped into the sea. The vessel being thus lightened, Xerxes was safely landed in Asia. As soon as he got on shore, he rewarded the pilot with a golden crown for preserving the life of the king; but, as he had caused so many Persians to perish, he cut off his head."—BELOE.

ANECDOTE OF QUEEN NITOCRIS.

"Nitocris had her tomb constructed in the upper part of one of the principal gateways of the city, high above the heads of the passers-by, with this inscription cut upon it:—'If there be one among my successors on the throne of Babylon who is in want of treasure, let him open my tomb, and take as much as he chooses; not, however, unless he be truly in want, for it will not be for his good.'

This tomb continued untouched until Darius came to the kingdom. To him it seemed a monstrous thing that he should be unable to use one of the gates of the town, and that a sum of money should be lying idle, and moreover inviting his grasp, and he not seize upon it. Now he could not use the gate, because, as he drove through, the dead body would have been over his head.

Accordingly, he opened the tomb; but, instead of money, found only the dead body, and a writing which said:—'Hadst thou not been insatiate of pelf, and careless how thou gottest it, thou wouldst not have broken open the sepulchres of the dead.'"

CUSTOMS OF THE BABYLONIANS.

"Of their customs, whereof I shall now proceed to give an account, the following is in my judgment the wisest. Once a year, in each village, the maidens of age to marry were collected all together into one place; while the men stood round them in a circle. Then a herald called up the damsels one by one, and offered them for sale. He began with the most beautiful. When she was sold for no small sum of money, he offered for sale the one who came next to her in beauty. All of them were sold to be wives.

The richest of the Babylonians who wished to wed, bid against each other for the loveliest maidens; while the humbler wife-seekers, who were indifferent about beauty, took the more homely damsels with marriage-portions. For the custom was that when the herald had gone through the whole number of the beautiful damsels, he should then call up the ugliest—a cripple, if there chanced to be one—and offer her to the men, asking who would agree to take her with the smallest marriage-portion. And the man who offered to take the smallest sum, had her assigned to him. The marriage-portions were furnished by the money paid for the beautiful damsels, and thus the fairer maidens portioned out the uglier.

No one was allowed to give his daughter in marriage to the man of his choice, nor might any one carry away the damsel whom he had purchased without finding bail really and truly to make her his wife. All who liked might come, even from distant villages, and bid for the women.

The Babylonians have no physicians; but when a man is ill, they lay him in the public square, and the passers-by come up to him, and if they have ever had his disease themselves or have known any one who has suffered from it, they give him advice, recommending him to do whatever they found good in their own case, or in the case known to them. And no one is allowed to pass the sick man in silence without asking him what his ailment is."—RAWLINSON.

Thucydides, on whom the mantle of Herodotus descended, was born in a village of Attica about 471 B.C. We may believe that he received a polite education, and became proficient in military science at an early age. It was in the prime of manhood, if the oft-repeated story is to be credited, that the history of Herodotus, read before an assembled throng, brought tears to his eyes and fired him with a desire to emulate its distinguished author. Greece was then on the eve of the Peloponnesian War, in which the rival states Athens and Sparta figured as chief actors. Thucydides anticipated the impending storm, and discerned his opportunity; this war should be his subject, and even before it began he was busy collecting preliminary information.

Nor did he serve his country merely in the capacity of historian. He engaged actively in the contest, and received as his reward the command of an Athenian squadron. But he committed an unpardonable sin by failing to save a town, which surrendered to the Spartans before he could arrive with assistance. Instigated by Cleon, his countrymen deprived him of his position and cast him forth an exile.

Thucydides retired to Thrace, where he had a valuable interest in certain gold-mines, and there devoted himself to the preparation of his history, narrowly watching the progress of events and gathering intelligence with the utmost care. His exile of twenty years was indeed "the Muses' blessing;" it enabled him to pursue his studies without interruption. Long after his death, the plane-tree in whose shadow he was accustomed to compose, was pointed out to travellers.

Thucydides traced the Peloponnesian War to the middle of its twenty-first year (411 B.C.), leaving it to be finished by another. Why he did not complete it himself, being in possession of the necessary materials, does not appear. After the Athenian power was broken by Sparta (404 B.C.), the decree of banishment was revoked; but whether Thucydides ever returned to Athens is a matter of doubt. According to one account, he went back to fall the victim of a conspiracy; from another we are led to infer that he died a natural death in Thrace about 391 B.C.

The "History of the Peloponnesian War" is remarkable for its accuracy and impartiality. Truth was the great object of its author, who, dispassionate and unprejudiced, ignores the ingratitude of his country, betrays no resentment even when he speaks of Cleon, and does full justice to his Spartan foes. He intended his work to be an authority, "a possession for everlasting." In it we find the first attempts to treat the philosophy of history, to trace events to their ultimate causes, and deduce from the past lessons for the future. His style is nervous, concise, stately, and even rises to the sublime; but lacks harmony, and is sometimes obscure. About one fourth of his work is composed of speeches, which indeed make an agreeable variety, but are often involved, and in parts all but unintelligible. Antithesis is a frequent figure.

Despite its faults, the history of Thucydides has always been a favorite. Charles V. was never without a copy when on a campaign, and the philosopher Hobbes declared that he valued its eight books above all the rest of Greek historical literature. The extract selected is a description of the plague which broke out at Athens in the year 430, while the Lacedæmonians were ravaging Attica, and which the historian contracted himself, but fortunately survived.

THE PLAGUE AT ATHENS.

"While the nature of this distemper was such as to baffle all description, and its attacks were almost too grievous for human nature to endure, it was still in the following circumstance that its difference from all ordinary disorders was most clearly shown. All the birds and beasts that prey upon human bodies either abstained from touching them (though there were many lying unburied), or died after tasting them. In proof of this, it was noticed that birds of this kind actually disappeared; they were not about the bodies, or indeed to be seen at all. But of course the effects which I have mentioned could best be studied in a domestic animal like the dog.

Meanwhile the town enjoyed an immunity from all the ordinary disorders; or, if any case occurred, it ended in this. Some died of neglect, others in the midst of every attention. No remedy was found that could be used as a specific; for what did good in one case, did harm in another. Strong and weak constitutions proved equally incapable of resistance, all alike being swept away, although dieted with the utmost precaution.

By far the most terrible feature in the malady was the dejection which ensued when they felt themselves sickening; for the despair into which they instantly fell took away their power of resistance, and left them a much easier prey to the disorder. Besides which, there was the awful spectacle of men dying like sheep, through having caught the infection in nursing each other. This caused the greatest mortality. On the one hand, if they were afraid to visit each other, they perished from neglect: indeed, many houses were emptied of their inmates for want of a nurse: on the other hand, if they ventured to do so, death was the consequence.

This was especially the case with such as made any pretensions to goodness: a sense of honor prevented them from sparing themselves in their attendance at their friends' houses, where even the members of the family were at last worn out by the moans of the dying, and succumbed to the force of the disaster. Yet it was with those who had recovered from the disease that the sick found most compassion. These knew what it was from experience, and had now no fear for themselves; for the same man was never attacked a second time—never at least fatally. And such persons not only received the congratulations of others, but themselves also in the elation of the moment half entertained the vain hope that they were for the future safe from any disease whatever.

An aggravation of the existing calamity was the influx from the country into the city, and this was especially felt by the new arrivals. As there were no houses to receive them, they had to be lodged at the hot season of the year in stifling cabins, where the mortality raged without restraint; bodies lay one upon another in the agonies of thirst, and half-dead creatures reeled about the streets and round all the fountains in their longing for water. The sacred places, also, in which they had quartered themselves, were full of corpses of persons that had died there.

All the burial rites before in use were entirely upset, and they buried the bodies as best they could. Many from want of the proper appliances, through so many of their friends having died already, had recourse to the most shameless sepultures: sometimes getting the start of those who had raised a pile, they threw their own dead body upon the stranger's pile and ignited it; sometimes they tossed the corpse, which they were carrying, on the top of another which was burning, and so went off.

Nor was this the only form of lawless extravagance which owed its origin to the plague. Men now coolly ventured on what they had formerly done in a corner, and not just as they pleased, seeing the rapid transitions produced by persons in prosperity suddenly dying and those who before had nothing succeeding to their property. So they resolved to spend quickly and enjoy themselves, regarding their lives and riches as alike things of a day. Perseverance in what men called honor was popular with none, it was so uncertain whether they would be spared to attain the object; but present enjoyment, and all that contributed to it, was laid down as both honorable and useful. Fear of gods or law of man there was none to restrain them. As for the first, they judged it to be just the same whether they worshipped the gods or not, as they saw all alike perishing; and for the last, no one expected to live to be brought to trial for his offences, but felt that a far severer sentence had been already passed upon them and hung even over their heads, and before this fell it was only reasonable to enjoy life a little.

Such was the nature of the calamity, and heavily did it weigh on the Athenians; death raging within the city and devastation without. Among other things which they remembered in their distress was, very naturally, the following verse, which the old men said had long ago been uttered:

'A Dorian war shall come, and with it death.'"

RICHARD CRAWLEY.

Xenophon, who in his "Hellenica" continued the story of the Peloponnesian War left unfinished by Thucydides, and carried the history of Greece as far as the battle of Mantine'a, 362 B.C., was born at Athens shortly after the middle of the fifth century. Of his early life we know nothing, save that he was the friend and pupil of Socrates; who, it is related, prepossessed with his intelligent countenance, once stopped him in a narrow way and demanded where men were made good and honest. Confused by the unexpected inquiry from so great a teacher, the boy hesitated; whereupon, the philosopher exclaimed, "Follow me and learn." Xenophon obeyed, and became a faithful student of his master's moral and philosophical doctrines. Together they braved the perils of the Peloponnesian War; and in the battle of De'lium (424 B.C.), where the flower of Athens' chivalry fell, Xenophon's life is said to have been saved by Socrates.

At the solicitation of his friend, Proxenus the Bœotian, Xenophon joined as a volunteer the famous Expedition of the Ten Thousand, made in the interest of Cyrus the Younger against his elder brother Artaxerxes, who occupied the Persian throne. Feeling the necessity of securing soldiers superior in bravery and discipline to the barbarian hordes through which he must cut his way to the capital, Cyrus supported the Spartans in the Peloponnesian War, in order to secure their aid in dethroning Artaxerxes. Accordingly, at his summons, about 10,000 Spartans and other Greeks, deceived at first as to the real object of the campaign, flocked to his standard, and in the spring of 401 B.C., with 100,000 Eastern troops, entered the confines of the Persian Empire.

On the plain of Cunaxa, ninety miles from Babylon, the decisive battle took place between the brothers, Artaxerxes having at his back an army of nearly a million men. Superior numbers, however, availed little against the superior discipline of the Greeks, who quickly routed the wing opposed to them; but Cyrus, already hailed as king, imprudently spurred into the disordered ranks of the foe, and was struck down while engaged in a furious hand-to-hand conflict with Artaxerxes.

The fall of Cyrus was the signal for his Asiatic troops to disperse, and the victors found themselves deserted in the heart of the enemy's country, more than 1,200 miles from home. Their generals were soon after seized at a conference and put to death. In this crisis, by the advice of Xenophon, inspired as he tells us by a dream, new leaders were chosen, he himself in the place of his friend Proxenus, one of the murdered chiefs. A retreat was determined upon; and during fifteen months of indescribable hardships, he was the patient guide, the sympathetic but vigilant and prudent commander. At last, from a mountain height, the glittering Euxine broke upon the view of the van, a glad shout rent the air—"the Sea! the Sea!"—proclaiming that their sufferings were over, while officers and soldiers wept in each other's arms. Here, in the neighborhood of Greek settlements, they were safe, and the march home was easy. The 8,600 survivors owed their lives to Xenophon.

This "Retreat" of the Greeks is the subject of Xenophon's graphic and interesting history in seven books, the "Anabasis" (*march up*, though most of the work is occupied with what happened on the march *down*). The chaste, simple style of the author, who throughout modestly speaks of himself in the third person, recommends his pages to readers of every class. He writes to the point; there is no straining for effect. We extract the passage relating to

XENOPHON'S DREAM.

"After the generals were made prisoners, and such of the captains and soldiers as had accompanied them were put to death, the Greeks were in great perplexity, reflecting that they were not far from the king's residence; that there were around them, on all sides, many hostile nations and cities; that no one would any longer afford them opportunities of purchasing provisions; that they were distant from Greece not less than ten thousand stadia; that there was no one to guide them on the way; that impassable rivers would intercept them in the midst of their course; that the Babylonians who had gone up with Cyrus had deserted them; and that they were left alone, having no cavalry to support them.

Reflecting, I say, on these circumstances, and being disheartened at them, few tasted food that evening, few kindled fires; and many did not come to the place of arms during the night, but lay down to sleep where they severally happened to be, unable to sleep for sorrow and longing for their country, their parents, their wives and children, whom they never expected to see again. In this state of mind they all went to their resting-places.

When this perplexity occurred, Xenophon was distressed as well as the other Greeks, and unable to rest; but having at length got a little sleep, he had a dream, in which, in the midst of a thunder-storm, a bolt seemed to him to fall upon his father's house, and the house in consequence became all in a blaze. Greatly frightened, he immediately awoke, and considered his dream as in one respect favorable, inasmuch as, being in troubles and dangers, he seemed to behold a great light from Jupiter; but in another respect he was alarmed, because the dream appeared to him to be from Jupiter, who was a king, and the fire to blaze all around him, lest he should be unable to escape from the king's territories, but should be hemmed in on all sides by inextricable difficulties.

What it betokens, however, to see such a dream, we may conjecture from the occurrences that happened after the dream. What immediately followed was this. As soon as he awoke, the thought that first occurred to him was, 'Why do I lie here? The night is passing away. With daylight it is probable that the enemy will come upon us; and, if we once fall into the hands of the king, what is there to prevent us from being put to death with ignominy, after witnessing the most grievous sufferings among our comrades, and enduring every severity of torture ourselves? Yet no one concerts measures or takes thought for our defence, but we lie still, as if we were at liberty to enjoy repose. From what city, then, do I expect a leader to undertake our defence? What age am I waiting for, to come to myself? Assuredly I shall never be older, if I give myself up to the enemy to-day.' After these reflections he arose, and called together, in the first place, the captains that were under Proxenus.

When they were assembled, he said, 'For my part, captains, I cannot sleep, nor, I should think, can you; nor can I lie still any longer, when I consider in what circumstances we are placed. For it is plain that the enemy did not openly manifest hostility toward us, until they thought that they had judiciously arranged their plans; but on our side no one takes any thought how we may best maintain a contest with them. Yet if we prove remiss, and fall into the power of the king, what may we not expect to suffer from a man who cut off the head and hand of his own brother by the same mother and father, even after he was dead, and fixed them upon a stake? What may not we, I say, expect to suffer, who have no relative to take our part, and who have marched against him to make him a subject instead of a monarch, and to put him to death if it should lie in our power? Will he not proceed to every extremity, that by reducing us to the last degree of ignominious suffering, he may inspire all men with a dread of ever taking the field against him? We must, therefore, try every expedient not to fall into his hands.

For myself, I never ceased, while the truce lasted, to consider ourselves as objects of pity, and to regard the king and his people as objects of envy; as I contemplated how extensive and valuable a country they possessed, how great an abundance of provisions, how many slaves and cattle, and how vast a quantity of gold and raiment. But since they have put an end to peace, their own haughtiness and our mistrust seem likewise to be brought to an end; for the advantages which I have mentioned lie now as prizes between us, for whichsoever of us shall prove the better men. And the gods are the judges of the contest, who, as is just, will be on our side; since the enemy have offended them by perjury, while we, though seeing many good things to tempt us, have resolutely abstained from all of them through regard to our oaths; so that, as it seems to me, we may advance to the combat with much greater confidence than they can feel.

We have bodies, moreover, better able than theirs to endure cold and toil; and we have, with the help of the gods, more resolute minds; while the enemy, if the gods, as before, grant us success, will be found more obnoxious to wounds and death than we are. But possibly others of you entertain the same thoughts; let us not then, in the name of Heaven, wait for others to come and exhort us to noble deeds, but let us be ourselves the first to excite others to exert their valor. Prove yourselves the bravest of the captains, and more worthy to lead than those who are now leaders. As for me, if you wish to take the start in the course, I am willing to follow you; or, if you appoint me to be a leader, I shall not make my youth an excuse, but shall think myself sufficiently mature to defend myself against harm.'"—WATSON.

For his sympathy with Sparta, and possibly for sharing the opinions of his beloved teacher Socrates, Xenophon was banished from Athens; but he was recompensed by the Lacedæmonians with a house and piece of land in E'lis. Here, amid lovely meadows and woodlands, he built a temple to the goddess Diana in fulfilment of a vow he had made when encircled by dangers in Asia. Here, free from the cares of public life, he passed many years, happy in the society of his wife, children, and friends, dividing his time among his farm, his hunting-parks, and his study. He died at the age of ninety.—Of his two sons, one fell on the field of Mantinea, after dealing the great Epaminondas his death-blow.

Besides the "Anabasis" and "Hellenica," Xenophon wrote the "Cy'ropædi'a" (*education of Cyrus*—the elder Cyrus, king of Persia), a semi-didactic, semi-historical fiction, illustrating a model system of education and setting forth his ideal of government—a perfect monarchy. He is also the author of several works written in defence of Socrates or as expositions of his philosophy, of which the "Memorabilia" (*memoirs*) is particularly interesting, teeming as it does with sayings and anecdotes of the sage.

In addition to his merits as an historian, Xenophon may justly claim the distinction of having been the first essayist: we have from his pen essays on the Policy of Lacedæmon, on the Chase, Horsemanship, and Cavalry Tactics, not to mention several political treatises ascribed to him. A creditable representative of elegant Attic prose, Xenophon has been called *the Attic Muse.*

Ctesias, a Greek physician attached to the Persian court, who dressed the wounds of Artaxerxes after the battle of Cunaxa, compiled a history of Persia in twenty-three books, a description of India, and a variety of other works. Of his writings, which were in the Ionic dialect, little has survived.

Theopompus (probably 378–304 B.C.) is also worthy of mention as an historian. He wrote a History of Greece from 411 to 394 B.C., and "Philippica," in fifty-eight books, in which he sketched the character of Philip of Macedon. Of the latter

K 2

work numerous fragments remain. Ancient critics give him credit for general accuracy, though he took rather too rose-colored views of his hero Philip as the promoter of Grecian civilization.

PHILOSOPHY.

The earliest philosophical investigations were made by Ionians, and THALES of Miletus is recognized as the founder of Greek philosophy. To him and to Pythagoras the various systems may all be traced.

The Ionic School of Thales, devoted to physical science, rapidly developed, theory after theory being brought forward to explain the universe and the nature of Deity. One philosopher made the Supreme Being an all-pervading, divine air; another, Heracli'tus "the Obscure," represented God as a subtile flame, and reduced the universe to an eternal fire.

A notable step in advance was taken by ANAXAGORAS (500–428 B.C.), who succeeded to the leadership of this school. The first to make the study of philosophy fashionable at Athens, he became the instructor of some of her great men, Socrates among the number. He represented God as a divine *mind*, acting on the material world with intelligence and design. Well did Aristotle say that Anaxagoras was like a sober man among stammering drunkards, when compared with earlier philosophers. As an astronomer, he anticipated some of the discoveries of more recent times; he correctly explained eclipses, taught that the sun was a molten ball, that from it the moon borrowed her light, that the lunar surface was diversified with mountains and valleys, and that the earth itself had been the scene of terrible convulsions.

The Italic School had meanwhile been founded by PYTHAG'ORAS, of Samos, born about 540 B.C. He settled in Croto'na, a Greek town of southern Italy, and there imparted to his disciples the philosophical principles which he had gathered in other lands, particularly Egypt.

Pythagoras modestly styled himself a lover of wisdom (*philosopher*), not a wise man (*sophist*). Among his doctrines were the mysterious theory that *number* is the first principle of all things, the transmigration of souls, and a system of future rewards and punishments. He forestalled Copernicus in his discovery of the true theory of the solar system — that the sun, and not the earth, as was then believed, is its centre ; he taught that the moon was inhabited ; and described the heavenly bodies as producing harmonious tones in their passage through ether, from which his followers were accustomed to say that to him the gods had revealed "the music of the spheres."

With such perfect confidence did his disciples regard their master, who usually gave his instructions from behind a thick curtain, that when any one called their doctrines in question they deemed it sufficient to reply, "He said so" (*ipse dixit*). Indeed, they invested him with supernatural powers, nor, according to his early biographers, did he deny the soft impeachment. On one occasion, we are told, to convince his pupils that he was a god, he showed them his thigh, which was of gold, and declared that he had assumed the form of humanity only the more readily to impart his lessons to mankind.

Pythagoras was the inventor of the monochord, a one-stringed instrument designed to measure musical intervals,— and also of the more useful, if humbler, Multiplication Table. He is the first who practised mesmerism ; at least so we may account for his subduing a fierce Daunian bear, and taming beasts and birds by gently passing his hands over their bodies.

There are no genuine remnants of this author. The celebrated "Golden Verses," long attributed to him, there is reason for supposing to have been inspired by his teachings, but written by one of his pupils :—

FROM THE GOLDEN VERSES.

"Ne'er suffer sleep thine eyes to close
   Before thy mind hath run
O'er every act, and thought, and word,
   From dawn to set of sun;
For wrong take shame, but grateful feel,
   If just thy course hath been;
Such effort, day by day renewed,
   Will ward thy soul from sin."

As the Ionics made physics everything, so the Pythagoreans regarded mathematical science as the *summum bonum.* In their master's eyes the world was "a living arithmetic," and virtue a proportion of all the faculties of the soul. A mystical relation between mathematical and moral truths was a principle of his philosophy.

Prominent among the followers of Pythagoras was EMPEDOCLES, of Agrigentum in Sicily (450 B.C.), who combined the previous theories of nature in his own, viz., that four elements—earth, air, fire, and water—enter into the constitution of the universe, and that these are constantly animated by the two opposing forces of Love and Strife. A peculiar doctrine of his was that like is perceived only by like; thus our knowledge of other bodies is due to minute emanations from their substance which enter the pores and impress corresponding elements in our own frames.

Empedocles is said to have arrogated to himself the importance of a god, going about in a purple robe confined with a belt of gold, performing wonderful cures. According to an old legend, he sought to create the belief that he had been translated to heaven, by secretly throwing himself into the crater of Mt. Etna; but the volcano, in a subsequent eruption, cast forth one of his brazen sandals and so exposed the fraud. He probably lost his life by accident while examining the crater.

From the Italic School sprung the sects known as Eleatic,

Epicurean, and Skeptic. The Eleatic School was founded by XENOPH'ANES (600–500 B.C.), a contemporary of Pythagoras, and derived its name from the town of E'lea in southern Italy.

Xenophanes asserted the unity of the Deity. "There is one god," he said, "among gods and men the greatest: unlike to mortals in outward shape, unlike in mind and thoughts." This was truly a sublime stand to take in an age of polytheism; he who feared not to face a superstitious people with such a doctrine, and ridicule even their divine Homer for his degrading pictures of the deities, deserves to be ranked among the greatest philosophers of Greece.

FRAGMENTS FROM XENOPHANES.

"If sheep, and swine, and lions strong, and all the bovine crew,
Could paint with cunning hands, and do what clever mortals do,
Depend upon it, every pig with snout so broad and blunt,
Would make a Jove that like himself would thunder with a grunt;
And every lion's god would roar, and every bull's would bellow,
And every sheep's would baa, and every beast his worshipped fellow
Would find in some immortal form, and naught exist divine
But had the gait of lion, sheep, or ox, or grunting swine."

"Homer and Hesiod, whom we own great doctors of theology,
Said many things of blissful gods that cry for large apology—
That they may cheat, and rail, and lie, and give the rein to passion,
Which were a crime in men who tread the dust in mortal fashion."

"All eyes, all ears, all thought, is God, the omnipresent soul;
And free from toil, by force of mind, he moves the mighty whole."

BLACKIE.

The noble conception of Deity entertained by Xenophanes was soon perverted. We find his pupil PARMEN'IDES "the Great" in the next century doing away with the personality of God, and confounding the divine nature with pure being, which he made equivalent to thought.

DEMOC'RITUS, of Abde'ra in Thrace (460–357 B.C.), known

as the laughing philosopher from his constantly deriding the weaknesses of men, put forth the *atomic theory*,—that the universe is made up of countless minute, intangible atoms, and that in the motion of such atoms, round and fiery, consisted the movements of the mind and soul. God had no place in this philosophy; matter, time, space, and motion, were eternal. Bodies were formed by the fortuitous concurrence of atoms; and by the affinities and motions of atoms in the vacuum that made up the universe, all natural phenomena were produced.

Such was the wisdom of one who laughed at the follies of his fellows, and is stated to have put out his own eyes that nothing might distract the current of his thoughts.

School of Epicurus.—The materialism of Democritus was at a later day elaborated by EPICURUS (born on Samos about 340 B.C.) into a system of philosophy which gained so many converts that we are told whole cities could not contain the friends and followers of its author. According to the Epicurean philosophy, chance governed the world of atoms; there was no life beyond the grave. The gods were immortal, but were mere figure-heads, enjoying an emotionless inactivity, indifferent alike to the vices and fortunes of men: most likely Epicurus did not believe in any gods at all, but allowed their existence, as nonentities, that he might not shock the prejudices of the Athenians. Pleasure he made the chief end of life; but with him pleasure was not sensual indulgence; it lay in freedom from pain, the sober exercise of reason, and the nobler enjoyments of man's higher nature. Such a doctrine, it is plain, was but too easy of perversion. The pure, high-toned "pleasure" of the moral Epicurus degenerated with the voluptuaries and profligates that adopted his tenets into the vilest excesses, and the very name *epicure* is applied to one unduly addicted to the gratifying of the appetite.

The Skeptical Philosophy.—PYRRHO, who flourished about

300 B.C., was the father of the Skeptics. They held that there was no standard of truth appreciable by the human mind; nothing can therefore be asserted as true. Pyrrho doubted everything; his disciples used to follow him, lest, in practically applying his theory, he should be run over in the streets or walk off a precipice.

The Socratic School.—When Socrates (470–399 B.C.) came upon the stage in the golden period of Athens, it was to denounce the atheistical philosophy of his predecessors, and take the field against the Sophists, who made endless disputation, fallacious but specious, the head and front of their system. "These word-snapping quibblers," says Felton, "were prodigious favorites with the Athenians,—men who proved that right was wrong, and wrong right, and that there was neither wrong nor right; that knowing one thing is knowing everything, and that there is no such thing as knowing anything at all; that as the beautiful exists by the presence of beauty, so a man becomes an ass by the presence of an ass; and so on, ringing myriads of changes, like the fools in Shakespeare, upon these quirks of jugglery."

Socrates had an effective way of dealing with these gentry. By cunningly contrived questions, which at first seemed to have no bearing on the point at issue, he led them on from admission to admission, until he involved them in absurdities and convicted them out of their own mouths.

For one like Socrates, the mythology of Greece was too gross, the speculations of the philosophy then current were too unreal and hollow. He aspired to something better. At length the unity of God, the soul's immortality, and the moral responsibility of man, dawned upon his mind—sublime truths which he might well have drawn from revelation itself. The practice of virtue he inculcated as indispensable to happiness and true religion. A *demon*, or secret influence, he said, constantly attended him, and was his director in the work of social reform no less than in the every-day affairs of life. Whether he deceived himself in this belief or strove to deceive others into it that he might gain credence for his doctrines, certain it is that his teachings exercised a most wholesome influence. All subsequent Greek philosophy is stamped with their impress.

In his domestic relations, Socrates was not happy. Believing it incumbent on him to devote every moment to philosophical inquiry or exhortations of the people to practical morality, he was wont to neglect his legitimate business of stone-cutting, and leave his family to provide for its own support. This was too much for his good wife Xantippe. Something of a shrew even under the best of circumstances, we may imagine that she made his household rather hot, particularly when he brought guests home to dinner and there was nothing in the larder. On one occasion she went so far as to give emphasis to her reproaches with a shower of dish-water. The dripping philosopher, not in the least disturbed, calmly remarked, "I thought after so much thunder, we should have some rain."

Socrates declined the invitation of a Macedonian prince to live in luxury at his court, with the characteristic reply, "At Athens meal is two-pence the measure, and water may be had for nothing." He clung to Athens to the last, and so doing won a martyr's crown. Accused of impiety in corrupting the religious belief of the young committed to his charge, he was condemned to drink the fatal hemlock. Surrounded by sorrowing disciples, who had bribed the jailer and vainly urged him to fly while there was yet time, he calmly placed the cup to his lips, and soon after passed away with not a doubt as to "the undiscovered country." "I derive confidence," said he, "from the hope that something of man remains after death, and that the condition of good men will then be much better than that of the bad."

Socrates failed to commit his philosophy to writing; it is from the pages of Xenophon and Plato, his most devoted admirers, that we have learned his doctrines.

The principal schools that originated in the Socratic were the Academic, Peripatetic, Cynic, and Stoic.

Academic School. — Plato. — The Academic School was founded by Socrates' pupil, Plato, and derived its name from the grove of Acade′mus, a public garden at Athens in which this philosopher was accustomed to deliver his lectures. Beneath its planes and olives flowed the stream Cephissus;

GROVE OF ACADEMUS.

statues and temples were scattered through its shade, and solitary paths invited to rest and meditation.

Plato was noble-born, tracing his descent from King Codrus through one parent and from Solon through the other. His great genius was early seen. After mastering the elementary branches, he turned his attention to painting and poetry; but when he compared an epic on which he had tried his hand with Homer's, he threw it into the fire in disgust. Chancing to hear Socrates discourse, he forthwith resolved to forsake the ornamental arts and study philosophy. So, when only twenty, Plato attached himself to Socrates; his admiration quickly ripened into an abiding affection; and for eight years he sat at the philosopher's feet as a pupil, though now and then obtruding new theories of his own. In the dark days of his master's trial and condemnation, he was still faithful; and when the judges silenced his speech in defence of Socrates, he would have resorted to the money-argument, which then, as now, seldom failed, had not the high-minded sage refused to secure life by such ignoble means.

After the execution of Socrates, Plato pursued his studies in foreign lands. He visited Italy, Sicily, and Egypt, carefully examining their different systems of philosophy, and possibly even making the acquaintance of the Hebrew Scriptures. During this tour he is related to have been sold into slavery at the instigation of Dionysius, tyrant of Syracuse, whom he had offended by his bold expressions.

On his return to Athens, in accordance with a long-cherished plan, Plato opened an humble dwelling in the grove of Academus for the reception of pupils, and founded the famous Academic School. He soon became the most popular man in Athens. Crowds thronged to his lectures and dialogues, which were free to all; and even ladies assumed male attire, that they might mingle unnoticed with the listeners and drink in the eloquence which flowed from his lips. His fame went abroad also. Foreign potentates sought his aid in adjusting political difficulties; and twice, by request, he returned to the

Syracusan court to effect a reform in the government—but in this case, without success.

On his eighty-second birthday, while he was pursuing his accustomed occupation, the stylus suddenly fell from Plato's hand, and he expired. Under the trees so long associated with his kindly instruction, he found a final resting-place; an admiring country preserved his memory by altars and statues; and the verdict of succeeding generations has been that Plato was the greatest philosopher of antiquity.

PLATO'S PHILOSOPHICAL SYSTEM.—Plato was an enthusiast in the pursuit of truth. He believed in a personal God, rational, immutable, eternal. He realized that man could never attain absolute wisdom, possible to God alone; and looked upon philosophy as "a longing after heavenly wisdom." He sought to correct abuses, to elevate humanity; and made man's highest duty consist in searching out God and imitating the perfection of the Almighty as his rule of conduct. The four cardinal virtues were wisdom, temperance, courage, and justice; but none could be virtuous without aid from on high.

The soul, an emanation from the Supreme Mind, was immortal. It existed before its union with the body, and all earthly knowledge is but the recollection of what it possessed in some former state. When, disembodied, it stood face to face with kindred immaterial essences, it acquired those *ideas*, or *forms*, which figure so prominently in the Platonic system—interpreted by some to mean veritable objective existences too subtile to be discerned by the eye of flesh, and by others explained as mere intuitions or generalizations having no objective reality.

Plato regarded men as free agents, to be rewarded or punished in a future life for their deeds in this. His poetical fancy fixed on some distant star as the abode of the blessed. The earth he supposed to occupy the centre of the universe.

It was not eternal, but was made by an intelligent God, who breathed into it a soul; so it was a living creature, self-active, and gifted with the beautiful form of the sphere.

Nor did the philosopher forget to train the reasoning powers, by the study of mathematics. The importance he attached to this science may be inferred from the sign on his school: "Let no one enter here who is a stranger to geometry." Plato has the honor of having been the inventor of geometrical analysis.

PLATO'S WORKS, which have descended to us unimpaired, are in the form of dialogues—a delightful method of conveying philosophical instruction, when, as in Plato's case, the personages introduced as speakers are salient characters, and their idiosyncrasies are maintained throughout with discrimination. The dull lessons of dialectics are thus enlivened by graphic portraitures and happy strokes of humor. Plato's language is the perfection of Attic prose, beautified by a poetical tinge. "If Jupiter should speak Greek," said ancient critics, "it would be Plato's." What Socrates dreamed on the night before the young Plato entered his school—that a cygnet came from the grove of Academus, and, after nestling on his breast for a time, took its flight heavenward, singing sweetly as it rose—is recorded as presaging his pupil's sweet mastery of words.

The Platonic Dialogues, thirty-five in number, discuss various subjects. One of the finest is "Phædo," written to prove the immortal nature of the soul. It derives its name from the beloved disciple of Socrates, who is here made by Plato, prevented from being present himself, to describe their master's death-scene and repeat his last discourse. Full of sublime and poetical conceptions, the "Phædo" aims at lifting the mind above the sensual to the spiritual and eternal; at foreshadowing the joys of the heavenly state, and painting death as a thing to be desired rather than feared, since it is the portal of bliss. The philosopher Cleom'brotus, on reading this Dialogue, is said to have thrown himself into the sea to exchange this life for the better one pictured by Plato.

EXTRACT FROM PHÆDO.

(Socrates, having proved the immortality of the soul to the satisfaction of all present in the prison, addresses them as follows.)

"Then, Cebes, beyond question, the soul is immortal and imperishable, and our souls will truly exist in another world!"

"I am convinced, Socrates," said Cebes, "and have nothing more to object; but if my friend Simmias, or any one else, has any further objection, he had better speak out, and not keep silence, since I do not know to what other season he can defer the discussion, if there is anything which he wants to say or have said."

"I have nothing more to say," replied Simmias; "nor can I see any reason for doubt after what has been said. But I still feel and cannot help feeling uncertain in my own mind, when I think of the greatness of the subject and the feebleness of man."

"Yes, Simmias," replied Socrates, "that is well said; but O my friends! if the soul is really immortal, what care should be taken of her, not only in respect of the portion of time which is called life, but of eternity! And the danger of neglecting her from this point of view does indeed appear to be awful. If death had only been the end of all, the wicked would have had a good bargain in dying, for they would have been happily quit not only of their body, but of their own evil together with their souls. But now, inasmuch as the soul is manifestly immortal, there is no release or salvation from evil except the attainment of the highest virtue and wisdom. For the soul, when on her progress to the world below, takes nothing with her but nurture and education; and these are said greatly to benefit or greatly to injure the departed, at the very beginning of his pilgrimage in the other world.

"Wherefore, Simmias, seeing all these things, what ought not we to do that we may obtain virtue and wisdom in this life? Fair is the prize, and the hope great!

"A man of sense ought not to say that the description which I have given of the soul and her mansions is exactly true. But I do say that, inasmuch as the soul is shown to be immortal, he may venture to think that something of the kind is true. The venture is a glorious one, and he ought to comfort himself with words like these, which is the reason why I lengthen out the tale.

"Wherefore, I say, let a man be of good cheer about his soul, who has cast away the pleasures and ornaments of the body as alien to him, and has followed after the pleasures of knowledge in this life; who has arrayed the soul in her own proper jewels, which are temperance, and justice, and courage, and nobility, and truth—thus adorned, she is ready to go on her journey to the world below when her hour comes.

"You, Simmias and Cebes, and all other men, will depart at some time or other. Me already, as the tragic poet would say, the voice of fate calls. Soon I must drink the poison; and I think that I had better repair to the bath first, in order that the women may not have the trouble of washing my body after I am dead."

When he had done speaking, Crito said: "And have you any commands for us, Socrates? anything to say about your children, or any other matter in which we can serve you?"

"Nothing particular," he said: "only, as I have always told you, I would have you look to yourselves; that is a service which you may always be doing to me and mine as well as to yourselves."

"We will do our best," said Crito; "but in what way would you have us bury you?"

"In any way that you like; only you must get hold of me, and take care that I do not walk away from you."

Then he turned to us, and added with a smile:—"I cannot make Crito believe that I am the same Socrates who have been talking and conducting the argument; he fancies that I am the other Socrates whom he will soon see, a dead body—and he asks, How shall he bury me? And though I have spoken many words in the endeavor to show that when I have drunk the poison I shall leave you and go to the joys of the blessed, these words of mine, with which I comforted you and myself, have had, as I perceive, no effect upon Crito.

"You must be my surety to him that I shall not remain, but go away and depart; and then he will suffer less at my death, and not be grieved when he sees my body being burned or buried. I would not have him sorrow at my hard lot, or say at the burial, 'Thus we lay out Socrates,' or 'Thus we follow him to the grave or bury him;' for false words are not only evil in themselves, but they infect the soul with evil.

"Be of good cheer then, my dear Crito, and say that you are burying my body only, and do with that as is usual, and as you think best."—JOWETT.

In his "Republic," Plato indulges in a political dream, sketching an ideal government and embodying his conception of absolute justice. In his "Atlantis," he describes a large island lying west of Europe, which some have tried to connect with America.

The Academic School long survived its founder; but little if any advance was made by his successors. Its fundamental tenets outlived Greece and Rome, to reappear in the schools of modern times. Many of them are in wonderful harmony with Christian doctrines; and such a resemblance to the Jewish Scriptures has been detected in the writings of their author that he has been called "the Attic Moses."

Peripatetic School.—Aristotle.—The Peripatetic was an offshoot from the Academic School, its founder Aristotle having for twenty years studied under Plato. Its influence cannot be estimated; for 1,800 years, up to the revival of letters in modern times, its author was recognized as the supreme authority on every subject, whether by Moslem or Christian.

ARISTOTLE (384–322 B.C.) was born at the Thracian town of Stagi'ra. Inheriting from his father literary tastes as well as the means to gratify them, he selected Athens as the scene of his labors, and there, at the age of seventeen, he entered the Academy of Plato. So energetically did he apply himself, not as a servile follower but often as a pioneer in new paths of his own, that his master said he required the bit rather than the spur, and styled him the Intellect of the school. On one occasion, when none but this ardent pupil was present to hear his lecture, Plato proceeded as usual, saying that "so long as he had Aristotle for an audience, he had the better half of Athens." His industry was proverbial; he grudged the time needed for repose, and used to sleep with a ball in his hand, that when it fell from his grasp by the relaxing of the muscles the noise would awaken him.

When Plato died, Aristotle retired from the Academy; and in 342 B.C. he received the following letter from Philip of Macedon, whose court he had visited as an ambassador:—

> "PHILIP to ARISTOTLE, wisheth health:
> Be informed that I have a son, and that I am thankful to the gods, not so much for his birth, as that he was born in the same age with you; for if you will undertake the charge of his education, I assure myself that he will become worthy of his father, and of the kingdom which he will inherit."

There was no declining such an invitation. At Stagira, his

native town, Philip provided a school and the accustomed grove for instruction, in which the philosopher moulded the mind of Alexander the future Conqueror. The king of Macedon was more than satisfied with the results; and the royal pupil owned his indebtedness to his teacher, exclaiming, "Philip only gave me life, but Aristotle has taught me the art of living well!"

When, on the assassination of Philip, Alexander mounted the throne and embarked on that expedition which extended the sway of Macedon over half the known world, he showed his gratitude by making his instructor a munificent present equivalent to nearly $1,000,000, and employed two or three thousand men to fill his cabinets with specimens. Thus supplied with material and funds, Aristotle, established in Athens since 335 B.C. as a distinguished teacher despite his traditional lisp and insignificant appearance, vigorously prosecuted his scientific labors. At the Lyce'um, Apollo's temple, he gave instruction to his disciples, walking up and down in the covered paths (*peripatoi*) about the building—whence the name of his school, *Peripatetic.* He mastered all existing knowledge, regarding learning as "an ornament to men in prosperity, a refuge in adversity;" and for thirteen years divided his time between his pupils and his literary work.

The news of Alexander's sudden death was the signal for Aristotle's enemies, no longer restrained by fear of his royal friend, to show their hand. Impiety was alleged against him; but mindful of the fate of Socrates, and, as he said, to prevent the Athenians from sinning a second time against philosophy, he retired to Chalcis on the island of Eubœa, where he died within a year.

PHILOSOPHY AND WRITINGS OF ARISTOTLE.—While to some extent following his master, from several of Plato's doctrines Aristotle felt compelled to dissent; truth, he said, was dearer to him than any friend.* He did not accept the Ideal theory, but inclined to materialism or to pantheism, making *reason* divine and omnipresent. He doubted his own immortality, holding that the soul could not exist apart from the body, and that there is "nothing good or bad beyond to the dead." His style was dry, elliptical, and full of technicalities; if we compare it with Plato's, we have the opposite poles of the magnet.

Plato was all imagination, Aristotle was thoroughly practical. The inspiration of the one was a passionate love of wisdom; the forte of the other was power of analysis, a wonderful faculty of systemizing knowledge. The master captivated the heart; the pupil convinced the reason. "The philosophy of Plato," says Dr. Draper, "is a gorgeous castle in the air; that of Aristotle is a solid structure laboriously founded on rock."

Aristotle's style is devoid of ornament, and his subjects are too abstruse for the general run of readers; but he was a keen observer and a close reasoner. A few paragraphs from his Rhetoric, in which he analyzes the peculiarities of old age, will show how well he understood human nature.

THE DISPOSITION OF THE OLD.

"Those who are advanced in life, having been deceived in a greater number of instances, err in everything more on the side of defect than they ought. And they always *suppose*, but never *know* certainly; and, questioning everything, they always subjoin a *perhaps*, or a *possibly*. And they are apt to view things in an unfavorable light; for a disposition thus to view things, is the judging of everything on the worse side.

Moreover, they are apt to be suspicious from distrust, and they are distrustful from their experience. And on this account they neither love nor hate with great earnestness; but, conformably to the remark of Bias, they both love as though about to hate, and hate as though about to love. And they are pusillanimous, from their hav-

---

* Hence probably the origin of the proverb, "Amicus Plato, sed magis amica veritas"—"*Plato is dear, but truth is dearer.*"

ing been humbled by the course of life; for they raise their desires to nothing great or vast, but to things only which conduce to the support of life.

And they are illiberal; for property is one of the necessaries; and they are at the same time aware, from their experience, of the difficulty of its acquisition, and of the ease with which it is lost. They are timid and apprehensive of everything; for their disposition is the reverse of that of the young; for they have been chilled by years, but the young are warm in their temperament; so that their age has paved the way to timidity; for fear is a certain kind of chill.

And they are attached to life, and particularly at its last closing day, from the circumstance that desire is of some object which is absent, and that men more especially desire that of which they stand in need.

They have self-love more than is fitting; for this too is a kind of littleness of spirit. And they live in a greater degree than they ought by the standard of expediency, and not of what is honorable, by reason of their self-love: for what is expedient is good *relatively* to one's self, but what is honorable is good *absolutely*.

Again, they are not easily inspired with hope, on account of their experience; for the majority of things are but paltry; wherefore the generality turn out inferior to the expectation; and once more, on account of their timidity they are apt to despond. And they live more in memory than in hope; for the remnant of life is brief, but what has passed is considerable; and hope indeed is of what is to come; whereas memory is of things gone by. The very reason, this, of their garrulity; for they never cease talking of that which has taken place, since they are delighted in awakening the recollections of things.

And their anger is keen, but faint. And some of their desires have abandoned them. Others are faint; so that neither are they liable to the influence of desire, nor apt to act in conformity to it, but with a view to gain; on which account men of this age appear to be naturally temperate, for both their desires have relaxed, and they are enslaved to gain.

The old have moreover a tendency to pity, but not on the same principle with the young; for the latter are thus disposed from their love of human nature; the former from their imbecility. Whence they are querulous, and neither facetious nor fond of mirth; for querulousness is the very reverse of fondness for mirth. Such is the disposition of those in advanced life."—THEODORE BUCKLEY.

The writings of Aristotle exhausted the fields of art and science; 400 treatises, most of which have perished, at one time bore his name. Rhetoric, psychology or mental science, and natural history, owed to him their origin. In his "Organon" was first presented the method of *deduction*,—the process by which the mind reasons down from general propositions to particular cases, by means of the *syllogism*, the *organ* or instrument of reasoning. Men had thus arrived at conclusions for ages, without any knowledge of Aristotle's formulæ, just as they had talked correctly though ignorant of analytical grammar. It was reserved for the Stagirite to discover the laws by which they drew conclusions, and thus at once to found and perfect LOGIC. This was the science of *reasoning*, as contrasted with Plato's *dialectics* or method of *discussing*.

Nor was Aristotle unacquainted with Induction, the great lever of modern philosophy. This process, which reverses the steps of deduction,* and reasons from particular cases up to general laws, was employed in his researches, but was not fully developed till twenty centuries later in the "Novum Organon" of Lord Bacon, opening the way to a new era in scientific investigation.

Aristotle willed his writings to his disciple Theophrastus, whom we shall next consider; and for many years they were kept from the world, while numerous imitations and forgeries gained the popular ear through the prestige of Aristotle's name. It was not till 50 B.C. that a complete edition of the genuine works was published, and then at Rome. Meanwhile the Lyceum had waned; its later heads were men of mediocre ability,

---

* The difference between reasoning by Deduction and by Induction may be made clearer by the following examples:—

DEDUCTION.—Dogs are quadrupeds.
Tray is a dog.
Therefore, Tray is a quadruped.

INDUCTION.—Tray is a quadruped; Carlo is a quadruped; Fan is a quadruped; Pet is a quadruped; etc.
Tray, Carlo, Fan, Pet, etc., are dogs.
Therefore, *all* dogs are quadrupeds.

and the Peripatetic School was superseded in popular estimation by the Epicurean and the Stoic.

Theophrastus, of Lesbos (374–287 B.C.), a pupil of Plato and afterward of Aristotle, succeeded the latter, by his appointment, as head of the Lyceum. During his time, he maintained the high reputation of the school, attracting many to it from all parts of Greece by his eloquence. That he might address a still larger audience, he wrote numerous treatises on philosophy and natural history.

His "Moral Characters," which have descended to us, show up in lively colors such representative personages as the Gabbler, the Niggard, the Noodle, the Grumbler, the Swell, the Poltroon, the Slanderer, the Newsmonger, the Clown, etc., from whom, it seems, that Greek society was not exempt any more than our own. These were the first character-sketches ever made; they served as models to La Bruyère in French, to Sir Thomas Overbury and others in English literature. As specimens, we cull the most pointed portions of the sections on the Flatterer and the Unseasonable Man.

THE FLATTERER.

"Flattery may be considered as a mode of companionship, degrading but profitable to him who flatters.

The Flatterer is a person who will say as he walks with another, 'Do you observe how people are looking at you? This happens to no man in Athens but you. A compliment was paid to you yesterday in the Porch. More than thirty persons were sitting there; the question was started, Who is our foremost man? Every one mentioned you first, and ended by coming back to your name.'

Then he will request the company to be silent while the great man is speaking, and will praise him, too, in his hearing, and mark his approbation at a pause with 'True;' or he will laugh at a frigid joke, and stuff his cloak into his mouth as if he could not repress his amusement.

He will request those whom he meets to stand still until 'his Honor' has passed. He will buy apples and pears, and bring them in, and give to the children in the father's presence; adding, with kisses, 'Chicks of a good father.' Also, when he assists at the purchase of slippers, he will declare that the foot is more shapely than the shoe. If his patron is approaching a friend, he will run forward and say, 'He is coming to you;' and then, turning back, 'I have announced you.'

He is the first of the guests to praise the wine; and to say, as he reclines next the host, 'How delicate is your fare! and (taking up something from the table) 'Now this—how excellent it is!' He will say that his patron's house is well built, that his land is well planted, and that his portrait is a good likeness."—JEBB.

MR. MALAPROP.

"Unseasonable behavior is such a manner of conversation as is very troublesome to those with whom you converse.

A man that acts unseasonably will intrude himself upon his friend, when he is engaged in earnest business, and consult him about his own private concerns. When his mistress lies dangerously ill of a fever, he'll make her a visit and carry himself gayly. If he stands in need of a surety, he begs that favor of one who has just smarted for being bound to another. If he is summoned for a witness in any cause, he appears in court immediately after judgment has been given.

When he is invited to a wedding, he takes the opportunity to rail at the fair sex. If he meets a friend who has just come home from a long journey, he'll press him to take a walk. He is ever ready and punctual, as soon as a shop-keeper has sold his goods, to help him to a customer that would have given more.

If he happens to be in a place where a servant is chastised, all the comfort he gives him is to tell him that he also had formerly a boy whom he chastised in the same manner, and that the poor lad so resented this usage that he immediately made way with himself. If he is accidentally present at an arbitration, where the contending parties desire to have the matter in dispute between them amicably settled, instead of promoting a reconciliation, he sets them together by the ears, and makes the difference ten times greater than it was before."—GALLY.

The Stoic School was so called from the Painted Portico (*stoa*) at Athens, where its founder ZENO, the Cyprian, taught for fifty-eight years (318–260 B.C.). It was based on high moral principles, but was not free from errors. Duty was all in this philosophy; virtue alone, happiness. Mastery of self, contempt alike for pleasure and pain, were leading doctrines.

Fate governed the world, even God himself. Yet Zeno did not allow this doctrine to excuse shortcomings or interfere with individual responsibility. When his slave, detected in theft, besought exemption from chastisement on the plea that it was fated for him to steal, he replied, "Yes, and it was also fated for you to be flogged."

Suicide, in Zeno's creed, was justifiable when a man had outlived his usefulness, and the great philosopher practised as he preached; for, having received a severe fall at the age of ninety-eight, he quietly remarked, "I obey the summons," and went and hanged himself.

Zeno enjoyed public confidence at home as well as the respect of foreign princes; among his disciples were enrolled some of the greatest men of Greece and Rome. Nothing remains of his writings.

The Cynics derived their name from the gymnasium of *Cynosarges*, near the Lyceum, where they gathered to listen to Antisthenes, a pupil of Socrates. This extremist perverted his master's theory of virtue, which he made to consist in a comfortless life, a renunciation of pleasure, and a contemptuous and even shameless independence of manners. Yet Socrates saw pride even through the holes of Antisthenes' shabby robe.

Antisthenes was not much in metaphysics. He was puzzled by abstract generalizations, and to Plato's Idealism opposed an uncompromising Realism. "Plato," he said, "I can see a horse, and I can see a man, but horsehood and manhood I cannot see."—"True," replied Plato, "you have the eye that can see a horse and a man; but the eye which can see horsehood and manhood you lack."

Of the many works of this first Cynic philosopher, scarcely anything is left. They were probably steeped in gall, for his powers of sarcasm were unsurpassed; he dealt trenchant blows at what he considered folly, wherever he found it. He ridiculed the want of judgment displayed at Athens in the selection of generals, by counselling the Athenians to vote their asses horses. "That is absurd," was the reply. "No more so," he retorted, "than to think you have made ignoramuses generals, by simply lifting up the hand." Once when annoyed at a speaker's dilating on the joys of the future state, he abruptly demanded, "Why don't you die, then?"

His successor, DIOGENES, carried out the rôle. Soured by the disgraceful failure of his father, he turned to the ascetic philosophy of the Cynics, and took a morbid pleasure in outraging society by his infringements on decency. His satirical remarks, which cut to the quick, earned him the title of "the Dog" by way of eminence. He slept wherever he happened to be, on stoops or in a tub; and eschewing artificial wants, he felt so rebuked when he saw a boy drinking through his hands and receiving his pottage in a hollowed loaf, that he threw away his cup and platter.

Into such snarling, insolent, and offensive misanthropes did the Cynics degenerate, that the name of their sect was popularly traced to the *dogs* (in Greek *cynes*) they so much resembled.—To this complexion did the noble philosophy of Socrates come at last.

ORATORY.

Political Eloquence, like the drama, history, and philosophy, attained perfection in the golden age. Public speaking was a natural accomplishment of the Greeks; and from the days of Homer down, soldiers, legislators, and statesmen, had been distinguished as orators. In Pericles, who made eloquence a study, we are introduced to one of the world's most polished speakers.

But the cultivation of rhetoric and oratory as an art was first popularized by Gorgias of Leonti'ni (see Map, p. 304), who about 427 B.C. transplanted it from Sicily and saw it flourish in Athenian soil as it had never flourished before. Gorgias founded a school of eloquence at Athens, which was thronged by the great men of the time, eager to acquire the persuasive arts of the Sicilian teacher. Thus rhetoric became a fashionable accomplishment; and to such account was it turned by the taste and genius of the Attic Greeks that they soon produced the greatest orators of history.

Among these was the graceful and elegant LYSIAS (*lish'e-ăs* —458–378 B.C.), compared by Quintilian to a pure fountain rather than a great river; and ISÆUS, the leading barrister of Athens and preceptor of Demosthenes. Greater than either as a teacher and writer of orations for others, though through timidity he rarely appeared in public himself, was ISOCRATES, founder of a school from which Cicero said, "as from the Trojan horse, princes only proceeded;" to use his own figure, he was a whetstone which imparted the power of cutting to other things, but cut not itself. Finally, to this category belonged the great rivals Æschines and Demosthenes, foremost of the Attic orators.

Demosthenes (384–322 B.C.—it is worth remembering that his dates are identical with Aristotle's) stands alone in the power of his eloquence. Born in Attica, he was left fatherless at the age of seven, but inherited a large fortune. The bulk of this his guardians made away with; although they engaged the best talent in the land to superintend the education of their ward. When Demosthenes arrived at his majority, he brought suit against them, and wrote his maiden speeches with such skill as to obtain a judgment in his favor.

The study of oratory now became the passion of his life. By indomitable perseverance he overcame what to many would have proved insuperable difficulties—shortness of breath, a sickly constitution, a weak and stammering utterance, and awkwardness in gesticulating. He practised on the seashore till his voice rose clear and full above the breakers; he placed pebbles in his mouth while declaiming to correct his articulation, and improved his breathing by running up steep hills. A friendly mirror helped him to make his gestures effective; and he spent months at a time in a room underground, occupied in study, or in copying the history of Thucydides to strengthen his style. Thus, in spite of every natural disadvantage, he placed himself by his own efforts "at the head of all mighty masters of speech." He lived to receive the homage, not only of those Athenians who had hissed the early performances of "the stammerer," but of crowds gathered from all quarters of Greece.

Conciseness, precision, clearness, compact reasoning, power of invective, and vehemence compared to that of a torrent carrying everything before it, were characteristic of the orations of Demosthenes. Sixty-one of these (probably not all genuine) are still extant, the most famous being the twelve "Philippics," delivered against Philip of Macedon, who was insidiously plotting the subversion of Grecian liberty. Demosthenes penetrated his designs, disdained his bribes, and for fourteen years struggled nobly against him. His impassioned utterances at last roused the slumbering patriotism of his countrymen, and, joined by the Thebans, they met Philip at Chæronea—but only to be hopelessly defeated. The fate of Greece was sealed. Demosthenes fled from the field and escaped to Athens, where he delivered the funeral eulogy on the slain.

The success of Philip strengthened the Macedonian sympathizers in Athens, at the head of whom was the orator Æschines, accused by Demosthenes of being in the pay of Macedon. When, therefore, Ctesiphon proposed that the services of Demosthenes be rewarded with a golden crown, Æschines opposed the measure. After a delay of six years, during which we may be sure both orators strained every nerve to prepare for the decisive struggle, the final contest took place before a vast and excited concourse. The fiery vigor of Demosthenes, in the most splendid effort of ancient eloquence, swept away like feathers the arguments, the wit, the sarcasm, of his opponent; Æschines was utterly discomfited.

The elaborate speech "On the Crown" is the masterpiece of Demosthenes; we give parts of the peroration.

FROM DEMOSTHENES' ORATION ON THE CROWN.

"Do you then, Æschines, ask me for what merit I claim public honors? I will tell you. It is because, when all the statesmen in Greece had been corrupted, beginning with yourself, first by Philip and then by Alexander, I was never induced nor tempted by opportunity, nor by fair speeches, nor by the magnitude of proffered bribes, nor by hope, nor by fear, nor by favor, nor by any other consideration, to swerve a hair's-breadth from the course which I believed to be right and for the public good. Never, in weighing my public counsels, have I, like you, inclined to the scale in which hung my private advantage; but all that I have done has been done straightforwardly, incorruptly, and with singleness of purpose. While I have been charged with affairs of greater magnitude than any of my contemporaries, the whole of my administration has been pure, honest, disinterested. These are the grounds on which I claim to be honored.

As for the fortifications and intrenchments which you have sneered at, I deem myself entitled to thanks and gratitude on that behalf. Wherefore should I not? But I am far, indeed, from placing such services in the same category with my general policy. It is not with stones nor with bricks that I have fortified Athens; it is not upon such works that I chiefly value myself; but if you would truly appreciate my fortifications, you will find them in arms, cities, territories, harbors, ships, and men to avail themselves of these advantages. These are the outworks which I have thrown up before Attica, according to the best of human foresight; by these have I fortified the whole country, not merely the circuit of the Piræus and the city. Nor was I defeated by the calculations or preparations of Philip; far from it: but the generals and the forces of our allies were defeated by Fortune. * * *

If my measures had been successful—O heaven and earth! we must, beyond all question, have become a first-rate power, as we well deserved to be. If they have failed, we have left to us our honor. No reproach can attach to the state or to its policy, but Fortune must bear the blame, who has so ordered our affairs. Never, never, will the patriotic citizen desert his country's cause, and, hiring himself to her foes, watch his opportunities of injuring her; never will he malign the statesman who in his utterances and his measures has consistently maintained his country's honor; nor will he nurse and treasure up resentment for private wrongs; nor, lastly, will he maintain a dishonest and a treacherous silence, as you have often done. * * *

No part, Æschines, have you taken in any measure for strengthening the country's resources. What alliance has been ever obtained for the state through your instrumentality? What succor? What acquisition of good-will from others, or credit for ourselves? What embassy? What public service that has added to our national renown? What public affairs, whether domestic, Hellenic, or foreign, have been brought by you to a successful issue? What ships have you furnished? What arms? What dockyards? What fortifications? What cavalry? In what one respect have you been useful? What pecuniary contribution have you ever made upon public grounds for the benefit of either the rich or the poor? None.

You were not deterred by your poverty, but by your anxiety to do nothing opposed to the interests of those for whose benefit all your policy has been designed. But what are the occasions of your brilliant displays, the exhibition of your youthful vigor? When aught is to be spoken against your countrymen, then is your voice best tuned, then is your memory most accurate; then you act your part to perfection. * * *

Every well-affected citizen, Athenians, (in such terms I am able to speak of myself least invidiously) is bound to possess two qualities: when in authority, the fixed resolve to maintain the honor and pre-eminence of his country; under all circumstances and at all times, loyalty. This Nature can command—to another power belong strength and success. By this spirit you find me to have been uniformly actuated.

Observe—never when I was demanded for extradition, nor when Amphictyonic suits were prosecuted against me, nor when threats, nor when promises were brought to bear upon me, nor when these miscreants were let loose like wild beasts upon me—never was I induced to abandon one jot or tittle of my loyalty to you. From first to last I took the straight and true path of statesmanship—that of complete devotion to the maintenance and furtherance of the honor, the power, and the glory of my country. Never was I beheld strutting about the Forum, radiant with joy and exultation at foreign success, gesticulating congratulations to those who might be expected to report them elsewhere. Nor have I heard the tidings of our good fortune with dismay and lamentations, and prostration to the earth, like these impious men who inveigh against their country without perceiving that their invective is directed against themselves, whose eyes are cast abroad, who felicitate themselves on foreign success purchased by the calamities of Greece, and avow their anxiety to secure its permanence.

Never, O ye Heavenly Powers! never may such designs obtain favor at your hands! Rather, if it be possible, inspire even these men with better thoughts, and turn their hearts; but if their moral plague be incurable, cut them off from among us, and drive them forth to destruction, sure and swift, over land and over sea: while to us who are spared ye vouchsafe the speediest deliverance from our impending alarms, and abiding security!"—SIR ROBERT COLLIER.

Twice after the reverse of Chæronea Demosthenes succeeded in arraying his country against Macedon — at the assassination of Philip and on the death of Alexander. When news of Alexander's decease reached Greece, the orator was in exile, having been unjustly convicted of taking Macedonian treasure; yet he did his utmost to arm the Grecian cities, and was in consequence recalled to Athens by the fickle people. But it was all in vain.

At last, marked for destruction by the Macedonian regent Antip'ater, and doomed to death by his cowardly fellow-citizens whose necks were now under the tyrant's heel, he fled to the temple of Neptune on Calaure'a and there found relief from his troubles in a quill of poison which he kept ready for an emergency. In Demosthenes, Athens lost an incorruptible patriot—antiquity, one of her noblest characters. The Athenians erected to his memory a brazen statue on which was inscribed:—

> "Had you for Greece been strong, as wise you were,
> The Macedonians had not conquered her."

Æschines (389–314 B.C.), of whose early life little is known, after his defeat at the hands of Demosthenes, went into exile. We are told that his victorious rival magnanimously forgave him, and even offered him money for the journey; which led Æschines to exclaim: "How I regret leaving a country where I have found an enemy so generous that I must despair of ever meeting with a friend who shall be like him!"

Æschines afterward established himself as a teacher of oratory in Rhodes. Here he once repeated to his pupils his famous oration against Ctesiphon in the contest for the crown, which filled them with wonder that so able an orator should have been defeated. But when at their request he read the reply of Demosthenes, his audience rose to their feet with eager acclamations; and the orator, forgetting all jealousy in his admiration, cried: "What would you have said, had you heard the wild beast himself roaring it out?"

The oration against Ctesiphon is one of three familiarly known in antiquity as "the Three Graces"—a title indicative of the refinement and easy flow of the author's style, deficient as it was in the energy and vehemence of his great rival.

MINOR DRAMATIC AND LYRIC POETS.

ION (flourished 450 B.C.): a history and lyrics, as well as tragedies; called "the Eastern Star," from the first words of an ode he was composing when death overtook him.

ACHÆUS (born 484 B.C.): tragic and satirical pieces.

AG'ATHON the Athenian: received his first tragic prize, 416 B.C.; his masterpiece was "the Flower."

CALLIS'TRATUS (flourished 420 B.C.): author of the convivial ode celebrating the memory of Harmodius and Aristogiton (p. 158).

CRATI'NUS (519–423 B.C.): called the *Cup-lover* from his excesses; 21 comedies; 9 prizes; with his last comedy, "the Wine-flask," he gained the first prize, triumphing over "the Clouds" of Aristophanes.

EU'POLIS: 15 plays; his first comedy was represented 429 B.C.

CRATES (450 B.C.): 14 comedies; the first poet to represent drunkenness on the Athenian stage.

METON, the Athenian astronomer (flourished 430 B.C.): founder of the Lunar Cycle of 19 solar years, which he discovered to be nearly equal to 235 revolutions of the moon round the earth. From the "Metonic Cycle" the Greeks computed their festivals; it is still used by the Western churches in fixing Easter.

HIPPOC'RATES (460–357 B.C.), born on the island of Cos, "the Father of Medicine:" knew little of anatomy; discovered the critical days in fevers.

NOTES ON GREEK EDUCATION, ETC.

Education recognized as all-important in ancient Greece, and even made compulsory by the great lawgivers. In Homer's time, children taught obedience, respect for the aged, and modesty of deportment; sons instructed in the use of weapons and gymnastic exercises; daughters, in domestic economy and virtue. Homer's epics long the chief text-books on all subjects.

Reading and writing, accomplishments of the earliest periods. An ignorant Greek an anomaly. Even among the Spartans, who affected contempt for literature, reading and writing were practised. The magistrates and their officers were provided with wooden cylinders of the same size; when one desired to communicate, he wound a strip of parchment round his cylinder and wrote his message thereon; then, removing the strip, he sent it to the other party, who was enabled to read it by rolling it upon his own cylinder in the same folds.

In the golden age, common schools were the glory of Greece; the rudiments of education everywhere taught. The importance of grammar urged by Plato, who was the first to explain the difference between nouns and verbs; articles and conjunctions distinguished by Aristotle, and also differences of number and case. The foundation of scientific grammar laid by the Stoics, who recognized eight parts of speech. Those who could afford it completed their education at the Lyceum, Academy, or some other celebrated school, often paying most extravagantly for instruction in rhetoric and philosophy. Some teachers charged their pupils as much as $2,000 apiece for a course of lectures. Foreign languages were never studied by the Greeks.

Many private libraries were established during the golden age, but no circulating or public libraries. As early as 400 B.C. Athens carried on quite a trade in manuscripts, one quarter of the market-place being called "the book-mart." Books were generally abundant and cheap, being copied by slaves, but rare works were very costly. Plato paid $1,600 for three books, and Aristotle $3,000 for a few volumes.

Wooden tablets for accounts sold for 18 cts. each about 400 B.C. A small blank book of two wax tablets was worth less than a penny. Pencils are said to have been invented 408 B.C. by Apollodorus, the self-styled "Prince of Painters."

CHAPTER VI.

THE ALEXANDRIAN PERIOD.

Decline of Letters.—The triumph of the Doric states over Athens in the Peloponnesian War (431–404 B.C.) gave the first blow to the intellectual power of Greece. Literary decay forthwith set in; its progress was hastened by internal dissensions, and completed when liberty was hopelessly extinguished by Philip of Macedon and his successors.

Alexander indeed benefited the East by introducing the Greek language and culture, and building magnificent cities in return for her hordes of barbarians slain; but his policy left out of view the interests of Greece. While Athens remained the seminary of Europe for several centuries after his death, Alexandria, founded by him at the mouth of the Nile, became the intellectual as well as commercial capital of the world. From this city, the period we are about to consider derives its name. It extends from the death of Alexander the Great (323 B.C.) to the conquest of Egypt by the Romans (30 B.C.).

The Alexandrian Age produced no grand masterpieces. No glorious struggle for freedom inspired the historian; there was no further need for the efforts of the orator; science and criticism flourished instead of poetry; and a host of imitators usurped the place of the mighty originals of the olden time. The national taste had sadly deteriorated; an affected obscurity was fashionable; and gaudy tinsel was more highly valued than true gold.

Yet one bright bloom gladdened this waste—Idyllic Poetry, which expanded into a perfect flower in the hands of Theoc'ritus the Sicilian. A new school of comedy was also established by Menander and Phile'mon; and many seeds of Greek genius that Alexander had scattered broadcast over the earth sprung up on foreign soil, and yielded fruit—but fruit inferior to that ripened under its native sun.

DRAMATIC POETRY.

The New Comedy dealt with the follies and vices of society at large, not with individuals, the actor no longer venturing, since the downfall of political liberty, to imitate Aristophanes in representing living characters. Its simple plot was generally based on some love-intrigue. Though the broad fun of the Old Comedy was wanting, quiet humor contrasted happily with pathos, the grave with the gay; the audience, provoked by turns to laughter and to tears, were all the time learning some useful principle or moral lesson. Cicero styled the New Comedy "the mirror of real life."—The chorus now ceased to take part in the representation, and the play was divided into acts separated by intervals of time.

Of the sixty-four poets associated by the ancients with the New Comedy, the greatest were Menander and Philemon, both citizens of Athens, though Philemon was foreign-born. Not until both had passed from the stage of life was the meed of superior excellence awarded to Menander.

Menander (341–291 B.C.) dramatized love-stories for the young with elegance and dignity; while the undercurrent of wisdom that flowed through his plays recommended them to the old. Out of a hundred comedies of which he was the author, only a few fragments are left; but these Goethe pronounced "invaluable." So perfectly did he delineate character that Aristophanes, the grammarian, asked whether Menander copied life, or life Menander.

His talent early displayed itself, securing him a crown while he was yet a mere youth, but subjecting him to the displeasure of his defeated rivals, who accused him of presumption in vying with experienced poets. Menander replied to the charge by appearing on the stage with an armful of new-born puppies, which he cast into a tub of water. Bidding the audience mark how they swam, he exclaimed: "You ask me, Athenians, how at my years I can have the knowledge of life required in the dramatist; I ask you under what master and in what school these creatures learned to swim?"

Despite his superior merit, however, Menander obtained the dramatic prize but eight times, owing to the greater influence of his rival Philemon with the masses. It is stated that this injustice at length led the poet to drown himself. His plays long served as models to the comic stage. The Romans, Plautus and Terence, helped themselves freely from his treasury, and through their dramas our modern comedy may be traced back to Menander himself.

FRAGMENTS FROM MENANDER.

"When thou would'st know thyself, what man thou art,
Look at the tombstones as thou passest by:
Within those monuments lie bones and dust
Of monarchs, tyrants, sages, men whose pride
Rose high because of wealth, or noble blood,
Or haughty soul, or loveliness of limb;
Yet none of these things strove for them 'gainst time:
One common death hath ta'en all mortal men.
See thou to this, and know thee who thou art."
SYMONDS.

"The sum of all philosophy is this—
Thou art a man, than whom there breathes no creature
More liable to sudden rise and fall."

"Of all bad things with which mankind are cursed,
Their own bad tempers surely are the worst."

"The maxim 'Know thyself' does not suffice;
Know others!—know them well—that's my advice."

Philemon exhibited the first of his ninety-seven comedies when Menander was a boy of eleven. Nine years later Menander's first piece appeared, and the rivalry between the poets began. In their subsequent contests, Philemon sometimes stooped to unworthy means to defeat his opponent; still, that his countrymen really admired him is evident from the legend current of his death. As he was concluding a comedy in his ninety-ninth year, nine beautiful maidens were said to have entered his chamber and beckoned him away. They were the Muses, about to wing their flight from Athens forever, and with them departed the soul of Philemon—the last of the Athenian poets.

FRAGMENTS FROM PHILEMON.

"Have faith in God, and fear; seek not to know him,
For thou wilt gain naught else beyond thy search:
Whether he is or is not, shun to ask:
As one who is, and sees thee, always fear him."

"All are not just because they do no wrong,
But he who will not wrong me when he may,
He is the truly just. I praise not them
Who, in their petty dealings, pilfer not;
But him whose conscience spurns a secret fraud,
When he might plunder and defy surprise.
His be the praise who, looking down with scorn
On the false judgment of the partial herd,
Consults his own clear heart, and boldly dares
To be, not to be thought, an honest man."

PASTORAL POETRY.

Theocritus (flourished 283–263 B.C.). — The pastoral, or bucolic, poetry of the Greeks, which originated in the rude songs of Laconian and Sicilian shepherds, was matured and elevated into a new department of polite composition in the idyls of Theocritus. Born in Sicily, as he tells us in an epigram intended to preface his works, he was tempted to the court of Ptolemy Philadelphus. Here his refreshing pictures of rural scenery were the delight of the Alexandrians, shut in by the walls of their city from the beauties of nature. Theocritus eventually returned to Sicily, and ended his days amid his native fields.

The poetry of Theocritus exhibits originality and refinement, the Doric dialect in which he wrote lending the charm of picturesqueness to his descriptions. Pope commends him for simplicity and truthfulness to nature; Dryden, for "the inimitable tenderness of his passions" and the skill with which he disguised his art. As a delineator of natural scenery, he has no superior among ancient or modern poets.— There are extant thirty idyls and twenty-two epigrams of this poet. We present below Idyl VIII.

THE TRIUMPH OF DAPHNIS.

"Daphnis, the gentle herdsman, met once, as rumor tells,
Menalcas making with his flock the circle of the fells. [play;
Both chins were gilt with coming beards, both lads could sing and
Menalcas glanced at Daphnis, and thus was heard to say:

'Art thou for singing, Daphnis, lord of the lowing kine?
I say my songs are better, by what thou wilt, than thine.'
Then in his turn spake Daphnis, and thus he made reply:
'O shepherd of the fleecy flock, thou pipest clear and high;
But come what will, Menalcas, thou ne'er wilt sing as I.'

MENALCAS.

This art thou fain to ascertain, and risk a bet with me?

DAPHNIS.

This I full fain would ascertain, and risk a bet with thee.

MENALCAS.

But what, for champions such as we, would seem a fitting prize?

DAPHNIS.

I stake a calf: stake thou a lamb, its mother's self in size.

MENALCAS.

A lamb I'll venture never: for aye, at close of day,
Father and mother count the flock, and passing strict are they.

DAPHNIS.

Then what shall be the victor's fee? What wager wilt thou lay?

MENALCAS.

A pipe discoursing through nine mouths I made, full fair to view;
The wax is white thereon, the line of this and that edge true.
I'll risk it: risk my father's own is more than I dare do.

DAPHNIS.

A pipe discoursing through nine mouths, and fair, hath Daphnis too;
The wax is white thereon, the line of this and that edge true.
But yesterday I made it: this finger feels the pain
Still, where indeed the rifted reed hath cut it clean in twain.
But who shall be our umpire? who listen to our strain?

MENALCAS.

Suppose we hail yon goatherd; him at whose horned herd now
The dog is barking—yonder dog with white upon his brow.

Then out they called: the goatherd marked them, and up came he;
Then out they sang; the goatherd their umpire fain would be.
To shrill Menalcas' lot it fell to start the woodland lay:
Then Daphnis took it up. And thus Menalcas led the way.

MENALCAS.

Ye god-created vales and streams! Oh! if Menalcas e'er
  Piped aught of pleasant music in your ears;
Then pasture, nothing loath, his lambs; and let young Daphnis fare
  No worse, should he stray hither with his steers.

DAPHNIS.

Ye joy-abounding lawns and springs! If Daphnis sang you e'er
  Such songs as ne'er from nightingale have flowed;
Lend to his herd your fatness; and let Menalcas share
  Like plenty, should he wend along this road.

MENALCAS.

'Tis springtide all and greenness, and all the udders teem
  With milk, and all things young have life anew,
Where my sweet maiden wanders: but parched and withered seem,
  When she departeth, lawn and shepherd too.

DAPHNIS.

There sheep and goats twin-burdened abound, and honey-bees
  Peopling the hives, and oaks of statelier growth,
Where falls my darling's footstep: but hungriness shall seize,
  When she departeth, herd and herdsman both.

MENALCAS.

Storms are the fruit-tree's bane; the brook's, a summer hot and dry;
  The stag's, a woven net; a gin, the dove's;
Mankind's, a soft sweet maiden. Others have pined ere I:
  Zeus! Father! hast not thou thy lady-loves?

Thus far, in alternating strains, the lads their woes rehearsed:
Then each one gave a closing stave. Thus sang Menalcas first:—

MENALCAS.

O spare, good wolf, my weanlings! their milky mothers spare!
Harm not the little lad who hath so many in his care!
What, Firefly, is thy sleep so deep? It ill befits a hound,
When ranging with his master, to slumber over-sound.
And, wethers, of this tender grass take, nothing coy, your fill:
So, when the after-math* shall come, will none be weak or ill.
So! so! feed on, that ye be full, that not an udder fail:
Part of the milk shall rear the lambs, and part shall fill my pail.

Then Daphnis flung a carol out, as of a nightingale:—

* Second crop of grass.

DAPHNIS.

Me from her grot but yesterday a girl of haughty brow
Spied as I passed her with my kine, and said, 'How fair art thou!'
I gave for answer not so much as one disdainful word,
But, looking ever on the ground, paced onward with my herd.
For sweet the heifer's music, and sweet the heifer's breath;
Sweet things to me the youngling calf, sweet things her mother saith;
And sweet is sleep by summer brooks upon the breezy lea:
And acorns they grace well the oak, apples the apple-tree,
Her calves the cow; the herdsman, but for his herd cares he.

So sang the lads; and thereupon out spake the referee:—

GOATHERD.

O Daphnis! lovely is thy voice, thy music sweetly sung;
Such song is pleasanter to me than honey on my tongue.
Accept this pipe, for thou hast won. And, should there be some notes
That thou couldst teach *me*, as I plod alongside with my goats;
I'll give thee for thy schooling this ewe, that horns hath none:
Day after day she'll fill the can, until the milk o'errun.

Then how the one lad laughed, and leaped, and clapped his hands
for glee!
A kid that bounds to meet its dam might dance as merrily.
And how the other inly burned, struck down by his disgrace!
A maid first parting from her home might wear as sad a face.

Thenceforth was Daphnis champion of all the country side:
And won, while yet in topmost youth, a Naiad for his bride."

C. S. CALVERLEY.

Bion of Smyrna, a contemporary of Theocritus, emigrated to Sicily for the purpose of studying pastoral poetry in its native haunts. What little we know respecting his life is gathered from the elegy written by his pupil, the delicate and graceful MOSCHUS, a bucolic poet of Syracuse ranked with Theocritus and Bion, but inferior to both. "The Lament for Bion" intimates that he died from the effects of poison, administered perhaps by jealous rivals.

Bion's love-songs and pastorals are characterized by sweetness and finish; they are less life-like, however, than those of Theocritus. The "Lament for Adonis" is the poet's best effort; but as it is uninteresting to the general reader, we give a free paraphrase of

THE BIRD-CATCHER AND LOVE.

A young bird-catcher sat 'neath a wide-spreading tree,
Where the breath of the summer breeze sported free,
Looking round on the neighboring bushes with care,
To see if a songster were lingering there.
At length, in the distance, he something espies—
A creature with wings of unusual size—
"Aha! what a treasure!" he joyously cries;
"To catch such a bird would indeed be a prize!"
And then sets to work with his rods all together,
To take the huge bird without spoiling a feather.

But the creature, alarmed, from its perch quickly flew;
The boy, all excited, still kept it in view
Till it lit on a box-tree—then followed his prey;
Alas! with a cry, it again flew away.
At length he grew tired of this profitless chase,
And turned toward his home with a wearisome pace.
But ere long, on the road, an old farmer he met,
Who had taught him his snares for the songsters to set.
And he told how the bird all his skill had evaded,
And to go see this wonder the farmer persuaded.

At length they drew near; in a thicket of trees,
Whose tops gently waved in the murmuring breeze,
On a dwarf laurel-bush, on the verge of the grove,
In beauty bewitching, there sat errant Love!
His pinions hung prettily down by his side,
And his features, the Cyprian goddess's pride,
Were as lovely as ever, more roguish by half,
For he scarce could refrain from a boisterous laugh.
And as soon as he saw him, the husbandman, smiling,
Knew at once the young Love-god the boy was beguiling.

Then said he to the boy: "Quick, away from this grove!
The bird thou art seeking is mischievous Love!
Though brilliant his hues as the butterfly's wings,
And melody dwells on the strain that he sings,
Yet a dangerous prize to the catcher he'll prove.
Then away with thy birdlime, nor follow this Love!
When he flies, seize thy chance and escape if thou can,
For in vain wilt thou shun him when grown to a man.
Then thou'lt be the bird—he, the catcher, 'll pursue thee;
Though now he evades, then he'll quickly fly to thee."

LINES TO HESPER.

"Hesper, thou golden light of happy love,
Hesper, thou holy pride of purple eve,
Moon among stars, but star beside the moon,
Hail, friend! and since the young moon sets to-night
Too soon below the mountains, lend thy lamp
And guide me to the shepherd whom I love.
No theft I purpose; no wayfaring man
Belated would I watch and make my prey;
Love is my goal, and Love how fair it is,
When friend meets friend sole in the silent night,
Thou knowest, Hesper!"—SYMONDS.

FROM MOSCHUS'S LAMENT FOR BION.

"Ye mountain valleys, pitifully groan!
Rivers and Dorian springs, for Bion weep!
Ye plants, drop tears; ye groves, lamenting moan!
Exhale your life, wan flowers; your blushes deep
In grief, anemonies and roses, steep;
In whimpering murmurs, hyacinth! prolong
The sad, sad woe thy lettered petals keep;
Our minstrel sings no more his friends among—
Sicilian Muses! now begin the doleful song.

Ye nightingales! that 'mid thick leaves set loose
The gushing gurgle of your sorrow, tell
The fountains of Sicilian Arethuse
That Bion is no more; with Bion fell
The song—the music of the Dorian shell.
Ye swans of Strymon! now your banks along
Your plaintive throats with melting dirges swell,
For him who sang like you the mournful song;
Discourse of Bion's death the Thracian nymphs among—

The Dorian Orpheus, tell them all, is dead.
His herds the song and darling herdsman miss,
And oaks, beneath whose shade he propped his head.
Oblivion's ditty now he sings for Dis;
The melancholy mountain silent is;
His pining cows no longer wish to feed,
But moan for him; Apollo wept, I wis,
For thee, sweet Bion! and in mourning weed
The brotherhood of Fauns and all the Satyr breed.

The tears by Naiads shed are brimful bourns;
Afflicted Pan thy stifled music rues;
Lorn Echo 'mid her rocks thy silence mourns,
Nor with her mimic tones thy voice renews;
The flowers their bloom, the trees their fruitage lose;
No more their milk the drooping ewes supply;
The bees to press their honey now refuse;
What need to gather it and lay it by,
When thy own honey-lip, my Bion! thine is dry?"
CHAPMAN.

The Museum.—While the Muses who fled with the spirit of Philemon were never induced to return to Hellas, in the East the Greek mind, stimulated by the architectural wonders, the new religious systems, the proficiency in many departments of knowledge, which it encountered, entered upon a new phase of development. Alexandria witnessed its proudest achievements in science.

This city was embellished with temples and palaces, with parks, fountains, and monuments, until it eclipsed in beauty all others of its time. Our interest, however, centres in its marble Muse'um, or Temple of the Muses, begun by the first Ptolemy and finished by his son Philadelphus, which sent forth the greatest scientists of antiquity. In its halls, those hungering for knowledge were more than satisfied; up and down its corridors the professors walked as they gave instruction; while its botanical and zoölogical gardens afforded opportunities for delightful relaxation. An observatory and the best astronomical instruments of the day invited to the study of the heavens, and a dissecting-room was at the disposal of the anatomist. Chemical investigations were facilitated by a laboratory, where thus early the science of alchemy was born, and Philadelphus himself eagerly experimented in search of the elixir of life. To this brilliant centre of letters, the first university in the world, learned men were attracted from all quarters. At one time, 14,000 students were under instruction.

The Alexandrian Library.—The Museum was the seat of a

great library, collected in accordance with Ptolemy's command that all the writings of the earth should be brought to Egypt to be transcribed. But once there, the originals seldom parted company with the pictures and statues in Ptolemy's sculptured alcoves, the owners being obliged to content themselves with fac-similes of their treasured rolls made by the royal copyists.

GREEKS OF THE ALEXANDRIAN PERIOD.

The Egyptian kings often paid roundly for valuable manuscripts. It is stated that Philadelphus borrowed at Athens the plays of Euripides to have them copied for his library, depositing about $10,000 as security for their return. But when the work was done, he sent back the transcript, preferring to lose his money rather than part with the originals.

Philadelphus left 100,000 volumes in the library. These quadrupled after his death, and filled the Museum to overflowing, so that in the Temple of Sera'pis was opened "the Daughter Library" for the reception of additional volumes. The number of these ultimately reached 300,000, making 700,000 in all.

When, after the assassination of Pompey, Cæsar fired Alexandria (47 B.C.), the flames enwrapped the Museum, and its library perished. Antony subsequently gave Cleopatra the Pergamene Collection of parchment books (see p. 24); which, with his kingdom, Attalus III. had bequeathed to the Romans (133 B.C.). This, added to the rolls in the Temple of Serapis, formed at once an extensive library. It was increased by constant additions, but in the end served as fuel for the four thousand baths of the city, when Alexandria fell before the Mohammedan arms (640 A.D.), and the bigoted caliph decided that "if the Greek writings agreed with the Koran, they were useless and need not be preserved; if they disagreed, they were pernicious and ought to be destroyed."

POETRY AT ALEXANDRIA.

The first school of poetry at Alexandria was founded by Phile'tas (330–285 B.C.), the elegiac writer, so dwarfish and emaciated that the jesters of his time declared he had to wear leaden shoes to keep the wind from blowing him away. Philetas was the instructor of Theocritus. But the greatest names associated with the Museum are those of Callim'achus and Apollonius Rhodius.

Callimachus (250 B.C.) shines not only as a lyric and epic poet, but also as a critic and grammarian. From the position of a suburban schoolmaster he rose to that of librarian at the Museum, and made himself "the literary dictator and universal genius of his age."

Callimachus exercised his talents in all the departments of

poetry, and wrote as well in prose. His works reached the number of 800; which is not to be wondered at when we remember his remark, "A great book is a great evil." Such of his hymns and epigrams as time has spared, bear the marks of study rather than genius.

Apollonius, called **Rhodius** from his long residence in Rhodes, was born at Alexandria, and studied under Callimachus. But the master grew jealous of his pupil, and a quarrel arose between them. When, at the instigation of Callimachus, his epic poem on the Argonautic Expedition was unfavorably received by the Alexandrians, Apollonius, in his mortification, left the city and opened a school of rhetoric in Rhodes. Here he revised his poem, and became justly renowned for his brilliant attainments. After the death of Callimachus, he was recalled to Alexandria, read his epic a second time to the people, and had the satisfaction of receiving their warmest commendations with the honorable office of librarian (194 B.C.).

The "Argonautica," in four books, is all that is left of his works. We take from it the passage which describes the impression made on Medea by Jason, the leader of the expedition; compare the history of Medea as sketched in connection with the play of Euripides bearing her name, page 210.

MEDEA IN LOVE.

"Thus Medea went, her soul absorbed
In many musings, such as love incites,
Thoughts of deep care. Now all remembered things
In apparition rose before her eyes:
What was his aspect; what the robe he wore;
What words he uttered; in what posture placed,
He on the couch reclined; and with what air
He from the porch passed forth. Then red the blush
Burned on her cheek; while in her soul she thought
No other man existed like to him:
His voice was murmuring in her ears, and all
The charming words he uttered. Now, disturbed,

She trembled for his life; lest the fierce bulls,
Or lest Æe'tes should, himself, destroy
The man she loved.* And she bewailed him now
As if already dead; and down her cheeks,
In deep commiseration, the soft tear
Flowed anxiously. With piercing tone of grief
Her voice found utterance: 'Why, unhappy one!
Am I thus wretched? What concerns it me,
Whether this paragon of heroes die
The death, or flee discomfited? And yet
He should unharmed depart. Dread Hecate!
Be it thy pleasure! let him homeward pass,
And 'scape his threatened fate; or, if his fate
Beneath the bulls have destined him to fall,
First let him know that in his wretched end
Medea does not glory.' So disturbed,
Mused the sad virgin in her anguished thoughts."

ELTON.

PROSE WRITERS.

Science.—The influence of the Alexandrian university in shaping modern science was all-potential. Among its ornaments are numbered the mathematicians Euclid and Archime'des, the astronomer Eratos'thenes, Hero the inventor of a steam-engine, and Ctesibius who devised water-clocks, pumps, and other ingenious machines.

EUCLID (300 B.C.) compressed in one volume all the geometrical knowledge extant, adding several original theorems. His "Elements" has been translated into many languages, and though it has attained the venerable age of 2,200 years, its clear demonstrations are still standards in our schools.

ARCHIMEDES was educated in Alexandria, but afterward lived in Syracuse, where his mathematical genius challenged the admiration of the world. In geometry and mechanics he was the master-mind of antiquity; and until the star of Newton rose twenty centuries after, Europe saw not his equal.

* An allusion to the hostility of Æetes, Medea's father, and his fire-breathing bulls, which Jason was required to tame before he could get possession of the Golden Fleece.

Many important discoveries in physical science are due to Archimedes,—the principle of the lever, which led him to exclaim, "Give me a place to stand on, and I will move the world;" the process of finding the specific gravity of bodies; the hydraulic screw and the pulley. Of his many mathematical works, written in Doric Greek, eight survive.

ERATOSTHENES (276–196 B.C.) was the founder of geodesy and chronology, as well as a proficient in astronomy, grammar, and poetry. The ancients styled him *Pentathlos* (*quintuple athlete*); also, from his determining the magnitude of the earth, "Measurer of the Universe." His most important works are "Chronographies," and geographical and mathematical writings.

HIPPARCHUS (150 B.C.), an astronomer of the Alexandrian age, deserves mention as the inventor of the planisphere and as the first to make a catalogue of the stars. He devised the method of locating places by latitude and longitude.

Grammar. — The Museum was especially eminent as a school of grammar and criticism, the principal occupation of its scholars being the revision and correction of the texts of the old authors.

The most distinguished of the Alexandrian critics were—ZENOD'OTUS, the first librarian and critical editor of Homer's epics; ARISTOPHANES OF BYZANTIUM, his pupil (200 B.C.), the inventor of Greek accents and punctuation; ARISTARCHUS (156 B.C.), "the arch-grammarian of Greece," who divided Homer's poems into books, revised the Alexandrian canon, and was the author of 800 commentaries; and CRA'TES, head of a grammatical school at Pergamus, and the first to make grammar a popular study at Rome.

History.—POLYBIUS (204–122 B.C.) was the chief historian of the Alexandrian age. Brought to Rome a prisoner after the battle of Pydna (168 B.C.), in which the king of Macedon was overthrown by Paulus Æmilius, he became the intimate friend of Scipio Africanus the Younger. Seventeen years elapsed before Polybius was permitted to return to Greece. Then he went back the firm friend of the Romans; and had his countrymen heeded his counsels, the sack of Corinth might have been averted and Greece might have preserved her independence. So, at least, declared the inscription on his statue: "Hellas would have been saved had she followed the advice of Polybius."

Polybius accompanied Scipio in several of his campaigns, and saw Carthage burned to the ground. In his travels, which were varied and extensive, he stored his mind with useful information for his "Universal History," the grand work of his life. Its forty books impartially narrated the history of Rome and the contemporary nations between the years 220 and 146 B.C., but in a style devoid of attractions. Polybius, as Macaulay said, lacked "the art of telling a story in an interesting manner." The first five books of his work, and a few fragments of the others, have been preserved.

As all eyes have recently been turned on Constantinople, whose important situation has long made its acquisition the traditional policy of Russia, it may not be uninteresting to present the view which Polybius takes of this ancient city, then known as

BYZANTIUM.

"Byzantium, of all the cities in the world, is the most happy in its situation with respect to the sea, being not only secure on that side from all enemies, but possessed also of the means of obtaining every kind of necessaries in the greatest plenty. But with respect to the land, there is scarcely any place that has so little claim to these advantages.

With regard to the sea, the Byzantines, standing close upon the entrance of the Euxine, command so absolutely all that passage that it is not possible for any merchant to sail through it, or return, without their permission; and hence they are the masters of all those commodities which are drawn in various kinds from the countries that lie round this sea, to satisfy the wants or conveniences of other men. For among the things that are necessary for use, they supply the Greeks with leather, and with great numbers of very serviceable slaves. And with regard to those that are esteemed conveniences, they send honey and wax, with all kinds of seasoned and salted meats; taking from us in exchange our own superfluous commodities, oil and every sort of wine. They sometimes also furnish us with corn, and sometimes receive it from us, as the wants of either may require.

Now it is certain that the Greeks must either be excluded wholly from this commerce, or be deprived at least of all its chief advantages, if ever the Byzantines should engage in any ill designs against them. For as well by reason of the extreme narrowness of the passage as from the numbers of barbarians that are settled around it, we should never be able to gain an entrance through it into the Euxine.

Though the Byzantines, therefore, are themselves possessed of the first and best advantages of this happy situation, which enables them to make both an easy and a profitable exchange of their superfluous commodities, and to procure in return, without any pain or danger, whatever their own lands fail to furnish; yet since, through their means chiefly, other countries also are enabled to obtain many things that are of the greatest use, it seems reasonable that they should always be regarded by the Greeks as common benefactors, and receive not only favor and acknowledgments, but assistance likewise to repel all attempts that may be made against them by their barbarous neighbors.

And with these barbarous tribes they are involved in constant war. For when they have taken great pains to cultivate their lands, which are by nature very fertile, and the rich fruits stand ready to repay their labors, on a sudden the barbarians, pouring down, destroy one part and carry away the rest; and leave to the Byzantines, after all their cost and toil, only the pain of beholding their best harvests wasted, while their beauty aggravates the grief, and renders the sense of their calamity more sharp and insupportable."—HAMPTON.

MAN'ETHO in Egypt, BERO'SUS at Babylon, and TIMÆUS in Sicily, wrote the annals of their several countries.

The Septuagint.—Finally, to the Museum we owe the Septuagint (p. 104), or Greek version of the Old Testament, made by learned Jews employed by Ptolemy. The Jews no longer spoke the ancient Hebrew with fluency, and their version in various parts betrays an imperfect knowledge of the original. The Septuagint served as a basis for translations into many different tongues.

THE SEVEN PLEIADES.

THEOCRITUS: the idyl-writer.	ARA'TUS: author of a popular astronomical poem; from him St. Paul quoted the expression with reference to the Deity, "in whom we live, and move, and have our being."
CALLIMACHUS: poet, grammarian, etc.	NICANDER, a physician: two didactic medical poems on poisons and their antidotes.
LYC'OPHRON, the Obscure: author of "Cassandra," "the dark poem," and 64 tragedies.	
APOLLONIUS RHODIUS.	
HOMER THE YOUNGER.	

EUPHO'RION, author of three heroic poems and a celebrated grammar—APOLLODORUS, the didactic poet—and MELEA'GER THE EXQUISITE, flourished in the Alexandrian age. Meleager's "Garland" was the first anthology, or collection of epigrams. AN'YTE of Arcadia, "the female Homer," and NOSSIS, the Locrian poetess (300 B.C.), wrote epigrams. CLEANTHES, the persevering disciple of Zeno (300–220 B.C.), composed moral treatises and a hymn to Jupiter full of lofty sentiments.

CHAPTER VII.

LATER GREEK LITERATURE.

Extinction of Greek Genius.—The long period which now engages our attention is marked by a further decline, and the ultimate extinction of letters. Roman despotism was inimical to literature; Greece lay prostrate and broken-spirited; night was fast settling down on the world. Poetry, a faint shadow of its former self, appeared principally in epigrams. The prose of the early Christian centuries exhibits some exceptional gleams, but they are only the flickerings of a dying flame.

About the Christian Era is gathered a group of geographical and historical writers with Stra'bo, Diodo'rus Sic'ulus, and Dionysius of Halicarnassus as the prominent figures.

The first century after Christ presents to us the authors of the New Testament; Clement of Rome, an eminent authority with the early Christians; and Josephus, the Jewish historian, all of whom wrote in Greek. Plutarch, the eminent biographer, born about 50 A.D., lived through the first twenty years of the second century, which was also adorned with the names of Lucian and Pausanias the geographer. In the third century flourished Longi′nus, the greatest rhetorician of this later age; while the writings of the Christian fathers extend over a period of several hundred years, from the time of Clement just named.

After the fall of Rome (476 A.D.), Constantinople became the sole centre of letters, and there for nearly a thousand years they languished. After Mahomet II. carried the city by storm in 1453, the native scholars dispersed over Europe, and by awakening an interest in classical studies contributed not a little to the revival of letters.

THE FIRST CENTURY BEFORE CHRIST.

Diodorus Siculus (*the Sicilian*) was the author of "the Historical Library," which cost him thirty years of labor. Unfolding the story of the human race from remote antiquity to the time of Julius Cæsar, his work contains much valuable information.

Dionysius of Halicarnassus.—The longest production of this writer is his "Roman Antiquities," a history of Rome prior to the Punic wars, pervaded by an evident partiality for Greece and her institutions. Dionysius was also a rhetorician of the highest rank, as his critical essays on the eloquence of Demosthenes, the style of Thucydides, and other subjects, testify.

Strabo, of Pontus in Asia Minor, must be remembered in connection with his "Geography," still extant, an interesting work in seventeen books, for which he prepared himself by travels in Asia, Africa, and Europe. It is not a mere tissue of names and statistics, but is lighted up with sketches of social life, pleasant stories, and epitomes of political history, thus entertaining at the same time that it instructs.

What this lively writer records of India may interest the reader:—

THE WONDERS OF INDIA.

"Between the Hydaspes and the Acesi'nes is the country of Porus, an extensive and fertile district, containing nearly three hundred cities. Here also is the forest in which Alexander cut down a large quantity of fir, pine, cedar, and a variety of other trees fit for ship-building, and brought the timber down the Hydaspes. With this he constructed a fleet near the cities which he built on each side of the river, where he had crossed it and conquered Porus. One of these cities he called Bucephalia, from the horse Bucephalus, which was killed in the battle with Porus. The name Bucephalus (*ox-headed*) was given to the animal from the breadth of his forehead.

In the forest before mentioned it is said there is a vast number of monkeys, as large as they are numerous. On one occasion the Macedonians, seeing a body of them standing in array on some bare eminences, prepared to attack them as real enemies.

The chase of this animal is conducted in two different ways. The hunters, when they perceive a monkey seated on a tree, place in sight a basin containing water, with which they wash their own eyes; then, instead of water, they put a basin of bird-lime, go away, and lie in wait at a distance. The animal, being an imitative creature, leaps down, and besmears itself with the bird-lime, and when it winks, the eyelids are fastened together. The hunters then come upon it, and take it. The other method of capturing them is as follows: the hunters dress themselves in bags like trousers and go away, leaving behind them others which are downy, with the inside smeared over with bird-lime. The monkeys put them on, and are easily taken.

A very singular usage is related of the high estimation in which the inhabitants of Cathaia (the tract between the Hydaspes and Acesines) hold the quality of beauty. They elect the handsomest person as king. A child, two months after birth, undergoes a public inspection. They determine whether it has the amount of beauty required by law. The presiding magistrate then pronounces whether it is to be allowed to live, or to be put to death. The bride and the husband are respectively the choice of each other, and the wives, it is related, burn themselves with their deceased husbands. The reason assigned for this practice is, that the women sometimes fell in love with young men, and deserted or poisoned their husbands.

This law was therefore established in order to check the practice of administering poison; but neither the existence nor the origin of the law is probable.

The dogs in this territory are said to possess remarkable courage. Alexander received from Sopeithes, the monarch, a present of one hundred and fifty of them. To prove them, two were set at a lion; when these were mastered, two others were set on; when the battle became equal, Sopeithes ordered a man to seize one of the dogs by the leg, and to drag him away; or to cut off his leg, if he still held on. Alexander at first refused his consent to the dog's leg being cut off, as he wished to save the dog. But on Sopeithes saying, 'I will give you four in the place of it,' Alexander consented; and he saw the dog permit his leg to be cut off by a slow incision rather than loose his hold.

Nearchus is surprised at the multitude and the noxious nature of the reptiles. They retreat from the plains to the settlements at the period of inundations, and fill the houses. For this reason the inhabitants raise their beds from the ground, and are sometimes compelled to abandon their dwellings. Charmers go about the country, and are supposed to cure wounds made by serpents. This seems to comprise nearly their whole art of medicine, for disease is not frequent among them, owing to their frugal manner of life, and to the absence of wine. Whenever diseases do occur, they are treated by the Sophists (*wise men*).

All the Indians are frugal in their mode of life, and are happy on account of their simple manners. They never drink wine but at sacrifices. Their beverage is made from rice instead of barley, and their food consists for the most part of rice pottage. The simplicity of their laws appears from their having few lawsuits. Theft is very rare among them. Their houses and property are unguarded. These things denote temperance and sobriety. Others of their customs no one would approve; as their eating always alone, and their not having all of them one common hour for their meals, but each taking food as he likes. As an exercise of the body they prefer friction in various ways, but particularly by making use of smooth sticks of ebony, which they pass over the surface of the skin. They marry many wives, who are purchased from their parents, and give in exchange for them a yoke of oxen.

Megasthenes divides the philosophers into two kinds, the Brahmans and the Garmanes. The Brahmans are held in greater repute. They do not communicate their philosophy to their wives, for fear they should divulge to the profane anything which ought to be concealed. They discourse much on death, and discipline themselves to prepare for it. According to the Brahmans, the world was created and is liable to corruption; it is of a spheroidal figure; the god who made and governs it, pervades the whole of it; the earth is situated in the centre of the universe. Many other peculiar things they say of the principles of generation and of the soul. They invent fables also, after the manner of Plato, on immortality and on the punishment in Hades; and other things of this kind."—FALCONER.

THE FIRST THREE CHRISTIAN CENTURIES.

Josephus, born A.D. 37 at Jerusalem, was the scion of a noble line. At the early age of fourteen he astonished the chief priests by his mental power and familiarity with the intricacies of Jewish law. We next hear of him as spending three years in the desert with a hermit, and then as joining the Pharisees.

The revolutionary tendencies of his countrymen brought on a war with the Romans, in the course of which Josephus, after the brave defence of a city under his command, was made prisoner by the Roman general Flavius Vespasian. Prophesying that Vespasian would one day wear the purple of the emperors, he alone of the captives was spared; the fulfilment of this prediction about three years later insured him the favor of the Flavian family, whose name he prefixed to his own. Vespasian's son, Titus, he accompanied to the siege of Jerusalem, receiving at the hands of the victorious general after its capture the lives of two hundred and forty of his friends, together with the sacred volumes which he greatly prized.

From the desolation of his country, Josephus returned to Rome as the honored guest of the emperor and his sons, during whose reigns he produced his great works,—"the History of the Jewish War" and "Jewish Antiquities." These interesting standards, though written in a style which has led to their author's being called "the Grecian Livy," are yet tinged with vanity and skepticism.

Plutarch (50–120 A.D.), the great biographer of antiquity, was born in Chæronea, a Bœotian town. After completing his education at Athens, he sailed to Egypt, and in Domitian's reign (81–96 A.D.) visited Rome, where his lectures won golden opinions from the learned.

From Italy, Plutarch returned to his native city, and there passed the last twenty or thirty years of his life, happy in the society of his wife, a paragon of good sense, economy, and virtue. Literature was henceforth his pursuit; but believing it a duty to devote part of his time to the public good, he accepted office from his fellow-townsmen, and was finally made chief-magistrate of Chæronea. He tells us with relish how his neighbors often laughed at his doing what they considered beneath his dignity. When they wondered that so great a man should carry fish from market in his own hands, he told them, "Why, it's for myself;" and when they found fault with him for personally superintending the building of public edifices, he silenced them with the reply, "This service is not for myself, but for my country." "The meaner the office you sustain," said Plutarch, "the greater the compliment you pay to the public."

In his delightful retreat at Chæronea, Plutarch compiled from two hundred and fifty authorities the work that has given him a niche in the Temple of Fame—"Parallel Lives"—sparkling with interest and animation, as it is underlaid by good judgment. His plan was to present the biography of a distinguished Greek, follow it with that of some Roman, and then critically compare the two characters. But the "Lives," as we have it, is not the complete work its author probably left at his death, inasmuch as a number of biographies and parallels are wanting. Though Plutarch's passion for story-telling sometimes carries him beyond the bounds of the probable, yet his work is an invaluable storehouse; his capital literary portraits have stood the test of time, and are still universally admired. The charms of a book in which are recorded "the greatest characters and most admirable actions of the human race" can never fade.

Among the best of Plutarch's Parallels is his

COMPARISON OF DEMOSTHENES AND CICERO.

"Omitting an exact comparison of their respective faculties in speaking, yet thus much seems fit to be said: That Demosthenes, to make himself a master in rhetoric, applied all the faculties he had, natural or acquired, wholly that way; that he far surpassed in force and strength of eloquence all his contemporaries in political and judicial speaking, in grandeur and majesty all the panegyrical orators, and in accuracy and science all the logicians and rhetoricians of his day: That Cicero was highly educated, and by his diligent study became a most accomplished general scholar in all these branches, having left behind him numerous philosophical treatises of his own on Academic principles; as, indeed, even in his written speeches, both political and judicial, we see him continually trying to show his learning by the way.

One may discover the different temper of each of them in their speeches. For the oratory of Demosthenes was without any embellishment or jesting, wholly composed for real effect and seriousness; not smelling of the lamp, as Pytheas scoffingly said, but of the temperance, thoughtfulness, austerity, and grave earnestness of his temper. Whereas Cicero's fondness for mockery often ran him into scurrility; and in his love of laughing away serious arguments in judicial cases by jests and facetious remarks, with a view to the advantage of his clients, he paid too little regard to what was decent: saying, for example, in his defence of Cælius, that he had done no absurd thing in indulging himself so freely in pleasures, it being a kind of madness not to enjoy the things we possess, especially since the most eminent philosophers have asserted pleasure to be the chief good. So also we are told that when Cicero, being consul, undertook the defence of Murena against Cato's prosecution, by way of bantering Cato, he made a long series of jokes upon the absurd *paradoxes*, as they are called, of the Stoic sect; so that, a loud laugh passing from the crowd to the judges, Cato, with a quiet smile, said to those who sat next him, 'My friends, what an amusing consul we have!'

Cicero was by natural temper very much disposed to mirth and pleasantry, and always appeared with a smiling and serene countenance. But Demosthenes had constant care and thoughtfulness in his look, and a serious anxiety, which he seldom, if ever, laid aside; and, therefore, he was accounted by his enemies, as he himself confessed, morose and ill-mannered.

It is very evident, also, from their several writings, that Demosthenes never touched upon his own praises but decently and without offence when there was need of it, and for some weightier end; but, upon other occasions, modestly and sparingly. But Cicero's immeasurable boasting of himself in his orations argues him guilty of an uncontrollable appetite for distinction, his cry being evermore that arms should give place to the gown, and the soldier's laurel to the tongue. And at last we find him extolling not only his deeds and actions, but his orations also, as well those that were only spoken as those that were published; as if he were engaged in a boyish trial of skill, who should speak best, with the rhetoricians Isocrates and Anaximenes, not as one who could claim the task to guide and instruct the Roman nation, the

Soldier full-armed, terrific to the foe.

Moreover, the banishment of Demosthenes was infamous, upon conviction for bribery; Cicero's very honorable, for ridding his country of a set of villains. Therefore when Demosthenes fled his country, no man regarded it; for Cicero's sake, the senate changed their habit and put on mourning, and would not be persuaded to make any act before Cicero's return was decreed.

Cicero, however, passed his exile idly in Macedonia. But the very exile of Demosthenes made up a great part of the services he did for his country; for he went through the cities of Greece, and everywhere, as we have said, joined in the conflict on behalf of the Grecians, driving out the Macedonian ambassadors, and approving himself a much better citizen than Themistocles and Alcibiades did in the like fortune. After his return, he again devoted himself to the same public service, and continued firm in his opposition to Antipater and the Macedonians. Whereas Lælius reproached Cicero in the senate for sitting silent when Cæsar, a beardless youth, asked leave to come forward, contrary to the law, as a candidate for the consulship; and Brutus, in his epistles, charges him with nursing and rearing a greater and more heavy tyranny than that they had removed.

Finally, Cicero's death excites our pity; for an old man to be miserably carried up and down by his servants, flying and hiding himself from that death which was, in the course of nature, so near at hand—and yet at last to be murdered. Demosthenes, though he seemed at first a little to supplicate, yet, by his preparing and keeping the poison by him, demands our admiration; and still more admirable was his using it. When the temple of the god no longer afforded him a sanctuary, he took refuge at a mightier altar, freeing himself from arms and soldiers, and laughing to scorn the cruelty of Antipater."—CLOUGH.

A moralist as well as a biographer, Plutarch wrote many ethical and philosophical essays. The death of his daughter called forth a feeling letter to his wife,—"the Consolation,"—in which he affectionately bids her not give way to extravagant grief, but submit with resignation to the blow, comforting her with thoughts of immortality; it may be added that he held Plato's views on this subject as on others.

In his "Essay on Inquisitiveness" he condemns all eagerness to learn news and impatience in opening letters, or "biting the strings in two, as many will if they do not succeed at once with their fingers." As an example of dignified patience, he instances Rusticus at Rome, who in the midst of a lecture received a letter from the emperor Domitian, but would not open it till Plutarch had finished speaking.

Lucian (probably 120–200 A.D.), one of the wittiest of Greek writers, was a native of Syria, and passed his boyhood on the banks of the Euphrates. Doubtless his favorite amusement of moulding wax into figures weighed with his parents, no less than their own poverty, when they bound him as an apprentice to his mother's brother to learn the sculptor's art. The young Lucian enthusiastically fell in with their decision, fondly anticipating the time when he should astonish his playfellows with little gods cut from the marble by his own hands. But his maiden attempt in the statuary's shop resulted in a broken slab and a cruel whipping at the hands of his uncle. "The first wages I earned," he said, "were tears"—but they were also the last. He never returned to the chisel and mallet.

After picking up a rhetorical education, by what means he does not tell us, Lucian established himself at Antioch as a lawyer; but failing of success, he set out on a lecture tour through Europe. In Gaul, where rhetoric, the art he taught, was in special demand, he accumulated a fortune; with which he retired from his profession in the prime of life, and took up his residence at Athens. Here he prosecuted his literary studies, exchanged his Syrian Greek for pure Attic, and is believed to have written his finest Dialogues.

At the age of seventy, Lucian found himself so reduced as to be obliged to accept from the Roman emperor the clerkship of the Alexandrian courts. This position, which allowed him to continue his literary labors, he is said to have enjoyed until his death.

LUCIAN'S STYLE AND WRITINGS.—Piquant humor, inimitable power of satire, and wonderful versatility, are Lucian's strong points. His style is clear and graceful. Of his voluminous writings the most popular are the "Dialogues" on various subjects, serious and humorous. He attacked falsehood and trickery, folly and superstition; and the deadly blows he rained upon his country's mythology, which led to his being called "the Blasphemer," indirectly, though unintentionally, helped the spread of Christianity.

In the "Dialogues of the Gods," the deities talk over the domestic affairs of the Olympian household, gossip, and wrangle, and pry into one another's secrets, quite after the manner of humans. Such a belittling of the national divinities could not be without an unsettling effect on the popular faith.—The "Dialogues of the Dead" are equally rich with humor and ridicule.

Against the philosophers of his day, whom he looked upon as miserable charlatans, Lucian launched the laughable Dialogue entitled "the Sale of the Philosophers," in which the founders of the old schools are disposed of at auction by Jupiter in a slave-market, Mercury playing the part of auctioneer. Pythagoras is put up first and sells for $175; Diogenes, the next, brings less than sixpence; while Socrates commands the high price of two talents. Pyrrho, the universal doubter, will not believe that he has been sold, even after he has seen himself paid for and delivered. The laughing Democritus and weeping Heraclitus fail to find a purchaser. The attempted sale of these two philosophers is thus depicted:—

"JUPITER.—Bring out another. Stay—those two there, that fellow from Abdera, who is always laughing, and the Ephesian, who is always crying; I've a mind to sell them as a pair.

MERCURY.—Stand out there in the ring, you two.—We offer you here, sirs, two most admirable characters, the wisest we've had for sale yet.

CUSTOMER.—By Jove, they're a remarkable contrast! Why, one of them never stops laughing, while the other seems to be in trouble about something, for he's in tears all the time. Holloa, you fellow! what's all this about? What are you laughing at?

DEMOCRITUS.—Need you ask? Because everything seems to me so ridiculous—you yourselves included.

CUSTOMER.—What! do you mean to laugh at us all to our faces, and mock at all we say and do?

DEMOCRITUS.—Undoubtedly; there's nothing in life that's serious. Everything is unreal and empty—a mere fortuitous concurrence of indefinite atoms.

CUSTOMER.—You're an indefinite atom yourself, you rascal! Confound your insolence, won't you stop laughing? But you there, poor soul [*to Heraclitus*], why do you weep so? for there seems more use in talking to you.

HERACLITUS.—Because, stranger, everything in life seems to me to call for pity and to deserve tears; there is nothing but what is liable to calamity; wherefore I mourn for men and pity them. The evil of to-day I regard not much: but I mourn for that which is to come hereafter—the burning and destruction of all things. This I grieve for, and that nothing is permanent, but all mingled, as it were, in one bitter cup—pleasure that is no pleasure, knowledge that knows nothing, greatness that is so little, all going round and round, and taking their turn in this game of life.

CUSTOMER.—What do you hold human life to be then?

HERACLITUS.—A child at play, handling its toys, and changing them with every caprice.

CUSTOMER.—And what are men?

HERACLITUS.—Gods—but mortal.

CUSTOMER.—And the gods?

HERACLITUS.—Men—but immortal.

CUSTOMER.—You speak in riddles, fellow, and put us off with puzzles. You are as bad as Apollo Loxias, giving oracles that no man can understand.

HERACLITUS.—Yea; I trouble not myself for any of ye.

CUSTOMER.—Then no man in his senses is like to buy you.

HERACLITUS.—Woe! woe to every man of ye, I say! buyers or not buyers.

CUSTOMER.—Why, this fellow is pretty near mad—I'll have naught to do with either of them, for my part.

MERCURY [*turning to Jupiter*].—We shall have this pair left on our hands too."—COLLINS.

"The Sale of the Philosophers" has a sequel in "the Resuscitated Professors." Permitted to return to earth for a day to revenge themselves on Lucian, the Philosophers capture him, and bring him to trial before the goddess of philosophy. He clears himself by showing that he has not attacked the venerable sages themselves, but only the impostors who cheat the world under their great names. In the beginning of the Dialogue, Lucian is thus assailed by the belligerent Socrates and his *confrères* :—

"SOCRATES.—Pelt the wretch! pelt him with volleys of stones—throw clods at him—oyster-shells! Beat the blasphemer with your clubs—don't let him escape! Hit him, Plato! and you, Chrysippus! and you! Form a phalanx, and rush on him all together. As Homer says—'Let wallet join with wallet, club with club!' He is the common enemy of us all, and there is no man among ye whom he has not insulted. You, Diogenes, now use that staff of yours, if ever you did! Don't stop! let him have it, blasphemer that he is! What! tired already, Epicurus and Aristippus? Aristotle, do run a little faster! That's good! we've caught the beast! We've got you, you rascal! You shall soon find out whom you've been abusing! Now what shall we do with him? Let us think of some multiform kind of death that may suffice for all of us, for he deserves a separate death from each.

PHILOSOPHER A.—I vote that he be impaled.

PHILOSOPHER B.—Yes—but be well scourged first.

PHILOSOPHER C.—Let his eyes be gouged out.

PHILOSOPHER D.—Ay—but his tongue should be cut out first.

SOCRATES.—What think you, Empedocles?

EMPEDOCLES.—He should be thrown down the crater of some volcano,* and so learn not to revile his betters.

PLATO.—Nay—the best punishment for him will be that, like Pentheus or Orpheus,

'Torn by the ragged rocks he meet his fate.'

LUCIAN.—Oh! no, no, pray! spare me, for the love of Heaven!

SOCRATES.—Sentence is passed: nothing can save you."

COLLINS.

Lucian is also famous in another line. His "True History," a burlesque on the Munchausen stories of the old poets and historians, recounts the stirring adventures of a party of voyagers who sail westward from the Pillars of Hercules

* An allusion to the fate of Empedocles himself; see p. 236.

(Strait of Gibraltar). It describes their visit to the moon, their sojourn in a country where wine flowed in rivers, their twenty months' experience inside of a sea-monster that swallowed their vessel, and their discovery of "the Island of the Blest," with its golden-paved city and vines loaded with monthly fruitage. The lunarians happened to be engaged in war with the people of the sun, at the time of Lucian's arrival, and he had the good fortune to witness a grand review of the lunar army. There were cavalry mounted on lettuce-winged birds, darters of millet-seed, garlic-fighters, wind-coursers, and archers who rode elephantine fleas. Spiders as large as islands hovered on their flanks. On the side of the sun were mustered horse-ants that covered two acres, archers on colossal gnats, slingers who discharged fetid radishes, and dog-headed men astride of winged acorns.—Had novel-writing been in vogue in Lucian's time, he would no doubt have excelled in that department of fiction.

Pausanias, the Lydian geographer, was a contemporary of Lucian's. It has been said that "no writer of antiquity except Herodotus has stored away so many valuable facts in a small volume" as he in his "Itinerary of Greece." Pausanias made art items a special feature of his Itinerary.

Other Writers of the Second Century.—In the second century, CLAUDIUS PTOLEMY, the astronomer, put forth his theory of the universe: that the earth is stationary and the centre of eight huge, hollow, crystal spheres, placed one within another. The moon he located in the nearest sphere, Mercury in the next, Venus in the third, the Sun in the fourth, Mars in the fifth, Jupiter in the sixth, and Saturn in the seventh. The eighth sphere he appropriated to the stars, which, despite their distance, were still visible through the transparent crystal. All these heavenly bodies he believed to revolve in their respective spheres around the earth. Ptolemy's "Syntaxis," or "Construction," embodying these views, was received as authority until Copernicus, fourteen hundred years later, taught the true theory of the solar system.

In this century, also, JUSTIN MARTYR wrote his "Apologies" in defence of Christianity against paganism; and POLYCARP, bishop of Smyrna, his "Epistle to the Philippians"—both sealing their faith with their blood. From IRENÆUS, bishop of Lyons, we have inherited a valuable legacy in his "Treatise against Heresies."

Origen, the gifted pupil of Cle'mens the Alexandrian, an ardent Christian philosopher, flourished in the third century. Among his writings, which, including his discourses, were numbered by thousands, are "Commentaries on the Scriptures," in the preparation of which he was assisted by clerks who wrote in short-hand from his dictation. Origen also replied effectively to CELSUS, an Epicurean philosopher who some years before had attacked Christianity in his "True Story," a powerful and much-read work of the time.

Neo-Platonism.—The Academic philosophy, modified by its later professors and wrapped in a veil of mysticism, gave rise to the eclectic school of the Neo-Platonists, which was popular among the learned till the time of Constantine. The seeds of this philosophy were planted by Philo the Jew, mentioned on page 104 as attempting to reconcile Plato's doctrines with the teachings of the Hebrew Scriptures.

AMMONIUS, of Alexandria, was the real founder of Neo-Platonism, which, as it left his hand, was a medley of Plato's and Aristotle's tenets harmonized with the leading doctrines of Christianity. Though Ammonius enjoined his disciples to keep the mysteries of his philosophy to themselves, PLOTI'NUS, one of his distinguished pupils, unfolded them in his writings and taught them publicly at Rome, where he went to live 244 A.D.

After Plotinus, PORPHYRY became a shining light of the Neo-Platonists; but he was an outspoken opponent of Christianity, maintaining that the world was without beginning, and denying the divinity of our Saviour. His work "Against the Christians" was afterward burned by order of the Roman emperor Theodosius the Great.

IAMBLICHUS, a successor of Porphyry, went back to the mystical speculations of Pythagoras, and, taking quite a different view from the early Neo-Platonists, turned his philosophy to the support of paganism. The emperor Julian the Apostate was one of his converts.

EUSEBIUS, the learned ecclesiastical historian, bishop of Cæsare'a in the fourth century, was among those who repelled the assaults of Porphyry on the Christian faith. He was a favorite of Constantine, whose life he wrote.

Longinus (213–273 A.D.) was the greatest critic and most learned philosopher of his age. He studied and taught at Athens, and by reason of his extensive information was styled "the Living Encyclopædia." The most distinguished of his pupils was Zenobia, queen of Palmyra, a woman of refined tastes and unusual talent. By his advice, she revolted from Rome; overpowered by the emperor Aurelian, 273 A.D., she sought to exculpate herself by throwing the blame upon her counsellor, and Longinus was put to death.

Part of this author's "Treatise on the Sublime" is all that remains of his many works.

Athanasius.—A century after Longinus, lived Athanasius, one of the main pillars of the early Christian Church. His life was spent in contentions with Arius and his followers, who denied the equality of Christ with the Father; in controversy with them, his vigorous pen was constantly employed.

St. Chrysostom (*golden-mouthed*, so called from his eloquence —350–407) was the most famous of the Greek fathers. He was archbishop of Constantinople, and a voluminous writer of homilies, epistles, and commentaries. His language is elegant, and his fund of figures inexhaustible.

LIGHT LITERATURE.

Novel-Writers.—The novel and romance are not unrepresented in Greek literature. HELIODO'RUS, a Phœnician by birth, who lived toward the close of the fourth century, obtained a well-deserved reputation as the author of "Æthiopica," a touching, pure-toned, but somewhat sensational, romance. Its heroine, Charicle'a, an Ethiopian princess, exposed by her mother in infancy and brought up in ignorance of her birth, with her lover Theagenes, falls into the hands of pirates and undergoes a variety of adventures. The tale ends happily, quite in the modern style.

Heliodorus, later in life, gave up novel-writing for a mitre, being made bishop of Tricca in Thessaly.

Another Greek novelist, perhaps a contemporary of Heliodorus, perhaps belonging to a later generation, was LONGUS, author of the "Loves of Daphnis and Chloë." The scene of this pastoral love-story is laid in the groves of Lesbos, where the hero and heroine have grown up together in the bonds of innocent affection, *à la* "Paul and Virginia."

The "Story of Leucippe and Cli'tophon," by ACHILLES TA'TIUS, an Alexandrian rhetorician who flourished about 500, stands next to the "Æthiopica" among the Greek novels.

Hierocles.—The "Facetiæ" of Hierocles (5th century) must not be forgotten in this connection. Though a Neo-Platonist, grave and learned enough to discuss "Providence and Fate" and make a volume of profound commentaries on the Golden Verses of Pythagoras, he evidently enjoyed a good joke. He has left us twenty-eight brief stories of *Scholastici*, or bookworms so unsophisticated and unused to the ways of the world that we may call them simpletons. A few of these are given as samples of his humor; from which it may be seen that some of the wit that passes for modern is as old as Hierocles.

STORIES OF SIMPLETONS.

A simpleton, wishing to swim, was nearly drowned; whereupon he swore that he would never touch the water until he had learned how to swim.

A simpleton, visiting a sick person, inquired about his health. He, however, was not able to reply. Thereupon the simpleton, being angry and scolding the man, said: "I hope that I shall be sick some of these days, and then when you come to ask how I am, I will not answer."

A simpleton, wishing to teach his horse to be a small eater, gave him no food at all. At length the horse having starved to death, he exclaimed: "I have suffered a great loss, for now that he had just learned not to eat he has died."

A simpleton, looking out of the window of a house which he had bought, asked the passers-by whether the house was becoming to him.

A simpleton, having dreamed that he had trodden on a nail and that the wound pained him, on waking bound up his foot. Another simpleton, having learned the cause, remarked: "It served you right, for why do you sleep without sandals?"

A simpleton, meeting a doctor, hid himself behind a wall. Some one asking the cause, he answered: "I have not been sick for a long time, and therefore I am ashamed to come into the sight of a physician."

A simpleton had sealed up a vessel of Aminæan wine which he had. His servant, having made a hole in the vessel beneath and drawn off some of the wine, he was astonished to see the contents diminished while the seals remained unbroken. A neighbor having told him to look whether it had not been taken out from below, he replied: "Why, you fool, it's the upper part, not the lower, that is missing."

A simpleton, meeting another simpleton, said, "I heard you were dead."—"And yet," replied the other, "you see that I am still alive." —"Well," said the first in perplexity, "I don't know what to believe, for he who told me is much more deserving of confidence than you."

A simpleton, learning that the raven would live more than two hundred years, bought one and brought it up, that he might test the matter.

Of twin brothers, one died. A simpleton, thereupon, meeting the survivor, asked, "Is it you that died, or your brother?"

A simpleton, in danger of being shipwrecked, called for his tablets that he might make his will. Seeing, thereupon, his slaves lamenting their lot, he said, "Do not grieve, for I am going to set you free."

A simpleton, wishing to cross a river, went on board the boat on horseback. When some one asked the reason, he answered that he wanted to get over in a hurry.

A simpleton and a bald man and a barber, travelling together, agreed to keep watch in turn four hours each while the others slept. The barber's turn came first. He quietly shaved the head of the sleeping simpleton, and when the time elapsed awoke him. The latter, scratching his head as he got up, and finding it bare, cried out: "What a rascal that barber is; he's waked the bald man instead of me!"

BYZANTINE LITERATURE.

The list of sophists, grammarians, historians, and other writers belonging to the Byzantine period, contains names without number and without lustre. A love-song of the Justinian era (527–565 A.D.), by the emperor's privy-councillor, will give an idea of the poetry of this age.

THE DRENCHED LOVER.

"The voice of the song and the banquet was o'er,
And I hung up my chaplet at Glycera's door,
When the mischievous girl from a window above,
Who looked down and laughed at the offering of love,
Filled with water a goblet whence Bacchus had fled,
And poured all the crystal contents on my head.
So drenched was my hair, three whole days it resisted
All attempts of the barber to friz it or twist it;
But the water (so whimsical, Love, are thy ways!)
While it put out my curls, set my heart in a blaze."

J. H. MERIVALE.

THE GREEK ANTHOLOGY.

The Anthology (*bunch of flowers*) is a collection of more than four thousand short pithy poems, from the pens of about three hundred Greek writers.

Melea'ger was the first gatherer of these literary flowers; his "Garland" contained choice morsels of poetry from the time of Sappho down, many of the best pieces being the work of his own hand. "Meleager's poetry," says Symonds, "has the sweetness of the rose, the full-throated melody of the nightingale." Others added to Meleager's collection, the last ancient anthologist being the historian Aga'thias, who flourished at Constantinople in the reign of Justinian.

The pieces of the Greek Anthology are epigrams and fugitive verses, amatory, witty, and didactic. Some of them compare favorably with the best efforts of the writers already considered; while not a few are plainly the sources of some of the household sayings and proverbial philosophy of modern times.

FLOWERS FROM THE ANTHOLOGY.

A PIOUS ACT REWARDED.

"While from the strand his line a fisher threw,
Shoreward a shipwrecked human head he drew.
His moistened eyes soft drops of pity shed,
While gazing on the bald and trunkless head.
No spade he had; but while his active hands
Scraped a small grave among the yielding sands,
A store of gold, there hid, he found. Yes! yes!
Heaven will the just man's pious actions bless."
CARPHYLLIDES.

"Enjoy your goods as if your death were near;
Save them as if 'twere distant many a year.
Sparing or spending, be thy wisdom seen
In keeping ever to the golden mean."—LUCIAN.

THE PARTNERSHIP.

"Damon, who plied the undertaker's trade,
With Doctor Cra'teas an agreement made.
What linens Damon from the dead could seize,
He to the Doctor sent for bandages;
While the good Doctor, here no promise-breaker,
Sent all his patients to the undertaker."

"Swift kindnesses are best; a long delay
In kindness takes the kindness all away."

THE LESSON OF THE TOPS.

"An Atarne'an stranger once to Pittacus applied,
That ancient sage, Hyrradius' son, and Mytilene's pride;
'Grave sir, betwixt two marriages I now have power to choose,
And hope you will advise me which to take and which refuse.
One of the maidens, every way, is very near myself;
The other's far above me, both in pedigree and pelf.

Now which is best?' The old man raised the staff which old men bear,
And with it pointed to some boys that then were playing there,
Whipping their tops along the street: 'Their steps,' he said, 'pursue,
And look and listen carefully; they'll tell you what to do.'
Following them, the stranger went to see what might befall,
And 'Whip the top that's nearest you!' was still their constant call.
He, by this boyish lesson taught, resigned the high-born dame,
And wed the maiden 'nearest him.' Go thou and do the same."

ENVY.

"Poor Diophon of envy died,
His brother thief to see
Nailed near him, to be crucified,
Upon a higher tree."

THE FLEAS OUTWITTED.

"A countryman once who was troubled with fleas,
Jumped up out of bed in a thundering breeze,
And triumphantly cried, as he blew out the light,
'Now I have you, you rogues, you can't see where to bite!'"

LUCIAN.

CURES FOR LOVE.

"Hunger, perhaps, may cure your love,
Or time your passion greatly alter;
If both should unsuccessful prove,
I strongly recommend a halter."—CRATES.

"Too much is always bad; old proverbs call
E'en too much honey nothing else than gall."

THE RAVEN LOCKS.

"Chloe, those locks of raven hair—
Some people say you dye them black;
But that's a libel, I can swear,
For I know where you buy them black."

LOVE SONG.

"The winecup is glad: dear Zenophilè's lip
It boasts to have touched, when she stooped down to sip.
Happy winecup! I wish that, with lips joined to mine,
All my soul at a draught she would drink up like wine."

"Short is the rose's bloom; another morn
Will show no rose, but in its stead, a thorn."

HELIODORA'S GARLAND.

"I'll frame, my Heliodora! a garland for thy hair,
Which thou, in all thy beauty's pride, mayst not disdain to wear;
For I, with tender myrtles, white violets will twine—
White violets, but not so pure as that pure breast of thine:
With laughing lilies I will twine narcissus; and the sweet
Crocus shall in its yellow hue with purple hyacinth meet:
And I will twine with all the rest, and all the rest above,
Queen of them all, the red, red Rose, the flower which lovers love."

MELEAGER.

GEMS OF GREEK THOUGHT.

HOMER.

"Mob rule is not good; let there be one monarch.—Victory changes oft her side.—Pray, for all men require aid from on high.—Even the fool is wise after the event.—The man whom Jove loves, is a match for many.—Wine leads to folly.—The force of union conquers all.—Too much rest itself becomes a pain.—Noblest minds are most easily bent.—Few sons are equal to their sires.—To sorrow without ceasing is wrong."

HESIOD.

"Emulation is good for mortals.—The best treasure among men is a frugal tongue.—Idleness, not labor, is disgraceful."

PINDAR.

"Mirth is the best physician for man's toils.—The guilty souls of those who die here must pay the penalty in another life.—Point thy tongue on the anvil of truth."

ÆSCHYLUS.

"He hears but half that hears one party only.—To know and to conjecture differ widely.—To be without evil thoughts is God's best gift."

SOPHOCLES.

"Clamorous sorrow wastes itself in sound.—Quick resolves are often unsafe.—What good man is not his own friend?—In a just cause, the weak subdue the strong."

EURIPIDES.

"The Deity helps him who helps himself.—Gold has greater power over men than ten thousand arguments.—Temperance, the noblest gift of Heaven!—To form devices, quick is woman's wit.—In darkness a runaway has mighty strength.—Death is a debt that all mortals must pay."

ARISTOPHANES.

"To fear death is a great folly.—Old men are boys twice over.—Poverty is a sister of beggary."

HERODOTUS.

"Rash haste ever goes before a fall.—Men are dependent on circumstances, not circumstances on men.—The god loves to cut down all towering things. The god suffers none but himself to be haughty.—The hand of a king is very long.—Self-restraint brings blessings, not seen at the moment perhaps, yet found out in due time."

XENOPHON.

"The sweetest of all sounds is praise.—It is impossible for a man attempting many things to do them all well."

PLATO.

"A boy is the most ferocious of animals.—Wisdom is the true and unalloyed coin.—Much learning brings danger to youth.—The race of fools is not to be counted.—Those are profane who think that nothing exists except what they can grasp with their hands.—Dogs are like their mistresses.—Let no one speak evil of another.—Self-conquest is the greatest of victories."

ARISTOTLE.

"One swallow does not make a spring.—We ought rather to pay a debt to a creditor than give to a companion.—Of this alone is even God deprived, the power of making that which is past never to have been.—The beginning is said to be half the whole.—All flatterers are mercenary.—No one loves the man whom he fears."

DEMOSTHENES.

"Success tends to throw a veil over the evil deeds of men.—What we wish, that we readily believe.—To find fault is easy."

MENANDER.

"A daughter is an embarrassing and ticklish possession.—He whom the gods love, dies young.—Evil communications corrupt good manners (*quoted by St. Paul*).—Whoever blushes seems to be good.—Nobody sees his own faults, but every one is lynx-eyed to those of his neighbor.—Love blinds all men.—Silence has many advantages.—He is well cleansed that hath his conscience clean.—There is nothing more daring than ignorance.—Truth, when not sought after, sometimes comes to light."

POLYBIUS.

"Nothing happens without a cause.—Royalty, aristocracy, and democracy, must combine to make a perfect government.—Many know how to conquer; few are able to use their conquest aright."

PLUTARCH.

"Absolute monarchy is a fair field, but has no outlet.—What one does not need, is dear at a penny.—Often, while we are delighted with the work, we regard the workman with contempt.—Dead men do not bite."

MINOR WRITERS AND THEIR WORKS.

OPPIAN (second century): didactic poems on fishing and hunting.

ARRIAN (second century): masterpiece, "Expedition of Alexander the Great."

DION CASSIUS, a Roman senator (born 155 A.D.): "History of Rome" in 80 books, from the earliest ages to 229 A.D.

ÆLIAN (second century): a zoölogy and a miscellaneous history.

APPIAN of Alexandria (second century): a "Roman History" in 24 books.

HERO'DIAN (180–238 A.D.): "History of the Roman Emperors."

DIOGENES LAERTIUS: his "Lives of the Philosophers" contains a valuable summary of the Epicurean tenets.

GA'LEN (second century), one of the world's greatest physicians: medical treatises.

MUSÆUS (fifth century): the poem "Hero and Leander."

TRYPHIODO'RUS (fifth century): poems on the Battle of Marathon and the sack of Troy; a lipogrammatic Odyssey, from the first book of which, styled *Alpha*, the letter *a* was excluded; from *Beta*, the second, *b*; and so the several letters in turn through its 24 books. This work is lost.

QUINTUS SMYRNÆUS (500 A.D.): his poem, "Things Omitted by Homer," a continuation of the Iliad.

NONNUS (sixth century): "the Dionysiaca," an Epic on Bacchus in 48 books.

PROCO'PIUS (flourished 550), the Byzantine historian: "History of his Own Times."

PART III.

ROMAN LITERATURE.

CHAPTER I.

LATIN AND ITS OLDEST MONUMENTS.

Italy Peopled.—While watching the rise, meridian splendors, and glowing sunset of Grecian letters, we have left unnoticed the dawn of literary taste in Italy, the sister of Hellas, peopled, as we have seen, by kindred Phrygian tribes who spoke dialects of the Phrygo-Hellenic tongue (p. 133). Whether they were the first of human kind to wake the echoes of the Italian solitudes, must ever remain a matter of doubt. Some believe that the Alps had proved an insuperable barrier to previous emigrants from the East; others, that the adventurous Pelasgians, on descending their slopes, found a Turanian population already in possession of the peninsula. If the latter theory be correct, the Turanian aborigines were speedily overpowered by the new-comers and became incorporated with their conquerors.

When Rome was founded, 753 B.C., the predominant Italian races were distinguished as Latin and Umbrian (embracing the Oscans); their languages were closely related, and have been called *Italic*. The Etruscans, who lived west of the Tiber, though probably of Aryan origin, differed in many respects from the Umbrians and Latins.

[See the above map for the various localities mentioned in connection with Roman Literature.]

The Latin Language, in its most ancient form, was probably spoken by the people of Latium at least twelve hundred years before the Christian Era. For many centuries it remained harsh and unpolished, nor did its roughness materially wear away until it came in contact with the Greek, about 250 B.C. Then its vocabulary was enriched, and it gradually acquired elegance and beauty. A knowledge of Greek came to be regarded as indispensable to a polite education, and Roman children were taught this language before their own.

A reaction, however, ultimately set in, and the foisting of foreign words and idioms on the native tongue was condemned as strongly as it had once been favored; a strange expression was now compelled to run the gantlet of merciless criticism before it was admitted as part of the language. Cæsar advised to shun a new term as one would a reef; Augustus frankly acknowledged that, though he was emperor of the world, he could not make a Latin word; and Tiberius was thus pointedly rebuked by a Roman grammarian for a verbal error: "Thou, O Cæsar! canst confer Roman citizenship on men, but not on words."

When the rest of Italy submitted to the arms of Rome, it accepted the language of the conqueror. Latin also supplanted the Carthaginian tongue in Africa and Spain, Celtic in Gaul and Britain, and finally was spoken in greater or less purity throughout the empire.

In its perfection, which it attained during the first century B.C., Latin was characterized by energy, dignity, and precision, its power and gravity compensating for the lack of "Attic grace." According to its system of grammar, six cases and two numbers were distinguished; nouns, pronouns, and adjectives, were declined; and verbs were varied in form through the tenses and moods of two voices. Thus the Latin had one more case-form than the Greek, but lacked the dual number and middle voice of Greek and Sanscrit.

The Latin alphabet, consisting originally of twenty-one letters, was borrowed from the Greeks through a Dorian colony at Cumæ. Its resemblance to the Greek may be seen by turning to page 87. The Roman system of notation was an Etruscan invention.

Ancient Latin Relics.—During the five centuries that followed the founding of Rome, the literary history of the city is all but a blank. Curious specimens of its antique tongue are preserved in fragments of laws and a few inscriptions; but the songs of the first Latin bards are lost forever. The legends of Romulus, the seizure of the Sabine women, the stories of Lucretia and Virginia, of Coriolanus and Horatius, —these, with many similar traditions, were doubtless the subjects of irregular ballads and heroic poems.

The rough simple verse in which they appeared was called *Saturnian*;* it is supposed to have been adopted from the Etruscan poets, and charmed the ears of the Romans until they listened to the more tuneful measures of the Greeks. The time-honored Saturnian verses were then thrust aside, with the old lays that told the proud conquerors of Italy of their humble origin and early struggles. This ballad-poetry may never have been written; sung from generation to generation, it was kept alive to grace in after-days the epic of Ennius and the pages of the historian Livy.

The oldest existing Latin poetry is inscribed on a tablet exhumed at Rome in 1778. It is a chant of the *Arval Brothers*, an association of priests founded under the Roman kings, and consists of an invocation to Mars, the god of war, to avert pestilence. Almost as venerable is a fragment from a *Salian Hymn*, sung by the Salian (*dancing*) priests in honor of Ja'nus.

Extracts from the Laws of the Twelve Tables (450 B.C.), which were destroyed in the early wars, have been collected from the works of later writers. The old Latin, however, is very obscure; so much did the language afterward change that in the golden age the Salian poems were enigmas to the Romans themselves.

There are also traces of an ancient Umbrian literature, which has perished.

Age of native minstrelsy, 753–250 B.C.: early poetry composed of hymns, festal and religious, banquet songs and funeral odes in commemoration of heroes,

---

* From *Saturn*, an ancient Italian god fabled to have instructed the people in agriculture. The metre was accommodated to the rapid beats of the foot in the country dances at harvest-time.

rude satiric verses, and, according to Niebuhr, epic poems surpassing the works of later times "in power and brilliance of imagination." No remnants of all this literature.—In prose, a primitive oratory.

CHAPTER II.

DAWN OF ROMAN LITERATURE.

As Italy received her first lessons in reading and writing from the Greeks, in law-making from Solon, in art from Phidias and Praxiteles, so in polite literature she drew her inspiration from the same source. The early Roman writers not only took their cue from Greek authors, but were in some cases downright imitators and mere translators.

A Greek slave, Livius Andronicus, who may be called the father of Roman classical literature, translating the Odyssey into Saturnian verse, introduced his captors to the literary treasures of his country. Enraptured Rome eagerly snatched the crown of letters as it fell from the head of her elder sister, and for a time the borrowed jewels sparkled on her brow. But she paid dearly for her brilliant ornaments; for, with Greek taste and culture, came also Greek effeminacy and vice.

The aim of the first Latin writers was to give their tongue the same polish as the model from which they copied; but an excess of foreign graces was repugnant to the genius of their more stately language, and it was soon seen that the refinement of the Greek would prove fatal to the vigor of Latin. Accordingly the Roman orators set their faces against any further "Grecizing," and struggled as manfully to preserve the purity of their vernacular as they did to maintain the moral purity of the nation, fast drifting into the dangerous quicksands of sloth and self-indulgence.

The sixth and seventh centuries of Rome, the period covered by the present chapter, saw the birth of the regular drama and its decline; the earliest attempts at epic and satiric poetry; and the rise of a vigorous prose. Livius Androni'cus paraphrased Greek tragedies; Nævius and Ennius not only contributed to dramatic literature, but called epic poetry into being; Plautus and Terence set forth a feast of good things in their comedies; Lucilius, the father of Roman satire, lashed vice and corruption unsparingly in his hexameters; and Cato laid the foundations of Latin prose.

DRAMATIC POETRY.

The Roman Drama.—While in the later and more developed stages of Roman literature the plastic influence of Greece is everywhere perceptible, in the earlier days there were original elements, devoid of polish indeed, but possessing the rude vigor that distinguished the nation. There was a sort of drama, for instance, native to Italy. It appeared in its primitive guise in the Fescennine* dialogues—metrical songs accompanied with rustic dances—which were long the delight of the mirth-loving Italian country-folk. When, however, the improvised jests and satires of these entertainments opened the door to malicious personal abuse, it was found necessary to prohibit libellous verses by law.

The merry songs called *Saturæ* (from the *satura lanx*, dish of various fruits offered to the gods) were brought upon the Roman stage in the fourth century B.C. A flute accompaniment and Etruscan actors, who through ignorance of the Roman language merely played the part of dancers and pantomimists, rendered the Saturæ highly attractive. At a later period, these medleys formed the afterpieces to regular dramas.

From the Oscan town Atella in Campa'nia, the so-called

* From Fescennium, an Etruscan town.

Atellane Fables derived their name—pieces with simple plots, that pictured ancient village-life in Italy, with its inevitable characters of the chatterbox, the sharper, and the long-eared glutton. It was no disgrace for young nobles, appropriately masked, to improvise the dialogue of the Atellane Fable, or sing the songs in Saturnian verse.

The regular Roman drama was a copy of the Greek, and first saw the light at the grand celebration over the downfall of Carthage, when (240 B.C.) a real tragedy and comedy were represented. Their author was

Livius Andronicus (about 285–204 B.C.), who fell into the hands of the Romans when his native city, Tarentum in southern Italy, submitted to their arms. Brought to their capital as a slave, he succeeded in obtaining his liberty and opened a school for his support. The wants of his pupils led him to translate Homer's Odyssey into Latin; he thus not only provided the Roman schools with a text-book which held its place for centuries, but inspired the people generally with a strong desire to become acquainted with the Greek masterpieces, and gave a spur to the development of a national literature.

Andronicus was no less successful as a literary caterer, when he put upon the Roman stage his Latin versions of certain Greek plays; yet, though the public relished higher and more dignified dramatic performances than the Fescennines and Saturæ, they loved the latter too much to dispense with them entirely. The vulgar off-hand humor of the amateur actors in these performances was long exceedingly popular.

Andronicus had a rough theatre assigned him on the Aventine Mount. In accordance with the fashion of his day, he played entire parts without assistance, until an injury to his voice obliged him to delegate the recitative passages to a boy, who sung them to the accompaniment of the flute, while he made the appropriate gestures. Thus originated a custom which thereafter prevailed at Rome,—that of having two actors, one to declaim and the other to gesticulate.

Livius Andronicus kindled the first spark of literary ambition in Rome, and paved the way for her future progress in letters. He enjoyed the respect of his contemporaries, and was honored by succeeding generations, though Cicero pronounced his plays unworthy of a second reading. If we except a few doubtful lines, posterity knows his dramas only by their titles.

Cneius Nævius (269–204 B.C.), a Campanian by birth, after serving in the First Punic War, took up his residence at Rome and there made dramatic literature his profession. His first play was represented about 235 B.C.

The Greek dramatists furnished Nævius with the material for his tragedies and comedies, in the latter of which—better adapted to his genius, and therefore more original—he particularly excelled. Closing his eyes to the danger of satirizing the patrician houses, he fearlessly revived the personal attack of Aristophanes in his ridicule of Scipio and the Metelli. His lampoons directed against the latter cost him dear. The verse of the poet,—"It is fate, not merit, that has made the Metelli always consuls of Rome,"—stung them to the quick, and they procured his imprisonment. Nævius employed the time in writing comedies; and after his liberation, nowise daunted by his previous bad fortune, he let fly his shafts at the nobility as recklessly as ever. Rome could no longer tolerate him, and sent him forth from her gates to die in exile.

The fate of Nævius proved a warning to future comic poets. None were ambitious to assume the rôle which he had played; but, taking Menander for their model rather than Aristophanes, they sought their subjects in the follies and foibles of society at large.

So far as we can judge from the scanty fragments that remain, the style of Nævius, though unpolished (for he still wrote in the old Saturnian verse), was nervous, bold, and pointed. His works were for centuries the delight of the Romans, who admired his independence; while succeeding authors did not regard it unworthy of their genius to borrow the spirited thoughts of Rome's first native poet. His epitaph read as follows:—

> "If gods might to a mortal pay the tribute of a tear,
> The Muses would shed one upon the poet Nævius' bier;
> For when he was transferred unto the regions of the tomb,
> The people soon forgot to speak the native tongue of Rome."

Sellar thus puts in English the old Roman's description of a flirt, which survives from one of his comedies:—

> "Like one playing at ball in a ring, she tosses about from one to another, and is at home with all. To one she nods, to another winks; she makes love to one, clings to another. Her hand is busy here, her foot there. To one she gives a ring to look at, to another blows a kiss; with one she sings, with another corresponds by signs."

The ablest work of Nævius is an epic poem, which will be described hereafter.

Ennius, partly Greek, partly Oscan by descent, was born in Rudiæ in southern Italy, 239 B.C. After serving with honor in the Roman army in Sardinia, he was induced to visit Rome by Cato the Censor, who appears at one time to have been his patron.

Filled with a desire to refine the taste of his countrymen, Ennius drew upon Euripides for their benefit. The titles of twenty-five of his tragedies survive; but the fragments that are preserved of these, as well as of several comedies, show them to be mere copies of Greek pieces. Though gifted with poetical genius and possessed of remarkable learning, Ennius found imitation easier than original composition.

In the following fragment from one of his plays, Ennius denies the providence of God:—

> "Yes! there are gods; but they no thought bestow
> On human deeds, on mortal bliss or woe;
> Else would such ills our wretched race assail?
> Would the good suffer? Would the bad prevail?"

It is not, however, as a dramatic poet that Ennius has won distinction. His renown is based on his "Annals," or "Metrical Chronicles," of all their poems the favorite with the Romans, in whose minds they were associated with the heroic achievements they commemorated. The "Annals" must be reserved for the present, while we view the progress of comedy in the works of Plautus and Terence.

Titus Maccius Plautus (254–184 B.C.), a contemporary of Ennius, was the first great comic poet of Rome. A boorish country-boy, he left his home among the mountains of Umbria to seek his fortune in the capital, and was at first quite successful as a stage-carpenter and decorator. The sobriquet *Plautus*, by which he is universally known, was significant of his large flat feet; nor do his personal peculiarities generally, judging from a self-painted portrait in one of his comedies, appear to have been of a very prepossessing type:—

> "A red-haired man, with round protuberant stomach,
> Legs with stout calves, and of a swart complexion:
> Large head, keen eyes, red face, and monstrous feet."

Unthrifty as he was uncomely, Plautus before long found himself reduced to the menial employment of grinding corn for a baker, to keep body and soul together; but his hardships were the making of the man. While thus engaged, during his unoccupied hours he tried his hand at writing comedies. He struck the right vein; play followed play in rapid succession; the author rose in public estimation, and during the rest of his life reigned without a peer on the comic stage.

Modern imitations of his comedies prove how lasting has been their popularity.

The Greek poets inspired the pen of Plautus; but he paints Roman manners, breathes Roman sentiments, and employs the idiomatic conversational Latin of his time. The tone of his dramas is far from elevating; his humor, though bold and sprightly, is coarse; and his Greek pictures of imbecile fathers, dissipated sons, intriguing slaves, jealous husbands, hungry parasites, and disreputable female characters (for all other female characters, except servants, were studiously kept in the background), had their effect in undermining the stern old Roman virtue. Yet the style of Plautus is flowing and animated; his plays are full of bustle and fun; and we can but admire his fertility of invention and wonderful command of language. Some of his characters are not unworthy of Shakespeare.

Plautus prefaced most of his comedies with prologues, which served the purpose of modern play-bills in that they contained brief analyses of the pieces. Curious requests appear in some of these: women are asked to refrain from disturbing the house by gossiping, children are desired to keep quiet, and mothers are besought not to bring infants to the theatre.

Twenty comedies of Plautus are extant, of which the finest is "the Captives." Its plot is as follows:—

During a war between Elis and Ætolia, Hegio, a rich Ætolian, buys at a sale of captives Philoc'rates and Tyndarus his slave, hoping to possess himself of a prisoner of rank to exchange for a son, who has fallen into the enemy's hands. To effect the negotiation, he proposes to send the slave to Elis with a message to the father of Philocrates, who, he learns, is a man of wealth and standing. The devoted Tyndarus, however, seizes the opportunity to restore Philocrates to liberty, allowing him to go on the journey and remaining in his stead, a change of apparel having been made, to impose upon Hegio. The parting scene between the two, in the presence of their master, is among the best passages of the play. The disguised Philocrates, about to leave, has inquired what message he shall carry to the captive's father:—

> "TYNDARUS (*habited as Philocrates*).—Say I am well; and tell him this, good Tyndarus,
> We two have lived in sweetest harmony,
> Of one accord in all things; never yet
> Have you been faithless, never I unkind.
> And still, in this our strait, you have been true
> And loyal to the last, through woe and want,
> Have never failed me, nor in will nor deed.
> This when my father hears, for such good service
> To him and to his son, he cannot choose
> But give you liberty. I will insure it,
> If I go free from hence. 'Tis you alone,
> Your help, your kindness, your devoted service,
> Shall give me to my parents' arms again.
> PHILOCRATES (*as Tyndarus*).—I have done this: I'm glad you should remember;
> And you have well deserved it: for if I
> Were in my turn to count up all the kindness
> That you have shown to me, day would grow night
> Before the tale were told. Were you my slave,
> You could have shown no greater zeal to serve me."

Hegio is moved to tears, and exclaims:—

> "O ye gods!
> Behold the honest nature of these men!
> They draw tears from me. Mark how cordially
> They love each other! and what praise the servant
> Heaps on his master!"

Hegio, however, soon discovers the trick, and condemns Tyndarus to the quarries—a punishment whose horrors the young man compares to "the torments of the damned." He is freed from bondage on the return of Philocrates with Hegio's son—to learn that he also is a son of Hegio, stolen by a slave in his infancy and mourned as lost for twenty years. It had been his good fortune to be bought by the father of

Philocrates, and to grow up the companion of the young noble.

After this happy dénouement, the play closes with an address to the audience, valuable for the view it gives of the characters in the popular comedy.

> "Gallants, this play is founded on chaste manners;
> No amorous intrigues, no child exposed,
> No close old dotard cheated of his money,
> No youth in love, making his mistress free
> Without his father's knowledge or consent.
> Few of this sort of plays our poets find,
> T' improve our morals, and make good men better.
> Now if the piece has pleased you, with our acting
> If you're content, and we have not incurred
> Displeasure by it, give us then this token:
> All who are willing that reward should wait
> On chaste and virtuous manners, give applause."
>
> WARNER.

Among the best-known of our author's comedies are "the Twins" and "the Three Silver Pieces." In the former a series of laughable incidents grows out of the resemblance of twin brothers, separated for many years and suddenly brought together. To this play Shakespeare owed the plot of his "Comedy of Errors." The second derives its name from three coins paid to a man to disguise himself as a foreigner, and pretend to bring a dowry of a thousand gold pieces to the heroine from her father, who is abroad at the time. The unexpected arrival of the father changes the aspect of affairs; but the marriage takes place, and everything ends happily.

The best of the remaining plays of Plautus are,

THE BOASTFUL SOLDIER (*Miles Gloriosus*).
THE HAUNTED HOUSE (*Mostellaria*).
THE SHIPWRECK (*Rudens*).
AMPHITRYON.
THE YOUNG CARTHAGINIAN (*Pœnulus*).
THE POT OF GOLD (*Aulularia*).
THE TWIN SISTERS (*Bacchides*).
THE LOST CHILD (*Epidicus*).
THE PARASITE (*Curculio*).
THE TRICKSTER (*Pseudolus*).

Terence, "the Prince of the Roman Drama," flourished between 195 and 159 B.C. Of his life the accounts are scanty and unsatisfactory. He appears to have been a Carthaginian slave-boy, the property of a Roman senator, who treated him with great kindness, gave him an education, and at last set him free. The youth's mind matured early; and when only twenty-one he submitted his first comedy, "the Andrian Maid," to the ædiles, who superintended dramatic representations, for their acceptance. Referred by them to Cæcilius, a comic poet of distinction, he repaired to the house of the latter at supper-time, and, humbly seated on a stool, began to read his play. The first few verses revealed to Cæcilius the genius of the young author; he beckoned Terence to a seat beside him, heard him through, and accepted his comedy at once.

On the performance of "the Andrian Maid," the reputation of Terence was secured. His plays paid him handsomely, and gave him the entrée to the highest literary circles. The great men of Rome became his intimates; among others, Scipio, the future destroyer of Carthage. They are thought to have encouraged Terence with the view of elevating the masses through his dramas, and are even suspected of having lent him a helping hand in their composition.

After completing six comedies, Terence sailed for Greece, to travel and study there. He is believed to have translated over one hundred of Menander's plays. None of these versions survive, and they are supposed to have been lost, together with the poet himself, on the return voyage.

Terence, Carthaginian though he was, is distinguished for the exceptional purity of his Latin and the beauty of his style. His taste was cultivated; his sentiments were pure; and his plays put to shame many a licentious comedy of the English stage. In lively humor and comic effect, however, he falls short both of Plautus and his Greek originals. It was in allusion to the source whence he borrowed his plots that Julius Cæsar addressed him as "thou half-Menander."

The masterpiece of Terence is "the Self-Tormentor," a copy of one of Menander's lost plays. Its title is derived from the self-inflicted punishment of Menede'mus, an Athenian, who, having refused his consent to the nuptials of his son Clin'ia with a poor but virtuous Corinthian girl, Antiph'ila, and thus driven Clinia to enlist as a mercenary, is stricken with remorse, leaves the city, and imposes on himself the severe toil of farm-life.

Chremes, a neighboring country gentleman, noticing how hard Menedemus works when there is apparently no necessity for it, inquires the reason. The first scene represents a conversation between the two, in which Menedemus, after asking his neighbor how he found time to pry into other people's affairs, and receiving the memorable answer,—"I am a man, and I have an interest in everything that concerns humanity,"*—acquaints him with the state of affairs as told above.

The love-sick Clinia now returns, and, reluctant to go to his father's house, becomes the guest of Chremes' son, Clit'-ipho, the friend of his youth. At his entreaty, Clitipho sends a slave for Antiphila; but the cunning fellow brings at the same time the lady-love of Clitipho himself, the dashing beauty Bacchis, introducing her to the family as Clinia's mistress, and passing off the modest Antiphila as one of her servants. The slave thus describes to Clinia, Antiphila and her employments when he came suddenly upon her, and announced her lover's return:—

"Busily plying the web we found her,
Decently clad in mourning. She had on
No gold or trinkets, but was plain and neat,
And dressed like those who dress but for themselves.
No female varnish to set off her beauty;
Her hair dishevelled, long, and flowing loose
About her shoulders."

---

* When the Roman audience heard this sentiment, they shook the theatre with their applause.

Chremes finds Bacchis a very expensive guest, and, announcing to Menedemus the next morning the return of his son, tries to put him on his guard against the extravagant tastes of Clinia's supposed mistress, but without producing any effect on the father thus relieved of his anxiety:—

"CHREMES.—First, she's brought with her half a score of maids,
Tricked out, the jades, with gold and jewelry;
Why, if her lover were an Eastern prince,
He couldn't stand it—how on earth can you?
MENEDEMUS.—Oh! is she here, too?
CHREMES.— Is she here, do you ask?
Oh! yes, she's here. There's no doubt as to that.
I know it to my cost. They've had one dinner,
She and her party. If I give another
Such as last night, why—I'm a ruined man.
She's very curious, mind you, as to her wines;
Knows the best brands—and drinks them. 'Ha!' she'd say,
'This wine's not dry enough, old gentleman—
Get us some better, there's a dear old soul!'
I had to tap my oldest casks. My servants
Are driven almost wild. And this, remember,
Was but one evening. What's your son to do,
And you, my friend, that will have to keep her always?
MENEDEMUS.—Let him do what he will: let him take all,
Spend, squander it upon her; I'm content,
So I may keep my son."—COLLINS.

The play is full of amusing incidents,—the intrusions of the eager Clitipho on the pretended love-making of his adored Bacchis and Clinia—the indignation of Chremes at his son's seeming want of politeness—the cozening of Chremes by the clever slave out of a large sum for his young master to give to Bacchis. The discovery that Antiphila is Chremes' own daughter, whom, at her birth, his wife had given to a Corinthian woman to expose, adds fresh interest to the plot. The marriage takes place to the delight of all parties. Chremes is persuaded to forgive his son, who promises to abandon Bacchis for a more modest wife. The "Self-Tormentor" is happy at last, and can afford to indulge in a hearty laugh at the misfortunes of his neighbor.

"I don't profess myself to be a genius—
I'm not so sharp as some folk—that I know;
But this same Chremes—this my monitor,
My would-be guide, philosopher, and friend,
He beats me hollow. Blockhead, donkey, dolt,
Fool, leaden-brains, and all those pretty names—
They might suit *me;* to him they don't apply:
His monstrous folly wants a name to itself."

The extant comedies of Terence are,

THE ANDRIAN MAID (*Andria*).
THE MOTHER-IN-LAW (*Hecyra*).
THE SELF-TORMENTOR (*Heautontimoroumenos*).
THE EUNUCH (*Eunuchus*).
PHORMIO (*taken wholly from a Greek comedy of Apollodorus*).
THE BROTHERS (*Adelphi*).

Decline of the Drama.—While the comedies of Terence were drawing crowded houses, tragedy, which Ennius attempted to popularize, that the heroic examples of early times might be emulated by his countrymen, was successfully cultivated by his nephew PACUVIUS "the Learned" (220–132 B.C.). The thirteen tragedies of Pacuvius (an accomplished painter as well as poet) were long favorites, particularly with the educated classes. The finest of them, "Orestes in Slavery," contained the famous scene between the bosom friends Py'lades and Orestes, in which each offers his life for the other. At its representation, the audience leaped to their feet and shouted their applause.

But Rome was no genial home for the tragic drama, and both tragedy and comedy soon began to languish. With Terence, the glory of the Roman theatre expired. Rope-dancing, buffoonery, and the games of the circus, offered superior attractions; and as the Republic lapsed into the Empire, the degenerate taste of the people sought gratification in the sports of the arena, where gladiators fought together or with wild beasts hardly more of brutes than themselves. In this first period of the national literature, the history of the Roman drama is written.

EPIC POETRY.

Nævius, meanwhile, ventured to appeal to the popular taste in a new department of poetry, with his epic, "the (First) Punic War"—in which contest, it will be remembered, the poet took an active part. It was written during his banishment at Utica, after he had signalized himself as a dramatist at Rome, and was a work which Cicero said "afforded him a pleasure as exquisite as the finest statue ever chiselled by Myron."

"The Punic War" entitles Nævius to the claim of originality as well as genius. The episode of Dido and Æneas, the career of Regulus, and other soul-stirring stories, were told in its Saturnian lines; and it must ever be a matter of regret that so interesting a poem is virtually lost to literature. Nævius is called "the last of the native minstrels."

Ennius (239–169 B.C.).—In Ennius we are introduced to a greater epic poet, and the founder of a new school. Brought to Rome, as we have seen, by Cato, he taught the young nobles Greek, translated dramas from that tongue, and devoted his leisure to poetical composition. A panegyric on Scipio decided his destiny; he rapidly rose in the estimation of the distinguished men of the time, and in 184 B.C. was made a Roman citizen—an honor to which Livius Andronicus had never aspired, and which Nævius sought in vain.

Though a friend of the wealthy and powerful, Ennius himself seems never to have been rich in this world's goods. A genial *bon vivant,* he spent his earnings in extravagant living; and much of his poetry was written while he was confined by the gout, a disease brought on by intemperate habits. Horace, perhaps, exaggerates his failing when he tells us that "Father Ennius never sung battles unless intoxicated." The family tomb of his friend Scipio became the final resting-place of Ennius; and from his time the name of poet was honored by the aristocracy of Rome.

Ennius owes his fame chiefly to his "Annals," an historical epic, the work of his old age. Here he wove together the ancient legends and folk-lore of the Romans handed down in Saturnian ballads, with later accredited events, and contemporary history, accomplishing the difficult task of adapting the old Latin to dactylic hexameters. Greek metres henceforth superseded the irregular Saturnian verse, the syllables being arranged according to quantity, and not as before by accent. Moreover, the language was indebted to him not only for this improved versification, but for fresh elements of strength, and grammatical changes for the better. Thus Ennius introduced a new era in Roman literature, laying solid foundations on which his successors built. He is recognized as "the father of Latin song," and it has been well said: "Whatever in the later poets is most truly Roman in sentiment and morality, appears to be conceived in the spirit of Ennius."

Ennius had a high opinion of his own talents; he deemed himself the Roman Homer, and claimed, in accordance with the Pythagorean doctrines, that the soul of the Greek bard had passed into his frame from the intermediate body of a peacock. And indeed his spirited battle-scenes, his "verses fiery to the heart's core," sometimes recalled his sublime prototype; while an air of antiquity breathed in his picturesque style and archaic forms.

The poet's self-praise was echoed by his countrymen. Cicero proudly styled him "our own Ennius;" Virgil enriched the Æneid with his most musical verses; Horace hailed him as "the Calabrian Muse." The triumphs of Rome and her heroes were often told in the verse that he made familiar; even during the Dark Ages his works remained favorites, until in the thirteenth century they gradually sunk into obscurity.

The versatile genius of Ennius displayed itself in satires,

epigrams, and didactic poems, as well as in epics and dramas. A curious specimen of his composition was his metrical treatise on edible fish, a compilation from a number of existing works on the subject.

From the fragments that remain of "the Annals" (600 lines in all) we present one of the most pleasing passages,— that in which the vestal Il'ia tells her elder sister a dream she has had, foreshadowing her great destiny as the mother of Romulus, founder of Rome.

ILIA'S DREAM.

Quick rose the aged dame, with trembling limbs
The light to bring; and Ilia then, from sleep aroused,
With tears and terror tells her wondrous dream:—
"Child of Eurydice, by our sire beloved,
Through all my fibres fail my strength and life.
A goodly man, methought, bore me away
Through pleasant willow-groves and places strange.
Next, all alone I seemed to wander desolate,
And slowly, sister, to retrace my steps,
Thee seeking but not finding; nor did path
Steady my steps. Soon a familiar voice—
My father's—thus with pitying accents spoke:
'Daughter, 'tis thine deep sorrow to endure;
This borne, thy great good fortune then is sure!'
He spoke, and suddenly departing, gave
To my fond yearning arms no sweet embrace.
Alas! I saw him not, though eagerly
To the blue vault of heaven I stretched my hands,
And called on him with loving tones. At last,
With aching heart sleep left me, and I woke."

The "Annals" were continued, and Homer's Iliad was rendered into Latin hexameters, by imitators of Ennius. But they were third or fourth rate men, and epic poetry really slumbered after Ennius passed from the stage, till it wakened to new triumphs at the call of Virgil.

SATIRIC POETRY.

In this era, we have to chronicle the birth of a new plant in the parterre of Roman literature—Satirical Poetry. It was no exotic, but native-born. The germ appeared in Nævius, the bud in Ennius, the full-blown blossom in Lucilius, the ripe fruit in the golden age of Augustus; the leaves were still green in the declining days of the empire.

Lucilius (148–103 B.C.), a Roman knight who fought under Scipio at the siege of Numantia, converted the *miscellanies* (*saturæ*) of Ennius into true satire. Though a mere youth, he was intimate with Rome's greatest statesmen, who were accustomed to doff their dignity in his lively society, and even to frolic with him before dinner. Shielded by them, and taking as his standard the stern morality and lofty patriotism of the fathers, he assailed with impunity prevalent social vices, ridiculed superstition, and denounced political corruption.

In bold relief against this dark background he brought out the noble qualities of Scipio. Always arrayed on the side of virtue, he devoted his brilliant talents to the improvement of the public morals. Yet he occasionally stooped to abuse, if we may believe the story that, having once sued a person for attacking his character, he lost his case because it was shown that he himself was not above similar practices.

The satires of Lucilius were embraced in thirty books, many fragments of which are extant. His style is forcible and not without elegance, though some of his verses are harsh and occasional Greek words lower the standard of his Latinity. He composed with haste, often standing on one foot while he dictated two hundred verses. His satires, had they been preserved, would have been valuable as a mirror of Roman manners.

VIRTUE AS DEFINED BY LUCILIUS.

"Virtue, Albinus, consists in being able to give their true worth to the things on which we are engaged, among which we live. The virtue of a man is to understand the real meaning of each thing: to understand what is right, useful, honorable, for him; what things are good, what bad, what is unprofitable, base, dishonorable; to know the due limit and measure in making money; to give its proper worth to wealth; to assign what is really due to honor; to be a foe and enemy of bad men and bad principles; to stand by good men and good principles; to extol the good, to wish them well, to be their friend through life. Lastly, it is true worth to look on our country's weal as the chief good; next to that, the weal of our parents; third and last, our own weal."—SELLAR.

EARLY LATIN PROSE.

In her prose, Rome owed but little to Greece. Had she never known the Greek masters, she might not have produced a poetical literature, but she would have had her great orators and historians. Statesmanship was the natural profession of her nobles and educated men; jurisprudence and oratory were essential accomplishments of the aspirant to public honors; and Latin was peculiarly adapted to prose composition, which appears to have been practised very early in Latium. The development of this primitive, yet nervous, prose was not left to Greek slaves and freedmen, but called forth the efforts of the foremost citizens,—Cato the Censor, Lælius and Scipio, the Gracchus brothers, Crassus and Antonius, Hortensius. In the period under consideration it began to lose its ruggedness, and acquire polish, grace, and harmony.

Cato (234–149 B.C.).—The early historians of Rome, following the example of FABIUS PICTOR, the first of her prose annalists, employed the Greek language. It was the elder Cato, the Censor and moralist, the inflexible enemy of all that was Greek, whose warning voice foretold the national corruption that must follow the introduction of Hellenic literature; it was Cato, the philosopher, orator, and historian, who dignified Latin prose by embodying in it his vigorous thoughts.

Inured from boyhood to hard toil and simple fare on his father's Sabine farm, Cato took an active part in the war against Hannibal, returning after the conflict to his humble rustic life. But his country soon demanded his services in another field; at her bar he won even greater glory, and she rewarded him with every office in her gift. Cato nobly discharged his various trusts; but it is as the uncompromising foe of effeminacy and vice that we know him best. His political life, a model of economy and uprightness, was a ceaseless battle with corruption — a struggle to banish the luxury he despised and restore the stern virtue of his fathers. But it was one man against a nation, and the current was too strong for one alone to stem. He served Rome to the bitter end, and fell in the traces at the age of ninety, his energies unimpaired, his purpose unshaken.

Amid all his active duties, Cato, whose constitution like his will was of iron, found time for literary work. He is known to have written at least one hundred and fifty orations, not without faults of style, for the amenities he was too apt to disregard, but cogent in their reasoning, clear and powerful in expression. Mutilated remains of his practical hand-book "on Agriculture" are extant, which show him to have been familiar with all the details of the farm and garden. In a work on medicine, dedicated to his son, he exclaims against the Greek physicians, and recommends the simple remedies which he had always found efficacious. His prejudice against medical men was founded on the belief that their introduction from Greece was a deep-laid plot to poison his fellow-citizens; moreover, he knew that Rome had thriven marvellously for five centuries, in blissful ignorance of the medical faculty.

Cato's chief work was his "Origines" (in seven books), a history of his country, deriving its name from the first three books, which discussed the origin of Rome and the Italian states. The aged patriot prepared this treatise just before his death, to throw it into the scale against Greek influence; but not a hundred Catos could have turned the balance then. The loss of the "Origines" is an irreparable one to archæology.

SPECIMENS OF CATO'S STYLE.

"For myself, I think well of a merchant as a man of energy and studious of gain; but it is a career that leads to danger and ruin. Farming, however, makes the bravest men and the sturdiest soldiers; and of all sources of gain is the surest, the most natural, and the least invidious. Those who are busy with it have the fewest bad thoughts."—TREATISE ON AGRICULTURE.

"Buy not what you want, but what you must have; what you don't want is dear at a farthing."—"Men are worn out by hard work; but if they do no work, rest and sloth injure them more than exercise."

HEROISM OF CÆDICIUS.

During the First Punic War the Roman army was surprised and threatened with destruction, when Cædicius the Tribune promptly volunteered to engage the enemy with 400 men, while the rest escaped. The little band was cut down to a man.

"The immortal gods," said Cato, "granted the tribune a lot according to his valor. For thus it came to pass. Though he had received many wounds, none proved mortal; and when his comrades recognized him among the dead, faint from loss of blood, they took him up and he recovered. But it makes a vast difference in what country a generous action is performed. Leonidas of Lacedæmon, who performed a similar exploit at Thermopylæ, is praised. On account of his valor, united Greece testified her gratitude in every possible way, and adorned his exploit with monumental records, pictures, statues, eulogies, histories. The Roman tribune gained but faint praise, and yet he had done the same and saved the republic."—ORIGINES.

Lælius and **Scipio** followed Cato, and improved upon his rude eloquence. Their speeches, which were committed to writing, bore the impress of learning and genius.

The Gracchi (169–121 B.C.), sons of the noble Cornelia, Scipio's daughter, to whom they owed their early education, introduced a new era in Roman eloquence, and have been called "the founders of classical Latin." Both gave up their lives in the interest of the Commons.

Tiberius, the elder, was the impersonation of clear-headed, dispassionate, argumentative oratory. Caius, the younger, of greater intellectual power, declaimed with such impetuosity that it was his custom to keep a slave at his side to remind him with the note of a flute when his vehemence became immoderate. Cicero inclined to the belief that, had not Caius Gracchus met an untimely death, he would have been the most brilliant representative of Roman eloquence. Nothing remains of the speeches of Tiberius, and the few fragments we possess of Caius indicate a want of finish.

Antonius and **Crassus** were the most distinguished speakers of the period that separated the Gracchi from Cicero. Both were diligent students of Greek literature, though both sought to conceal their indebtedness to it. Crassus excelled in the elegance of his language; Antonius, in gesture.

Hortensius (114–50 B.C.).—Crassus, in the last year of his life, highly complimented the young Hortensius, whose promise as an orator he was quick to discern. After the death of Antonius (87 B.C.), Hortensius became "prince of the Roman bar," a position which he enjoyed until eclipsed by the superior genius of Cicero (70 B.C.). During his early manhood he labored with untiring industry, turning his remarkable memory to good account. His style was ornate, his voice perfect; his gestures were so graceful that actors came to learn their art from him; never before had Rome listened to a flow of language so copious and elegant. As a matter of course his services were in great demand, and hardly a day passed in which he did not either speak or prepare a speech.

Thus Hortensius accumulated a vast fortune, which proved his stumbling-block. Wealth begot a love of luxury, his energy gave way to indolence, and he quietly yielded the first place to his youthful rival. His luxurious villas, with their deer-parks, and gardens whose plants he watered with wine, were more to Hortensius than the victories of the forum. In these charming retreats he loved to entertain his friends, and exhibit to them his menagerie and tame fish—for which he showed more concern than for his servants. The death of a favorite lamprey affected him to tears. At his luxurious mansion in Rome, the nucleus of the future imperial palace, peacocks were served for the first time at a feast.

The orator's tastes, however, were æsthetic as well; he wrote poetry, and expended large sums on statues and paintings. His orations are lost. Only the merest fragments of all the above prose writers survive.

MINOR DRAMATIC POETS.

LAVINIUS, the rival of Terence, who jealously interrupted the performance of the "Eunuch," denouncing its author as a plagiarist; yet this play brought Terence more than had ever before been paid for a comedy.

TURPILIUS (125 B.C.), a popular comic poet.

ACCIUS (170–94 B.C.), the last of the tragic poets; 37 tragedies, borrowed to a great extent from the Greek; diction majestic and eloquent.

Early Roman theatres, temporary wooden structures; first stone theatre built by Pompey (55 B.C.), capable of accommodating 40,000 spectators. Pompey's example promptly followed by others. The orchestra reserved for the chief men of Rome, and not occupied by the chorus as in ancient Greece. Awnings for theatres invented by the Romans. The vast size of the later theatres obliged the actors to wear masks with features much larger than life and arranged at the mouth so as to give additional force to the voice.

MINOR PROSE WRITERS.

HISTORIANS.

FABIUS PICTOR: "Annals" of Rome, from the founding of the city to the end of the Second Punic War; careless and inaccurate.

CINCIUS (210 B.C.): a truthful and diligent annalist.

ACILIUS GLABRIO (180 B.C.): History of Rome.

CALPURNIUS PISO: "Annals;" style barren and lifeless.

SISENNA (119–67 B.C.): History of Rome from the destruction of the city by the Gauls.

ORATORS.

GALBA (180–136 B.C.): first master of Greek rhetoric; vehemence and artifice his characteristics.

CARBO (164–119 B.C.): an unscrupulous, but sweet-voiced and powerful pleader.

RUTILIUS (158–78 B.C.): a distinguished jurist.

CATULUS: graceful and elegant; a master of pure Latin.

COTTA: soft-spoken and courteous; his eloquence of the sweet, persuasive kind.

Study of grammar introduced by Crates, who, fortunately for the Romans, broke his leg while on an embassy to their city from the king of Pergamus (156 B.C.), and during his convalescence lectured on philology at Rome. The earliest works on Roman law were produced during this period.

CHAPTER III.

GOLDEN AGE OF ROMAN LITERATURE.

(B.C. 80–14 A.D.)

Divisions and Ornaments.—The Golden Age, which now engages our attention, is naturally divided into two distinct periods, bearing the names of Cicero, the greatest of Roman writers, and Augustus, the founder of the empire and patron of letters.

In the Ciceronian Period (80–43 B.C.), a stormy era of conspiracy as well as conquest—marked by Catiline's formidable attempt to destroy the commonwealth, by the civil war of Cæsar and Pompey, and the murder of these renowned leaders—political eloquence and history monopolized the attention of the master minds of Rome. As a consequence, Latin prose matured early in the golden age; while poetry boasted of no ornaments until, at the close of the Ciceronian Period, Lucretius penned his philosophical poem "On the Nature of Things," and Catullus produced his erotic odes and elegies.

In the Augustan Period (B.C. 42–14 A.D.), the greatest of Roman poets, Virgil and Horace, lived and wrote, prose playing a secondary part. Tibullus and Propertius put forth their sweet elegies, and Ovid his amatory pieces. Even the pages of Livy's history are aglow with poetical coloring. But the blossom was as transient as it was beautiful, and expanded only to die.

PROSE WRITERS OF THE CICERONIAN PERIOD.

Marcus Tullius Cicero (106–43 B.C.) was born at Arpi'num, a Latian town south-east of Rome. As his family (of equestrian rank) had never distinguished itself, he is known as a *novus homo* (*new man*). Detecting unusual talent in the boy, his father resolved to develop it by a thorough education, which he himself superintended at Rome. The most accomplished teachers were secured, the Greek poet Ar'chias among the number, and the youth was thoroughly grounded in grammar, rhetoric, and Grecian literature. This early

training Cicero sedulously supplemented with a course on Roman law under Scævola, avoiding the whirl of dissipation that surrounded him, and even relinquishing social pleasure for the labors of his closet or to study in the forum the style of the first public speakers. "Who can blame me," he asked in his oration for Archias, "if while others are gazing at festal shows and idle ceremonies, exploring new pleasures, engaged in midnight revels, in the distraction of gaming, the madness of intemperance, I dedicate *my* time to learning and the Muses?"

At twenty-five Cicero made his début; and within two years he rose to the highest rank at the Roman bar by ably pleading the cause of one Roscius against a friend of the terrible Sulla. Successful in this case, to escape the vengeance of the dictator as well as to recruit his failing health, Cicero went abroad. At Athens he pursued the study of philosophy with Pompo'nius Atticus, the companion of his boyhood and ever after his warmest friend. In the schools of Asia Minor, as well as at Rhodes, then a great literary centre, he studied under distinguished teachers, storing his memory with valuable knowledge at the same time that he made himself proficient in the rhetorical art. The death of Sulla having removed all danger, at the age of thirty he went back to Italy, thoroughly restored by his travels, and fired with the noble ambition of making himself the Demosthenes of Rome. Step by step he approached the realization of his hopes, and when, in the prosecution of Verres, the rapacious governor of Sicily, he triumphed over Hortensius, who conducted the defence (70 B.C.), his end was practically achieved.

Cicero served his country in many capacities, but in none more effectively than as consul; since, while holding this office (63–62 B.C.), he saved the republic from a dangerous conspiracy, headed by the profligate Catiline. The consul's tact and courage were sorely tried, but prevailed. Four crushing orations laid bare the plans of the traitor and drove him from the city, to fall in a desperate battle with the Roman legions, while a grateful nation greeted the vigilant Cicero as "the Father of his Country."

But the Roman people were fickle, and at the instigation of an enemy banished Cicero from the city he had saved, 58 B.C. The next year, however, the decree was revoked, and he returned. When the civil war between Cæsar and Pompey was imminent, Cicero's indecision told powerfully against him.* At last he joined Pompey, who, provoked at his vacillation, exclaimed: "I wish that Cicero would go over to the other side; perhaps he would then be afraid of us." The battle of Pharsalia (48 B.C.) overthrew the hopes of the party whose cause he had espoused, and Cicero, returning to Italy, accepted the rule and friendship of Cæsar, and settled down to a literary life.

Shortly after, a plot is laid against the dictator; the fatal Ides (15th) of March (44 B.C.) arrive; the assassins do their bloody work in the senate-house; and Brutus, flourishing his traitorous dagger, cries to Cicero: "Rejoice, O Father of our Country, for Rome is free!"

But it was grief, not joy, that the dagger of Brutus brought to the Republic; another Pompey and another Cæsar arose to contend for the mastery of the world. Marc Antony aspired to the dead dictator's place; but Cicero, now the foremost statesman in Rome, regarding him as the enemy of liberty, upheld the cause of the people and of Octavius, Cæsar's young nephew. Into the struggle that ensued, he entered with all the spirit of his youth, thundering against Antony his grand "Philippics," in the second of which are concentrated all his powers of invective, passion, and eloquence. It is Cicero's mightiest effort.

FROM THE SECOND PHILIPPIC.

"When, therefore, this fellow (*Antony*) had begun to wallow in the treasures of that great man, he began to exult like a buffoon in a

---

* A Roman knight, Laberius, who had lost caste by appearing on the stage, made a good hit at Cicero, for his political non-committalism. As he was going to his place in the theatre one day, Cicero, who was seated in the orchestra, called out to him, "Laberius, I would make room for you, if we were not so crowded here."—"You crowded!" answered Laberius. "Why, how is that? you generally manage to sit on two stools."

play, who has lately been a beggar and has become suddenly rich.* But, as some poet or other says,

'Ill-gotten gains come quickly to an end.'

It is an incredible thing, and almost a miracle, how he in a few, not months, but days, squandered all that vast wealth. There was an immense quantity of wine, an excessive abundance of very valuable plate, much precious apparel, great quantities of splendid furniture, and other magnificent things in many places, such as one was likely to see belonging to a man who was not indeed luxurious, but who was very wealthy. Of all this in a few days there was nothing left. What Charybdis was ever so voracious? Charybdis, do I say? Charybdis, if she existed at all, was only one animal. The ocean, I swear most solemnly, appears hardly capable of having swallowed up such numbers of things so widely scattered, and distributed in such different places, with such rapidity.

Nothing was shut up, nothing sealed up, no list was made of anything. Whole storehouses were abandoned to the most worthless of men. Actors seized on this, actresses on that; the house was crowded with gamblers, and full of drunken men; people were drinking all day, and that too in many places; there were added to all this expense (for this fellow was not invariably fortunate) heavy gambling losses. You might see, in the cellars of the slaves, couches covered with the most richly embroidered counterpanes of Cneius Pompey. Wonder not, then, that all these things were so soon consumed. Such profligacy as that could have devoured, not only the patrimony of one individual, however ample it might have been, but whole cities and kingdoms.

And then his houses and gardens! O the cruel audacity! Did you dare to enter into that house? Did you dare to cross that most sacred threshold? and to show your most profligate countenance to the household gods who protect that abode? A house which for a long time no one could behold, no one could pass by, without tears! Are you not ashamed to dwell so long in that house—one in which, stupid and ignorant as you are, still you can see nothing which is not painful to you?

When you behold those beaks of ships in the vestibule, and those warlike trophies, do you fancy that you are entering into a house which belongs to you? It is impossible. Although you are devoid of all sense and all feeling, still you are acquainted with yourself, and with your trophies, and with your friends. Nor do I believe that you, either waking or sleeping, can ever act with quiet sense.

It is impossible but that, were you ever so drunk and frantic, as in

* Allusion is here made to Antony's purchase of the goods of Pompey the Great, at auction, after the defeat of the latter in the civil war.

truth you are, when the recollection of the appearance of that illustrious man comes across you, you should be roused from sleep by your fears, and often stirred up to madness if awake. I pity even the walls and the roof."—YONGE.

The patriot paid for his stanch defence of freedom with his life. Octavius and Antony, becoming reconciled, formed with Lepidus the Second Triumvirate, or board of three, to govern the Roman world; and Cicero knew that the sun of liberty had set. The triumvirs agreed upon a general proscription of their enemies. A reign of terror deluged Italy with blood, but the noblest of those who fell was Cicero.

Antony demanded his life, and Octavius covered himself with infamy by yielding it. The orator met his fate near his villa at Formiæ; timid throughout his life, in the last scene he exhibited manly fortitude. He is said to have been calmly reading the "Medea" of Euripides in his litter when Antony's myrmidons overtook him; a desperado who owed him many favors, while even his brutal companions covered their eyes, struck the fatal blow. The head and hands of the murdered orator were cut off and sent to Antony, whose inhuman wife, as she fondled the ghastly head in her lap, maliciously thrust her bodkin into the tongue that had denounced her husband. —True as it was, it ill became the time-serving Octavius to say, when afterward wielding the sceptre of the world as Augustus Cæsar, "Cicero was a good citizen, who really loved his country."

CICERO'S WORKS.—Cicero was emphatically a many-sided man, and filled a wide space in Roman literature. Though he excelled chiefly in oratory, he has left us, besides fifty-nine orations, a number of philosophical treatises, essays, and many letters to his friend Atticus, his brother, and other correspondents. While deeply absorbed in public duties, he found opportunities, without neglecting these, to pursue the study of philosophy, having in view not only his own relaxation, but also the moral advancement of his countrymen. His works on this subject, some of which, for the sake of interest and variety, he wrote in the form of dialogues, present a valuable survey of the Greek systems. They assert his belief in the existence of one Supreme Creator and the immortality of the soul.

Cicero's chief philosophical writings are "the Tusculan Disputations," imaginary discussions of various practical questions at the author's Tusculan villa,—the scorn of death, the endurance of suffering, etc.; "the Offices," a moral essay; treatises "On Friendship" and "On Old Age," justly considered as among the most charming productions of their class in any literature; political dissertations "On the Republic" and "On Laws;" and a theological disquisition "On the Nature of the Gods."

THE END OF LIFE.

[From Cicero's Treatise on Old Age.]

"An old man, indeed, has nothing to hope for; yet he is in so much the happier state than a young one; since he has already attained what the other is only hoping for. The one is wishing to live long, the other has lived long. And yet, good gods! what is there in man's life that can be called long? To my mind, nothing whatever seems of long duration, in which there is any end. For when that arrives, then the time which is past has flowed away; that only remains which you have secured by virtue and right conduct. Hours indeed depart from us, and days, and months, and years; nor does past time ever return, nor can it be discovered what is to follow.

Whatever time is assigned to each to live, with that he ought to be content: for neither need the drama be performed entire by the actor, in order to give satisfaction, provided he be approved in whatever act he may be; nor need the wise man live till the *plaudite*.* The short period of life is long enough for living well and honorably; and if you should advance farther, you need no more grieve than farmers do, when the loveliness of spring-time hath passed, that summer and autumn have come. For spring represents the time of youth, and gives promise of the future fruits; the remaining seasons are intended for plucking and gathering those fruits. Now the harvest of old age, as I have often said, is the recollection and abundance of blessings previously secured.

* The last word of the play, which invites the applause of the audience.

In truth, everything that happens agreeably to nature is to be reckoned among blessings. What, however, is so agreeable to nature as for an old man to die? which even is the lot of the young, though nature opposes and resists. And thus it is that young men seem to me to die, just as when the violence of flame is extinguished by a flood of water; whereas old men die, as the exhausted fire goes out, spontaneously, without the exertion of any force. And as fruits when they are green are plucked by force from the trees, but when ripe and mellow drop off, so violence takes away their lives from youths, maturity from old men; a state which to me indeed is so delightful that, the nearer I approach to death, I seem as it were to be getting sight of land, and at length, after a long voyage, to be just coming into harbor."—EDMONDS.

Cicero also wrote a treatise "On Glory," now lost. It was once in the possession of Petrarch, who commends it in the most flattering terms. The Italian poet was induced to lend it to his aged preceptor; but the latter, driven by poverty, secretly put the work in pawn and died without making known its whereabouts. It never saw the light afterward; although it is supposed to have been destroyed two centuries later by a plagiarist, who had helped himself to some of its fine periods.

As a letter-writer, Cicero excels all others. It was the custom of his countrymen to bestow as great pains on private correspondence as on works intended for publication; and his epistles, eight hundred of which survive, are simple, elegant, and glow with wit, though some of them were written so fast as to be almost illegible. They cast important light on the history of his day.

Our author also turned his hand to history and poetry, but with indifferent success. His works were extremely popular among his contemporaries, some of them selling by the thousand.

CICERO'S STYLE.—Cicero has always been commended for the cadence of his periods. The art of framing harmonious balanced sentences was his special study, and the Latin language, which he perfected in beauty and richness, was well adapted to his purpose. His style is often exuberant, for he cultivated the flowers of rhetoric. Character he sketched with a powerful pen, and his speeches are enlivened with abundant illustrations drawn from the wonderful storehouse of his memory. Too often, however, vanity crops out, to mar the effect.

Quintilian declared that as an orator Cicero combined "the force of Demosthenes, the copiousness of Plato, and the elegance of Isocrates." Through all his works flows a current of mingled majesty and sweetness. Merivale aptly styles him "the most consummate specimen of the Roman character under the influence of Hellenic culture."

CICERO ON PROVIDENCE.

[From the Treatise on the Nature of the Gods.]

"There are and have been philosophers who have given it as their opinion that the gods exercise no superintending care whatever over human affairs. Now, if the opinion of these men be true, what becomes of piety? what of public worship? what of religion itself? For all these marks of homage are to be rendered in a pure and holy spirit unto the majesty of the gods, only in case they are observed by these same, and in case any favor has been bestowed by the immortal gods on the race of men. If, however, the gods are neither able nor willing to assist us; if they take no care whatever of us; if they mark not what we do; if there is nothing that can come from them and exercise an influence on the lives of men,—what reason is there why we are to pay any adoration, render any honors, offer any prayers, to the immortal gods?

Piety, just as much as the other virtues, cannot exist in outward show and empty feignings; while along with piety, both public worship and religion itself must of necessity be done away with. Remove these, and a great disturbance and total confusion of life ensue. Nay, indeed, I do not know whether, if piety toward the gods be removed, good faith also, and every social tie that binds together the human race, and justice too, that most excellent of all virtues, would not be removed along with it."—CHARLES ANTHON.

Varro (116–28 B.C.).—The great central sun of the Republican Era was Cicero, compared with whom the brightest of his contemporaries seem but as lesser luminaries whose light is swallowed up in his. Of these, Marcus Terentius Varro was perhaps the greatest. Years of incessant application, which a boyhood passed among the Sabine mountains at Reate (*re'ă-te*) had prepared him to endure, won for Varro the proud title "Most Learned of the Romans."

During the civil war, Varro sided with Pompey. After the triumph of Cæsar, he retired from public life to his favorite studies, the victor magnanimously recognizing his merit by placing him in charge of the public library at Rome. The material results of his literary labors enabled him to live like a prince, and we find him the proprietor of three sumptuous country-seats, one of which was celebrated for its costly marble aviary of three thousand song-birds—Varro's pets.

All this wealth did not escape the notice of the rapacious triumvirs after the assassination of Cæsar. The name of Varro, then more than seventy, was placed on the proscription list; his property was confiscated; and Antony sacked his beautiful villa at Casi'num, committing his invaluable library to the flames. The old man owed his life to friends, who concealed him from his implacable foe till the order for his murder was countermanded. Augustus afterward restored his fortune, but Varro always keenly missed the society of his books. At the advanced age of eighty, he composed, in dialogue form, an admirable work "On Husbandry," written in a brisk and entertaining style.

The genius of Varro was remarkably versatile; as over six hundred different books on various subjects, in both prose and verse, abundantly testify. In fertility he surpassed all other Romans; and we can but wonder, with St. Augustine, how he found time to write so much. His most creditable work was his "Antiquities Divine and Human," a lost treasure, of which the present age, with its profound interest in the religions of the past, severely feels the want.

Varro also prepared a treatise "On the Latin Language," edited a popular encyclopædia of the liberal arts, and wrote on history. Throughout his works he appears as a pure patriot, a defender of ancient simplicity and virtue. His satires on effeminacy and affectation are caustic; no one can help enjoying his humorous etchings of the spruce dandy, the dainty epicure, and the finical poet who gargles his throat before reciting his pieces. In every kind of writing that he attempted (and there was little he did not attempt) he is worthy of respect: the familiar line from Dr. Johnson's epitaph on our own Goldsmith, would apply with equal force to Varro—"He touched nothing that he did not adorn."

Little survives of Varro's writings beyond the treatise on agriculture, and a part of that on the Latin language.

Julius Cæsar.—July 12th, 100 B.C., was the birthday of Caius Julius Cæsar, by some believed to be, as Shakespeare styled him, "the foremost man of all this world." The period at which he lived was a critical one in history. Roman virtue had depreciated, justice was bought and sold, luxury had sapped the vigor of the nation, and vice ran riot. Only one-man power, and that wielded by a clear head and powerful arm, could save the state. The times demanded a statesman who would not shrink from taking upon himself all needful responsibilities; and in Julius Cæsar that statesman was forthcoming.

Cæsar's whole career evinces ambition, courage, and determination. Sulla himself he feared not to defy, when ordered to divorce his wife for political reasons; and he was adroit enough to escape the vengeance of the ruthless dictator who saw in "the loose-girt boy" many Mariuses. Leaving Rome for the East, he acquitted himself with signal ability, though only twenty-two, in a campaign against Mytilene; and when captured by pirates on the high seas, he paid them an extortionate ransom, but promptly turned the tables on them by overhauling their vessel with a small fleet, and nailing them to crosses on the coast of Asia Minor.

At Rhodes he studied oratory and rhetoric. On his return to Rome he gave evidence of his powers in the forum, and was hailed as second in eloquence to Cicero only. His readiness to protect the poor and the oppressed, together with his insinuating manners, made Cæsar the idol of the people, who bestowed upon him various offices and finally raised him to the consulship. At the expiration of his term, he was intrusted with the government of the two Gauls; and the military skill he displayed in this position, during nine years of active service (58–50 B.C.), proved him to be one of the world's great captains. Overpowering many fierce tribes, he carried the terror of the Roman eagles into the forests of Germany and even across the Channel. A million human beings are computed to have been sacrificed in his Gallic campaigns.

Jealous of these brilliant successes, and recognizing in Cæsar a dangerous opponent of his schemes for political aggrandizement, Pompey prevailed on the senate to demand the resignation of his victorious rival. This brought matters to a crisis. Cæsar with his legions crossed the Rubicon, which separated Cisalpine Gaul from Italy (49 B.C.), and was soon in Rome, whence Pompey and his friends had fled. The battle of Pharsalia the next year decided the question in favor of Cæsar; Pompey's party was overthrown in Africa and Spain, and the Roman world remained the prize of the conqueror.

Not long, however, did he enjoy it. Fearing his ambition, or pretending to do so, a number of "liberators" conspired against his life. On the 15th of March, 44 B.C., he fell pierced by their daggers at the foot of Pompey's statue, as that last cry, wrung from his heart by the ingratitude of a trusted friend, resounded through the senate-house,—"Thou, too, Brutus, my son!"

We can hardly see how, amid the excitements of such a career, Cæsar found any time to devote to literary pursuits; yet his name is hardly less eminent in letters than for statesmanship and military genius. He seems to have had the rare ability of "employing at the same time his ears to listen, his eyes to read, his hand to write, and his voice to dictate." While crossing the Alps, on one occasion, he wrote a grammatical treatise of no little merit.

The greatest of Cæsar's works are his "Commentaries" on the Gallic and the Civil War—the former in seven books, to which an eighth was added at the author's request by his fellow-soldier HIRTIUS. In "the Gallic War," Cæsar not only recounts his successes and feats of engineering skill, but also entertains us with pleasing descriptions of the countries he visited and the tribes he encountered. He always aims at justifying himself, and so plausibly defended his course in "the Civil War" as to carry conviction even to the prejudiced.

In Cæsar's style, conciseness goes hand in hand with simplicity and perspicuity. Dispensing with ornament, he uses every word to the best advantage—and this despite the fact that he wrote with amazing rapidity. Though, perhaps, he lacks vivacity and energy, there is no purer Latin than his. We subjoin some interesting paragraphs from the Commentaries on the Gallic War, relating to the customs of

THE ANCIENT GAULS AND GERMANS.

"The whole nation of Gauls is extremely addicted to superstition; whence, in threatening distempers and the imminent dangers of war, they make no scruple to sacrifice men, or engage themselves by vow to such sacrifices. In these they make use of the ministry of the Druids: for it is a prevalent opinion among them that nothing but the life of man can atone for the life of man, insomuch that they have established even public sacrifices of this kind. Some prepare huge colossuses of osier twigs, into which they put men alive, and setting fire to them, those within expire amid the flames. They prefer for victims such as have been convicted of theft, robbery, or other crimes, believing them the most acceptable to the gods; but, when criminals are wanting, the innocent are often made to suffer.

Mercury is the chief deity with them; of him they have many images, account him the inventor of all arts, their guide and conductor in their journeys, and the patron of merchandise and gain. Next to him are Apollo and Mars, Jupiter and Minerva. Their notions in regard to these are pretty much the same as those of other nations. Apollo is their god of physic, Minerva of works and manufactures; Jove holds the empire of heaven, and Mars presides in war. To this last, when they resolve on a battle, they commonly devote the spoil. If they prove victorious, they offer up all the cattle taken, and set apart the rest of the plunder in a place appointed for that purpose; it is common in many provinces to see these monuments of offerings piled up in consecrated places. Nay, it rarely happens that any one shows so great a disregard of religion as either to conceal the plunder or pillage the public oblations; and the severest punishments are inflicted on such offenders.

The Gauls fancy themselves to be descended from the god Pluto; which, it seems, is an established tradition among the Druids. For this reason they compute the time by nights, not by days; and, in the observance of birthdays, new moons, and the beginning of the year, always commence the celebration from the preceding night. In one custom they differ from almost all other nations, that they never suffer their children to come openly into their presence until they are old enough to bear arms; for the appearance of a son in public with his father before he has reached the age of manhood is accounted dishonorable.

Whatever fortune the woman brings, the husband is obliged to equal it out of his own estate. This whole sum, with its annual product, is left untouched, and falls always to the share of the survivor. The men have power of life and death over their wives and children; and, when any father of a family of illustrious rank dies, his relations assemble, and, on the least ground of suspicion, put even his wives to the torture like slaves. If they are found guilty, iron and fire are employed to torment and destroy them. Their funerals are magnificent and sumptuous, according to their quality. Everything that was dear to the deceased, even animals, are thrown into the pile; and, formerly, such of their slaves and clients as they loved most sacrificed themselves at the funeral of their lord.

The Germans differ widely in their manners from the Gauls; for neither have they Druids to preside in religious affairs, nor do they trouble themselves about sacrifices. They acknowledge no gods but those that they can see, and by whose power they are apparently benefited: the sun, the moon, fire. Of others they know nothing, not even by report. Their whole life is addicted to hunting and war; and from their infancy they are inured to fatigue and hardships. Agriculture is little regarded among them, as they live mostly on milk, cheese, and the flesh of animals. Nor has any man lands of his own, or distinguished by fixed boundaries. The magistrates and those in authority portion out yearly to every canton and family such a quantity of land, and in what part of the country they think proper; and the year following remove them to some other spot.

Many reasons are assigned for this practice; lest, seduced by habit and continuance, they should learn to prefer pillage to war; lest a desire of enlarging their possessions should gain ground, and prompt the stronger to expel the weaker; lest they should become curious in their buildings, in order to guard against the extremes of heat and cold; lest avarice should get footing among them, whence spring factious and discords; in fine, to preserve contentment and equanimity among the people, when they find their possessions nothing inferior to those of the most powerful.

It is accounted honorable for states to have the country all around them lie waste and depopulated; for they think it an argument of valor to expel their neighbors, and suffer none to settle near them; at the same time that they are themselves also the safer, as having nothing to apprehend from sudden incursions. When a state is engaged in war, either offensive or defensive, they make choice of magistrates to preside in it, whom they arm with the power of life and death. In time of peace there are no public magistrates; but the chiefs of the several provinces and clans administer justice, and decide differences within their respective limits. Robbery has nothing infamous in it when committed without the territories of the state to which they belong; they even pretend that it serves to exercise their youth, and prevent the growth of sloth. The laws of hospitality are held inviolable among them. All that fly to them for refuge, on whatever account, are sure of protection and defence."—DUNCAN.

Sallust (86–34 B.C.).—Another historian, whose name is as familiar as Cæsar's to classical students, is Caius Sallustius Crispus, popularly known as Sallust. From his native town Amiternum, in the country of the Sabines, he came to Rome, ambitious of public honors, and gradually worked his way up to a seat in the senate. Alleged immorality, however, caused his expulsion from that body, and not until he had rendered important service to Cæsar in the civil war did he recover his good standing. Cæsar made him governor of the rich province of Numidia (46 B.C.), which Sallust pretty thoroughly plundered during his one year of office, returning to Rome with fabulous riches. It was fortunate for him that, when a Numidian commission arrived to prosecute him for extortion, his powerful patron interposed to save him from punishment.

On the assassination of Cæsar, Sallust retired from public life and devoted part of his ill-gotten gains to the erection of a splendid mansion on one of the seven hills. It was surrounded by lovely pleasure-grounds, adorned with baths, statues, and other magnificent works of art, prominent among which, on exquisitely chiselled columns, rose a temple, paved in mosaic, and set off with Grecian marbles. "The Gardens of Sallust" were preferred by many of the Roman emperors to the imperial palace itself.

Here or at his Tiburtine villa, our author, thoroughly convinced of the vanity of political honors, and filled with remorse for his youthful indiscretions, spent the last nine years of his life in the compilation of historical works which give us a high opinion of his abilities. His first effort was "the Conspiracy of Catiline," the facts of which were vividly impressed upon his memory, since, when a student at Rome, he was a witness of its thrilling scenes. "The Jugurthine War," which followed, treats of the struggle which the Roman people carried on with Jugurtha, king of Numidia. This unscrupulous prince had made his way to an undivided throne over the murdered bodies of his two cousins, allies of the Romans, securing impunity for a time by buying up the senate. Having, however, caused the assassination of another kinsman in the very streets of Rome, whither he had been summoned, on the pledge of the public faith, to expose those who had taken his bribes, he was ordered to quit Italy. It was on leaving the capital that Jugurtha, looking back, uttered those words so significant of the prevalent corruption: "O venal city and destined soon to perish, if you can but find a purchaser!"

A Roman army followed him into Africa; but little was effected until the consul Metellus assumed the command, and, proof against Numidian gold, prosecuted the war in earnest. After five years' continuance, it was successfully terminated by Marius. Sallust's history ends with the betrayal of Jugurtha to the Romans, and the triumph of the consul Marius, "on whom the hopes of the state were then placed." Plutarch adds that, after figuring in the procession, Jugurtha was set upon by the people, who tore the rings from his ears and even stripped him of his clothes; then he was pushed into a damp dungeon to starve, shuddering as he cried to the bystanders with a maniacal laugh, "How cold is this bath of yours!"

Another work of Sallust was a History of Rome from 78 to 66 B.C., fragments of which remain.

SALLUST'S STYLE, modelled after that of Thucydides, is sententious, energetic, and an improvement on the original in clearness. Condensation without obscurity is its crowning excellence; and its finish, though too plainly showing marks of labor, is always attractive.

The forte of Sallust lay in delineating character; his portraits of Catiline and Jugurtha are as vivid as if the men themselves stood before us. Especially striking are his pictures of remorse. Catiline, who murdered his own son to induce an infamous beauty to become his wife, "at peace with neither gods nor men, finds no comfort either waking or sleeping; his complexion is pale, his eyes haggard, his walk sometimes quick and sometimes slow, and distraction is apparent in every look." Jugurtha, red with the blood of many victims, "fears his subjects and his enemies alike, is ever on the watch, starts from his sleep to seize his arms, and is so agitated by terror as to appear under the influence of madness."

Sallust also affects the moralist, and throughout his works is as loud in the praises of virtue as in his life he was careless of her interests. From "the Jugurthine War" we take an interesting account of the

CAPTURE OF A NUMIDIAN FORT.

"Not far from the river Mulucha, which separated the kingdoms of Jugurtha and Bocchus, there stood, in the midst of a plain, a small fort, on a rock of considerable breadth, and of prodigious height, naturally as steep on every side as art or labor could render it; it had no access, except at one place, and that was by means of a narrow path. As the king's treasure was deposited in this place,

Marius exerted his utmost efforts to reduce it; and succeeded, more by accident than by prudent management.

The castle was abundantly provided with men, arms, provisions, and a spring of water; its situation rendered it impossible to make use of mounds and turrets, and the machinery usually employed in a siege; the path to it was very narrow, with a precipice on each side. The moving galleries were pushed forward with infinite hazard, and to no purpose; for, when they advanced toward the garrison, they were either destroyed by fire or crushed by prodigious stones. The soldiers could neither maintain their footing nor make use of their batteries without exposing themselves to continual danger. The most adventurous were either slain or wounded, and the rest were greatly discouraged.

Marius, having thus spent many toilsome days, now hesitated whether he should abandon his enterprise, which had proved unsuccessful, or wait the interposition of fortune, which had so frequently befriended him. While these reflections day and night occupied his mind, a Ligurian, a common soldier of the auxiliary cohorts, who had gone out of the camp in search of water, happened to observe, not far from the opposite side of the castle, some periwinkles creeping among the rocks; gathering one, then another, and still climbing to procure more, he was led insensibly almost to the top of the mountain, where, perceiving all was quiet in that quarter, the natural desire of viewing unknown objects prompted him to proceed.

It chanced that an oak-tree, of considerable magnitude, here grew out of the side of the rock, and, bending its trunk downward near the root, then taking a turn, mounted upward, as is natural to trees in such situations.

By the help of this, the Ligurian, laying hold of the branches of the tree or of the prominences of the rock, was at length enabled to survey the whole plan of the castle, without being disturbed by the Numidians, who were all engaged on that side on which the attack had been made. Having carefully examined whatever he thought would be useful to him in the execution of his design, he returned the same way; not hastily, as he went up, but pausing at every step, and observing everything with the utmost care.

On his return to the camp, he hastened to Marius, informed him of what he had done, pressed him to make an attempt on the castle on that side where he himself had mounted, and promised that he would lead the way, and be the first to face the danger. Marius despatched some of those who attended him, accompanied by the Ligurian, to examine the spot; and, although their reports varied as to the facility or the difficulty of the undertaking, the consul, encouraged by the hope of success, determined to make the attempt. He accordingly selected, from among the trumpeters and cornet-blowers of the line, five of the most active and enterprising men, together with four centurions to support them, and, putting the whole under the command of the Ligurian, he ordered them to be in readiness to set out on the following day.

At the time appointed the party left the camp, having previously taken such measures as were necessary for the expedition. The centurions, according to the instructions which they had received from their guide, had changed their arms and dress, and marched with their heads and feet bare, that they might have the freer prospect, and climb with more facility. Their swords and bucklers were slung across their shoulders; the latter, of the Numidian kind, and covered with hides, as well for the sake of lightness, as that all noise might be avoided if they struck against the rock.

The Ligurian, leading the way, fixed cords about the stones, and such roots of trees as appeared proper for the purpose, to assist the soldiers in climbing; stretching his hand, from time to time, to such as were discouraged at so rugged a march. When the ascent was more steep than ordinary, he would send them up before him unarmed, and then follow himself with their arms. Wherever it appeared more dangerous to climb, he went foremost; and, by ascending and descending several times, encouraged the rest to follow him, and retired to make way for them. At length, after much tedious labor, they gained the castle, which was quite deserted on that side, the Numidians being all employed in the opposite quarter.

When Marius was informed of the success of the Ligurian, although he had kept the garrison employed the whole day by a continued attack, he now, encouraging the soldiers, sallied from under the moving galleries, and, drawing up his men in the form of a shell, rushed forward to the castle; while the slingers and archers poured their volleys from a distance, and the engines incessantly played on the besieged. The Numidians, who had often before broken to pieces and even burned the Roman galleries, did not now defend themselves within their battlements, but passed whole days and nights without their walls; they railed at the efforts of the Romans, upbraided Marius with madness, and in the height of their exultation threatened to make our men slaves of Jugurtha.

While both sides were warmly engaged in this vigorous struggle for glory and empire on the one hand, and life and liberty on the other, the trumpets on a sudden sounded in the enemy's rear. The women and children, who had come out to see the engagement, first fled in dismay; after them, such as were nearest the walls; and at last the whole, armed and unarmed, fairly gave way. The Romans now pressed onward with greater vigor, overthrowing the enemy, and wounding most of them; then, advancing over the heaps of slain, they flew to the walls, all thirsting for glory, and each striving to be foremost, without regard to plunder. Thus did accidental success justify the rashness of Marius, while his imprudence contributed to heighten his glory."

Cornelius Nepos (74–24 B.C.), though inferior to the writers just treated, deserves mention for his "Lives of Eminent Commanders," his only extant work. These sketches, especially the biography of Pomponius Atticus, are clearly written and furnish valuable information respecting the times to which they relate; but Nepos was not an accurate compiler, and dependence cannot always be placed on his statements. As a specimen of his style, we quote from his "Lives"

THE CHARACTER OF ALCIBIADES.

"Nature seems to have tried in him what she could do. For it is agreed upon among all who have written about him, that nobody was more extraordinary than he, either in vices or in virtues; being born in a very great city, of a great family, much the handsomest man of his time, fit for all things, and abounding in judgment for the management of affairs. For he was a very great commander, both by sea and land; so eloquent that he mightily prevailed in speaking; and such was the plausibility of his elocution and language that in haranguing nobody was able to stand before him.

The same man, when occasion required, was laborious, hardy, generous, splendid no less in his equipage than his diet, affable, fawning, very cunningly serving the times. The same, when he had unbent himself, and there was no reason why he should take upon him any labor of thought, was found to be luxurious, dissolute, and intemperate, in so much that all wondered that in the same man there should be so much unlikeness to himself, and natures so different." —JOHN CLARKE.

POETS OF THE CICERONIAN PERIOD.

Lucretius (95–55 B.C.).—Meanwhile Italy produced two poets of high rank, Lucretius and Catullus. Of Lucretius we have little trustworthy information. A native of Italy, he appears, in accordance with the common practice, to have studied philosophy at Athens, where he became the classmate of Memmius. From his poetry, we may infer his indifference to all things transient, alike to social pleasures and the stormy sea of politics that surged around him; his life was probably one of deep thought, tinged with sadness. In dignity he was a true Roman; in sympathy for his kind, a true man. With nature he must have held frequent converse, for Homer alone of ancient writers excels him in description. His life ended with suicide.

The only work of Lucretius was what Macaulay styles "the finest didactic poem in any language," "On the Nature of Things." It was dedicated to his school-friend Memmius, at whose suggestion it is said to have been written. The old story that, having been crazed by a love-philter administered through the jealousy of his wife, the poet composed this work during the temporary returns of reason, is now discredited as a fabrication of later times.

The poem is divided into six books, and embodies the dogmas of Epicurus, which Lucretius vivified with the spirit of poetry and beautified with its most attractive drapery. Pleasure, the chief end of existence, is to be sought by banishing care and distressing thoughts. God created not; but eternal atoms, variously and ceaselessly active, constitute all existing things. The soul is material, and dies with the body; it behooves us, therefore, to make the most of the little time allotted us out of eternity, by dividing it between moderate enjoyment and philosophical contemplation.

Lucretius also accounted for the origin of the universe, whose government by a Divine Being he scouted; for that of plants, men, and animals, teaching the survival of the fittest; for that of language and the arts. To elevate his readers above degrading superstitions and the cowardly fear of death is his primary aim; and "the constant presence of this practical purpose imparts to his words that peculiar tone of impassioned earnestness to which there is no parallel in ancient literature." In one of many passages on the subject, he thus speaks of

THE DREAD OF DEATH.

"Were then the Nature of Created Things
To rise abrupt, and thus repining man
Address:—'O mortal! whence these useless fears?
This weak, superfluous sorrow? why the approach

Dread'st thou of death? For if the time elapsed
Have smiled propitious, and not all its gifts,
As if adventured in a leaky vase,
Been idly wasted, profitless, and vain—
Why quitt'st thou not, thou fool! the feast of life
Filled, and with mind all panting for repose?
But if thyself have squandered every boon,
And of the past grown weary—why demand
More days to kill, more blessings to pervert,
Nor rather headlong hasten to thine end?'
Were Nature thus to address us, could we fail
To feel the justice of her keen rebuke?
So true the picture, the advice so sage!
But to the wretch who moans the approach of death
With grief unmeasured, louder might she raise
Her voice severe:—'Vile coward! dry thine eyes—
Hence with thy snivelling sorrows, and depart!'
Should he, moreo'er, have passed man's mid-day hour—
'What! thou lament, already who hast reaped
An ample harvest? By desiring thus
The past once more, the present thou abhorr'st,
And life flies on imperfect, unenjoyed,
And death untimely meets thee, ere thy soul,
Cloyed with the banquet, is prepared to rise.
Leave, then, to others bliss thy years should shun;
Come, cheerful leave it, since still leave thou must.'
Justly, I deem, might Nature thus reprove:
For, through creation, old to young resigns,
And this from that matures; nor aught descends
To the dread gulfs, the fancied shades of hell.
The mass material must survive entire
To feed succeeding ages, which, in turn,
Like thee shall flourish, and like thee shall die;
Nor more the present ruins than the past.
Thus things from things ascend; and life exists
To none a freehold, but a use to all.
Reflect, moreo'er, how less than naught to us
Weighs the long portion of eternal time
Fled ere our birth: so, too, the future weighs
When death dissolves us. What of horror, then,
Dwells there in death? what gloomy, what austere?
Can there be elsewhere slumber half so sound?"

JOHN MASON GOOD.

Lucretius reasons plausibly, but on some points, it is too evident, unsatisfactorily even to himself. His work contains much that is worthy of praise, but this only makes its atheistical tendencies more dangerous. It was left unfinished at the poet's death, to be revised and edited by other hands.

The style of Lucretius is not uniformly harmonious; some of his verses lack polish, and he inclines to antique forms. Yet it is dignified, luminous, and animated; glows with all the poet's enthusiasm, and is marked by tenderness and pathos. The pictures drawn are so real as to awaken the emotions that would be experienced on beholding the originals. Schlegel gives Lucretius high praise: "As a painter and worshipper of nature, he is the first of all the poets of antiquity."

In the extract given below, the touching description of the cow searching for her calf that has been offered in sacrifice, will show how he dignifies commonplace subjects:—

VARIETY IN NATURE.

"Thus Nature varies; man, and brutal beast,
And herbage gay, and silver fishes mute,
And all the tribes of heaven, o'er many a sea,
Through many a grove that wing, or urge their song
Near many a bank of fountain, lake, or rill,
Search where thou wilt, each differs in his kind,
In form, in figure differs. Hence alone
Knows the fond mother her appropriate young,
The appropriate young their mother, 'mid the brutes,
As clear discerned as man's sublimer race.
Thus oft before the sacred shrine, perfumed
With breathing frankincense, the affrighted calf
Pours o'er the altar, from his breast profound,
The purple flood of life. But wandering wild
O'er the green sward, the dam, bereft of hope,
Beats with her cloven hoof the indented dale,
Each spot exploring, if, perchance, she still
May trace her idol; through the umbrageous grove,
With well-known voice, she moans; and oft reseeks,
Urged by a mother's love, the accustomed stall.
Nor shade for her, nor dew-distended glebe,
Nor stream soft gliding down its banks abrupt,
Yields aught of solace; nor the carking care
Averts, that preys within; nor the gay young
Of others soothe her o'er the joyous green:
So deep she longs, so lingers for her own.
Thus equal known, thus longed for, seek, in turn,

The tender heifer, tremulous of voice,
And the gay bleating lamb, their horned dams,
Lured by the milky fount that nurtures life."

Catullus (87–54 B.C.).—Verona in Cisalpine Gaul gave birth to Catullus, the first great Roman lyrist. It was no doubt to avail himself of the superior advantages Rome offered, that while still in the greenness of his youth he exchanged his provincial quarters for the capital. Here we catch occasional glimpses of him—moving among the *élite* as the equal of men like Nepos, Hortensius, and Cicero; or as the reckless sensualist throwing himself at the feet of some dissolute siren.

Upon the notorious "Lesbia," who stole, our poet sung,

"The charms most rare of every fair
To frame a perfect whole,"

Catullus wasted alike his love and the finest lyrics of which the Latin boasts. The coquettish beauty at first gloried in her conquest of Rome's most popular poet, and appears for a time to have been true. Then she grew cold, and cast him off for new admirers. But Catullus, though outraged by her fickleness, could not overcome his unworthy passion:—

"I curse her every hour sincerely,
Yet hang me—but I love her dearly."

At last, however, he renounced his faithless mistress, bidding her adieu in an ode which closes with one of his most beautiful similes:—

"Nor give that love a thought which I
So nursed for thee in days gone by,
Now by thy guile slain in an hour,
E'en as some little wilding flower,
That on the meadow's border blushed,
Is by the passing ploughshare crushed."

Catullus spent his hours of relaxation at his villa in the suburbs of the Latian town of Ti'bur, or at his favorite Sirmio on a lovely lake in northern Italy, the subject of one of his most graceful odes. Toward the close of his life, in the hope of refilling a purse which his extravagance had depleted, he went to Bithynia in Asia Minor as a staff-officer of the prætor Memmius, to whom Lucretius inscribed his poem. But in consequence of the selfishness of his superior, Catullus came back with wallet still lighter. Of two friends who went to Spain on a similar errand, he archly inquired:—

> "And have you netted—worse than worst—
> A good deal less than you disbursed;
> Like me, who following about
> My prætor, was—in fact—cleaned out?"

The death of a brother to whom he was devotedly attached plunged Catullus in grief; and now with nothing to live for, sated with worldly pleasure, in which he found the vanity of vanities, he longed for the fate that soon overtook him.

THE STYLE OF CATULLUS, called by the ancients "the Accomplished," is lively, graceful, and vigorous; he writes in the language of nature, and excels in suiting his words to the sentiments expressed. The musical measures of the Greeks, adapted by him to his native tongue, lent intensity to his words, and there were "lutes in his very lines." From the Greek writers, particularly Sappho and Callimachus of Alexandria, he borrowed largely. One of his odes to Lesbia is evidently an imitation of Sappho's celebrated love-song quoted on p. 169:—

TO LESBIA.

> "The equal of a God he seems to me,
> Surpassing wealth doth his blessed lot appear,
> Who, sitting often opposite to thee,
> May gaze and hear.
>
> The radiance of thy smile from me hath reft,
> From miserable me, all sense away,
> For when I look on Lesbia naught is left
> That Love can say.
>
> My tongue is dumb, while through each trembling limb
> The thin flame mounts, till self-wrought murmurs rise
> To fill mine ears, and night grown doubly dim
> Veils o'er mine eyes."—C. N. GREGORY.

His book of poems, 116 in number, was dedicated to Cornelius Nepos. Their subjects are as various as the metres in which they are written, for they reflect the passing emotions of the poet, now lighted with gayety, now clouded with sorrow, anon ablaze with love.

Among the other pieces of Catullus must be mentioned his cutting satires, in which even Cæsar was not spared; his exquisite *epithalamia*, or marriage-hymns; and the "Atys," a weird poem remarkable for its metrical effects. Our poet's lyric powers may be further judged of by the following

ELEGY ON LESBIA'S SPARROW.

"Loves and Graces, mourn with me,
Mourn, fair youths, where'er ye be!
Dead my Lesbia's sparrow is,
Sparrow, that was all her bliss,
Than her very eyes more dear;
For he made her dainty cheer,
Knew her well, as any maid
Knows her mother, never strayed
From her lap, but still would go
Hopping round her to and fro,
And to her, and her alone,
Chirrup'd with such pretty tone.
Now he treads that gloomy track,
Whence none ever may come back.
Out upon you, and your power,
Which all fairest things devour,
Orcus' gloomy shades, that e'er
Ye should take my bird so fair!
Oh! poor bird! Oh! dismal shades!
Yours the blame is, that my maid's
Eyes, dear eyes! are swoll'n and red,
Weeping for her darling dead."

THEODORE MARTIN.

POETRY OF THE AUGUSTAN AGE.

As prose reached its highest development in the last years of the Republic, so many causes contributed to perfect Latin verse in the reign of the first Roman emperor, Augustus. Secured upon the throne by his triumph at Actium (31 B.C.),

Augustus pursued a conciliatory course, with a view to winning the love of his subjects, and he was eminently successful. All classes, tired of civil war and its attendant proscriptions and massacres, hailed with delight the return of peace; and under the patronage of the emperor, seconded by his minister Mæcenas, poetry revived.

Augustus was as fortunate in finding at Rome a number of youthful poets, many of them in humble circumstances and of provincial origin, as in the possession of a minister who could appreciate and foster their talents. Mæcenas knew the value of genius too well to let it die of neglect; and his name, as the patron of art and letters, has passed into a proverb. His luxurious gardens were the haunt of poets and savants, and round his sumptuous table sat an inspired circle who poured their grateful tributes into the ears of their master and his.

Thus the munificence of Augustus and Mæcenas, themselves both critics and writers, combined with the political quiet that gave leisure for literary pursuits, to make their period the golden age of poetry. Prose, on the other hand, declined. Political eloquence was powerless in the face of despotism; while the veracious historian must needs tread a dangerous path, or seal his lips.

The poets of the Augustan era were deficient, as a rule, in that creative genius which characterized the age of Pericles in Greece, their works being rather the fruits of art and industry. A long and careful training, in which Greek studies played a prominent part, prepared them for their high profession; Horace tells us that at the age of twenty-three he was still "seeking the truth among the groves of Academus." Works on various subjects could now be consulted in the public libraries of Rome; and Alexandrian models helped to mould the literary taste of the day.

The Augustan poets will now be considered in turn.

Virgil.—In the little village of Andes near Mantua, on the

P 2

ROMANS OF THE AUGUSTAN AGE.

15th of October, B.C. 70, Rome's greatest poet, Virgil (Publius Virgilius Maro), first saw the light. His boyhood was spent on the banks of the winding Mincio in a quiet round of rural pursuits; his father, as owner of a small farm, being among those whom the poet subsequently pictured as the happiest of men.

Alive to the importance of education, Virgil's parents set aside a portion of their slender means to provide for his instruction; and when he reached the age of twelve, his father entered him in a school at Cremona. In his seventeenth year he went to Rome, and there prosecuted the higher studies, familiarizing himself with the Greek poets, and spending his leisure in the composition of lyric pieces. Having completed his education, Virgil returned to his native place, where, amid the natural attractions that surrounded him, he conceived the idea of rivalling Theocritus in bucolic poetry, and in 42 B.C. began his Eclogues.

After the victory of the Triumvirs in the civil war, the lands about Cremona and Mantua were divided among the soldiers who had served against Brutus, and the estate of Virgil, neutral though he had been, was taken from him. On the poet's application to Octavius, however, it was restored, and in one of his Eclogues he gave utterance to his sincere gratitude. Shortly after, Virgil was ejected again, and this time narrowly escaped with his life by swimming the Mincio. Nor does he appear to have ever been reinstated. Octavius, however, loaded him with favors; and a house in Rome near the palace of his friend Mæcenas, with a lovely villa in the suburbs of Naples, where the climate agreed better with his delicate constitution than the damp air of the north, reconciled him to the loss of his boyhood's home.

The Eclogues, published about 37 B.C., established Virgil's reputation as a pastoral poet, and gained him no mean place among the literary and political celebrities that crowded the house of Mæcenas. It was by the advice of this statesman that the poet undertook the most finished and original of all his productions,—the Georgics,—a work which, though only about 2200 lines in length, occupied him for seven years.

Having declared in this poem that "he would wed Cæsar's glories to an epic strain," Virgil was held to his promise by the emperor, at whose solicitation he gave the rest of his life (eleven years) to the composition of the Æneid. In this great epic, like the Odyssey a sequel to the Iliad, the origin of Rome is traced back to ancient Troy, and the genealogy of Augustus to her greatest surviving hero, "the pious Æneas." Death stopped the poet's pen when three years' labor was yet necessary, in his estimation, to perfect his work.

It appears that in the year 19 B.C. Virgil undertook a tour through Greece and Asia Minor, to acquaint himself with the geography of the countries described in the Æneid; but meeting Augustus at Athens, he changed his plans and started with the emperor for Rome. On the way he was seized with a mortal illness, and only lived to reach the harbor of Brundisium in southern Italy. On his death-bed, Virgil besought his friends to bring him the manuscript of his epic, that he might consign it to the flames; but they wisely saved a masterpiece which the modesty of its author would have condemned to oblivion.

Virgil was interred at Naples. A simple vault, overgrown with ivy and wild myrtle, still marks his grave. On a marble slab set in the rock opposite is the inscription which Dryden has thus rendered:—

> "I sung flocks, tillage, heroes: Mantua gave
> Me life; Brundisium, death; Naples, a grave."

Virgil has been described as a tall, dark-complexioned man, careless of his dress, and with awkward country airs. His life was that of a student; and despite the fact that he was a martyr to dyspepsia and pulmonary disease, he did not allow his delicate health to interfere with his literary labors. Of gentle, unassuming manners, he would fly from the admiring crowds that followed him in the streets; and none would have inferred from his appearance or conversation that he was a great poet. He was more than a great poet—he was a pure, unselfish, honest man, uncontaminated by the prevailing vices. Not the least among his virtues was filial piety. His countrymen felt how great and noble he was, when they rose in the theatre and paid him equal honor with the emperor himself.

Had he lived, it was Virgil's purpose, after completing the Æneid, to study philosophy, the love of which he had imbibed in early life from the verses of Lucretius. The investigation of truth was his highest aim; and there are reasons for believing that he had in mind the preparation of a grand philosophical poem that might have cast into the shade the stately treatise "On the Nature of Things."

Such liberality had Virgil experienced from his friends that he left a fortune of $400,000, to be divided, as he never married, among his brother, Augustus, Mæcenas, and others of his associates.

THE ECLOGUES.—Virgil was the first Roman writer to cultivate pastoral poetry, and his Eclogues (*selections*), or more properly Bucolics (*shepherd poems*), are mostly dialogues, in imitation of the idyls of Theocritus. Various subjects are charmingly discussed by imaginary shepherds, in whom one sometimes recognizes the poet and his friends.

The least understood of Virgil's Eclogues is the one entitled "Pollio," from the name of the consul to whom it is addressed. It was written B.C. 40, and predicts the coming of a wondrous Child, whose birth would usher in a golden age of peace and happiness. Some have seen in this child an unconscious allusion to the Babe of Bethlehem, whose advent the Sibylline oracles are believed to have foretold. Perhaps Virgil had heard of the Hebrew prophecies indirectly through the Alexandrian Greeks, and recast them in Latin verse; perhaps it was but a Roman infant—Pollio's child—whose birth he sung in an exaggerated strain. However this may be, we may remember that the heathen as well as the Jewish world at this time expected a great reformer, who should restore the innocence and bliss of by-gone ages.

EXTRACT FROM THE POLLIO.

"Comes the Last Age, of which the Sibyl sung—
A new-born cycle of the rolling years;
Justice returns to earth, the rule returns
Of good King Saturn; lo! from the high heavens
Comes a new seed of men. Lucina chaste,
Speed the fair infant's birth, with whom shall end

Our age of iron, and the golden prime
Of earth return; thine own Apollo's reign
In him begins anew. This glorious age
Inaugurates, O Pollio, with thee;
Thy consulship shall date the happy months;
Under thine auspices the Child shall purge
Our guilt-stains out, and free the land from dread.
He with the gods and heroes like the gods
Shall hold familiar converse, and shall rule
With his great father's spirit the peaceful world.
For thee, O Child! the earth untilled shall pour
Her early gifts, the winding ivy's wreath,
Smiling acanthus, and all flowers that blow.
The ground beneath shall cradle thee in blooms,
The venomed snake shall die, the poisonous herb
Perish from out thy path.
So, when the years shall seal thy manhood's strength,
The busy merchant shall forsake the seas—
Barter there shall not need; the soil shall bear
For all men's use all products of all climes.
The glebe shall need no harrow, nor the vine
The searching knife, the oxen bear no yoke;
The wool no longer shall be schooled to lie,
Dyed in false hues; but, coloring as he feeds,
The ram himself in the rich pasture-lands
Shall wear a fleece now purple and now gold,
And the lambs grow in scarlet. So the Fates,
Who know not change, have bid their spindles run,
And weave for this blest age the web of doom."

W. L. COLLINS.

THE GEORGICS.—Having shown his powers in the Eclogues, Virgil was not unwilling to put them to a further proof, when Mæcenas suggested a work on husbandry, which should dignify that ancient art and revive a love for the simple pursuits of the fathers of the Republic.

Taking Hesiod's "Works and Days" as his model, he added the artistic Georgics (*agricultural poem*) to the works of Cato and Varro on rural life. No less elevated in tone than theirs, it possesses an additional attraction in its dress of verse, glows with the author's love of nature, and displays his ardent zeal to check the national decay. Virgil labored upon the Georgics for seven years, it being his habit to rise betimes and dictate in the early morning verses which he spent the rest of the day in polishing and condensing.

The Georgics is a didactic poem, and as such, with the work of Lucretius, represents the only department in which the Romans excelled both the Greeks and all modern nations. The first of its four books is devoted to tillage; it gives directions for ploughing (early and often, was Virgil's motto), sowing, and fertilizing, and explains the signs of the weather. We learn from it that the pests of the modern farmer were not unknown to the old Roman husbandman:—

"With ponderous roller smooth the level floor,
And bind with chalky cement o'er and o'er;
Lest springing weeds expose thy want of art,
And worn in many a chink the surface part:
There builds the field-mouse underneath the ground,
And loads her little barn with plunder crowned;
There works the mole along her dark abode,
There in its hollow lurks the lonely toad,
There wastes the weevil with insatiate rage,
There the wise ant that dreads the wants of age."

Arboriculture is treated minutely in the second book, the vine receiving the principal share of attention. Here we have the most beautiful of those digressions which lend an enchanting variety to the style of the Georgics — the poet's glowing eulogy of his native land.

PRAISES OF ITALY.

"Yet nor the Median groves, nor rivers, rolled,
Ganges, and Hermus, o'er their beds of gold,
Nor Ind, nor Bactra, nor the blissful land
Where incense spreads o'er rich Panchaia's sand,
Nor all that fancy paints in fabled lays,
O native Italy! transcend thy praise.
Though here no bulls beneath the enchanted yoke
With fiery nostril o'er the furrow smoke,
No hydra teeth embattled harvest yield,
Spear and bright helmet bristling o'er the field;
Yet golden corn each laughing valley fills,
The vintage reddens on a thousand hills,

Luxuriant olives spread from shore to shore,
And flocks unnumbered range the pastures o'er.
Hence the proud war-horse rushes on the foe,
Clitumnus! hence thy herds, more white than snow,
And stately bull, that, of gigantic size,
Supreme of victims, on the altar lies,
Bathed in thy sacred stream oft led the train
When Rome in pomp of triumph deck'd the fane.
Here Spring perpetual leads the laughing Hours,
And Winter wears a wreath of summer flowers:
The o'erloaded branch twice fills with fruits the year,
And twice the teeming flocks their offspring rear.
Yet here no lion breeds, no tiger strays,
No tempting aconite the touch betrays,
No monstrous snake the uncoiling volume trails,
Or gathers orb on orb his iron scales.
But many a peopled city towers around,
And many a rocky cliff with castle crowned,
And many an antique wall whose hoary brow
O'ershades the flood that guards its base below.
All hail, Saturnian earth! hail, loved of fame,
Land, rich in fruits and men of mighty name!
For thee I dare the sacred founts explore,
For thee, the rules of ancient art restore,
Themes once to glory raised again rehearse,
And pour through Roman towns the Ascræan verse."

SOTHEBY.

The raising of cattle and the management of bees form the subjects of the remaining books of the Georgics.

THE ÆNEID narrates in epic verse the adventures of Æneas, the legendary ancestor of the Romans. Virgil sums up his plot in the opening lines :—

"Arms and the man I sing, who first,
By Fate of Ilian realm amerced,
To fair Italia onward bore,
And landed on Lavinium's shore:—
Long tossing earth and ocean o'er,
By violence of heaven, to sate
Fell Juno's unforgetting hate:
Much labored too in battle-field,
Striving his city's walls to build,
And give his Gods a home.
Thence come the hardy Latin brood,
The ancient sires of Alba's blood,
And lofty-rampired Rome."

Æneas, the son of Venus by the Trojan shepherd Anchi'-ses, escaped from burning Troy with his aged father, little son, and household gods. He lay concealed for a time in the mountains; and, when the victorious Greeks had all withdrawn, took ship with the remnant of his people to found a new Troy in the west. After seven years of hardships and mistakes, the Trojans embark from Sicily for "the Hesperian shore."

Here the Æneid takes up the story. In the first book we see the Trojan fleet driven by a tempest, sent at Juno's solicitation, on the opposite coast of Africa, near the rising walls of Carthage. Dido, its queen, whom the murder of her husband Sichæus by her unnatural brother had driven from Tyre, receives the strangers hospitably, and by the strategy of Venus conceives a passionate love for Æneas. At her request the Trojan prince tells the pathetic story—the fall of his native city through the wiles of the Greeks, and his subsequent trials.

Æneas returns Dido's love, but only at last to betray his confiding hostess, and fly with his vessels under cover of the night, in obedience to a warning from Mercury, the messenger of Jove. Too "pious" to disregard the heavenly command, he left Dido to end her sorrow on the funeral pyre.

After a temporary sojourn in Sicily, where he celebrates funeral games to his father's memory, Æneas at length reaches Cumæ in Italy, and at once seeks the Sibyl. She informs him that his trials are not over, and takes him to the lower world that he may hold an interview with his father Anchises. There he descries among other shades the injured Dido, to whom he endeavors to excuse his conduct.

"'Mid these among the branching treen
Sad Dido moved, the Tyrian queen,
Her death-wound ghastly yet and green.
Soon as Æneas caught the view
And through the mist her semblance knew,

Like one who spies, or thinks he spies,
Through flickering clouds the new moon rise,
The tear-drop from his eyelids broke,
And thus in tenderest tones he spoke.
'Ah Dido! rightly then I read
The news that told me you were dead,
Slain by your own rash hand!
Myself the cause of your despair!
Now by the blessed stars I swear,
By heaven, by all that dead men keep
In reverence here 'mid darkness deep,
Against my will, ill-fated fair,
I parted from your land.'"
CONINGTON.

But Dido averts her eyes "that neither smiled nor wept," and moves away in silence to join Sichæus, who "gives her love for love."

Æneas learns from the lips of Anchises the future of his race, and beholds the shadowy forms of kings, generals, and statesmen that are to shed glory on the Roman name. "Augustus Cæsar, god by birth," figures, as we should expect, the proudest of the throng. At last he espies the great Marcellus, "the Sword of Rome," glittering in the spoils of the Punic War; and by his side

"A youth full-armed, by none excelled
In beauty's manly grace."

In answer to the inquiry of Æneas, Anchises tells his son that this youth is "our own Marcellus," and eulogizes his virtues. Thus Virgil immortalized the name of a Roman prince of great promise, son of Octavia, the emperor's sister, whose premature death had filled the Roman world with sorrow. When, at the request of Augustus, the poet read this portion of his epic before the royal family, all were moved to tears, and the bereaved mother fainted. She afterward showed her appreciation of Virgil's genius by presenting him about $400 for each of the twenty-seven lines. The passage is well worth repeating here:—

VIRGIL'S TRIBUTE TO MARCELLUS.

"Seek not to know (the ghost replied with tears)
The sorrows of thy sons in future years.
This youth (the blissful vision of a day)
Shall just be shown on earth, then snatched away.
The gods too high had raised the Roman state,
Were but their gifts as permanent as great.
What groans of men shall fill the Martian field!
How fierce a blaze his flaming pile shall yield!
What funeral pomp shall floating Tiber see,
When rising from his bed, he views the sad solemnity!
No youth shall equal hopes of glory give,
No youth afford so great a cause to grieve.
The Trojan honor, and the Roman boast,
Admired when living, and adored when lost!
Mirror of ancient faith in early youth!
Undaunted worth, inviolable truth!
No foe, unpunished, in the fighting field
Shall dare thee, foot to foot, with sword and shield!
Much less in arms oppose thy matchless force,
When thy sharp spurs shall urge thy foaming horse.
Ah! couldst thou break through Fate's severe decree,
A new Marcellus shall arise in thee!
Full canisters of fragrant lilies bring,
Mixed with the purple roses of the spring:
Let me with funeral flowers his body strow;
This gift which parents to their children owe,
This unavailing gift, at least I may bestow!"—DRYDEN.

From Cumæ the Trojan chief sails to Latium, the land of his destiny, and there he receives from King Lati'nus the promise of his daughter Lavinia's hand. But this provokes a war with Turnus, a neighboring prince, to whom Lavinia had been secretly plighted by the queen-mother. Not until he had subdued Turnus and his Latin allies did Æneas make Lavinia his own and rule as king of Latium. The poem ends with the fall of Turnus in a duel between the rival chiefs. To finish the story, Alba Longa was built by Æneas' son Iulus, from whose royal line in later ages sprung Romulus, founder of Rome, the *Julian* family, and their great hero *Julius* Cæsar.

The passion of Dido, as portrayed in the fourth book of the

Æneid, is the most masterly piece of Virgil's handiwork. We present below the closing scenes that sealed her sad fate.

THE DEATH OF DIDO.

"Now, rising from Tithonus' bed,
The Dawn on earth her freshness shed:
The queen from off her turret height
Perceives the first dim streak of light,
The fleet careering on its way,
And void and sailless shore and bay;
She smites her breast, all snowy fair,
And rends her golden length of hair:
'Great Jove! and shall he go?' she cries,
'And leave our realm a wanderer's mock?
Quick, snatch your arms and chase the prize,
And drag the vessels from the dock!
Fetch flames, bring darts, ply oars!—yet why?
What words are these, or where am I?
Why rave I thus? Those impious deeds—
Poor Dido! how your torn heart bleeds.
Too late! it should have bled that day
When at his feet your sceptre lay.
Lo here, the chief of stainless word,
Who takes his household gods on board,
Whose shoulders safe from sword and fire
Conveyed his venerable sire!
Oh! had I rent him limb from limb
And cast him o'er the waves to swim,
His friends, his own Ascanius killed,
And with the child the father filled!
Yet danger in the strife had been:—
Who prates of danger here?
A death-devoted, desperate queen,
What foe had I to fear?
No, I had sown the flame broadcast,
Had fired the fleet from keel to mast,
Slain son and sire, stamped out the race,
And thrown at length with steadfast face
Myself upon the bier.

If needs must be that wretch abhorred
Attain the port and float to land;
If such the fate of heaven's high lord,
And so the moveless pillars stand;
Scourged by a savage enemy,
An exile from his son's embrace,

So let him sue for aid, and see
   His people slain before his face;
Nor when to humbling peace at length
   He stoops, be his or life or land,
But let him fall in manhood's strength
   And welter tombless on the sand.
Such malison to heaven I pour,
A last libation with my gore.
And, Tyrians, you through time to come
   His seed with deathless hatred chase:
Be that your gift to Dido's tomb:
   No love, no league 'twixt race and race.
Rise from my ashes, scourge of crime,
   Born to pursue the Dardan horde
To-day, to-morrow, through all time,
   Oft as our hands can wield the sword:
Fight shore with shore, fight sea with sea,
Fight all that are or e'er shall be!'

   She ceased, and with her heart debates
How best to leave the life she hates.
Then to Sichæus' nurse she cried
(For hers erewhile at Tyre had died):—
'Good nurse, my sister Anna bring:
O'er face and body bid her fling
   Pure drops from lustral bough:
So sprinkled come, and at her side
The victims lead: you too provide
   A fillet for your brow.
A sacrifice to Stygian Jove
I here perform, to ease my love,
And give to flame the fatal bed
Which pillowed once the Trojan's head.'
Thus she: the aged dame gives heed,
And, feebly hurrying, mends her speed.

Then, maddening over crime, the queen,
   With bloodshot eyes, and sanguine streaks
   Fresh painted on her quivering cheeks,
And wanning o'er with death foreseen,
Through inner portals wildly fares,
   Scales the high pile with swift ascent,
Takes up the Dardan sword and bares,
   Sad gift, for different uses meant.
She eyed the robes with wistful look,
   And, pausing, thought awhile and wept:
Then pressed her to the couch, and spoke
   Her last good-night or ere she slept.

'Sweet relics of a time of love,
  When fate and heaven were kind,
Receive my life-blood and remove
  These torments of the mind.
My life is lived, and I have played
  The part that Fortune gave,
And now I pass, a queenly shade,
  Majestic to the grave.
A glorious city I have built,
  Have seen my walls ascend,
Chastised for blood of husband spilt
  A brother, yet no friend.
Blest lot! yet lacked one blessing more,
That Troy had never touched my shore.'
Then as she kissed the darling bed,
'To die! and unrevenged!' she said,
'Yet let me die: thus, thus I go
Exulting to the shades below.
Let the false Dardan feel the blaze
That burns me pouring on his gaze,
And bear along, to cheer his way,
The funeral presage of to-day.'

Thus as she speaks, the attendant train
Behold her writhing as in pain,
Her hands with slaughter sprinkled o'er,
And the fell weapon spouting gore.
Loud clamors thrill the lofty halls:
Fame shakes the town, confounds, appalls:
Each house resounds with women's cries,
And funeral wails assault the skies:
E'en as one day should war o'erthrow
  Proud Carthage or her parent Tyre,
And fire-flood stream with furious glow
  O'er roof, and battlement, and spire."

CONINGTON.

Virgil's epic was the pride of his countrymen, who, with a pardonable national vanity, pronounced it superior to Homer's. Tenderness, grace, elegance, rhythmical perfection, brilliance of description, it certainly possesses; yet, with all its beauties, it is not faultless. We miss the wonderful imagination that plays through every page of the Iliad; indeed, Homer furnished the originals of many of its most striking figures. Nor did Virgil disdain levying on Latin authors also.

Whatever recommended itself to him in the poetry of others, he borrowed for his own. And yet he must not be regarded as a plagiarist; doubtless it was his intention to enshrine in a national epic literary monuments of all the great minds of his country.

Æneas, his hero, too often appears as the boaster or the heartless hypocrite, rather than as the ideal of greatness and piety it was designed to draw. The author himself seems to have felt the inferiority of his epic to the Iliad, and hence his wish to destroy it. We are told that it was first written in prose; and then the artist, having a clear conception of the whole, threw different portions into verse as the spirit moved him.

Horace (65–8 B.C.).—The great lyric poet of Rome was Horace (Quintus Horatius Flaccus), a freedman's son, of Venusia on the roaring Au'fidus. That he might enjoy the best educational advantages, his father took him to Rome at the early age of twelve. Here he was placed in charge of a famous schoolmaster, called by his pupils "the Flogger;" under whose rod the country lad made the acquaintance of Ennius and Homer. To the watchful care and liberality of his parent, who remained to guard him from the temptations of the metropolis, he gratefully acknowledged that he owed everything.

Horace was at Athens, finishing his course, when Cæsar fell beneath the daggers of the conspirators. With a number of hot-headed fellow-students he promptly espoused the cause of Brutus the Liberator, and served in the civil war as military tribune. But Horace's courage could not stand the touch of cold steel; he ignominiously fled from the field of Philippi, and his estate was confiscated as a reward for his patriotism. Poverty now compelled him to take a clerkship at Rome; and to add to his slender income he began writing verses. This brought him into notice, and in 38 B.C. he had the honor of an introduction to the social circle that gathered round Mæcenas. His little farm, fifteen miles from Tibur, the ruins of which are still pointed out to tourists, was the gift of his munificent patron.

This "Sabine farm" was at once Horace's joy and pride. Between Rome and Tibur, therefore, he made frequent journeys, and the simple country-folk, won by his affability, hailed with delight the occasions when, tired of city excitements, he sought relaxation among them. Beset by the throng of gossips and favor-seekers who haunted his footsteps as the friend of Mæcenas, Horace in his Sixth Satire breaks out into enthusiastic praises of his rural home, with its simple fare and freedom from annoyances:—

"This fortune's favorite son ('tis cried)
Is ever by Mæcenas' side,
Companion wheresoe'er he goes,
In rural sports or festal shows.
Should any rumor, without head
Or tail, about the streets be spread,
Whoever meets me gravely nods,
And says, 'As you approach the gods,
It is no mystery to you;
What do the Dacians mean to do?'
'Indeed I know not.'—'How you joke,
And love to sneer at simple folk.'
'Then, pr'ythee, where are Cæsar's bands
Allotted their long-promised lands?'
Although I swear I know no more
Of that than what was asked before,
They stand amazed, and think me then
The most reserved of mortal men.
Bewildered thus amidst a maze,
I lose the sunshine of my days,
And often wish: Oh! when again
Shall I behold the rural plain?
And when with books of sages deep
Sequestered ease and gentle sleep,
In sweet oblivion, blissful balm!
The busy cares of life becalm.
Oh! when shall Pythagoric beans
With wholesome juice enrich my veins?

And bacon, ham, and savory pottage,
Be served within my simple cottage?
O nights that furnish such a feast
As even gods themselves might taste!"
FRANCIS.

The loss of his friend Virgil cast a shadow over Horace's latter years. His own death was sudden. A short month before, Mæcenas had breathed his last; and thus the promise of the poet not to survive his patron was almost literally fulfilled. In an ode to Mæcenas, Horace had sung,

"Should you, alas! be snatched away,
Wherefore, ah! wherefore should I stay,
My value lost, no longer whole,
And but possessing half my soul?
One day (believe the sacred oath)
Shall lead the funeral pomp of both;
With thee to Pluto's dark abode,
With thee I'll tread the dreary road."

The remains of the poet were laid by the side of his friend; and thus, devoted to each other in life, they slept together in the grave.

Horace, in his youth, was a free liver, a voluptuary; such, indeed, were the men of his day, Virgil alone excepted. Time, however, corrected his tastes, and at the close of his life we find him playing the part of the moralist. If there is much to condemn in his character, there is also much to admire,—his even temper, contented disposition, and independent spirit. Quick to resent an affront, he was as ready to forgive an injury. His friends found him ever a genial, frank, warm-hearted companion.

As to his personal appearance, we may judge from his own accounts that he was gray in advance of his years, short, corpulent, and withal blear-eyed. This last defect furnished Augustus with a ready joke, when he had Horace on one side and the asthmatic Virgil on the other: "I sit between sighs and tears," he used to say.

WORKS OF HORACE.—The earliest poetical efforts of Horace were Satires, which, though written in hexameter verse, he called *prose-poems.* Holding up to contempt the follies of fashionable society, fortune-hunting, extravagance, avarice, etc., they pleased the Romans and rapidly grew in popularity. But Horace merely derides, he does not chastise, the vices of his day, evidently deeming ridicule a more effective weapon than denunciation.

In his Epodes, Horace aimed his blows at individuals with something like the force of Archilochus. But personal satire was not the author's forte, and his Epodes are hardly equal to his other productions.

It is to his Odes, in the lyric metres of Alcæus and Sappho, whose poetry he not only loved, but recast after his own ideas in his native tongue, that Horace owes his renown. Always brief and to the point, clear and elegant in their condensation, graceful, spicy, true to nature, these poems have been read with pleasure for nineteen centuries. They deal with a great variety of subjects—the grand as well as the commonplace; and, whatever the theme, their author is equally admirable. He paints pictures of moral beauty and sublimity with singular impressiveness. Nowhere in the classics is a nobler character sketched than that drawn by Horace of a man firm in the cause of justice (Book III., 3). Byron presents it in an English dress:—

"The man of firm and noble soul
No factious clamors can control;
No threat'ning tyrant's darkling brow
Can swerve him from his just intent:
Gales the warring waves which plough
By Auster on the billows spent,
To curb the Adriatic main,
Would awe his fixed, determined mind in vain.

Ay, and the red right arm of Jove,
Hurtling his lightnings from above,

With all his terrors then unfurled,
He would unmoved, unawed behold:
The flames of an expiring world
Again in crashing chaos rolled,
In vast promiscuous ruin hurled,
Might light his glorious funeral pile:
Still dauntless, 'mid the wreck of earth he'd smile."

Horace began writing his odes at the age of thirty-five, and was seven years in completing the first three books; they were issued 23 B.C. That he designed them to include all his lyric productions is evident from the following ode, with which the third book closes :—

"And now 'tis done: more durable than brass
My monument shall be, and raise its head
O'er royal pyramids: it shall not dread
Corroding rain or angry Boreas,
Nor the long lapse of immemorial time.
I shall not wholly die: large residue
Shall 'scape the queen of funerals. Ever new
My after-fame shall grow, while pontiffs climb
With silent maids the Capitolian height.
'Born,' men will say, 'where Aufidus is loud,
Where Daunus, scant of streams, beneath him bowed
The rustic tribes, from dimness he waxed bright,
First of his race to wed the Æolian lay
To notes of Italy.' Put glory on,
My own Melpomene, by genius won,
And crown me of thy grace with Delphic bay."
CONINGTON.

The odes of the fourth book were written at the request of Augustus, who commissioned the favorite poet to celebrate the victories of his step-sons over a German tribe. After publishing the original three books, Horace wrote his Epistles, the most finished of all his works. They bear the ripe fruits of his experience, and are full of wise reflections which do credit to his knowledge of men and manners. Sprightliness and wit constitute their charm. Their subjects are various, several of them being literary criticisms; the longest, called "the Art of Poetry," possesses the greatest value.

The works of Horace have maintained their popularity in all ages; his sententious sayings have become aphorisms; and to-day he is a greater favorite with scholars than ever. Few classical poets have been so fortunate in their translators.

ODE TO MÆCENAS.

"Strong doors, wakeful watch-dogs, securely had barred
Danaë in her tower of brass,
If Venus and Jove had not laughed at such guard
And the shower of gold caused to pass.

Through an army of guards will bright gold make its way;
It will pierce through the thickest of walls;
More power it has and may strike more dismay
Than the lightning from heaven that falls.

Through lucre the house of the Argive seer* fell:
Philip forced cities' gates with his gold;
The power of rivals with bribes he could quell:
We know, too, how fleets have been sold.

The increase of wealth ever brings with it care
And hungry ambition for more;
Thus, Mæcenas, O knight with whom none can compare!
Great fortune I ever forswore.

The more that a man to himself shall deny,
The more he shall have from the gods;
Poor, I seek for the home of contentment, and fly
With joy from the wealthy abodes.

With my stream of pure water, few acres of wood,
And secure that my harvest will pay,
A pleasure I have more substantial than could
Be to him that o'er Afric holds sway.

Though for me never works the Calabrian bee,
Though for me is no Formian wine,
Though no sheep in the pastures of Gaul feed for me,
Yet poverty never is mine.

* Amphiara'us, whose wife betrayed him for a pearl necklace, and was afterward murdered by her son.

Much must that man want ever who much shall demand;
What he gains whets the covetous vice;
Happy he to whom God with a niggardly hand
Has granted what yet will suffice."—YARDLEY.

TO PYRRHA.

"What scented stripling, Pyrrha, wooes thee now
In pleasant cavern, all with roses fair?
For whom those yellow tresses bindest thou
With simple care?

Full oft shall he thine altered faith bewail,
His altered gods; and his unwonted gaze
Shall watch the waters darken to the gale
In wild amaze,

Who now believing gloats on golden charms;
Who hopes thee ever kind and ever void;
Nor, hapless! knows the changeful wind's alarms,
Nor thee, untried.

For me, let Neptune's temple wall declare
How, safe escaped, in votive offering
My dripping garments own, suspended there,
Him Ocean-king."
GLADSTONE.

Varius (74–14 B.C.).—Older than Horace or Virgil in the Augustan galaxy was Varius, the friend who introduced them both to Mæcenas. An epic on the death of Cæsar, highly esteemed by his countrymen,—and a tragedy entitled "Thyestes," classed with the finest Greek dramas,—have won for Varius an enviable fame.

Both are lost; but we still have the benefit of the poet's labors as the editor of Virgil's Æneid.

Albius Tibullus (59–19 B.C.), another poet of the Augustan age, perfected the erotic elegy which Catullus had introduced from Greece. The meagre accounts that remain of his life inform us that he was a knight, and lost his estates near Rome for political reasons, after the overthrow of Pompey. These he partially recovered, it is supposed through the influence of

Messa'la, a noble of the old school, whose praises he never tired of sounding. As aide-de-camp, he accompanied Messala in his expedition against the rebellious Aquitanians, and doubtless figured in the triumph decreed his victorious friend by the emperor.

A peaceful life, however, was more in accordance with his tastes. The hills and dales, the corn-fields, vineyards, and meadows, possessed greater charms for him than the favor of Augustus, who vainly sought to attract Tibullus to his court. Hence we find the poet generally living at his country-seat, amid rural enjoyments.

The elegies of Tibullus preserve the names of two Roman beauties—"Delia," the early mistress of his heart, and "Nem'-esis," her successor. Delia, "with her queenly charms and golden locks," first brought him to her feet, and he wooed her in his most finished strains. But, like Catullus, he soon found occasion to lament his fair one's inconstancy. Delia jilted him for a richer lover, and Tibullus transferred his affections to the imperious Nemesis.

The style of Tibullus is sweet and polished. A pensive, almost melancholy tone pervades his verses. In the following plaintive elegy, the injured but forgiving poet recalls to his false one how tenderly he nursed her through a critical sickness, picturing his dream of happiness with her installed as the mistress of his rural home, and his rude awakening:—

ELEGY TO DELIA.

"Oh! I was harsh to say that I could part
From thee; but, Delia, I am bold no more!
Driven like a top, which boys with ready art
Keep spinning round upon a level floor.

Burn, lash me, love, if ever after this
By me one cruel, blustering word is said;
Yet spare, I pray thee by our stolen bliss,
By mighty Venus and thy comely head.

When thou didst lie, by fell disease o'erpowered,
  I rescued thee, by prayers, from death's domain;
Pure sulphur's cleansing fumes I round thee showered,
  While an enchantress sung a magic strain.

Yes—and another now enjoys the prize,
  And reaps the fruit of all my vows for thee:
Foolish, I dreamed of life 'neath golden skies,
  Wert thou but saved—not such great heaven's decree.

I said—I'll till my fields, she'll guard my store
  When crops are threshed in autumn's burning heat;
She'll keep my grapes in baskets brimming o'er,
  And my rich must expressed by nimble feet.

She'll count my flock; some home-born slave of mine
  Will prattle in my darling's lap and play:
To rural god ripe clusters for the vine,
  Sheaves for my crops, cates for my fold, she'll pay.

Slaves—all shall own her undisputed rule;
  Myself a cipher—how the thought would please!
Here will Messala come, for whom she'll pull
  The sweetest apples from the choicest trees;

And, honoring one so great, for him prepare
  And serve the banquet with her own white hands.
Fond dream! which now the east and south winds bear
  Away to far Armenia's spicy lands."

CRANSTOUN.

Propertius.—With the name of Tibullus is often linked that of Propertius, who was born about 50 B.C. at Assisium, among the Umbrian mountains. In this lovely spot he was prepared for the study of the law, which he afterward adopted as his profession at Rome. But Propertius found this calling distasteful; relinquishing it, accordingly, for the pursuits of literature, he aspired to be a Roman Callimachus, and grounded himself in the principles of Alexandrian verse. But too much study made him artificial, and his numerous mythological allusions and digressions encumber rather than embellish. He lacks the sweetness, simplicity, and tenderness, of Tibullus.

Catullus had his "Lesbia;" Tibullus, his "Delia;" and Propertius, profiting not by the example of his brother bards, lavished his affections on the accomplished but fickle "Cynthia," who played him false as soon as a rich prætor laid a fortune at her feet. Cynthia was the single theme of our poet's love-lays, all rapture or gentle reproach. In an elegy to Mæcenas, who had pressed him to attempt an epic, he sings:—

"You ask me why love-elegy so frequently I follow,
And why my little book of tender trifles only sings:
It is not from Calliope, nor is it from Apollo,
But from my own sweet lady-love my inspiration springs.

If in resplendent purple robe of Cos my darling dresses,
I'll fill a portly volume with the Coan garments' praise;
Or if her truant tresses wreathe her forehead with caresses,
The tresses of her queenly brow demand her poet's lays."

In another elegy he describes his Cynthia's charms:—

"'Twas not her face, though fair, so smote my eye
(Less fair the lily than my love: as snows
Of Scythia with Iberian vermeil vie;
As float in milk the petals of the rose);

Nor locks that down her neck of ivory stream,
Nor eyes—my stars—twin lamps with love aglow;
Nor, if in silk of Araby she gleam
(I prize not baubles), does she thrill me so,

As when she leaves the mantling cup to thread
The mazy dance, and moves before my view,
Graceful as blooming Ariadne led
The choral revels of the Bacchic crew."

The death of Propertius is supposed to have taken place about 15 B.C. Of his elegies, there is none better than

LOVE'S DREAM REALIZED.

"Not in his Dardan triumph so rejoiced the great Atrides,
When fell the mighty kingdom of Laomedon of yore;
Not so Ulysses, when he moored his wave-worn raft beside his
Beloved Dulichian island-home—his weary wanderings o'er;

As I, when last eve's rosy joys I ruminated over:
To me another eve like that were immortality!
Awhile before with downcast head I walked a pining lover—
More useless I had grown, 'twas said, than water-tank run dry.

No more my darling passes me with silent recognition,
Nor can she sit unmoved while I outpour my tender vow.
I wish that I had sooner realized this blest condition;
'Tis pouring living water on a dead man's ashes now.

In vain did others seek my love, in vain they called upon her,
She leaned her head upon my breast, was kind as girl could be.
Of conquered Parthians talk no more, I've gained a nobler honor,
For she'll be spoils, and leaders, and triumphal car to me.

Light of my life! say, shall my bark reach shore with gear befitting,
Or, dashed amid the breakers, with her cargo run aground?
With thee it lies: but if, perchance, through fault of my committing,
Thou giv'st me o'er, before thy door let my cold corse be found."

CRANSTOUN.

Ovid (43 B.C.–17 A.D.).—Publius Ovidius Na'so, the last of the Augustan poets, was a knight of Sulmo, an ancient Samnite town in the eastern part of Italy. Designed for the legal profession, he was sent to Rome to be educated; but the writing of verses was more congenial than rhetorical studies; and an eminent critic of the day, on hearing one of his early declamations, described it as "nothing else than poetry out of metre."

After the death of an elder son, his father consented that Publius should follow the bent of his own inclinations, and the poet went abroad to study in Greece and travel in Asia Minor. Returning to Rome, he began his literary career as the glory of the Augustan age was beginning to fade.

For twenty-two years Ovid wasted his talents on the composition of licentious love-poems. In the "Loves" (Amo'res), the earliest of his works, one Corinna is addressed throughout. The hearty reception with which these loose songs met at Rome is a sad comment on the degeneracy of the public taste and morals. They were followed by the "Hero'-

ides," a collection of twenty-one imaginary love-letters, inscribed by the heroines of the past to their absent or unfaithful lords—an original idea with Ovid. Penelope indicts an epistle to Ulysses, Medea to Jason, Sappho to Phaon, etc. In the one last named, translated by Pope, the Lesbian poetess informs the youth of her resolve to take the Lover's Leap.

"A spring there is, where silver waters show,
Clear as a glass, the shining sands below;
A flowery lotus spreads its arms above,
Shades all the banks, and seems itself a grove:
Eternal greens the mossy margin grace,
Watched by the sylvan genius of the place.
Here as I lay, and swelled with tears the flood,
Before my sight a watery virgin stood:
She stood and cried, 'O you that love in vain,
Fly hence, and seek the fair Leucadian main!
There stands a rock, from whose impending steep
Apollo's fane surveys the rolling deep;
There injured lovers, leaping from above,
Their flames extinguish and forget to love.
Hence, Sappho, haste! from high Leucadia throw
Thy wretched weight, nor dread the deeps below.'
She spoke, and vanished with the voice—I rise,
And silent tears fall trickling from my eyes.
I go, ye nymphs, those rocks and seas to prove:
And much I fear; but ah! how much I love!
To rocks and seas I fly from Phaon's hate,
And hope from seas and rocks a milder fate."

In the "Art of Love," Ovid again overleaped the bounds of propriety, and threw so brilliant a coloring into his pictures of vice that his readers were fain to linger over them, to enjoy, and to admire, with manifest danger to their own morals. When even a daughter of the imperial line was corrupted by them, Augustus, the professed defender of virtue, felt that it was time to stop the dissemination of such principles, and visited the poet with his displeasure. In consequence of a subsequent and more serious offence, in some way connected with the royal family, but the nature of which we can only conjecture, Ovid suddenly received notice to quit the capital forever, and retire to To'mi, a dreary and desolate village on the Black Sea, A.D. 9. Despite his urgent prayers, the decree of banishment was never revoked.

The works of his eight years' exile are the "Tristia," or Sorrows, "Letters from Pontus," and some shorter poems; they prove his genius to have been crushed, his spirit broken. Tomi gave Ovid a grave; even his request to be buried in Italy was refused.

The best of Ovid's works were the "Fasti," or Roman Calendar, a pleasant almanac in verse, and the "Metamorphoses," ingenious in both conception and expression. While engaged on the Fasti, which he intended to complete in twelve books, one dedicated to each month, the poet was surprised by the decree of banishment, and left his work unfinished.

The Metamorphoses, from which modern writers have largely drawn, gives an account of the transformations of ancient mythology, such as the changing of Io into a heifer, Daphne into a laurel, the sisters of Phaëton into the poplars of the Po, and Atlas into a mountain of stone by the gorgon-head of Perseus. One of the prettiest of these poems relates to the metamorphosis of the ivory statue wrought by Pygmalion, into a living bride, by the goddess of beauty, in answer to the sculptor's prayer :—

PYGMALION'S STATUE.

"The sculptor sought
His home, and, bending o'er the couch that bore
His Maiden's life-like image, to her lips
Fond pressed his own—and lo! her lips seemed warm,
And warmer, kissed again; and dimpling to his touch
The ivory seems to yield,—as in the sun
The waxen labor of Hymettus' bees,
By plastic fingers wrought, to various shape
And use by use is fashioned. Wonder-spelled,
Scarce daring to believe his bliss, in dread
Lest sense deluded mock him, on the form
He loves again and yet again his hand
Lays trembling touch, and to his touch a pulse

Within throbs answering palpable: 'twas flesh!
'Twas very life!—Then forth in eloquent flood
His grateful heart its thanks to Venus poured!
The lips he kissed were living lips that felt
His passionate pressure; o'er the virgin cheeks
Stole deepening crimson; and the unclosing eyes
At once on heaven and on their lover looked!"

HENRY KING.

With the death of Ovid, the flourishing period of poetry terminated. Among his contemporaries, we may mention, in passing, the epic poets ALBINOVA'NUS author of the These'id, and CORNELIUS SEVE'RUS, who wrote an heroic on the war between Augustus and Sextus Pompey. The didactic poets GRATIUS and MANILIUS also flourished in the Augustan age; the former memorable for his poem on hunting, the latter for his "Astronomica."

PROSE WRITERS.

Titus Livius.—The last ornament of the Augustan Era is the historian Livy, born at Pata'vium (now Padua) about 59 B.C.—the scion of a noble line that had figured proudly in the annals of the Republic. His was the uneventful life of the scholar, and few particulars of his biography have therefore been preserved. He appears to have begun his career as a rhetorician; to have come to the capital about B.C. 31, for what precise purpose we cannot say, and there to have gained a ready introduction at court. The emperor, already favorably impressed with his ability, is said to have placed at his disposal a suite of rooms in the palace.

Perhaps, as his importunities made the reluctant Virgil the great epic poet of Rome, so Augustus may have stirred the ambition of Livy to become its historian; whether he did or not, we find the rhetorician of Patavium, soon after taking up his abode at the imperial city, entering upon the composition of his "Annals," a work which progressed simultaneously with the Æneid. As the different decades (divisions of ten books) were completed, the author, after first reading them to Augustus and Mæcenas, published them for the perusal of his countrymen. They at once made his reputation, and became the received authority on the national history, raising Livy during his lifetime, as at the present day, to the rank of the most distinguished historians. The estimation in which they were held may be inferred from the story of Pliny—that a citizen of Cadiz came all the way to Italy merely to see the great writer the whole Roman world was talking about.

For forty years Livy labored on his history. At the time of his death, which took place in his native town, 17 A.D., he had finished 142 books, covering nearly seven and a half centuries from the founding of Rome. It is supposed that he intended to add eight more, embracing the entire reign of Augustus. Only thirty-five of the original books have been recovered.

The loss of the decades relating to the civil wars is much to be deplored, and it has ever been the hope of scholars that some day the missing parts would be found. Several times has the literary world been thrown into excitement by false rumors of their discovery. Once, we are told, a learned man detected in the parchment covering of a battledoor with which he was playing a page of the favorite historian; but on hastening to the maker of the toy, to rescue the prized manuscript to which it had belonged, he found that all had been utilized in a similar manner. A meagre synopsis of the books that have perished, serves only to make us regret their loss the more keenly.

Livy's "Annals" is a model of elegant historical writing, and a repertory of tales and traditions of early heroism, which have made Roman virtue and prowess the admiration of the world; yet his statements must be taken with many grains of allowance. Not that he wilfully misrepresented, but rather that he trusted too implicitly authorities of doubtful veracity, and shrunk from the labor of thorough original investigation. Moreover, a vein of exaggeration runs through his pages. It was doubtless his intention to be impartial; but carried away by a natural bias, he was too ready to color or cover over the blots on his country's escutcheon. That he stooped not to curry favor with his superiors is evident from the epithet applied to him by Augustus—"the Pompeyite"—by reason of his warm praises of Cæsar's rival. Ignorance of geography, military science, and even of the constitutional development of Rome, is conspicuous in his narrative.

As an artist, however, Livy was great. He excels in depicting character, whether directly by description, or indirectly in the actions or utterances of the old Roman worthies. Hence, artificial as they are and often smelling of the rhetorician's lamp, the speeches which Livy puts in the mouths of his different personages display his genius to advantage. One of the finest, given below, is that of the old Horatius, pleading with the people for the life of his son. According to the legend, in a war between Rome and Alba Longa, it was agreed by the contending parties, to save unnecessary bloodshed, that the question at issue should be decided by a hand-to-hand conflict between three champions on each side,—the brothers Horatii for Rome, the Curiatii for Alba. All fell save one Horatius. We leave the conclusion of the story to Livy:—

THE CRIME AND PUNISHMENT OF HORATIUS.

"Horatius advanced at the head of the Romans, bearing in triumph the spoils of the three brothers. Near the gate Capena he was met by his sister, a maiden who had been betrothed to one of the Curiatii; observing on her brother's shoulder the military robe of her lover, made by her own hands, she tore her hair, and with loud and mournful outcries called on the name of the deceased. His sister's lamentations, in the midst of his own triumph and of so great public joy, irritated the fierce youth to such a degree that, drawing his sword, he plunged it into her breast, at the same time upbraiding her in these words: 'Begone to thy spouse with thy unseasonable love, since thou couldst forget what is due to the memory of thy deceased brothers, to him who still survives, and to thy native country; so perish every daughter of Rome that shall mourn for its enemy!'

Both the senate and people were shocked at the horrid deed; but still, in their opinion, his recent merit outweighed its guilt: he was, however, instantly carried before the king for judgment. The king, unwilling to take on himself a decision of so melancholy a nature, summoned an assembly of the people, and then said: 'I appoint two commissioners to pass judgment on Horatius for murder, according to the law.' The law was of dreadful import: 'Let two commissioners pass judgment for murder; if the accused appeal from the commissioners, let the appeal be tried; if their sentence be confirmed, cover his head, hang him by a rope on the gallows, let him be scourged either within the Pomœrium* or without the Pomœrium.'

The two commissioners appointed were of opinion that, according to this law, they were not authorized to acquit him; and, after they had found him guilty, one of them pronounced judgment in these words: 'Publius Horatius, I sentence thee to punishment as a murderer; go, lictor, bind his hands.' The lictor had come up to him, and was fixing the cord, when Horatius, by the advice of Tullus, who wished to give the mildest interpretation to the law, said, 'I appeal;' so the trial on the appeal came before the Commons.

During this trial, the people were very deeply affected, especially by the behavior of Publius Horatius, the father, who declared that 'in his judgment his daughter was deservedly put to death; had it not been so, he would, by his own authority as a father, have inflicted punishment on his son.' He then besought them that 'they would not leave him childless, whom they had beheld, but a few hours ago, surrounded by a progeny of uncommon merit.' Uttering these words, the old man embraced the youth, and pointing to the spoils of the Curiatii, which were hung up in the place where now stands the Horatian column, exclaimed:—

'O my fellow-citizens! can you bear to behold him laden with chains, and condemned to ignominy, stripes, and torture, whom but just now you saw covered with the ornaments of victory, marching in triumph—a sight so horrid that scarcely could the eyes of the Albans themselves endure it? Go, lictor, bind the arms which but now wielded those weapons that acquired dominion to the Roman people; cover the head of that man to whom your city owes its liberty; hang him upon the gallows. Scourge him within the Pomœrium; but do it between those pillars to which are suspended the trophies of his victory. Scourge him without the Pomœrium; but do it between the graves of the Curiatii. For to what place can ye lead this youth, where the monuments of his glory would not redeem him from the ignominy of such a punishment?'

The people could not withstand either the tears of the father, or

* A consecrated ground in ancient Rome, on which it was unlawful to build.

the intrepid spirit of the youth himself, which no kind of danger could appall; and rather out of admiration of his bravery than regard to the justice of his cause, they passed a sentence of acquittal. Wherefore, that some expiation might be made for the act of manifest murder, the father was ordered to make atonement for his son at the public expense. After performing expiatory sacrifices, which continued afterward to be celebrated by the Horatian family, he laid a beam across the street, and, covering the young man's head, made him pass, as it were, under the yoke. The beam remains to this day, being constantly kept in repair at the expense of the public, and is called the Sister's beam. A tomb of squared stone was raised for Horatia on the spot where she fell."—BAKER.

In addition to the "Annals of Rome," Livy also wrote historical and philosophical dialogues, which we know only by name.

Pompeius Trogus, contemporary with Livy, produced a history of the world, extending from the founding of Nineveh to the Christian Era. Macedonia fills an important place in this work, an abridgment of which is still in existence.

A prominent rhetorician of the Augustan period was the elder SENECA, of Cordova, in Spain. Portions of his works (which consist of rhetorical exercises on imaginary cases, historical events, and circumstances in the lives of great men, written for the benefit of his sons) have survived; but nothing remains of a history of Rome ascribed to him.

The orators MESSALA and ASINIUS POLLIO graced the early years of the first emperor's reign; but, when political eloquence was interdicted, they retired to private life,—Pollio, to win new laurels by his tragedies and other literary compositions. Both were patrons of literature, and loved to gather round them the eminent poets of their day. Messala's orations, known to us only by a few fragments that remain, were regarded as almost equal to Cicero's; while Pollio, none of whose works have been preserved, was ranked by his contemporaries with Cicero as an orator, with Virgil as a poet, and with Sallust as an historian.

MINOR POETS AND PROSE WRITERS.

HELVIUS CINNA (50 B.C.): author of the lost epic "Smyrna," the fruit of nine years' labor. In one of his Eclogues, Virgil compared himself in the company of Cinna and his friend Varius to a goose among swans.

LICINIUS CALVUS (82-47 B.C.): poet and orator; elegies, epigrams, and love-songs in the style of Catullus; an epic "Io;" no remains.

VALGIUS RUFUS, a friend of Horace: an epic and elegiac poet.

ÆLIUS GALLUS: a noted jurist.

TU'BERO (48 B.C.) the historian: contemporary with Sallust.

VERRIUS FLACCUS: a renowned grammarian; author of a voluminous Latin lexicon, which is lost. His work was subsequently condensed into twenty volumes.

VITRUVIUS POLLIO, the great architect of the Augustan Era: he prepared a comprehensive work on the science of architecture, long received as authority.

TITUS LABIE'NUS: an orator and historian.

NOTES ON EDUCATION, ETC., AMONG THE ROMANS.

Education never compulsory, as in Greece. Its chief aim in early times to make warriors and statesmen. Children usually grounded in the rudiments by their mother, the father occasionally doing service as a teacher of reading and writing. From the Greeks, the Romans adopted the custom of employing *pædagogi* to instruct their children or accompany them to and from school.

Private schools in Rome about 450 B.C.; Virginia insulted by Appius Claudius, while on her way to school. The youth instructed at these institutions in reading, writing, and arithmetic, and required to memorize the laws of the Twelve Tables. Grammar was next essayed; and a course in rhetoric and oratory completed the Roman boy's education. Many continued their studies at Athens, Rhodes, or Alexandria.

The teachers often provincials or freedmen. In the golden age, Greek tutors very generally the companions and flatterers of the wealthy Romans. During the reign of Augustus, great schools at Cordova and Marseilles rivalled the academy of Flaccus at Rome, the favorite of the emperor, who paid Flaccus a salary of $3,600, and offered special inducements in the way of prizes to such as would join his school. Under Vespasian the first Roman college, the Athenæum, was established; botany, zoölogy, and mineralogy, now became favorite studies.

Rome had its booksellers in the golden age, to supply the demand for standard authors and school manuals. Books multiplied rapidly by transcription, and were cheap in proportion. At the beginning of the first century B.C., many private libraries in Rome; every noble took pride in his collection of manuscripts. First public library founded by Asinius Pollio, whose example was followed by others.

Earliest known attempts at journalism, 59 B.C. The *Acta* of the senate and of the people, the first publications. The latter, a daily (*diurna*, whence *journal*), had an extensive circulation throughout the Roman territories. Stenography practised at this time by the Romans, and subsequently taught in their schools. Cicero said to have been the inventor of their system of short-hand. Sympathetic ink in use for writing love-letters and secret correspondence. For this purpose Ovid recommends milk, which may be made visible by dusting powdered charcoal on the letters. To keep mice from gnawing their papyrus and parchment rolls, some Roman writers mixed wormwood with their inks.

CHAPTER IV.

AGE OF DECLINE.

Silver Age of Roman Letters.—With the death of Augustus and the accession of his step-son Tiberius, despotism in its worst form was established at Rome, and, as in Greece, a decline of letters immediately followed. Symptoms of literary decay had already shown themselves in the reign of the first emperor, although he took care to conceal his assumption of absolute power under the mask of republican forms, and was known to all as a patron of learning. Tiberius, on the contrary, openly declared himself the enemy of freedom, both political and intellectual; and when, in 37 A.D., his attendants, no longer able to endure his rule of blood, smothered the monster with pillows, Latin literature was at its lowest ebb.

A brief renaissance, however, succeeded; so that the imperial fiend Nero was able to number among his victims an epic poet, Lucan, and a philosopher and dramatist of no common stamp, Seneca. Under the Cæsars, genius was hopelessly fettered; a chance word might condemn its author to the headsman; the poet, the historian, the orator, must needs suppress his sentiments or forfeit his self-respect by flattering the reigning despot.

A brighter day dawned with the mild rule of Nerva, Trajan, Hadrian, and the Antonines (96–180 A.D.). During this golden age of the Roman empire, poetry for a time recovered its vitality, and through the stinging satires of Juvenal denounced the abuses that had prevailed in the days of Nero and Domitian; while in the histories of Tacitus, prose indignantly broke its enforced silence, and held up to public detestation the despots of the past. But this revival was short-lived. Latin literature rapidly degenerated, for Latin genius was no more. In the later centuries of the empire, science and jurisprudence alone flourished on the soil where poetry had now ceased to bloom.

ERA OF THE CÆSARS (14-96 A.D.).

In the reign of Tiberius, we meet with the names of Velleius Paterculus, the court historian; Celsus, the scientist; and Phædrus.

Velleius Paterculus is memorable for his epitome of Roman history, a work in other respects meritorious, but marred by its author's servile praise of Tiberius. Yet we must remember that Velleius was not permitted to see the worst phase of this emperor's tyranny. When the treachery of the prime minister Seja'nus was exposed, the historian, though not implicated with him, was one of the first to be put to death. He was thus prevented from witnessing the murders of hundreds of other innocent persons—atrocities that might have altered his estimate of his ungrateful master.

Valerius Maximus, his contemporary and fellow-flatterer, prepared a cyclopædia of anecdotes gleaned from the history of Rome and foreign countries, entitled "Remarkable Deeds and Sayings." It was designed for the use of persons who had not the time or inclination to make original investigations, and, though written in an artificial style, contains much that is interesting.

Celsus was the author of a scientific encyclopædia, whose twenty books were devoted to farming, medicine, rhetoric, jurisprudence, and military tactics. The eight books on medicine still survive, constituting the great Roman authority on that subject.

Before his day the art of medicine and surgery had been almost entirely confined to Greek physicians; but Celsus dignified it as a calling worthy of Romans, not only practising with success among his countrymen, but committing to writing the results of his experience. He was the first ancient author who recommended the tying of blood-vessels for the purpose of checking hemorrhage.

Phædrus, the only noteworthy poet of Tiberius's reign, is known to us by his fables. Of his life, we have few facts. He is supposed to have been brought from Thrace to Rome, as a captive; and to have lived there as the slave of Augustus, who, recognizing his latent talent, gave him an education and finally his freedom.

In the sunshine of his patron's smiles, Phædrus led a happy life; but on the death of Augustus he was exposed to the persecutions of Sejanus, who virtually controlled the state under the succeeding emperor, and who affected to see in the poet's fables masked attacks upon his own vicious career. Phædrus, however, outlived all his enemies, and died at a good old age.

The fables of Phædrus, preserved in a single manuscript, were discovered in an abbey at Rheims (1561), and, after narrowly escaping destruction at the hands of some French fanatics, were published to the world. In the main translated or imitated from Æsop, whom their author thus made known to the Romans, they commend themselves for their conciseness and simplicity, as well as for the moral lessons they convey. His "pleasant tales" may be judged of by the following specimens:—

THE FOX AND THE GOAT.

"A crafty knave will make escape,
When once he gets into a scrape,
Still meditating self-defence,
At any other man's expense.
A fox by some disaster fell
Into a deep and fencèd well:
A thirsty goat came down in haste,
And asked about the water's taste,
If it was plentiful and sweet?
At which the fox, in rank deceit:—
'So great the solace of the run,
I thought I never should have done.
Be quick, my friend, your sorrows drown.'
This said, the silly goat comes down.
The subtle fox herself avails,
And by his horns the height she scales,
And leaves the goat in all the mire,
To gratify his heart's desire."

THE BALD MAN AND THE FLY.

"As on his head she chanced to sit,
A man's bald pate a gadfly bit;
He, prompt to crush the little foe,
Dealt on himself a grievous blow.
At which the fly, deriding, said:—
'You who would strike an insect dead
For one slight sting, in wrath so strict,
What punishment will you inflict
Upon yourself, whose heavy arm,
Not my poor bite, did all the harm?'
'Oh!' says the party, 'as for me,
I with myself can soon agree;
The intention of the act is all.
But thou, detested cannibal!
Bloodsucker! to have thee secured,
More would I gladly have endured.'
What by this moral tale is meant
Is, those who wrong not with intent
Are venial; but to those that do,
Severity is surely due."—CHRISTOPHER SMART.

The three great ornaments of Nero's reign (54–68 A.D.) were Persius the satirist, Seneca, and his nephew Lucan.

Persius.—Born at the Etruscan town of Volaterræ (34 A.D.), Persius was brought to Rome by his mother at the age of twelve, and there educated. In the Stoic, Cornu'tus, he found his ideal preceptor, and to this "best of friends" the poet pays a beautiful tribute in the following verses, among the finest he ever wrote :—

"When first I laid the purple* by, and free,
Yet trembling at my new-felt liberty,
Approached the hearth, and on the Lares hung
The bulla, from my willing neck unstrung;
When gay associates, sporting at my side,
And the white boss, displayed with conscious pride,
Gave me, unchecked, the haunts of vice to trace,
And throw my wandering eyes on every face,
I fled to you, Cornutus, pleased to rest
My hopes and fears on your Socratic breast;
Nor did you, gentle sage, the charge decline.
Then, dextrous to beguile, your steady line
Reclaimed, I know not by what winning force,
My morals, warped from virtue's straighter course.
Can I forget how many a summer's day,
Spent in your converse, stole unmarked away?
Or how, while listening with increased delight,
I snatched from feasts the earlier hours of night?
One time (for to your bosom still I grew),
One time of study and of rest we knew;
One frugal board where, every care resigned,
An hour of blameless mirth relaxed the mind."—GIFFORD.

Death overtook our poet in his 28th year (62 A.D.). All we have of his writings is six satires—only 650 hexameter lines. After his death these were published, and elicited unbounded admiration. Other works of his were torn up by his mother, who deemed them unworthy of his genius. Persius bequeathed to Cornutus his library of 700 manuscripts.

The satires of Persius were written in the interest of morality, and what gave them weight was that all knew their author

* An allusion to the change from the purple-bordered *toga* of the youth, to the *toga virilis*, or manly robe.

to be a man who practised the virtue he commended, a man of stainless character in an age of universal licentiousness. And yet we do not find him lashing vice as we should expect. Was he loath to do so, lest the very pictures he must draw might corrupt? Or, was Persius forced to hold his peace in the presence of a despot who revelled in the vilest excesses, whose policy it was to reduce his subjects to his own low level? Perhaps for both reasons he preferred to assail wickedness in the abstract. Certainly his "maidenly modesty" shrunk from portraying the hideous sins that flaunted around him, while his philosophical tenets inclined him to keep aloof from the world.

Poetasters and pedants that pandered to the perverted taste of the day, received the brunt of his attack in his First Satire. The Second discusses the proper subjects of prayer. How few, says the poet, would be willing to have their petitions made public:—

> "Hard, hard the task, from the low muttered prayer
> To free the fanes; or find one suppliant there,
> Who dares to ask but what his state requires,
> And live to heaven and earth with known desires!
> Sound sense, integrity, a conscience clear,
> Are begged aloud, that all at hand may hear;
> But prayers like these (half whispered, half suppressed)
> The tongue scarce hazards from the conscious breast:—
> 'O that I could my rich old uncle see
> In funeral pomp!'—'O that some deity
> To pots of buried gold would guide my share!'—
> 'O that my ward, whom I succeed as heir,
> Were once at rest! poor child, he lives in pain,
> And death to him must be accounted gain.'—
> 'By wedlock thrice has Nerius swelled his store,
> And now—is he a widower once more!'"

The Second Satire concludes with these noble lines:—

> "No; let me bring the immortal gods a mind,
> Where legal and where moral sense are joined
> With the pure essence; holy thoughts, that dwell
> In the soul's most retired and sacred cell;

A bosom dyed in honor's noblest grain,
Deep-dyed—with these let me approach the fane,
And Heaven will hear the humble prayer I make,
Though all my offering be a barley-cake."—GIFFORD.

Lucius Annæus Seneca, son of the rhetorician, was born at Cordova B.C. 7, but received his education at Rome under the supervision of his father. From the first he displayed great interest in his studies, and as he grew in years he indulged his natural bent for philosophical researches. So thorough a Pythagorean did he become that he even eschewed animal food, lest he should devour flesh that had once been animated by a human soul. On the remonstrance of his parent, however, he renounced vegetarianism and "lived as others lived" again. At a later period we find him the leader of the Stoics at Rome.

Seneca early made his mark as an orator. Hearing him plead eloquently on one occasion in the senate, Caligula, out of jealousy, threatened to have him executed, and was deterred only by the consideration that Seneca had the consumption and was not likely to live for any length of time.

But Seneca survived this imperial butcher, to become the instructor and moral guide of the youthful Nero. While Nero submitted to his counsels, Rome enjoyed a halcyon age, long remembered by her people as *the Five Years.* His influence led to the adoption of many salutary measures; it is thought to have been at his instigation that Nero despatched an expedition to explore the sources of the Nile—the first recorded in history. Well would it have been for Rome, had Nero continued to follow the advice of Seneca.

This, however, was not to be; a sudden change took place in the disposition of the prince, when his mother was charged with conspiring against him. It was her life or his; and Nero won. The taste of blood transformed him into a monster, and he forthwith entered upon a reign of horrors that has no equal in history. Virtue was now the surest road to ruin. Falsely accused of complicity in a conspiracy, Seneca was sentenced to put an end to his own life (65 A.D.). With perfect calmness he received the royal mandate, and caused his veins to be severed; but the blood flowing too slowly, he entered a vapor-bath and ended his sufferings by suffocation. His wife Paulina elected to die with him, and in the same manner; but Nero had her veins ligatured, and thus added several years of misery to her life. To his friends, Seneca was permitted to leave no more valuable legacy than his virtuous example.

Seneca was a great moral leader, the first of a class of philosophers who aimed at winning the people back to the virtue of primitive Rome. His teachings were in strange contrast to the age in which he lived; they bear a striking resemblance to those of the Gospel, with which he may have become acquainted through St. Paul. The fathers of the Church were loud in their praises of "the divine pagan," but there is no evidence that, as some have stated, Seneca was persuaded by the apostle to become a Christian.

Our philosopher is described as simple in his tastes. Though the envied possessor of a princely fortune, he could consistently write in support of temperance on his table of gold. A cupful of water from the brook was sweeter to him than beakers of Italy's choicest wines, and the fruits of the wild wood he preferred to the luxurious dishes fashion required him to spread before the rich and great. His fault was weakness, which betrayed him into flattery, and perhaps made him an unwilling accessory to some of his master's crimes.

Seneca was the author, not only of philosophical treatises, but also of ten tragedies, and one hundred and twenty-four moral epistles. He even attempted a satire on the stupidity of the emperor Claudius, representing him as transformed after death, not into a god, as the senate decreed, but into a pumpkin. Several other works from his pen are lost.

The best of Seneca's treatises are those on Anger, Providence, and Consolation. His style, labored, antithetical, and full of repetitions, has an artificial glitter about it that impresses the reader unfavorably.

EXTRACTS FROM SENECA'S WRITINGS.

ON ANGER.

"How idle are many of those things that make us stark mad! A resty horse, the overturning of a glass, the falling of a key, the dragging of a chair, a jealousy, a misconstruction. How shall that man endure the extremities of hunger and thirst, that flies into a rage only for the putting of a little too much water in his wine? What haste is there to lay a servant by the heels, or break a leg or an arm immediately for it? The answer of a servant, a wife, a tenant, puts some people out of all patience, and yet they can quarrel with the government for not allowing them the same liberty in public which they themselves deny to their own families. If they say nothing, 'tis contumacy; if they speak or laugh, 'tis insolence. Neither are our eyes less curious and fantastical than our ears. When we are abroad, we can bear well enough with foul ways, nasty streets, noisome ditches; but a spot upon a dish at home, or an unswept hearth, absolutely distracts us. And what's the reason, but that we are patient in the one place and peevish in the other?

Nothing makes us more intemperate than luxury. When we are once weakened with our pleasures, everything grows intolerable. And we are angry as well with those things that cannot hurt us as with those that do. We tear a book because it is blotted; and our clothes because they are not well made—things that neither deserve our anger nor feel it. The tailor perchance did his best, or had no intent to displease us. If so, first, why should we be angry at all? Secondly, why should we be angry with the thing for the man's sake? Nay, our anger extends even to dogs, horses, and other beasts.

Cyrus, in his design upon Babylon, found a river in his way that put a stop to his march. The current was strong, and carried away one of the horses that belonged to his own chariot; upon this he swore that, since it had obstructed his passage, it should never hinder that of another, and presently set his whole army to work on it, which diverted it into a hundred and fourscore channels, and laid it dry. In this ignoble and unprofitable employment he lost his time and the soldiers their courage; moreover, he gave his adversaries an opportunity of providing themselves, while he was waging war with a river instead of an enemy."

ON A HAPPY LIFE.

"It is dangerous for a man too suddenly or too easily to believe himself. Wherefore let us examine, watch, observe, and inspect our own hearts; for we ourselves are our own greatest flatterers. We should every night call ourselves to account—'What infirmity have I mastered to-day? What passion opposed? What temptation resisted? What virtue acquired?' Our vices will abate of themselves, if they be brought every day to the shrift. O the blessed sleep that follows such a diary! O the tranquillity, liberty, and greatness of that mind that is a spy upon itself, and a private censor of its own manners! It is my custom every night, so soon as the candle is out, to run over all the words and actions of the past day; and I let nothing escape me. What can be more reasonable than this daily review of a life that we cannot warrant for a moment?"—L'ESTRANGE.

MISCELLANEOUS SAYINGS.

"Those whom God loves, he disciplines.

We can never quarrel enough with our vices.

The day of death is the birthday of eternity.

There is no need to pray the ædile to admit you to the ear of an image, that so your petitions may be heard the better. God is near you; he is with you; a holy spirit resides within us, our constant guardian.

Let us be liberal after the example of our great Creator, and give to others with the same consideration that he gives to us.

How many are unworthy of the light; yet the day dawns.

The good-will of the benefactor is the fountain of all benefits.

To obey God is liberty.

Apply thyself to the true riches. It is shameful to depend for a happy life on silver and gold."

Lucan (39-65 A.D.), the nephew of Seneca, though born at Cordova, was brought up at Rome, and there became the fellow-pupil and favorite companion of Nero. But the superior genius of the Spanish youth provoked the jealousy of his royal master, who had rather too high an opinion of his own attainments, and was nettled by the public verdict that Lucan, then only twenty-three years of age, was the greatest of living poets. At length the awarding of the prize to Lucan in a literary contest between them so enraged the emperor that he forbade his former friend to recite any more pieces.

Lucan's indiscretion sealed his fate. Not content with libellous attacks upon Nero, he became implicated in a conspiracy against the government, upon the detection of which he was condemned to death. Nero allowing him to choose the manner in which he should suffer, the poet had his veins opened in a hot bath. Becoming faint from loss of blood, he recited a passage from his own "Pharsalia," descriptive of the death of a snake-bitten soldier :—

"So the warm blood at once from every part
Ran purple poison down, and drained the fainting heart.
Blood falls for tears, and o'er his mournful face
The ruddy drops their tainted passage trace.
Where'er the liquid juices find a way,
There streams of blood, there crimson rivers stray;
His mouth and gushing nostrils pour a flood,
And e'en the pores ooze out the trickling blood.
In the red deluge all the parts lie drowned,
And the whole body seems one bleeding wound"—

and so he passed away.

Lucan was interred at Rome in his own garden. An ancient monument in the church of Santo Paulo contains an inscription to his memory, probably placed there by order of Nero, who seems after all to have rendered secret homage to his genius and virtue. The talents of his wife have been highly commended; and it is probable that she assisted him in composing his work.

The epic "Pharsalia" is the only poem of Lucan's that we now possess. Its subject is the civil war between Cæsar and Pompey; and it receives its name from the place at which the decisive battle between the rival commanders was fought. Though inferior to the Æneid, it certainly displays talent of a high order. Critics have differed in their estimate of Lucan. That he has faults, none will deny who are familiar with his tumid style and love of tinsel. On the other hand, energy, exuberant imagination, and a fervent love of liberty, are his peculiar excellences. The defects of the Pharsalia are excusable in a youth of twenty-six. Had the author lived to revise and finish the work, it might have equalled Virgil's epic.

Lucan is partial to the supernatural; dreams, witches, and ghosts, enter freely into his machinery. In the sixth book of the Pharsalia, he makes Pompey's son consult the witch Erichtho on the eve of the battle. His picture of the weird woman is quoted here as one of the most imaginative passages in the whole range of classical poetry. Erichtho is the type of a class of impostors firmly believed in by the Romans of that day; the powers with which the poet endows her are simply those attributed to her by popular superstition.

THE WITCH ERICHTHO.

"Whene'er the proud enchantress gives command,
Eternal Motion stops her active hand;
No more heaven's rapid circles journey on,
But universal Nature stands foredone;
The lazy god of day forgets to rise,
And everlasting night pollutes the skies.
Jove wonders to behold her shake the pole,
And, unconsenting, hears his thunders roll.
Now, with a word she hides the sun's bright face,
And blots the wide ethereal azure space:
Loosely, anon, she shakes her flowing hair,
And straight the stormy lowering heavens are fair:
At once she calls the golden light again;
The clouds fly swift away, and stops the drizzly rain.

In stillest calms, she bids the waves run high;
And smooths the deep, tho' Boreas shakes the sky:
When winds are hushed, her potent breath prevails,
Wafts on the bark, and fills the flagging sails.
Streams have run back at murmurs of her tongue,
And torrents from the rock suspended hung:
No more the Nile his wonted seasons knows,
And in a line the straight Mæander flows.
The ponderous earth, by magic numbers struck,
Down to her inmost centre deep has shook;
Then, rending with a yawn, at once made way,
To join the upper and the nether day:
While wondering eyes, the dreadful cleft between,
Another starry firmament have seen.

Each deadly kind, by nature formed to kill,
Fears the dire hags, and executes their will:
Lions to them their nobler rage submit,
And fawning tigers crouch beneath their feet:
For them the snake foregoes her wintry hold,
And on the hoary frost untwines her fold;
The poisonous race they strike with stronger death,
And blasted vipers die by human breath.

But these, as arts too gentle and too good,
Nor yet with death or guilt enough imbrued,
With haughty scorn the fierce Erichtho viewed.
New mischief she, new monsters, durst explore;
And dealt in horrors never known before.
From towns and hospitable roofs she flies,
And every dwelling of mankind defies;
Through unfrequented deserts lonely roams,
Drives out the dead, and dwells within their tombs.
Grateful to hell the living hag descends,
And sits in black assemblies of the fiends.
Dark matted elf-locks dangling on her brow,
Filthy and foul, a loathsome burden grow:
Ghastly, and frightful pale, her face is seen;
Unknown to cheerful day and skies serene;
But, when the stars are veiled, when storms arise,
And the blue forky flame at midnight flies,
Then, forth from graves she takes her wicked way,
And thwarts the glancing lightnings as they play:
Where'er she breathes blue poisons round her spread,
The withering grass avows her fatal tread.

Oft in the grave the living has she laid,
And bid reviving bodies leave the dead:
Oft at the funeral pile she seeks her prey,
And bears the smoking ashes warm away;
Snatches some burning bone, or flaming brand,
And tears the torch from the sad father's hand.
Her teeth from gibbets gnaw the strangling noose,
And from the cross dead murderers unloose:
Her charms the use of sun-dried marrow find,
And husky entrails withered in the wind.

Where'er the battle bleeds, and slaughter lies,
Thither, preventing birds and beasts, she hies;
Nor then content to seize the ready prey,
From their fell jaws she tears their food away;
She marks the hungry wolf's pernicious tooth,
And joys to rend the morsel from his mouth:

Nor ever yet remorse could stop her hand,
When human gore her cursed rites demand.
When blooming youths in early manhood die,
She stands a terrible attendant by;
The downy growth from off their cheeks she tears,
Or cuts left-handed some selected hairs.
Oft, when in death her gasping kindred lay,
Some pious office would she feign to pay;
And, while close hovering o'er the bed she hung,
Bit the pale lips, and cropped the quivering tongue;
Then, in hoarse murmurs, ere the ghost could go,
Muttered some message to the shades below."

ROWE.

The Flavian Era is memorable for a few writers of note. Pliny the Elder, called also the Naturalist, was an intimate friend of the emperor Vespasian; while the names of Martial, Statius, and Quintilian, are associated with the reign of Domitian, Vespasian's son (81-96 A.D.).

Pliny the Elder (23-79 A.D.) was born at Como in Cisalpine Gaul, and there passed his boyhood. We find him afterward at Rome attending rhetorical lectures, and still later in his career serving as a soldier in Germany. Nero made him proconsul of Spain, and at the expiration of his term he returned to Rome to find his old friend Vespasian invested with the purple.

Pliny had already become distinguished as the author of a treatise on "the Use of the Javelin," a "History of the German Wars," and eight books on "Difficulties in the Latin Language." He now devoted himself to the compilation of his "Natural History," the only work we have left from his pen, which Cuvier pronounced "one of the most precious monuments that have come down to us from ancient times."

We might well wonder how, in the face of his onerous public duties, Pliny found time for literary pursuits so engrossing, did not his nephew, Pliny the Younger, describe to us his wonderful industry. His day's work began at 1 or 2 A.M., even in winter; sometimes at midnight. Before sunrise he repaired to the palace to chat informally with Vespasian, who like him was accustomed to rob the night of a few hours; after which he applied himself to business and study, devoting every spare moment to the accumulation of knowledge. "No book so bad but that something good may be gleaned from it," was his motto. To be without a volume and a portable writing-desk was a crime in Pliny's eyes. A slave constantly attended him, to take down his words in short-hand; during his meals he employed a reader, and even in his bath he dictated or listened. "I remember his chiding me," said his nephew, "for taking a walk, saying 'You might have saved three hours.' Compared with him, I am an idle vagabond."

Pliny the Elder was a martyr to science. In August, 79 A.D., while in command of the Mediterranean squadron, to which he had been appointed by Vespasian, word was brought him that Vesuvius was in a state of eruption. Desiring to investigate the phenomenon, he steered straight for the blazing mountain, pushed on through the rain of hot ashes and pumice-stones, and when advised by the pilot to turn back fearlessly replied, "Fortune favors the brave!" He effected a landing, but only to be suffocated by the sulphurous vapors that proved fatal to so many of the inhabitants of Herculaneum and Pompeii.

Pliny was the master-compiler of antiquity; and he was only a compiler, as he himself acknowledged. His Natural History, in thirty-seven books, is a storehouse of quaint lore, according to its author a condensation of two thousand volumes, relating to astronomy, geography, zoölogy, botany, mineralogy, diseases and their remedies, etc. A penchant for the marvellous, which shows him to have been a man of infinite credulity, was a weakness of Pliny; yet his stories were implicitly trusted in the Dark Ages, and many of them reappeared in the tales of the Arabian Nights. A few of his curious statements are subjoined :—

ECCENTRICITIES OF NATURE.

"Some individuals are born with certain parts of the body endowed with properties of a marvellous nature. Such was the case with King Pyrrhus, the great toe of whose right foot cured diseases of the spleen merely by touching the patient. We are also informed that this toe could not be reduced to ashes together with the other portions of the body.

India and Ethiopia abound in wonders. According to Megasthenes, on a mountain called Nulo there dwells a race of men who have their feet turned backward, with eight toes on each foot. On many of the mountains, again, there is a tribe of men who have the heads of dogs; instead of speaking they bark, and, furnished with claws, they live by hunting and catching birds. According to Ctesias, the number of this people is more than 120,000. This author speaks also of another race of men called Single-legs, who have only one limb, but are able to leap with surprising agility. The same people are also called Foot-shadowers, because they are in the habit of lying on their backs, and protecting themselves from the sun by the shade of their feet.

At the very extremity of India, near the source of the river Ganges, there is the nation of Mouthless people; their bodies are rough and overgrown with hair, and they cover themselves with a down plucked from the leaves of trees. These people subsist only by breathing and by the odors which they inhale through the nostrils. They support themselves upon neither meat nor drink; when they go upon a long journey, they carry with them only odoriferous roots and flowers, and wild apples, that they may not be without something to smell at. But an odor which is a little more powerful than usual easily destroys them."

HYDROPHOBIA.

"Canine madness is fatal to man during the heat of the Dog-star, and proves so in consequence of those who are bitten having a deadly horror of water. For this reason, during the thirty days that the star exerts its influence, we try to prevent the disease in dogs; or, if they are attacked by it, give them hellebore.

We have a single remedy against the bite, which has been but lately discovered—the root of the wild rose, which is called dog-rose. Columella informs us that if, on the fortieth day after the birth of a pup, the last bone of the tail is bitten off, the sinew will follow with it; after which the tail will not grow, and the dog will never become rabid."

REMEDIES FOR TOOTHACHE, ETC.

"Toothache is alleviated by scarifying the gums with bones of the sea-dragon, or by rubbing the teeth once a year with the brains of a dog-fish boiled in oil. It is a very good plan, too, for the cure of toothache, to lance the gums with the sting of the ray. This sting is pounded and applied to the teeth with white hellebore, having the effect of extracting them without the slightest difficulty. A decoction is made of a single frog boiled in two-thirds of a pint of vinegar, and the teeth are rinsed with it. It is generally thought that this recipe applies more particularly to the double teeth, and that the vinegar prepared as above mentioned is remarkably useful for strengthening them when loose. Ashes, also, of burnt crabs make an excellent dentifrice.

There is a small frog which ascends trees, and croaks aloud there; if a person suffering from cough spits into its mouth and then lets it go, he will experience a cure. For cough attended with spitting of blood, it is recommended to beat up the raw flesh of a snail, and to drink it in hot water."—RILEY.

Martial (43-117 A.D.).—The chief poet of Domitian's reign was Martial, master of the Latin epigram. Born in Spain, Martial came to Rome in Nero's time and began the study of law. But finding it uncongenial, he adopted literature as a profession, and rose to distinction under Titus and Domitian, his sordid flattery of the latter securing him wealth and honors.

The epigrams of Martial are pithy, pointed with satire, and not without elegance; but the pleasure of reading them is constantly interrupted by coarse allusions and even downright obscenity. Hence it has been justly said that Martial taught vice while reproving it. His poems, however, contain valuable pictures of Roman manners.

THE BEAU.

"They tell me, Cotilus, that you're a beau:
What this is, Cotilus, I wish to know.
'A beau is one who, with the nicest care,
In parted locks divides his curling hair;
One who with balm and cinnamon smells sweet,
Whose humming lips some Spanish air repeat;

Whose naked arms are smoothed with pumice-stone,
And tossed about with graces all his own.
A beau is one who takes his constant seat,
From morn to evening, where the ladies meet;
And ever, on some sofa hovering near,
Whispers soft nothings in some fair one's ear;
Who scribbles thousand billets-doux a day;
Still reads and scribbles, reads and sends away.
A beau is one who shrinks, if nearly pressed
By the coarse garment of a neighbor guest;
Who knows who flirts with whom, and still is found
At each good table in successive round.
A beau is one—none better knows than he
A race-horse and his noble pedigree.'—
Indeed? Why, Cotilus, if this be so,
What teasing trifling thing is called a beau!"

"With but one eye Philœnis weeps. How done
If you inquire, know she hath got but one."

Statius (61–96 A.D.), a contemporary and rival of Martial, was the author of the epic "Theba'is," based on the strife of the sons of Œdipus (see p. 200). Despite the fact that the poet gave a year's work to each of its twelve books, this epic has little to recommend it.

Statius began another poem on the life of Achilles, which he did not live to finish. His forte lay not in the line of epics, but in the improvising of short pointed pieces, thirty-two of which are preserved in the collection called "Silvæ." Juvenal bears witness to his popularity.

Statius was patronized by the emperor Domitian, but is said to have been stabbed by the latter with a stylus, in a fit of anger. The following tender lines are from a poem addressed to his wife Claudia.

STATIUS TO HIS WIFE.

"Whither could ocean's waves my bark convey,
Nor thou be fond companion of my way?
Yes—did I seek to fix my mansion drear
Where polar ice congeals the inclement year;

Where the seas darken round far Thule's isle,
Or unapproached recedes the head of Nile;
Thy voice would cheer me on. May that kind Power,
Who joined our hands when in thy beauty's flower,
Still, when the blooming years of life decline,
Prolong the blessing, and preserve thee mine!
To thee, whose charms gave first the enamoring wound,
And my wild youth in marriage fetters bound;
To thee submissive, I received the rein,
Nor sigh for change, but hug the pleasing chain.

And thou hast listened, with entranced desire,
The first rude sounds that would my lips inspire;
Thy watchful ear would snatch, with keen delight,
My verse, low-murmured through the live-long night.
To only thee my lengthened toils were known,
And with thy years has my Thebaid grown.
I saw thee, what thou art, when late I stood
On the dark verge of the Lethæan flood;
When glazed in death, I closed my quivering eyes,
Relenting Fate restored me to thy sighs;
Thou wert alone the cause, the Power above
Feared thy despair and melted to thy love."—ELTON.

Sulpitia.—We must not pass over the Roman lyric poetess Sulpitia, the Sappho of Domitian's age—a noble lady of exceptional genius, who claims that she

"First taught the Roman dames to vie
With Græcia's nymphs of lyric minstrelsy."

A short satire on Domitian's expulsion of the Greek philosophers from Italy, bearing the name of Sulpitia, still survives. It is valuable, as the only fragment we have from a Roman poetess. From it we extract the following apt simile:—

"It fares with Romans as with wasps, whose home
Is hung where Juno's temple rears its dome;
A bristling crowd, they wave their flickering wings,
Their yellow bodies barbed with quivering stings.
But not like wasps, thus tremblingly alive,
The bee, secure returning, haunts her hive;
Forgetful of the comb, by sloth oppressed,
The swarm, the queen, die slow in pampered rest:
And this the sons of Romulus have found,
Sunk in the lap of peace, in long perdition drowned."

Quintilian (35–95 A.D.), of Spanish parentage but Roman education, for many years taught eloquence successfully in the capital, numbering among his pupils the nephews of Domitian. He had the good fortune to enjoy the favor of the emperor, and filled a professorship to which was attached an annual salary of about $4,000.

Quintilian is honored as the author of the "Institutes of Oratory," an exhaustive rhetorical treatise in twelve books, devoted to the education of the orator from infancy. "No other author," it has been said, "ever adorned a scientific treatise with so many happy metaphors." No other author, it may be added, ever succeeded better in investing a dry subject with general interest. The "Institutes" may be read with profit by all who desire to improve their style.

Quintilian insists on virtue as a requisite of the perfect orator; yet with strange inconsistency excuses a falsehood if told in a good cause, and justifies the doing of evil that good may come. We present a few paragraphs on

THE EMBELLISHMENT OF STYLE.

"By polish and embellishment of style the orator recommends himself to his auditors in his proper character; in his other efforts he courts the approbation of the learned, in this the applause of the multitude. Cicero, in pleading the cause of Cornelius, fought with arms that were not only stout, but dazzling; nor would he, merely by instructing the judge, or by speaking to the purpose in pure Latin and with perspicuity, have caused the Roman people to testify their admiration of him not only by acclamations, but even by tumults of applause. It was the sublimity, magnificence, splendor, and dignity of his eloquence, that drew forth that thunder of approbation.

This grace of style may contribute in no small degree to the success of a cause; for those who listen with pleasure are both more attentive and more ready to believe; they are very frequently captivated with pleasure, and sometimes hurried away in admiration. Thus the glitter of a sword strikes something of terror into the eyes; and thunderstorms themselves would not alarm us so much as they do, if it were their force only, and not also their flame, that was dreaded. Cicero, accordingly, in one of his letters to Brutus, makes with good reason the following remark: 'That eloquence which excites no admiration, I account as nothing.' Aristotle, also, thinks that to excite admiration should be one of our greatest objects.

But let the embellishment of our style be manly, noble, and chaste; let it not affect effeminate delicacy, or a complexion counterfeited by paint, but let it glow with genuine health and vigor. Should I think a piece of land better cultivated, in which the owner should show me lilies, anemonies, and violets, and fountains playing, than one in which there is a plentiful harvest, or vines laden with grapes? Should I prefer barren plane-trees, or clipped myrtles, to elms embraced with vines, and fruitful olive-trees? The rich may have such unproductive gratifications; but what would they be, if they had nothing else?

Whatever may be attractive in conception, elegant in expression, pleasing in figures, rich in metaphor, or polished in composition, the orator, like a dealer, as it were, in eloquence, will lay before his audience for them to inspect, and almost to handle; for his success entirely concerns his reputation, and not his cause. But when a serious affair is in question, and there is a contest in real earnest, anxiety for mere applause should be an orator's last concern. Indeed, no speaker, where important interests are involved, should be very solicitous about his words."—WATSON.

Among the lesser lights of the first Christian century were QUINTUS CURTIUS, who compiled a "History of Alexander the Great;" COLUMELLA, a writer on agriculture; POMPONIUS MELA, the first Latin geographer; PROBUS, the grammarian; VALERIUS FLACCUS, who wrote the epic "Argonautica," in imitation of Apollonius Rhodius; and SILIUS ITALICUS, author of a third-rate epic on the Punic Wars.

AGE OF TRAJAN AND THE ANTONINES.

Juvenal (40–125 A.D.), the single poet of this age, ranks with Rome's great writers. The accounts of his life are fragmentary and obscure. A native of Aqui'num in Latium, he came to Rome, and was apparently a student of rhetoric, perhaps an advocate. A chance lampoon on an actor revealed to him his satirical talent, and forthwith he applied himself to that branch of poetry in which he became so eminent. Too modest at first to read his satires even before his friends, Juvenal postponed publishing them until his sixtieth year, when they took Rome by storm. Sixteen of them survive.

His fierce diatribes not unnaturally gave offence in high places; and at length the emperor Ha'drian* quietly sent their author off to Egypt, to command a Roman cohort stationed there—a disgrace which brought the old satirist in sorrow to the grave.

Juvenal probed Roman society to its very depths, laying bare vices of the blackest dye. In his day, the degenerate masters of the world even out-sodomed Sodom in depravity. Nobles and emperors openly perpetrated the vilest crimes. High-born ladies, in male attire, entered the arena to fight like gladiators; revelled in reckless extravagance; plunged into immoralities that call up a blush in the very recital, and even added the arts of the poisoner to their accomplishments. Thus the poet exclaims against these fashionable murderesses:—

"They see upon the stage the Grecian wife
Redeeming with her own her husband's life;
Yet, in her place, would willingly deprive
Their lords of breath, to keep their dogs alive!
Abroad, at home, the Belides † you meet,
And Clytemnestras swarm in every street;
But here the difference lies—those bungling wives
With a blunt axe hacked out their husbands' lives;
While now the deed is done with dexterous art,
And a drugged bowl performs the axe's part."

In the blaze of his satire Juvenal brought out the represent-

---

* Hadrian was for the most part a patron of literary men, and himself spoke and wrote with eloquence. Pope's paraphrase has made familiar his verse addressed to his soul:—

"Ah! fleeting spirit! wandering fire,
That long hast warmed my tender breast,
Must thou no more this frame inspire,
No more a pleasing, cheerful guest?
Whither, ah! whither art thou flying?
To what dark undiscovered shore?
Thou seem'st all trembling, shivering, dying,
And wit and humor are no more."

† The fifty daughters of Danaus, who stabbed their husbands on the marriage-night.

ative characters of his time. Parasites, hypocrites, and panders, upstarts, legacy-hunters, and gamblers, ballet-dancers and fortune-tellers, gluttons and sots,—defile before us in his pages till we turn with nausea from the revolting panorama. Well might the poet sigh:—

"Oh! happy were our sires, estranged from crimes;
And happy, happy were the good old times,
Which saw beneath their kings', their tribunes' reign,
One cell the nation's criminals contain!"

Juvenal's vividness of description and minuteness of detail show him to have been personally familiar with the vices he lashed; that he kept himself unspotted we can neither assert nor deny. His satires are full of moral precepts and virtuous sentiments; the Tenth, perhaps the gem of the collection, has lent more thoughts and expressions to modern times than any other Latin poem of equal length. It closes with a beautiful petition:—

JUVENAL'S PRAYER.

"O Thou who know'st the wants of human kind,
Vouchsafe me health of body, health of mind;
A soul prepared to meet the frowns of fate,
And look undaunted on a future state;
That reckons death a blessing, yet can bear
Existence nobly, with its weight of care;
That anger and desire alike restrains,
And counts Alcides' toils, and cruel pains,
Superior far to banquets, wanton nights,
And all the Assyrian monarch's soft delights!
Here bound, at length, thy wishes. I but teach
What blessings man, by his own powers, may reach.
The path to peace is virtue. We should see,
If wise, O Fortune, naught divine in thee:
But we have deified a name alone,
And fixed in heaven thy visionary throne!"

Brevity, intensity, and vigor, are conspicuous elements in our author's style. He always used "the best words in the right places." Said Dryden, his only peer in satiric poetry, "Juvenal gives me as much pleasure as I can bear." We extract from the Tenth Satire one of his most graphic passages:—

THE INSTABILITY OF FORTUNE.

[Illustrated by the fall of Sejanus.]

"Some, Power hurls headlong from her envied height;
Some, the broad tablet, flashing on the sight,
With titles, names: the statues, tumbled down,
Are dragged by hooting thousands through the town;
The brazen cars torn rudely from the yoke,
And, with the blameless steeds, to shivers broke—
Then roar the flames! The sooty artist blows,
And all Sejanus* in the furnace glows;
Sejanus, once so honored, so adored,
And only second to the world's great lord,
Runs glittering from the mould, in cups and cans,
Basins and ewers, plates, pitchers, pots, and pans.
'Crown all your doors with bay, triumphant bay!
Sacred to Jove, the milk-white victim slay;
For lo! where great Sejanus by the throng,
A joyful spectacle! is dragged along.
What lips! what cheeks! ha, traitor! for my part,
I never loved the fellow—in my heart.'
'But tell me, why was he adjudged to bleed?
And who discovered, and who proved the deed?'
'Proved!—a huge wordy letter came to-day
From Capreæ.' Good! what think the people? They—
They follow fortune, as of old, and hate,
With their whole souls, the victim of the state.
Yet would the herd, thus zealous, thus on fire,
Had Nursia† met the Tuscan's fond desire,
And crushed the unwary prince, have all combined,
And hailed Sejanus master of mankind!
Lured by the splendor of his happier hour,
Wouldst thou possess Sejanus' wealth and power;
See crowds of suppliants at thy levee wait,
Give this to sway the army, that the state;
And keep a prince in ward, retired to reign
O'er Capreæ's crags, with his Chaldean train?
Yes, yes, thou wouldst (for I can read thy breast)
Enjoy that favor which he once possessed,

---

* The wicked minister of the emperor Tiberius, who encouraged his master in the most detestable vices. At length, having engaged in a conspiracy with the view of usurping the empire, he was executed by Tiberius. The fate of the bronze statues raised in his honor is related by the poet.

† The Etruscan goddess of fortune.

Assume all offices, grasp all commands,
The Imperial Horse, and the Prætorian Bands.
'Tis Nature, this; e'en those who want the will,
Pant for the dreadful privilege to kill:
Yet what delight can rank and power bestow,
Since every joy is balanced by its woe!"—GIFFORD.

Tacitus (54–118 A.D.).—Foremost among the prose writers of this later period was Caius Cornelius Tacitus, by some considered the greatest of Roman historians. Of his early life we know nothing, though as a youth he seems to have mastered those arts which afterward made him a successful orator. In the reign of Vespasian he took to wife the daughter of Julius Agricola, the Roman governor of Britain, and began a public career which culminated under Nerva (97 A.D.) in the consulship. After this he probably confined his attention to literature, busying himself with the compilation of historical works until death put an end to his labors.

The first of these in the order of time was the "Agricola," an admirable biography of the author's father-in-law, "the hero of a hundred fights, the conqueror of those warlike islanders whom the mighty Julius left to their original freedom, and whom Claudius and his captains imperfectly subdued." It is particularly valuable for the light it casts on the history of Britain, and the influence of Roman institutions.

"Agricola," said Tacitus, "gave private encouragement and public aid to the building of temples, courts of justice, and dwelling-houses, praising the energetic and reproving the indolent. Thus an honorable rivalry took the place of compulsion. He likewise provided a liberal education for the sons of the chiefs, and showed such a preference for the natural powers of the Britons over the industry of the Gauls that they who lately disdained the tongue of Rome now coveted its eloquence. Hence, too, a liking sprung up for our style of dress, and the *toga* became fashionable. Step by step they were led to things which dispose to vice—the lounge, the bath, the elegant banquet. All this, in their ignorance, they called civilization."

The "Agricola" was followed by "the Germania," a treatise on the situation, customs, and tribes of Germany, in whose freedom-loving warriors Tacitus saw an enemy to be feared. What more caustic satires than his telling contrasts of their simple habits with Roman luxury, their stern morality with Roman profligacy? The Germania may be regarded as a warning from a patriotic historian to his vice-ridden, enervated countrymen — a warning which they would have done well to regard. Particularly pleasing are its picturesque sketches of German life, written in concise, vigorous language.

The remaining works of Tacitus are his "Histories," "Annals," and a Dialogue on "the Decline of Eloquence." The Histories covered the reigns of the Roman emperors from Galba to Domitian inclusive (69–96 A.D.); about one-third of the work is preserved. The genius of Tacitus did ample justice to the tremendous issues of this eventful period, described by him as follows :—

"I am entering on the history of a period rich in disasters, frightful in its wars, torn by civil strife, and even in peace full of horrors. Four emperors perished by the sword. There were three civil wars: there were more with foreign enemies: there were often wars that had both characters at once. Now, too, Italy was prostrated by disasters, either entirely novel or that recurred only after a long succession of ages. Cities in Campania's richest plains were swallowed up and overwhelmed; Rome was wasted by conflagrations, its oldest temples were consumed, and the Capitol itself was fired by the hands of citizens. Never, surely, did more terrible calamities of the Roman people, or evidence more conclusive, prove that the gods take no thought for our happiness, but only for our punishment."

In the "Annals" (sixteen books), which traced the history of the emperors from the death of Augustus up to the point at which the Histories had opened, the voice of the indignant satirist is everywhere heard. Portions of this work, which were published about 115 A.D., are lost. We extract the historian's vivid description of the burning of Rome.

THE BURNING OF ROME.

"There followed a dreadful disaster, whether fortuitously or by the wicked contrivance of the prince is not determined, for both are asserted by historians. But of all the calamities which ever befell this city from the rage of fire, this was the most terrible. It broke out in that part of the Circus which is contiguous to mounts Palatine and Cœlius, where, by reason of shops in which were kept such goods as minister aliment to fire, the moment it commenced it acquired strength, and being accelerated by the wind, it spread at once through the whole extent of the Circus. For neither were the houses secured by enclosures, nor the temples environed with walls, nor was there any other obstacle to intercept its progress; but the flame, spreading every way impetuously, invaded first the lower regions of the city, then mounted to the higher; then again ravaging the lower, it baffled every effort to extinguish it, by the rapidity of its destructive course, and from the liability of the city to conflagration in consequence of the narrow and intricate alleys, and the irregularity of the streets in ancient Rome.

Add to this the wailings of terrified women, the infirm condition of the aged, and the helplessness of childhood; such as strove to provide for themselves, and those who labored to assist others; these dragging the feeble, those waiting for them; some hurrying, others lingering; altogether created a scene of universal confusion and embarrassment. While they looked back upon the danger in their rear, they often found themselves beset before, and on their sides; or if they had escaped into the quarters adjoining, these too were already seized by the devouring flames; even the parts which they believed to be remote and exempt, were found to be in the same distress.

At last, not knowing what to shun or where to seek sanctuary, they crowded the streets, and lay along in the open fields. Some, from the loss of their whole substance, even the means of their daily sustenance, others, from affection for their relatives whom they had not been able to snatch from the flames, suffered themselves to perish in them, though they had opportunity to escape. Neither dared any man offer to check the fire: so repeated were the menaces of many who forbade to extinguish it; and because others openly threw fire-brands, with loud declarations 'that they had one who authorized them;' whether they did it that they might plunder with less restraint, or in consequence of orders given.

Nero, who was at that juncture sojourning at Antium, did not return to the city till the fire approached that quarter of his house which connected the palace with the gardens of Mæcenas; nor could it, however, be prevented from devouring the house, and palace, and everything around. But for the relief of the people thus destitute and driven from their dwellings, he opened the field of Mars, and even his own gardens. He likewise reared temporary houses for the reception of the forlorn multitude; from Ostia and the neighboring cities were brought household necessaries, and the price of grain was reduced to three sesterces (about 11½ cts.) the measure. All which proceedings, though of a popular character, were thrown away, because a rumor had become universally current, that at the very time when the city was in flames Nero, going on the stage of his private theatre, sung 'The Destruction of Troy,' assimilating the present disaster to that catastrophe of ancient times.

At length, on the sixth day, the conflagration was stayed by pulling down an immense quantity of buildings, so that an open space and, as it were, void air, might check the raging element by breaking the continuity. . . . But not all the bounties that the prince could bestow, nor all the atonements which could be presented to the gods, availed to relieve Nero from the infamy of being believed to have ordered the fire. Hence, to suppress the rumor, he falsely charged with the guilt and punished with the most exquisite tortures, the persons commonly called Christians, who were hated for their enormities.* Christus, the founder of that sect, was put to death as a criminal by Pontius Pilate, procurator of Judea, in the reign of Tiberius; but the pernicious superstition, repressed for a time, broke out again, not only through Judea, where the mischief originated, but through the city of Rome also, whither all things horrible and disgraceful flow from all quarters, as to a common receptacle, and where they are encouraged.

Accordingly, first those were seized who confessed they were Christians; next, on their information, a vast multitude were convicted, not so much on a charge of burning the city as of hating the human race. And in their deaths they were also made the subjects of sport, for they were covered with the hides of wild beasts and worried to death by dogs, or nailed to crosses, or set fire to, and when day declined burned to serve for nocturnal lights.† Nero offered his own gardens for that spectacle, and exhibited a Circensian game, indiscriminately mingling with the common people in the habit of a charioteer, or else standing in his chariot. Whence a feeling of compassion arose toward the sufferers, though guilty and deserving to be made examples of by capital punishment, because they seemed not to be cut off for the public good, but victims to the ferocity of one man."

Suetonius, a contemporary of Tacitus, appears to have been born in the reign of Vespasian. His literary labors began in Trajan's time; and under Hadrian he occupied the honorable

---

* Tacitus shared the unjust prejudice current among the Romans.

† This was the first of the ten persecutions of the Christians.

position of private secretary, which, however, he lost in consequence of disrespect to the empress.

The best-known of his works, and the only one that has been preserved entire, is his "Lives of the Twelve Cæsars," full, interesting, and trustworthy in its information, clear and vigorous in style. The "Cæsars" of Suetonius has always been a standard. The Romans dwelt on his stories with gusto; but in such frightful colors did he paint the deeds of Caligula that the tyrant Com'modus made death by wild beasts the penalty for reading his life of that emperor. After the invention of printing, editions of Suetonius multiplied rapidly.

EXTRACTS FROM SUETONIUS.

SUPERSTITION OF AUGUSTUS.

"Some signs and omens he regarded as infallible. If in the morning his shoe was put on wrong, the left instead of the right, that boded some disaster. If when he commenced a long journey, by sea or land, there happened to fall a mizzling rain, he held it to be a good sign of a speedy and happy return. He was much affected likewise with anything out of the common course of nature. A palm-tree which chanced to grow up between some stones in the court of his house, he transplanted into a court where the images of the household gods were placed, and took all possible care to make it thrive. He also observed certain days; as never to go from home the day after the market-days, nor to begin any serious business upon the nones."

CHARACTER OF CALIGULA.

"Caligula evinced the savage barbarity of his temper by the following indications. When flesh was only to be had at a high price for feeding his wild beasts, he ordered that criminals should be given them to be devoured. After disfiguring many persons of honorable rank, by branding them in the face with hot irons, he condemned them to the mines, to work in repairing the highways, or to fight with wild beasts; or, tying them by the neck and heels, would shut them up in cages, or saw them asunder.

Nor were these severities inflicted merely for crimes of great enormity, but for making remarks on his public games, or for not having sworn by the Genius of the emperor. He compelled parents to be present at the execution of their sons; and to one who excused himself on account of indisposition, he sent his own litter. He burned alive the writer of a farce, for some witty verse which had a double meaning. A Roman knight, who had been exposed to the wild beasts, crying out that he was innocent, Caligula called him back, and having had his tongue cut out, remanded him to the arena.

Even in the midst of his diversions, while gaming or feasting, this savage ferocity never forsook him. Persons were often put to the torture in his presence, while he was dining or carousing. At Puteoli, at the dedication of the bridge, he invited a number of people to come to him from the shore, and then suddenly threw them headlong into the sea; thrusting down with poles and oars those who, to save themselves, had got hold of the rudders of the ships. As often as he met with handsome men, who had fine heads of hair, he would order the back of their heads to be shaved, to make them look ridiculous. At a sumptuous entertainment, he fell suddenly into a violent fit of laughter, and upon the consuls', who reclined next to him, respectfully asking him the occasion, 'Nothing,' replied he, 'but that upon a single nod of mine, you might both have your throats cut.'

In profuse expenditure he surpassed all the prodigals that ever lived; inventing a new kind of bath, washing in precious unguents, both warm and cold, drinking pearls of immense value dissolved in vinegar, and serving up for his guests loaves and other victuals modelled in gold. He built two ships with ten banks of oars, the sterns of which blazed with jewels while the sails were of various colors. They were fitted up with baths, galleries, and saloons, and supplied with a great variety of vines and fruit-trees. In these he would sail in the daytime along the coast of Campania, feasting amidst dancing and concerts of music."

STUPIDITY OF CLAUDIUS.

"Among other things, people wondered at the indifference and absent-mindedness of Claudius. Placing himself at table a little after Messalina's death, he inquired, 'Why does not the empress come?' Many of those he had condemned to death, he ordered the day after to be invited to his table, and to game with him, and sent to reprimand them as sluggish fellows for not making greater haste. The following expression he had in his mouth at all hours, 'What! do you take me for a fool?'

A man engaged in litigation before his tribunal drew Claudius aside and told him, 'I dreamt I saw you murdered;' and shortly afterward, when the defendant came to deliver his plea to the emperor, the plaintiff, pretending to have discovered the murderer, pointed to him as the man he had seen in his dream: whereupon, as if he had been taken in the act, he was hurried away to execution."—Dr. Thomson.

Pliny the Younger (62–113 A.D.), nephew and adopted son of the naturalist, learned his early lessons from Quintilian and other celebrated rhetoricians. After figuring for a time as a successful advocate, he was elevated to the consulship, and in Trajan's reign, having served his second term as consul, received the appointment of governor of Bithynia.

Pliny took a prominent stand as the champion of the wronged, and delighted in compelling dishonest governors to disgorge their stolen spoils. The eloquent speeches identified with his name have perished, with the exception of a single specimen, a panegyric on Trajan. It is as a letter-writer that Pliny is entitled to a place among the worthies of Latin literature. His epistles to his friends and the emperor (in ten books) are among the most pleasing relics of antiquity, affording, as they do, many instructive glimpses of contemporary society. They are written with life and polish, and show their author to have been "the perfect type of a pagan gentleman."

While governor of Bithynia, Pliny corresponded frequently with Trajan on official business. We give below one of his letters in relation to the Christians, with Trajan's reply.

PLINY'S LETTER ON THE CHRISTIANS.

"I had never attended at the trial of a Christian; hence I knew not what were the usual questions asked them, or what the punishments inflicted. I doubted, also, whether to make a distinction of ages, or to treat young and old alike; whether to allow time for recantation, or to refuse all pardon whatever to one who had been a Christian; whether, finally, to make the name penal, though no crime should be proved, or to reserve the penalty for the combination of both. Meanwhile, when any were reported to me as Christians, I followed this plan. I asked them whether they were Christians. If they said yes, I repeated the question twice, adding threats of punishment; if they persisted, I ordered punishment to be inflicted. For I felt sure that whatever it was they confessed, their inflexible obstinacy well deserved to be chastised. There were even some Roman citizens who showed this strange persistence; those I determined to send to Rome.

As often happens in cases of interference, charges were now lodged more generally than before, and several forms of guilt came before me. An anonymous letter was sent, containing the names of many persons, who, however, denied that they were or had been Christians. As they invoked the gods and worshipped with wine and frankincense before your image, at the same time cursing Christ, I released them the more readily, as those who are really Christians cannot be got to do any of these things. Others, who were named to me, admitted that they were Christians, but immediately afterward denied it; some said they had been so three years ago, others at still more distant dates, one or two as long ago as twenty years. All these worshipped your image and those of the gods, and abjured Christ. But they declared that all their guilt or error had amounted to was this: they met on certain mornings before daybreak, and sung one after another a hymn to Christ as God, at the same time binding themselves by an oath not to commit any crime, but to abstain from theft, robbery, adultery, perjury, or repudiation of trust. After this was done, the meeting broke up; they, however, came together again to eat their meal in common, being quite guiltless of any improper conduct. But since my edict forbidding (as you ordered) all secret societies, they had given this practice up.

However, I thought it necessary to apply the torture to some young women who were called *ministræ* (deaconesses), in order, if possible, to find out the truth. But I could elicit nothing from them except evidence of some debased and immoderate superstition; so I deferred the trial, and determined to ask your advice. For the matter seemed important, especially since the number of those who run into danger increases daily. All ages, all ranks, and both sexes, are among the accused, and the taint of the superstition is not confined to the towns; it has actually made its way into the villages. But I believe it possible to check and repress it. At all events, it is certain that temples which were lately almost empty are now well attended, and sacred festivals long disused are being revived. Victims too are flowing in, whereas a few years ago such things could hardly find a purchaser. From this I infer that vast numbers might be reformed, if an opportunity of recantation were allowed them."

TRAJAN'S REPLY.

"I entirely approve of your conduct with regard to those Christians of whom you had received information. We can never lay down a universal rule, as if circumstances were always the same. They are not to be searched for; but if they are reported and convicted, they must be punished. But if any denies his Christianity and proves his words by sacrificing to our divinity, even if his former conduct may have laid him under suspicion, he must be allowed the benefit of his recantation. No weight whatever should be attached to anonymous communications; they are no Roman way of dealing, and are altogether reprehensible."—CRUTTWELL.

During the period under consideration, FLORUS abridged Livy's "Annals;" AULUS GELLIUS (125–175 A.D.) crowded into his "Attic Nights" (a work in twenty books, prepared by night at Athens) a vast store of historical anecdotes and extracts from works now lost; GAIUS, the jurist, composed his "Institutes;" and FRONTO wrote his epistles.

Apuleius.—Last of the writers of this age, but by no means least when we consider the influence of his tales upon modern fiction, is Apuleius, author of the romance of "the Golden Ass." Lucius, the hero, an enthusiast in the study of magic, having seen the sorceress Pam'phile transform herself into an owl by rubbing an ointment on her person, endeavors, with the help of her maid, to imitate her example. But the girl selects the wrong box of ointment from her mistress's cabinet; and Lucius, on applying it, is changed into a donkey.

Hardly, however, had the metamorphosis been effected when a band of robbers made a descent upon the house, loaded a portion of their plunder on the ass's back, and made good their escape, driving Lucius before them. In search of rose-leaves, which the maid told him would remove the spell, the hero meets with a series of marvellous adventures. Among the episodes introduced is the oft-repeated tale of Cupid and Psy'che. In the Decameron, Don Quixote, and Gil Blas, some of these old Roman stories are told over again.

The style of Apuleius is unnatural; his Latin is bad. Besides "the Golden Ass," he wrote a discourse on Magic, on "the God of Socrates," and the "Florida," a collection of paragraphs from his own orations.

LATER LATIN AUTHORS.

After its temporary revival under Trajan's kindly rule, Latin literature gradually sunk into a hopeless decline. In the long array of names that represent the last three centuries of the Roman Empire, we find none more worthy of respect than those of the Latin fathers. Greatest of these was

St. Augustine (354–430 A.D.), of whom Tulloch said "no single name has ever made such an impression upon Christian thought."

Impressed with the truth of the Gospel by the eloquence of Ambrose at Milan, where he had gone to teach rhetoric, Augustine at length received baptism, to the delight of his saintly mother Mon′ica, who had long prayed for his conversion. When raised to the bishopric of Hippo in Africa, Augustine zealously engaged in a controversy with Pela′gius and his followers, who entertained heterodox views in relation to grace and original sin. The bishop put forth fifteen treatises in refutation of the Pelagian heresies. His greatest works were "the City of God," a vindication of Christianity, "Confessions," and a treatise on the Trinity.

Ambrose, bishop of Milan, who lived in the last half of the fourth century, was the author of numerous epistles and hymns, the *Te Deum* being one of his compositions. His "Offices" defines the duties of Christian pastors.

St. Jerome (Hieronymus) (340–420), the great apostle of monasticism, from a convent at Bethlehem promulgated his Latin version of the Old and New Testaments, called the Vulgate (*common*) because designed for the use of the common people, who understood no language but Latin. Jerome's Bible, adopted as a standard version, was the first book ever put to press (1455).

St. Gregory, bishop of Constantinople, the last of the four great Latin fathers and the most poetical of early Christian writers, has left us a book of epistles, orations, and religious poems. He pressed into the service of Christianity the arts of Greek rhetoric, and assailed Julian the Apostate in two speeches that recall the invective of the Attic orators.

Tertullian (150–230), "the Master," one of the earlier Christian authors, is worthy of mention not only for his numerous practical treatises on Penance, Idolatry, Theatrical Exhibitions, etc., but also for his polemical works against unbelievers, and the "Apologeticus" in defence of Christianity. In after-life Tertullian joined a heretical sect.

Cyprian, bishop of Carthage, the pupil of Tertullian, defended his religion with an eloquent pen, and finally laid down his life for his faith (258).

Lactantius, "the Christian Cicero," was the most learned man of Constantine's age (306–337). His earliest effort, an hexameter poem, "the Banquet," gained him such reputation that the emperor Diocletian appointed him to give instruction in rhetoric at Nicomedia. The "Banquet" is lost; but several of the author's prose works remain, the greatest being his "Divine Institutions." In his treatise "On the Death of the Persecutors," Lactantius endeavors to prove the avenging hand of God in the violent ends of those emperors who had oppressed his people.

Boëthius.—Finally, we must notice the famous moral treatise "On the Consolation of Philosophy," by Boëthius, a Roman noble who outlived the fall of his country (476). A model of integrity and justice, Boëthius was loaded with honors by Theod'oric, the Ostrogothic king of Italy; but at last, falsely accused by his enemies of witchcraft and treason, he was executed by his suspicious master (525).

The above-mentioned work was much read during the Middle Ages. Alfred the Great rendered it into Anglo-Saxon; Chaucer, into English; and later writers have reproduced its sentiments.

SPECIMENS OF LATER POETRY.

As a favorable specimen of later Latin poetry, we quote a few verses from an eclogue on hunting by NEMESIAN (280), a favorite poet in the time of Charlemagne, extensively read in the schools:—

"The toil that should round lawn and forest spread,
Hemming the nimble prey in moveless dread,
Must with inwoven plumes its threads divide,
From every various wing diversely dyed.
This the keen wolf and flying stag shall scare,
The fox, the monstrous boar, and shaggy bear;
As if with lightning flash, aghast, confound,
And still forbid to pass the checkered bound.
This then, with various paint anointing, smear;
Let florid hues with snowy white appear,
And lengthen on the threads the alternate fear.
A thousand terrors from his painted wings,
To aid thy enterprise, the vulture brings.
The swan, the goose, the crane, and each that laves
His webbèd feet amid the stagnant waves.
Then rarer plumes shall brighter tints bestow,
Where scarlet deepens in its native glow:
Where flights of birds on blooming pinions rise,
And plumage reddens with its saffron dyes,
Or streaks in green its pied varieties.
Thy gear complete, when autumn's end is near,
And showery winter overhangs the year,
Begin: your hounds unkennel in the mead;
Begin: o'er champaign fields impel the steed.
Hunt, while the daybreak sheds its glimmering light,
And the fresh dews retain the scented tracks of night."

ELTON.

A different style was that of CLAUDIAN, the court poet in the reign of Theodosius the Great (379–395). Tawdry and artificial in general, it was displayed to the best advantage in his amatory pieces and marriage hymns; as in this description of

THE SLEEPING VENUS.

"It chanced, in quest of slumbers cool, the Queen
Of Love in vine-wrought grot retired unseen;
Her star-bright limbs on tufted grass were spread,
A heap of flowers the pillow for her head.
The Idalian maids lie round; the Graces twine
Their arms, and screened by spreading oak recline.
The wingèd boys, where shade invites, repose
On every side; unstrung their loosened bows;

While, on a neighboring branch suspended high,
With gentle flames their breathing quivers sigh.
Some wakeful sport, or through the thickets rove;
Climb for the nest, or blithely strip the grove
Of dewy apples for the Queen of Love;
Along the bough's curved windings creeping cling,
Or hang from topmost elm with light-poised wing."

AUSONIUS of Bordeaux, an affected verse-maker of the fourth century, wrote much that is second-rate, in the way of epigrams and idyls, too often of a licentious tone; but there is some merit in the following reflections on

ROSES.

"'Twas spring; the morn returned in saffron veil,
And breathed a bracing coolness in the gale.
Through the broad walks I trod the garden bowers,
And roamed, refreshed against the noontide hours.
I saw the hoary dew's congealing drops
Bend the tall grass and vegetable tops;
The sprinkled pearls on every rose-bush lay,
Anon to melt before the beams of day.
I saw a moment's interval divide
The rose that blossomed from the rose that died.
This with its cap of tufted moss looked green;
That, tipped with reddening purple, peeped between.
One reared its obelisk with opening swell,
The bud unsheathed its crimson pinnacle;
Another, gathering every purfled fold,
Its foliage multiplied, its blooms unrolled.
While this, that ere the passing moment flew,
Flamed forth one blaze of scarlet on the view,
Now shook from withering stalk the waste perfume,
Its verdure stript, and pale its faded bloom.
I marvelled at the spoiling flight of time,
That roses thus grew old in earliest prime.
E'en while I speak, the crimson leaves drop round,
And a red brightness veils the blushing ground.
These forms, these births, these changes, bloom, decay,
Appear and vanish in the self-same day.
One day the rose's age; and while it blows,
In dawn of youth, it withers to its close.
O virgins! roses cull while yet ye may;
So bloom your hours, and so shall haste away."

ELTON.

GEMS OF LATIN THOUGHT.*

PLAUTUS.

"Easy is sway over the good.—Man to his fellow-man is a wolf.—No one left to himself is sufficiently wise.—All things are not equally sweet to all.—No one is inquisitive without being ill-natured.—A woman who has good principles has dowry enough.—Courage in danger is half the battle.—Good fortune finds good friends.—Love is very fruitful in both honey and gall.—Flame is very near to smoke."

TERENCE.

"The strictest administration of law is often the greatest wrong.—Without danger no great and memorable deed is done.—Fortune favors the brave.—Many men, many minds.—Nothing in excess.—As we can, when we cannot as we would.—Nothing is said now that has not been said before.—Obsequiousness begets friends, truthfulness hatred."

VARRO.

"It is divine nature that has given the country, human art that has built cities.—As a state ought to worship the gods in its public capacity, so ought each family."

CICERO.

"Justice gives every one his due.—No one was ever great without divine inspiration.—The noblest spirit is the most strongly attracted by the love of glory.—One man is more useful in one thing, another in another.—Guilt lies in the very hesitation, even though the act itself has not been reached.—The chief recommendation comes from modesty.—Fear is no lasting teacher of duty.—Any man may err, but no one but a fool will persevere in error.—The memory of a well-spent life is everlasting.—Whatever you do, you should do it with your might.—Glory follows virtue like its shadow."

LUCRETIUS.

"The ring on the finger is worn thin by constant use.—It is pleasant, when winds roughen the sea with great waves, to behold from the shore another's arduous toil.—We are all sprung from heavenly seeds.—Weigh well with judgment; what seems true, hold fast; gird thyself against what is false.—We see that the mind strengthens with the body, and with the body grows old."

---

* For these "Gems," as well as those under Greek literature, we have drawn to some extent on the collections of Ramage.

CATULLUS.

"Nothing is sillier than a silly laugh.—What a woman says to her fond lover may well be written on the wind and rapid stream."

SALLUST.

"Every one is the architect of his own fortune.—The endowments of the mind form the only illustrious and lasting possession.—Fear closes the ears of the mind.—The mind is the leader and director of the life of mortals.—In grief and miseries, death is a respite from sorrows, not a punishment.—To have the same likes and dislikes, this in a word is firm friendship."

VIRGIL.

"Endure, and preserve yourselves for prosperous times.—We are not all able to accomplish all things.—Love conquers all things, and to love let us yield.—Praise large farms, cultivate a small one.—The only safety for the vanquished is to hope for no safety.—Accursed thirst for gold, what dost thou not drive mortal breasts to do?—Nowhere is faith safe.—Whatever shall happen, every kind of fortune is to be overcome by patient endurance.—Hug the shore; let others launch out into the deep."

HORACE.

"There is a mean in all things.—It is right for one craving forgiveness for his sins to grant it to others in turn.—There is nothing too high for mortals; in our folly we storm heaven itself.—Life has given nothing to mortals without great toil.—Avoid inquiring what is about to be to-morrow.—To die for one's native land is sweet and glorious.—Punishment presses on crime as a companion.—He has carried every point who has mingled the useful with the agreeable."

LIVY.

"Wounds cannot be cured unless they are touched and handled.—Necessity is the ultimate and strongest weapon.—In nothing do events less answer to men's expectations than in war.—It is safer that a wicked man should not be accused at all than that he should be acquitted.—In difficult and almost hopeless cases the boldest counsels are the safest."

TIBULLUS.

"There is a God who forbids that crimes should be concealed.—Happy thou who shalt learn by another's suffering how to avoid thine own.—While thy early summer-time is blooming, use it; it slips away with no slow foot."

PROPERTIUS.

"Neither is beauty a thing eternal, nor is fortune lasting to any; later or sooner death awaits everybody.—In maddening love nobody sees.—Let no one be willing to injure the absent.—Great love crosses even the shores of death."

OVID.

"A wounded member that cannot be healed must be cut off with the knife, lest the healthy part be affected.—It is the coward's part to wish for death.—Even the unconquered man grief conquers.—A mind conscious of rectitude laughs at the lies of rumor.—The reefed sail escapes the storms of winter."

NEPOS.

"No evil is great which is the last.—Peace is obtained by war.—The mother of a coward is not wont to weep."

PHÆDRUS.

"The poor man, striving to imitate the powerful, comes to grief.—The fair speeches of a bad man are full of snares.—Rashness is an advantage to few, a source of evil to many.—The learned man always has his riches within himself."

PLINY.

The Elder.—"Every one is pleased with his own, and wherever we go the same story is found.—No one of mortals is wise at all hours.—Our ancestors used to say that the master's eye is the best fertilizer for the field."

The Younger.—"Nothing seems as good, when we have gained it, as it did when we were wishing for it.—I deem him the best and most commendable who pardons others as if he himself daily went astray, yet abstains from faults as if he pardoned no one."

LUCAN.

"Great fear is concealed by daring.—The prosperous man knows not whether he is truly loved.—An offence in which many are engaged, goes unpunished."

PETRONIUS ARBITER.

"A physician is nothing more than a satisfaction to the mind.—Fear first made gods in the world.—There is no one of us that sinneth not; we are men, not gods.—Poverty is the sister of a sound mind."

TACITUS.

"Traitors are odious even to those whom they benefit.—When the state is most corrupt, the laws are most numerous.—There will be vices as long as there are men.—Everything unknown is magnified.—It is a peculiarity of the human mind to hate one whom you have injured."

JUVENAL.

"Rare is the combination of beauty and modesty.—Nature never says one thing, and wisdom another.—Himself being the judge, no guilty man is acquitted.—The anger of the gods, however great it may be, yet certainly is slow.—Less frequent enjoyment of them makes pleasures keener."

MINOR POETS AND PROSE WRITERS.

CREMU'TIUS CORDUS, the historian: "Annals." Cordus offended Tiberius by styling Cassius "the last of the Romans," and starved himself to death to escape the tyrant.

AUFID'IUS BASSUS: histories of the civil and German wars.

ASCO'NIUS PEDIA'NUS: a grammarian of Patavium; commentaries on Cicero's orations.

PETRO'NIUS ARBITER, the companion and victim of Nero: author of "Satyricon," a witty romance, of which a few fragments remain.

JULIUS FRONTI'NUS: a self-made man of the Flavian era; works on the Roman aqueducts, military tactics, the measurement of land, etc.

LICINIA'NUS (age of the Antonines): a history of republican Rome; style affected.

MARCUS AURELIUS, the emperor (161–180): a devoted Stoic; his "Meditations" (in Greek) full of noble sentiments.

PAPINIAN AND ULPIAN, the jurists (about 200): writers on law.

SPARTIA'NUS (300): "Biographies of the Roman Emperors."

ÆLIUS DONA'TUS (4th century): the preceptor of St. Jerome; his "Art of Grammar" once a popular text-book.

PRUDENTIUS CLE'MENS (4th century): a Christian poet; hymns, etc.

AVIE'NUS (4th century): poems on astronomical and geographical subjects.

AMMIA'NUS MARCELLI'NUS (died about 400): the last Latin historian; his "Thirty-one Books of Events," a continuation of the history of Tacitus through the reign of Valens (378).

SYMMACHUS (400): a high-minded opponent of Christianity; defeated by Ambrose in an attempt to restore the altar of Victory; orations, epistles.

RUTILIUS (5th century): poetical diary of a journey from Rome to Gaul; style terse and elegant.

PRISCIAN (6th century): the greatest of classical grammarians; the most complete Latin Grammar of antiquity.

INDEX.

www.ingramcontent.com/pod-product-compliance
Lightning Source LLC
LaVergne TN
LVHW021143110826
845150LV00005B/1115

* 9 7 8 1 4 2 5 5 4 8 1 4 8 *